from the Innovative Motivation Series
(Part of the *Music Motivation*® Series)

Who Are You?

Your Personal Success Goal Book

Discover who you really are and who you can become!

Get to know yourself, your strengths, weaknesses, goals, dreams, hopes, fears, and potential!

LIFE COACH and MUSIC MENTOR

JERALD SIMON

To my **sweetheart**, Zanny, with all my love.

Dedicated to the greatest teens and young adults alive!
You are our future and I believe our future is bright and beautiful.

Motivation at its Best.

Music Motivation®
http://musicmotivation.com

Who Are You?

Your Personal Success Goal Book

by JERALD SIMON

Music Motivation®, http://musicmotivation.com
P.O. Box 1000 Kaysville, UT 84037-1000 U.S.A.
info@musicmotivation.com; +1-801-444-5143

Copyright © 2018 by JERALD SIMON

All Rights Reserved — International Copyright Secured. No part of this book may be copied, reproduced, or duplicated or reproduced in any form by any means, electronic or mechanical, including photocopying, recording, or by any information storage and retrieval system, or other means known or hereafter invented without written permission from the author, Jerald Simon, except for the inclusion of brief quotations in a review.

For more promotional excerpt permission, contact:
Music Motivation®
P.O. Box 1000 Kaysville, UT 84037-1000
http://musicmotivation.com
info@musicmotivation.com

International Standard Book Numbers (ISBN)
Paperback - 978-1-948274-01-2
eBook - 978-1-948274-06-7
Audio Book Barcode - 191924596387
Library of Congress Control Number - 2017918228

Also available as an Audio Book, MP3 on iTunes, Amazon, CDbaby and all online music retailers. Visit your favorite online music retailer to download the MP3 audio book read by Jerald Simon.

Printed in the **United States of America**
Simon, Jerald
Jerald Simon's Who Are You? (Your Personal Success Goal Book) by Jerald Simon
Edited by Suzanne Simon and Wendy Cederlof

Motivation at its Best.

Direct Hire, Contract-to-Hire or Contract

When employers are seeking to fill an available position, they typically offer the position as a direct hire (DH), contract-to-hire (CTH or C2H) or contract position.

- **Direct hire** means the employer wants to hire you as a permanent full-time company employee.

- **Contract-to-hire** means the employer wants to hire you as a temporary contractor, but the employer plans to convert your contractor position to a permanent full-time company employee position after you successfully fulfill the time period of your contract obligation.

- **Contract** position means the employer wants to hire you as a temporary contractor with no plans to convert you over to a permanent full-time company employee.

When a company advertises a job opening on their company website, they normally offer that job as a direct hire position. Companies will also use staffing agencies to help them fill available positions. When companies use staffing agencies to help them in the recruiting process, companies oftentimes offer these jobs as direct hire, contract-to-hire or contract positions.

Direct Hire Worker

If you find a direct hire position through a staffing agency, and you are hired for the job, that staffing agency and recruiter who found you get paid their expected commission by the employer who hired you. This is where your business relationship with the staffing agency ends and your business relationship with your new employer begins. Once the staffing agency hands you off to your employer as a direct hire, you become that employer's permanent full-time company employee. All of your paychecks (including taxes withheld), company benefits and working relationship will be directly with that employer from that point on.

Since you were working through a staffing agency, the salary and benefits you negotiated with the staffing agency recruiter or account manager for that direct hire position will become your permanent salary and benefits with the employer once you are directly hired as a permanent full-time employee. Therefore, it is important that you negotiate as high an hourly rate or annual salary as possible with the staffing agency recruiter before you accept that direct hire job. You do not get a second chance or a do-over to renegotiate your salary with your employer after you agreed to that salary through the staffing agency. Also, ask the recruiter or check the client company's website about the type of company benefits you will receive before you sign the job offer letter for that position. Make sure your job offer letter includes a statement saying you will receive these company benefits.

You can be more direct and assertive in your salary negotiations with a staffing agency recruiter than you normally would when negotiating your salary with the hiring manager who is also the one interviewing you for that open position. Don't fret over the idea of negotiating your salary for now. I'll provide you plenty of details and examples as I explain to you the variety of ways to negotiate a higher annual salary or hourly rate in chapter 7. Once you're done reading through that section on negotiating your salary, recruiters will be calling you the Artful Dodger because you'll be picking their pockets clean.

Since we're momentarily on the subject of negotiating salaries, here's where I want to share with you this important truth.

Your highest raise is the salary you negotiate.

The highest raise you'll most likely ever receive in your current job is the salary you negotiated for that job.

Allow me to explain.

The time to increase your salary to where you want it to be at is not after you are in that job. The best time to increase your salary to a level you're satisfied with is while you negotiate your salary for that job before you sign the offer letter.

Some job seekers will accept whatever salary is offered to them for a particular job, hoping they can increase that salary with raises each year once they're hired. True, you'll increase your salary with annual raises, but this is not the best way to increase your salary to a high level.

The quickest way to increase your salary for a job is to start off by asking for the highest possible salary when you are first hired for that position. This strategy works better than accepting that job at a lower salary; and then expect to receive annual raises to increase your salary to the level you'd like it to be at.

When I was living in Europe, I accepted a direct hire position for a large US company in Europe. I accepted the position for a lower salary than I wanted. I took the job hoping after working there each year; the company would reward me with annual raises that would increase my salary to a higher level. What I discovered was that the raises were only for one or two thousand dollars each year. In my fourth year with this company, I realized my salary increases were happening at a much lower and slower rate than I expected with annual raises.

Then I tried something I'm telling you to do. I decided I would try to search for another job and ask for the salary I wanted during salary negotiations. What I discovered during salary negotiations with another company was that this new company was willing to pay me $30,000 more in salary than the salary I was currently making with my previous employer with the raises I received over a 4-year period.

This is what I mean by saying the highest raise you'll ever receive is the salary you negotiate.

I've used this salary-increasing strategy throughout my career for US government and corporate jobs to increase my salary faster and in greater amount than I could every possibly attain through normal raises that companies give their employees. Using this salary-blaster strategy, along with other tips I will show you throughout this guidebook, helped me attain 6-figure salaries I'm enjoying today.

The only other way to get a significant increase in salary within the same company is by accepting a position change within that company that pays a significantly higher salary. However, that may mean doing a job you may not enjoy. In that case, you're better off finding another job you like that pays you the higher salary you want than to move into another position you don't enjoy within the same company in order to get that higher salary.

Rock on ninja turtle; we're just getting started in your job-hunting ninja training.

Contract-to-Hire Worker

Contract-to-hire jobs are oftentimes referred to as CTH or C2H by staffing agency recruiters. If you find a contract-to-hire position through a staffing agency, and you are hired for the job, your business relationship continues with the staffing agency throughout your time working as a contractor for the company client that hired you. Although the source of the money you will be paid is coming from the company client, the staffing agency is your employer who pays your wages every payday.

In this arrangement, the employer who hired you (the primary company) does not pass the common-law employer control test; and therefore, under IRS rules, does not withdraw taxes from your wages.

The staffing agency who is paying your wages (the secondary company) passes the common-law employer control test over you; and are required by the IRS to withdraw taxes from your wages and report your earnings to the IRS at the end of the tax year. You will be working at the worksite of the primary employer who hired you for the job; taking directions from managers and leaders of that company; and working alongside permanent company employees there; but under IRS rules, you belong to the staffing agency—not the company that hired you—and are classified as one of the staffing agency's contractor workers.

At the end of your contract period, the hiring manager and other permanent full-time employees of the client company that hired you will evaluate your performance. If they like your performance, the hiring manager will offer you that same position as a full-time permanent company employee.

If the hiring manager decides to make you a permanent company employee, what typically happens is the hiring manager will approach you in private and ask you if you'd like to become a permanent company employee. If you tell the hiring manager you would like to become a company employee, the hiring manager will coordinate with his or her company's human resource (HR) department to make you an offer for the permanent employee position.

As with the staffing agency paying your hourly rate or annual salary as a contractor, you will again have to negotiate your hourly rate or annual salary with the client company. The company's HR department will send you an offer letter with a salary quote for that company employee position. You can either accept the offer or respond back to HR with a counter-offer asking for more money.

Here's what you need to know about this situation.

You are probably in the best position you could ever possibly be in when it comes to having leverage to ask for more money if you feel the salary in the job offer is too low.

LEVERAGE

What is leverage? Leverage is being in an advantageous position where you're able to use or expend lesser amount of something to gain a greater amount of something else. In other words, leverage gives you a greater return on your investment (ROI). Leverage puts you in an advantageous position to ask for more. When it comes to salary negotiations, leverage allows you to ask for more money or company benefits. Leverage gives you greater **power** and **control** at the bargaining table. The key to unlocking this power and control in salary negotiations is in knowing what your leverage is. I'll provide you that knowledge throughout this book.

Why do you have more leverage to ask for more money when a company's HR department sends you an offer letter for a full-time permanent position in a C2H position? Because you've already proven to the hiring manager and your co-workers of that company that you are an excellent person for the job. That's why they're offering you the full-time permanent employee position. In their eyes, you're a good technical fit and cultural fit for their company.

The hiring manger has been observing and evaluating your performance during your entire contract period, and liked what he or she saw in your work. You already have the hiring manager's seal of approval. *That's leverage.* Therefore, if you feel that the salary HR is offering you is too low, now is the best time you'll ever have to ask for more money in salary negotiations. HR is going to have a harder time saying no to the salary increase in your counter-offer when they know the hiring manager wants you for the position.

So how do you communicate to HR that you want more money? Thank HR for the job offer; let HR know that you appreciate the job opportunity; tell them you want to work for their company as a permanent employee, but you would like to see the compensation at a higher amount. Then tell them in your counter-offer what amount you want. In chapter 7, I'll teach you a variety of methods on negotiating your salary and asking for more money during those negotiations.

One thing that's important to realize though, is that contractors hired by employers to work temporarily in a position are oftentimes paid *more*—not less—money than company employees working in that same position doing the same amount of work. The reason for this comes down to that age old effect of supply and demand. The majority of employers and contractors know that not everyone is cut out to work in a temporary contract position. That means contractors are more in demand than permanent company employees. Companies save more money in the long run hiring someone temporarily for more money with little to no company benefits than they would by hiring someone permanently for less money with full company benefits. That may sound backwards but company balance sheets prove it's true.

Employers are willing to pay extra to attract qualified individuals to temporarily work in needed positions for their company. However, once that contract honeymoon is over; and the contract position is converted to a permanent employee position; that's when the reality of this arranged contract-to-hire marriage relationship sets in. So don't be surprised to discover your salary in the offer letter for the company employee position is actually lower than what you were making as a contractor. Just ask any breadwinner in a home if they had more money or less after being married. I rest my case. Welcome to the supply pool side of this supply and demand economy.

Depending on whether you are making above a 6-figure annual salary or below a 6-figure salary, the decrease from your contract salary to employee salary could be anywhere from $5K a year to $20K a year. Usually, the higher your salary is as a contractor, the more your salary could drop after you convert from a contractor position to a permanent employee position. This is another reason why you should negotiate as high an hourly rate or annual salary as possible for the contractor C2H position.

However, there is no reason why you can't ask for more money if you feel your salary has dropped too low for your liking when it comes time to convert from a contractor to a company employee position.

Many people who have been working as contractors for a while have come to realize that their contract salaries are higher than their company employee salaries; and prefer to remain a contractor if they have the choice. I worked for a private company where the employer hired both C2H contractors and company employees. At the end of the contract period, the contractors were given the opportunity to convert to a company employee or continue working as a contractor. Many of the contractors I worked with opted to remain as contractors because they knew their salary would decrease once they became a company employee.

If you are in a C2H contractor position with an employer who allows you to either convert to a company employee or remain as a contractor, you want to consider both the salary and company benefits when the time comes to make that decision. Your salary may decrease when you convert to a company employee, but your quality of company benefits (such as 401(k), stock options, health insurance, paid holidays, vacations and time off, sick leave, reimbursement for educations or certifications, etc.) will increase above the company benefits you typically receive as a contractor working through a staffing agency.

So how do you know if your company employee salary is going to be lower than your contractor C2H salary if you convert to a company employee?

There are two ways to learn if the company employee salary will be lower than your contractor salary:

1. The first way is simply waiting until you receive the offer letter from HR.

2. The second method is getting an indication from other contractors.

Let's clarify something first.

It's always bad form to either ask someone about their salary or to reveal your own salary to someone. When you and another person engage in a conversation about what each other make, you **RELEASE THE KRAKEN!** Sharing salary information always results in *The Clash of the Titans*.

This is a small social-media world in which we live and communicate. Sharing your salary with someone outside of work can quickly make its way through your connected friends to people in your workplace. Later I'll go into more detail why it's never a good idea to discuss what salaries you or your co-workers make. Trust me on this one for now—bad things can happen.

However, there's nothing wrong with asking a co-worker why they chose to remain a contractor instead of converting to a company employee. Asking a contractor colleague why they chose to remain a contractor is not a question about that person's salary; it's a career path question. If the person responds to your career path question with a contractor-to-employee salary comparison answer, you have the answer you were looking for without your co-worker revealing their salary.

That answer will typically be along the lines of "**The contractor salary pays more than the employee salary**".

Notice that in this answer, your colleague did not reveal their salary. Neither did you share your salary information. Your colleague only gave you an **indication** that contractor salaries are higher than employee salaries in that company. That's why I stated this second way is merely an indication from another colleague who decided to remain as a contractor.

Some recruiters will offer both a C2H hourly rate and a company employee salary.

In some rare instances, a staffing agency recruiter will offer you both a contractor hourly rate and a company employee annual salary for a contract-to-hire position. Typically, the hourly rate will be a higher amount than the annual salary.

For example, the recruiter might offer you an hourly rate of $55 an hour and an annual salary of $105K per year for a contract-to-hire position. The $55/hour rate will be used during your contract period. The $105K/year salary will be used once your contract position is converted to a permanent company employee. If you do the math, you will notice that $55/hour works out to be $114,400 per year as a contractor. This is

$9,400 more than the annual salary of $105,000 per year you will receive as a permanent full-time company employee.

In chapter 6, I'll show you how to easily convert an hourly rate to an annual salary, and vice versa.

For now though, I want you to understand that your permanent company employee salary is fixed the moment you agree to this hourly-to-salary job offer from the recruiter. The good news of this arrangement is you already know how far your contractor pay will decrease if you convert to a company employee at the end of your contract period. The bad news is you already know how far your contractor pay will decrease if you convert to a company employee at the end of your contract period.

You won't be given another chance to renegotiate your salary once you convert to a permanent company employee. In this pre-arranged contract-to-hire marriage relationship, you already know what the marriage is going to be like after the contract honeymoon period is over. Enjoy it while it lasts.

What do you mean I have to interview again?

Sometimes, employers will interview the contractor again for the permanent full-time position before providing the contractor an offer letter. However, at this point, it is simply a matter of company procedure. You're a shoe-in for the job. You've already interviewed with the hiring manager and other interviewers the first time. It will be the same people interviewing you again—the same hiring manager and interviewers—only this time these people now know you, have become your friends and enjoy working with you. That's why they want to hire you to a permanent position. You've been working with them over the past months, and over that time, they've become not only your co-workers; they are now your friends. So don't sweat this second interview.

Besides, I'll show you everything you need to know to successfully pass your interview with strength and confidence in chapters 8 and 9. The information, tips, advice and examples I'll show you in chapters 8 and 9 will put you at ease and empower you for every job interview from this moment forward.

Contract Worker

If you find a contract position through a staffing agency, and you are hired for the job, your business relationship continues with the staffing agency throughout your time working as a contractor for the company client that hired you. The client employer is the source of your income but the staffing agency will pay your wages. This is the same business relationship as the contract-to-hire position, only the employer does not plan to convert your temporary position to a permanent company employee position.

Although this position is only for a temporary contract period, this is not the time to let up on the pedal in putting your best foot forward in giving the employer your best performance and working hard as if you are being considered for a permanent company employee position. Why? First of all, it's the right thing to do. Secondly, the employer oftentimes has the option to either extend your contract out longer or convert your contract position over to a permanent company employee. However, the employer chose to advertise the job as only a temporary contract position for now. If that is the case, the employer will think twice before letting you go after your contract period is up if you put up a stellar performance.

W-2, W-4, W-9, 1099 and Corp-to-Corp Tax Forms

Working under a W-2

When a company passes the common-law employer control test, that company must withhold state and federal taxes, social security, Medicare and other pertinent taxes from each of your paychecks. These withholdings are shown in the W-2 tax form that the employer fills out and sends to their employees at the end of each tax year. The IRS requires employers to send the employee the W-2 form no later than February 1 so employees can file their state and federal income tax returns. Employees of companies typically use the W-2 tax form, whereas contractors may have the option to use the W-2, 1099 or Corp-to-Corp (C2C) tax forms.

Working under a W-4

When employees and contractors use the W-2 tax form, employers are required by the IRS to provide new workers the W-4 tax form to fill out at the start of their new job. The W-4 form employees and contractors fill out help the payroll department of the company figure out what amount to withhold from each person's paycheck each payday. The W-4 allows the employee or contractor to state how much federal income tax the employer should withhold from their paycheck based on certain factors such as marital status, allowances and exemptions.

If you withhold more taxes than needed by the IRS on the W-4, you'll receive less money each payday, but this typically results in you receiving a larger tax refund at the end of the tax year. If you don't withhold enough taxes than needed by the IRS, you'll receive more money each payday, but this means you may owe money back to the IRS at the end of the tax year. Keep in mind you can make changes to your W-4 withholdings any time throughout the tax year.

To help you determine your federal tax withholding, you can use a variety of W-4 withholding calculators found on the Internet.

Working under a 1099 or Corp-to-Corp (C2C)

Contractors can also elect to work under other tax forms, such as a 1099 or Corp-to-Corp (C2C). With these tax forms, the IRS makes the contractor—not the primary or secondary company employers—responsible for paying directly to the IRS the taxes due on the wages or payment the contractor receives. These are the taxes that would normally be withheld by employers using the W-2 and W-4 forms for your work.

Contractors using a 1099 or C2C tax form are required to maintain and keep track of their own records of financial transactions between them and the employer or paying client in order to determine their state and federal taxes, social security, Medicare and other pertinent taxes they owe at the end of the tax year. These records are used by the contractor when filing their income tax returns; and these returns can be audited by the IRS.

Working under a 1099

The 1099 tax form is used to classify yourself as a self-employed individual owning your own business, but your business is not incorporated such as a corporation company. This is considered the simplest business model. If you use the 1099 form, the IRS will tax all of your profits with self-employment tax and income tax. Using a 1099 also disqualifies you for unemployment compensation when you are laid off by the business customer.

Ok, enough of the bad news; now for some good news.

Since the 1099 classifies you as a business, you can take advantage of self-employment tax deductions on your business expenses, such as home office, vehicle and travel expenses; rent on the use of business property; costs for and depreciation of property and equipment; costs for education, training, publications and subscriptions; paying for business-related meals and entertainment; and fees to maintain insurance and retirement accounts, such as IRA or 401k accounts for you and the employees of your business.

Independent contractors oftentimes use the 1099 tax form. When vendors or independent contractors are hired by businesses, the business company will have the contractor fill out a W-9 tax form (for US citizens) or a W-8 form (for non-US citizens) to obtain tax information from the vendor or independent contractor. The W-9 is similar to the W-4 tax form that is initially filled out by company employees when they are hired by their employer.

The tax information on the W-9 includes the contractor's name, address, business name (if different from the contractor's name), business entity (such as sole proprietorship or S corporation) and social security or tax identification number. The business customer will use the information on the W-9 form to complete the 1099-MISC tax form for the independent contractor.

The 1099 states the amount businesses pay to contractors throughout the tax year; and the IRS uses that information to determine how much taxes the contractors owe Uncle Sam. Although the company client provides the 1099 form to the independent contractor at the end of the year to file their tax returns, the client does not withhold income tax, social security, Medicare or other taxes from the contractor's pay. The independent contractor is responsible for paying those taxes to the IRS. So don't spend it all in one place; Uncle Sam still wants his cut at the end of the tax year.

If you are hired as a company employee instead of an independent contractor, it is important you ensure you are filling out a W-4 tax form instead of a W-9 form used by independent contractors. If your new employer erroneously gives you a W-9 to fill out, notify the employer of the error and make them give you a W-4 instead. This will prevent you from being responsible for paying taxes to the IRS at the end of the tax year that your employer is supposed to withdraw from your paycheck each payday.

If someone thinks they're getting one over on their employer by falsely filling out a W-9 and receiving a tax-free salary, it's only a matter of time that full-blown clown-fest they're enjoying will come to an end. Once the IRS reviews that person's tax status on the W-9 for that tax year, the party's over and they're left with the tab.

Working under a Corp-to-Corp (C2C)

The Corp-to-Corp (C2C) tax form is used by one corporation providing services or products to another client corporation. In other words, to use the C2C form, you have to be a corporation company. Being a corporation provides you the same full protection of the law provided to any corporation, such as safeguarding your personal assets against lawsuits.

When you have a C2C business relationship with another company, your corporation—*not you*—is legally bound in agreement to the other company. This means your paycheck is actually paid to your business corporation, instead of to you, by the other client company. If you use the C2C form, the IRS won't hit you with self-employment taxes as with the 1099. However, you are still responsible for all of the bookkeeping and tax reporting requirements of C2C status by the IRS.

Using Tax Status as Leverage to Negotiate Your Salary with Staffing Agencies and Company Clients

Staffing agency recruiters will oftentimes offer jobs to contractors with the option of using a W-2, 1099 or Corp-to-Corp tax form. Contractors should understand their tax responsibilities and liabilities to the IRS when selecting one of these tax options. The W-2 and W-4 forms are the easiest to use for company employees and contractors because the employer is responsible for maintaining and keeping track of the contractor's state, federal and other taxes withheld. At the end of the year, the employee or contractor simply wait for the employer to provide them their completed W-2 form to file with their income tax return.

This information about W-2, 1099 and C2C tax forms is important during your salary negotiations with HR departments, hiring managers, and staffing agency recruiters and account managers. Since your federal and state taxes are not withheld from your salary when you use the 1099 and C2C tax forms, you can negotiate a much higher salary than you normally would using the W-2 tax form.

For instance, when staffing agency recruiters offer you a job opportunity, they will oftentimes tell you that you can work in this position either under a W-2 or C2C. Once the recruiter tells you that you have this option, they typically do one of two things:

1. The recruiter will tell you what the salaries are under the W-2 and C2C tax statuses for the position.

2. The recruiter will not tell you what the salaries are under the W-2 and C2C tax statuses for the position.

If the recruiter tells you what the salaries are for the W-2 and C2C, the first thing you will notice is that the salary quote under the C2C is higher than the salary quote under the W-2. That's because under the Corp-to-Corp and 1099 tax statuses, you (not the staffing agency or the company client) must pay your state, federal and other taxes from your earnings to the IRS at the end of the tax year. Therefore, the staffing agency and the company client offer a higher salary for the C2C and 1099 statuses knowing your gross salary amount will drop to a lower net amount after you subtract a portion of that salary to pay your taxes.

The challenge is trying to figure out how much salary under the C2C status would be enough after you subtract the amount needed for taxes. The key is finding the balance between the salary quote for the C2C position; the amount owed in taxes; your tax bracket; and the potential tax deductions you will have at the end of the year. This is where you may need an accountant to help you with those figures to come out on top with your net salary.

Regardless of how much you think you will need in salary to offset the taxes you must pay to Uncle Sam on your own, you want to ask for as high amount as possible to increase your salary while offsetting those taxes. That's where leverage comes into play. Your leverage in asking for more money in this situation is the fact that you have to deduct your taxes yourself from your earnings under the C2C or 1099 tax status.

If the recruiter does not tell you what the salaries are for the W-2 and C2C, you have to negotiate your salary for either the W-2 or C2C position depending on your preference for working under one of those tax statuses. I'll go into the details of negotiating your salary in chapter 7.

Working Hours

Not long after you joined the ranks of working people, you soon realized there are a variety of hours that people work. The concept of a standard 8-hour workday and 40-hour workweek was not started in America. It originated in Britain.

The harsh realities of child labor working 10–16 hours a day in Britain and other countries in Europe during the Industrial Revolution that emerged in 1760 through the 19th century sparked a need for child labor laws and a change in working hours and working conditions.

Children as young as 4 years old were forced to work to help support their poor families or to help pay off their family's debt while their parents rotted away in the deplorable conditions of debtor's prisons for unpaid bills. By 1810, roughly 2 million school-age children were being forced to work 50-hour to 80-hour workweeks, many of which were working on night shifts and on weekends. What about holidays? Poor children could not afford to take holidays off from their hard labor in coal mines, workshops and factories. Unfortunately, many of those children languished, perished and died under those unspeakable conditions.

Out of the Mouths of Babes

Even Charles Dickens, the author of 15 novels, 5 novellas including *A Christmas Carol*, Oliver *Twist, Great Expectations* and *A Tale of Two Cities*, and hundreds of short stories was a victim of Britain's harsh child labor practices. At the tender age of 12, he was forced to leave school and work in a shoe polish factory to help pay off the debt of his father who was wasting away in a debtor's prison. No doubt, Dickens' poor and difficult childhood gave him much of the material he drew upon in writing his emotionally-charged books, particularly his well-known book *Oliver Twist*; the story that has been retold in many films.

The United States followed suit with Europe in these cruel child labor practices all the way through the early 20th century. Think about it: the die that is cast today for your 8 hours a day, 40 hours a workweek was forged on the backs of little children. *"Out of the mouth of babies and infants, you have established strength."* Psalm 8:2 ESV

Fortunately for these children, the country that was at the forefront of these despicable child labor practices—Britain—was also at the forefront of regulating and later abolishing child labor.

As before, the US followed suit with Britain and other European countries in easing and later abolishing child labor. It wasn't until 1938 that the United States Congress passed the Fair Labor Standards Act for children. For the first time, the US government took action to establish laws regulating the minimum ages and hours of working children. With this Act, the US government set the minimum age of 16 for children who could work during school hours; the minimum age of 14 for children working certain jobs after school; and the minimum age of 18 years of age for young adults working dangerous jobs. As history has recorded, these child labor laws later developed into our current labor laws on working hours for all working people in the US today.

I say all of this to give you a bit of history and appreciation for the working hours you have available to you in our 21st century economy. Although many of us may have reason to complain about the hours we have to work at night or during the day, we've come a long way baby.

Fair Labor Standards Act (FLSA) and the 40-Hour Workweek

Today, the Fair Labor Standards Act (FLSA) under the US Department of Labor establishes minimum wage, overtime pay, hours worked, recordkeeping and child labor laws for all US employees in both government and private sectors.

The FLSA Act states you cannot work more than 40 hours a week without being compensated with at least one and one-half times your regular rate of pay for the overtime hours. This overtime pay rate is also referred to as "time and a half". For instance, if a person who makes $40 an hour works 50 hours during a workweek, that person would be paid $60 (40 x 1.5 = 60) for each hour worked beyond the 40-hour workweek. This overtime regulation is on a per week basis. By US law, you cannot transfer overtime hours from one workweek to another workweek.

If you are working beyond 40 hours per workweek, you may be entitled to extra money in your paycheck that you're missing out on. It's your right by law—not a privilege granted by employers—to receive this overtime pay from your employer.

Later in this chapter I'll go over exempt and non-exempt employees. This information will help you determine if your company is required by law to pay you time and a half overtime pay for the hours you work over 40 hours on a weekly basis.

Working hours and work schedules vary from job to job. The skies the limit on how businesses choose to split their daily working hours to reach the magical 40-hour workweek. Some workplaces use a work schedule of 8-hour days five days a week to obtain a 40-hour workweek. Other places use 10-hour shifts four days a week for a 40-hour workweek. Some employers give their personnel the option to flex their hours; letting their employees select what hours they work as long as they work 40 hours a week.

No matter what schedule of hours a company or office uses, the goal for all of them is to maintain a 40-hour workweek for full-time employees in order to stay within the limits of the law created by the FLSA Act.

Full-Time and Part-Time Hours

Full-time and part-time employees are defined by the IRS and employers, not the Fair Labor Standards Act. However, the same Department of Labor FLSA regulations apply to both full- and part-time workers.

The IRS defines a full-time employee as someone who works an average of at least 30 hours per workweek during a calendar month, or at least 130 hours per calendar month. Naturally, businesses want to squeeze every hour out of their employees in a workweek. Therefore, employers typically have their employees and contractors work the full 40 hours per week since a 40-hour workweek is the most employers can make you work without paying overtime.

Part-time employees typically work less than the 30 hours per workweek during a calendar month or less than 130 hours per calendar month. Many part-time workers are found among the seasonal or holiday workforce; and some part-time workers rotate their shifts with other part-time employees.

Employers save money by hiring part-time workers because employers typically do not provide full company benefits to part-time workers, if they provide any benefits at all to these workers. With the surge of consumer business during seasonal or holiday months, employers can easily supplement their workforce with additional part-time workers without incurring the overhead costs of paying for company benefits to these workers during this timeframe.

Despite the lack of company benefits, statistics show part-time work is on the rise as a popular form of employment. Statista, one of the world's most successful online statistics databases, shows part-time workers in the US rose from 26.68 million in September 2015 to 27.25 million in September 2016. Part-time work is beneficial to many people because it provides these workers more time for other responsibilities they may have in their lives, such as taking care of children or other family members; continuing their education while earning extra money; or supplementing their income they receive from a full-time job.

Wages for Alternative Working Hours

Alternative working hours include working outside the hours of a normal day shift job, such as a swing shift or night shift; or non-standard work days, such as working on weekends or holidays.

Employers also have their own versions of compensating their employees for working odd hours, such as double-time pay (a rate of twice a person's hourly wage for hours worked on holidays or weekends); swing-shift pay (an increase in one's wage, such as a 10% increase in pay for working from 2pm to 11pm); and mid-shift pay (an increase in one's wage, such as a 15% increase in pay for working from 11pm to 8am). These increases in your pay end after you come off those odd working hours. These compensations are initiated, implemented and controlled by the employer; they are not regulated by the FLSA Act or the IRS.

Using Odd Working Hours as Leverage to Increase Your Salary

Working odd hours is another opportunity to increase your salary. If you want to bump up your salary, take a swing shift or night shift that provides a stipend, such as a 10% or 15% increase in pay, respectively, for working those odd hours. If you are asked to work a swing shift or night shift, this is the perfect opportunity to ask your manager for an increase in your salary while you are working that swing or night shift. Employers know that working swing and mid shifts are less desirable to employees than working on day shifts. Your employer will be more willing to grant your requested increase for the duration you work those less desirable hours.

If a staffing agency recruiter offers you a job opportunity, ask the recruiter if that job requires some shift work. Some of these jobs that recruiters offer are rotating shifts where everyone on the team rotates through a day, swing and mid shift. If the recruiter tells you there is some shift work involved, that's the time to enter into salary negotiations with the recruiter by asking if there is differential pay or a stipend for working the swing and mid shifts. You should increase your salary by 10% to 15% more for that swing or mid shift job, respectively, than what you would normally take working on a day shift.

I've worked night shifts in past jobs in order to take advantage of the 15 percent increase in my salary. However, night shifts are not for everyone.

As you might imagine, working those late hours come with their own set of challenges. Working at night and sleeping during the day for long periods can take its toll on the body and some daytime activities, such as time for family, exercise, socializing and entertainment, making appointments, and so forth. If you're a light sleeper, the noise from other people inside or outside your home; the unwelcomed daylight that sneaks its way through your drawn curtains; and warm temperatures of the day may rob you of some of your precious sleep, drain your energy and strain relationships.

Seasonal or Holiday Jobs

While some people are rushing to buy that turkey on sale or gifts at discount prices during the holidays, other people are rushing to those seasonal or holiday jobs. Whether it's Easter, Thanksgiving and the following Black Friday, Christmas or New Years; finding jobs during these holiday seasons are all about timing, like catching a wave on a surfboard.

Before we dive into the specifics of finding jobs during the holiday seasons, let's first take a broader view of when employers are hiring throughout the year.

Ride the Wave of Seasonal Hiring

Statistics show that company hiring practices occur in cycles or waves throughout the year. According to most statistics, the two biggest times in the year when companies in the majority of industries hire people the most are January and February and late September and October. These are the months after the Christmas and New Year holidays (for January and February) and after the summer break (for September and October) when the demand for workers exceeds the supply of workers.

January is the month when most companies receive their approved budgets for the new financial year. Additionally, everyone—including hiring managers and interviewers—has returned back to work after the holidays. This means companies have the money and resources in place to start interviewing and hiring new people again.

Hiring picks up in September and October because workers are returning from summer vacations. Companies know if they're going to hire people, they have to do it before their employees—particularly hiring managers and interviewers—begin their next round of vacations during the November and December holiday months.

Towards the end of each year, companies are also seeking tax write-offs to reduce taxes they owe on their profits that year. One of the ways companies do this is through increasing their costs for recruitment which is a tax write-off. It makes sense for companies to pay for more recruiters and new employees during the September and October months because their hiring managers and other interviewers will be at work during these recruiting months before they start taking time off from work again during the holiday season in November and December.

This doesn't mean you can't find jobs outside of these months. It just means these are the biggest hiring months overall across most industries in the US.

This is important to know especially when you want to increase your salary in your next job search. These months are a good time for job-hunters to ask for that higher salary because demand exceeds supply during these months. This information is also important if you've been out of the job market for a while and want to know when is a good time to jump back into the job market and catch the biggest wave of hiring activity to increase your chances of being hired. It's right at the beginning of January or at the beginning of September.

Start your job search at the beginning of the hiring cycle.

For those who work in industries that rely on warm summer conditions, such as construction, air conditioning, amusement parks and tourism; the best time to get hired first before other job-seeking candidates is at the beginning of the summer hiring cycles in these industries.

The US Bureau of Labor Statistics (BLS) Job Openings and Labor Turnover Survey shows spring and summer job openings on average each year start rising from a low in March to a peak in April; and then drop again in May. Then job openings rise again from May to a peak in July, at which time job openings decline again in August.

So if you want to get hired in the spring months, start looking for work at the beginning of March until hiring peaks in April. If you want to get hired in the summer months, start looking for work at the beginning of May until hiring peaks in July.

The months of June, July and August can oftentimes be the toughest time to get an interview for a job because hiring managers and other members on the interview team are taking their summer vacations. When one or two key people are missing from the interview team, companies usually wait till everyone is back at work before starting the interview process. You can find jobs during these summer months, but just be prepared for greater delays in the interviewing process because of these reasons.

Although November (Thanksgiving and Black Friday) and December (Christmas and New Year) may see an increase in holiday jobs in retail, overall hiring during these months are usually at their lowest levels of the year across major industries due to businesses slowing down for the holiday season and workers taking holiday and vacation days off from work.

Catch the Holiday Wave of Hiring

A great way to supplement your income or have extra spending money during the holidays is to catch the holiday wave of hiring between Thanksgiving and Christmas.

Contrary to the information about the slowdown in hiring across most industries during November and December, these winter months also see a hiring increase in certain industries such as retail stores between

Thanksgiving and Christmas. Retailers in clothing, jewelry, sporting goods, electronics and holiday gifts increase their workforce during the higher volume sales months of November and December. Included in this list are restaurants, party suppliers, holiday decoration centrals, and winter attractions such as ski resorts. Other markets that seek out extra help during the winter holidays are post offices and other warehouse, fulfillment center, shipping and transportation companies, and online distributers because consumer spending has moved from brick-and-mortar toward click-and-order.

The National Retail Federation (NRF) provided the *2015 Holiday Trends and Expectations Survival Kit*, a report on holiday forecasts, consumer trends, historical retail sales data and employment data. This report shows holiday employment rose from a low 263.8 thousand workers when our US economy tanked in the 2008 recession to a high of over 700 thousand people working during the holidays in 2014 and 2015; and expected holiday hiring to reach 750 thousand people during the November and December months in 2016.

Many companies start preparing for this holiday rush by hiring more people for temporary work (part-time and full-time) as early as August or September for the final two months of the year. Most of these jobs are temporary because companies only need the extra personnel to handle the increase of customers during the holidays. Once the customer traffic and buying dies down, so do these positions.

The US Department of Commerce reported 2.9 million jobs were filled in the temporary help services industry in 2015. Although these jobs are only temporary, it gives many people an opportunity to gain experience and skills; network with people in the workforce; build their resume; and possibly open the door to a permanent position with the company. Don't forget the discounts you'll receive with many companies while working there.

Where to Look For Holiday Jobs

You don't have to search or drive far for holiday jobs because many of these retailers and other businesses are in your local neighborhood. Therefore, you don't necessarily have to search for these jobs at Internet job search websites. Just go to the retailer of your choice and ask about any job openings and apply for the job in person.

The following list is where you can apply for seasonal or holiday jobs for the November and December consumer rush. Don't wait until November to start applying for these jobs. Start inquiring about these holiday jobs in September and October.

- **Toys R Us**: They plan to hire around 40,000 seasonal workers in 2016.

- **Kohl's**: They plan to hire around 69,000 seasonal workers in 2016.

- **Target**: They plan to hire around 77,500 seasonal workers in 2016.

- **JCPenny**: They plan to hire around 49,000 seasonal workers in 2016.

- **Macy's**: They plan to hire around 83,000 seasonal workers in 2016.

- **Walmart**: If 2015 was any indication of how many people Walmart plans to hire in 2016 and beyond, you can expect Walmart to hire around 60,000 seasonal workers.

- **Party City**: They plan to hire around 35,000 seasonal workers in 2016.

- **Amazon**: If 2015 was any indication of how many people Amazon plans to hire in 2016 and beyond, you can expect Amazon to hire around 100,000 seasonal workers.

- **UPS**: They plan to hire around 95,000 seasonal workers in 2016; and even better news is that 37 percent of their seasonal hires in 2015 became regular UPS employees.

- **FedEx**: They plan to hire around 50,000 seasonal workers in 2016.

- **Santa Claus**: (I couldn't resist putting this in here.) According to an AARP article titled *12 Great Holiday Jobs* by Kerry Hannon, the contract pay range for Santas is from $10 to $200 an hour during the Christmas holiday season. Even Santa is making some jingle during the holiday season.

The following list is online job boards where you can find seasonal or holiday jobs:

- Snagajob
  http://www.snagajob.com/c/seasonal-jobs

- Backdoorjobs
  http://backdoorjobs.com

- CoolWorks
  http://www.coolworks.com

- Indeed
  http://www.indeed.com/q-Seasonal-jobs.html

- Go to the website of the company, such as Amazon.com, and apply on their career link.

Dress for Success When Applying for Seasonal Jobs

Even though it may be only a seasonal or holiday job at Walmart, JCPenny, Target or another retailer; you should always dress appropriately when inquiring about an available seasonal position. Rules about first impressions apply when people at that retail store, especially the hiring manager, meet you for the first time. It doesn't matter if you're applying for a job at Home Depot and everyone there wears jeans. You're not one of their employees dressed for work. You're a person on the outside looking for a job on the inside. Hiring managers, including Home Depot hiring managers, expect you to dress neatly when you ask for a job application to work at their store.

When inquiring about job openings at Walmart, JCPenny, UPS or other businesses, a business suit for men or a business outfit for women is not required. However, you should be dressed neatly in business-casual attire, such as conservative neat slacks, a collared shirt (a tie is appropriate for clothing stores and other retailers where workers wear ties) and polished shoes for men; and conservative neat slacks or dress, blouse and shoes for women.

In chapter 8 on Interview Preparation and Tips, I go over in great detail the appearance and attire that is acceptable for both men and women seeking jobs in US government and corporate sectors. The advice I give in that chapter is about the proper business attire men and women should wear for those types of job interviews. I recommend you look this chapter over because it also covers important ways to make a good impression in front of the hiring manager when interviewing for the job.

Exempt versus Non-Exempt Employees

The Fair Labor Standards Act (FLSA) entitles all workers to receive overtime pay except workers who are classified as exempt workers.

Exempt employees and contractors are not compensated for working overtime.

Being an exempt employee means you are exempt from the FLSA Act entitling workers compensation for working beyond the 40-hour workweek. In other words, when exempt employees have to work more than 40 hours in any given workweek, every minute of every hour beyond 40 hours they are working means they are working for free for their employer. They get to join the ranks of other people forced to work overtime without time and a half pay, like Santa Claus minus the milk and cookies. Christmas comes early each workweek for employers of exempt employees.

There are many jobs and many workplace situations that require people to stay longer at work for one reason or another. Perhaps there is a presentation they have to give; so they stay later at work to prepare or do more research. Maybe they have to help with a project or installation that requires them to come in at night or on a weekend with other team members. Then there's that person who is late to their shift at work; so the person on the previous shift has to remain at work until that late person arrives. Don't be that guy.

These planned or unplanned hours people work eventually add up to more than 40 hours at the end of the workweek. Those employees who are non-exempt from the FLSA regulation concerning overtime will be paid overtime wages for those extra hours. Those employees who are exempt from the FLSA policy on overtime are simply working those extra hours for their employer for free without any right to compensation, like Santa's little helper (not the greyhound pet dog on *The Simpsons*).

Many of us come in to work early and leave late to make a good impression and set a good example as a dependable and hard worker. There are also times when we don't mind staying a little longer to finish what we're doing at work before heading home. Those are extra minutes that could easily add up to an extra hour or two during a workweek. However, we chose to work those extra minutes or hours every workweek for free to make a good impression. Our employer isn't making us work those extra minutes or hours.

It's when your job oftentimes requires you to work an hour or so beyond your regular 40-hour workweek that your employer or job requirements make you fulfill. If you are a non-exempt employee, you have the option and right under the FLSA regulation to record those extra hours on your timesheet and receive compensation for those extra hours. If you are an exempt employee, you are not entitled to overtime pay. You simply have to suck it up every time, regardless of how many times those extra hours add up each workweek.

This is important to remember when you are job-hunting. When you are presented with a job opportunity, inquire if the positon is an exempt or non-exempt position.

Some employers or staffing agencies will slip in the "exempt employee" statement in your job offer letter without previously telling you the job you are accepting is an exempt position. Therefore, it is important to read your offer letter carefully to see if the word "exempt" is included in the offer language.

Many employers or staffing agencies representing employers will openly advertise a job opportunity as an exempt position. Employers do this to save money by not paying overtime to employees. The employer knows the job may sometimes require you to work beyond a 40-hour workweek. By openly offering the job as an exempt position, the employer is basically rolling the dice to see if they'll get any takers on the exempt position in order to take advantage of the FLSA regulation concerning overtime pay for exempt employees.

"But how do I know a job will actually have me working overtime?" you ask. *"Is there some crystal ball I'm supposed to look into to see the future to know this job will have me coming home later than planned?"*

It's quite elementary my dear Watson. The fact that the employer is advertising the position as an exempt position tells you there is some overtime hours involved with this job. As comedians Jeff Foxworthy and Bill Engvall would say: *"There's your sign."*

Using Overtime as Leverage to Increase your Salary

If you are contemplating pursuing a job opportunity that is an exempt position, and it has the potential of having you work hours beyond the normal 40 hours per workweek, take the time to consider if you are willing to work for free beyond the 40-hour limit in order to get the job.

Ask yourself, ***"Does the hourly rate or annual salary make this job worth the extra unpaid hours I may have to work?"***

If not, you can use the exempt status as leverage to ask for more money during salary negotiations. The job should pay you well enough that you don't mind working extra hours for free. After all, you are not in a love relationship with your employer; you're in a business relationship—unless of course, your employer is also your spouse. Then you're in trouble.

Knowing that the job is an exempt position—no compensation for overtime—gives you more leverage during salary negotiations to ask for a higher salary because you will not be compensated with overtime pay in a job that will potentially have you working over 40 hours per workweek. You can also use the exempt status to try and negotiate for more company benefits due to the exempt classification.

After you agree to take a position as an exempt employee and pass the job interview, the employer will send you an offer letter that will include a reference that you are an exempt employee. *There's your sign.* Once you sign that offer letter, you agree to work for free after the 40-hour mark is reached each workweek.

Stupid is What Stupid Does

By now, you're probably wondering: Shouldn't every worker be paid a decent day's wage for a decent day's work? Why should employers be allowed to pay overtime for some people and no overtime for others, especially if these employees are performing the same job? How can employers get away with offering jobs as exempt? Who came up with this stupid idea anyway; and why are some employees exempt and some are not?

The answer is quite simple.

It's because the same US government that created the FLSA Act to prevent employers from abusing their employees also empowered employers with the same FLSA regulation to take advantage of their employees.

Now before you do your Gump impression of *stupid is what stupid does*, let me explain.

The Fair Labor Standards Act defines what an exempt employee is.

It was the US government that came up with the idea of an exempt employee. The idea made sense back in 1938 during the Great Depression when the FLSA regulation was first passed by Congress and signed by President Franklin D. Roosevelt.

Back then, the FLSA Act initially set the minimum wage to 25 cents an hour and established a 44-hour maximum workweek which amounted to 11 dollars for a 44-hour workweek. That equates to an annual salary of about $572 back in 1938. This new law was also the Act that our government used to take concrete steps to abolish the harsh child labor practices by employers.

Besides protecting children from being exploited by employers looking for cheap labor, the original intent of the exempt provision in the FLSA

Act was to protect lower wage earners—not upper, higher-paid wage earners—from having to work overtime without compensation. Upper wage earners were considered better off with higher salaries, better benefits, job security and greater opportunities for advancement. Therefore, the government didn't need to provide them protection for working overtime. The government still feels the same way today about higher wage earners.

The FLSA law identifies three main categories of exempt workers: executive, administrative and professional (EAP) workers. Included in this group are jobs in driving (taxicab, truck, etc.), sales, science, engineering, math, maritime, radio, TV and motion pictures, and technology. These are mostly white collar workers but some are also blue collar workers.

In 2016, the FLSA regulation stipulates that an employer can classify workers (employees and contractors) as exempt employees if they meet the following three qualifying conditions:

- **Salary Basis Test**: The worker is paid a salary instead of an hourly rate of pay. This salary is constant regardless of the hours worked (more or less hours) each workday or workweek.

- **Salary Level Test**: The worker is earning more than $455 per week ($23,660 per year). According to the FLSA regulation, workers making less than $455 per week ($23,660 per year) are guaranteed time and a half overtime pay for hours worked in excess of 40 hours per workweek. (Again, this was meant to favor low income workers; not high income workers.)

- **Duties Test**: The worker is paid a full salary for every workweek regardless of the amount of hours worked.

The US government has reviewed these three qualifiers defining exempt employees since 1940. The last time the FLSA regulation was reviewed and updated was 2004 when the $455 per week ($23,660 annually) qualifier was set. Ten years later in 2014, it was reviewed and updated again.

In 2014, it was President Obama who directed the US Department of Labor to review and update the Fair Labor Standards Act again. The resulting review and update, called the Final Review, is effective December 1, 2016. Here's what changed in the three qualifying conditions for classifying a worker as an exempt employee:

- **Salary Basis Test**: Salary basis qualifier remains the same—the worker is paid a salary instead of an hourly rate of pay. However, for the first time, employers are now allowed to use bonuses and incentive payments, including commissions, to satisfy up to 10 percent of the employee's salary of the new salary level qualifier of $913. This amendment does not apply to highly compensated employees (HCE) employees.

- **Salary Level Test**: The worker is earning more than $913 per week ($47,476 per year). This increase from $455 to $913 per week is based on the lowest-wage Census Region—the South. This increase essentially provides overtime protection to a larger number of lower income families. Additionally, the total annual compensation requirement for highly compensated employees (HCE) is increased from $100,000 per year to $134,004. An HCE employee is considered one of the top wage earners in a company, such as the top 10 or 20 percent salaried workers of a company. FLSA regulation concerning HCE employees ensures most of these highly-paid full-time white collar workers are ineligible for overtime.

- **Duties Test**: No changes to the duties test. The worker is paid a full salary for every workweek regardless of the amount of hours worked.

In addition to these changes, the updated FLSA Act, effective December 1, 2016, will require that the salary and compensation levels mandated by the FLSA Act will be automatically reviewed and updated every three years starting on January 1, 2020.

The Department of Labor expects these overtime changes in December 2016 to positively impact a majority of the 4.1 million low income workers who currently are not eligible for overtime pay. The Labor Department also estimates that roughly 100,000 people will receive a raise in pay due to these new changes because employers will be attempting to maintain the exempt status of many of their employees by increasing their salaries above the $47,476 per year threshold. For more information about changes to the Fair Labor Standards Act (FLSA), go to http://bit.ly/1XmUYvA and https://www.dol.gov/featured/overtime.

The increase from $455 per week ($23,660 per year) to $913 per week ($47,476 per year) forces many employers to make a decision on how they will pay their employees and contractors. They can either pay people less than $913 per week and be required by law to make them non-exempt workers who are entitled to overtime wages; or they can increase their weekly rate above $913 and make them exempt workers who are not entitled to overtime pay. Either way, a greater number of lower income workers win—which was the original intent of the exempt status.

So you can see from this information that the US government gives employers the right to make you an exempt employee or contractor based on FLSA regulation, as long as you fall within the criteria of the qualifying factors. If you are paid a salary over $913 per week ($47,476 per year) after December 1, 2016, and your position falls into the executive, administrative and professional (EAP) categories of workers, the employer has the right to make you an exempt employee or contractor. You, on the other hand, have the right to refuse a job offer if you prefer overtime pay.

However, this new overtime rule received a lot of push-back from business groups, Congress and the courts to delay the new overtime rule; roll it out over several months; or scrap it altogether. On November 22, 2016, a federal judge in Texas issued a temporary injunction halting the overtime rule nationwide. This new overtime rule will now most likely be up to President Trump's administration to decide on its fate.

Salary Workers versus Hourly Workers

The money you are paid for the work you perform in a job can be paid to you as either a salaried worker or an hourly worker.

Salary Workers

Salaried workers are company employees or contractors that are paid a set annual salary, such as $70K, $90K or $140K per year, upon being hired. Although $43.27 an hour equals $90K per year, the salaried worker is not paid $43.27 an hour; they are paid a flat salary of $90,000 a year.

This annual salary can be paid out to the salaried worker in various ways, such as on a weekly, bi-weekly or monthly basis each payday. This set amount paid to the salary worker each payday does not change regardless of how many hours the person works. Whether the employee or contractor works more or less than 40 hours per workweek, the employee will still be paid the same amount of money each payday. Therefore, salary workers do not have to track their hours worked the way hourly workers do. Salary workers oftentimes do not have to sign a timesheet as do hourly workers.

The Fair Labor Standards Act classifies most salaried workers as exempt workers. Under the FLSA Act, exempt workers are not entitled to overtime pay. When salaried workers have to work overtime to fulfill their duties or responsibilities on the job, employers expect salaried workers to work those overtime hours for free to get the job done.

Hourly Workers

Hourly workers are company employees or contractors that are paid by the hour, such as $25, $43.27 or $60 an hour. Although you could correctly surmise that $43.27 an hour is equal to an annual salary of $90K, the worker's hourly wage is not computed or classified that way.

Unlike the salary worker, the hourly worker must work the full hour to receive the full $43.27. If the worker works less than an hour they will be paid less than $43.27 for that hour. When payday rolls around, the hourly worker could receive less than they normally would for a one-week or two-week pay period depending on each hour worked in that period. Hourly workers typically have to document each hour worked and sign their timesheet at the end of each pay period.

The Fair Labor Standards Act classifies most hourly workers as non-exempt workers. When hourly workers work overtime beyond the normal 40-hour workweek, they usually receive overtime pay. The FLSA Act gives hourly workers the right to be compensated with at least one and one-half times their regular hourly rate of pay for their overtime hours.

Salary and Hourly Positions Offered by Recruiters

Oftentimes, full-time company employees receive salaries while contractors receive hourly wages. When you are offered a job by a staffing agency recruiter or a company HR rep; always ask if the position is a salaried or hourly position. This will help you determine what are your rights concerning overtime pay and how your pay will be determined for each payday.

Salaried positions ensure you will receive the same amount each payday, but you probably will not be paid for overtime worked. Ask the recruiter offering you the job to confirm if the open position is a salaried or hourly position.

Hourly wages means you must track each hour worked to ensure you are properly compensated for with each hour of work. Most employers paying wages to hourly workers provide them an online timesheet where they can document their hours worked each workweek. As an hourly worker, you will most likely receive overtime pay when you work beyond 40 hours during the workweek. Again, clarify if this is an hourly or salary position with the recruiter before accepting the position.

I've worked both salaried and hourly positions. Typically, my deciding factor on whether or not I pursue a job opportunity is not based on whether it is a salaried or hourly job. I usually make my decision about working somewhere based on how interested I am in the work the company does; the responsibilities I will have on the team I'm working with; and the amount of money—salary or hourly—that I will make working in that job. If the hourly rate or salary is high enough, I don't care if I am not compensated for working overtime.

The choice is yours to make.

Company Benefits

The beauty of working as a full-time company employee is receiving the employer's version of a celebrity gift bag at the Academy Awards—company benefits. These bennies usually include health and dental insurance, vision care, 401(k), stock options, paid vacation, paid time off, and reimbursements for education, training or certifications. Not bad for a gift bag. Part-time employees are not provided all of these benefits but may be given other lesser perks by the company.

Full-time contractors that work for an employer other than a staffing agency are typically offered similar benefits being offered by employers to their permanent company employees. Full-time contractors whose hourly wage or annual salary is paid by a staffing agency usually receive fewer benefits than full-time company employees, but more benefits than part-time employees.

Whether you are looking for work as a contractor or company employee, the best thing to do is make a list of company benefits that you absolutely must have in order to accept a job opportunity. Then have another list of benefits that would be nice to have but is not a deal breaker if these benefits are not included with the job. When it comes time to negotiate your salary and benefits, you'll already know which benefits you must negotiate for and which ones you can live without.

It's important to ask recruiters if the contract position they are offering you comes with or without company benefits, such as health insurance, paid holidays, vacation or sick days. Some recruiters will offer you a job opportunity and not mention that the job does not come with any benefits. Some of these job opportunities may offer health insurance, but do not pay for any paid holidays, vacation, sick leave or time off. That means that while everyone else is taking a paid holiday off from work, you still have to be at work (if you want to be paid for that day) or take the holiday off without pay. If you're sick or one of your children is sick, and you need to remain home so you or your child can recover, you have to take that day or couple of days off without pay.

This doesn't mean the job opportunity with few or no benefits isn't worth taking. If the contract position does not come with benefits or very few company benefits, this gives you leverage over the recruiter and the employer to ask for a higher hourly rate or salary than what you would normally accept for that position if company benefits were offered.

Using Company Benefits as Leverage to Increase Your Salary

How much leverage is company benefits worth?

First of all, think about the cost of the benefits you stand to lose. Think about the lost pay you will incur from taking holidays, vacations or sick leave without pay. Think about the cost of buying health insurance out-of-pocket or having to pay IRS penalty fees if you don't have any health insurance. Think about the costs for treatment without health insurance or dental insurance. Think about the costs for your or your family member's eyeglasses without coverage. It doesn't matter if you have health or dental insurance from another source. The fact is this job doesn't provide these benefits, so you must factor in these costs when negotiating your salary. Think about the money or tax deductions you stand to lose from having no investment plan, such as a 401(k). All of these benefits are part of your justification for asking for more money in salary negotiations. That's plenty of leverage to ask for more money.

These company benefits amount to thousands of dollars. We're talking about leverage to ask for several thousand dollars more in annual salary. The amount you should ask above the salary you normally would ask for a job that comes with benefits should be equal in value to those benefits lost. This amount is subjective but could easily amount to $10,000 to $20,000 more than what you would normally ask in salary compensation.

Don't forget, this higher contractor salary will be reduced if you convert to a permanent company employee with this client employer. When your contractor position is converted to a company employee position, your new employer will justify the decrease in your salary by providing you all of these company benefits. So while you are negotiating your salary as a contractor, ask for as much money as the employer is willing to pay for that contractor position without benefits. In chapter 7 on salary negotiations, I'll go into more detail on how to ask for more.

People with other sources of income, such as another working spouse or military veterans with a pension and/or TRICARE health benefits, tend to benefit most from accepting job opportunities without benefits. They can ask for a higher salary because of the lack of benefits, but are still covered by their spouse's company benefits or by retirement benefits. As a retired military veteran with a pension and TRICARE health and dental benefits, I oftentimes will accept a job opportunity with no company benefits. I can tell a company to *show me the money*, lots of money, and still be covered with health benefits from another source.

Business Travel

Ellen Degeneres joked, *"My grandmother started walking five miles a day when she was 60. She's 97 now, and we don't know where the heck she is."*

Do you enjoy traveling? Do you like being on the road, traveling to different places, experiencing different surroundings and meeting new people? Then perhaps a job that includes traveling is right for you.

For others, traveling is right up there in the category of doing your taxes, having your teeth pulled or finding an eviction notice on your door.

In either case, that's why it's important to find out if the job you are pursuing involves travel. Some jobs might be advertised as "occasional travel" required. Some job descriptions will specifically state 25 percent travel is required with the job. Other jobs may ask you to travel 50 or 75 percent of the time. You may be on the road so often; people won't know where the heck you are from one month to the next.

When a job opportunity is presented to you by a recruiter, ask the recruiter how much travel is involved with the job. This way you can quickly assess if the amount of travel required by that job is acceptable for you, your personality, your family and your lifestyle.

For the more adventurous types, a job that requires some travel time is a welcomed opportunity to see and enjoy other people and places at the company's expense while on a business trip. After all, it's not all business when you're on the road. Companies are still required by law to limit your working hours to 40 hours per workweek (which amounts to 8 hours a day per week) regardless if you're at your desk at work or on the road. If you're traveling at your company's expense, the rest of your time off from work is free time to enjoy the sights like any other tourist or vacationer.

Before you decide for or against the idea of choosing a job that requires traveling, consider some of the basic pros and cons to business travel.

Pros to Business Travel

- Opportunity to get away from the daily grind at the office or workplace routine.

- Opportunity to travel and see different sites, try different foods, experience different cultures, meet new people; and add to your memories and social media posts—all at the company's expense.

- Opportunity to use company paid vacation along with business travel to extend your time away from work.

- Company paid expenses for travel, hotel, food, tips, entertainment, rental car and gas, taxi, Uber, Lyft, conference fees and miscellaneous items.

- Opportunity to rack up airline miles and hotel points.

- Use of a company credit card while traveling.

- Cash advances for travel.

- Tax deductions for business expenses not reimbursed by the company.

Cons to Business Travel

- Concern and costs for temporary care of pets, children or other family members while you are traveling.

- Sometimes hard on relationships; and the constant possibility of missing out on family or friend events.

- Long lines at airports, travel delays, TSA checkpoints, lost luggage and other travel inconveniences.

- Initial out-of-pocket expenses; having to maintain receipts for all purchases related to business travel; and delays in company reimbursements for your out-of-pocket travel expenses.

- Having to live out of a suitcase while traveling; unhealthy eating habits and poor exercise while traveling; and stress on the body from loss of sleep or change of time zones.

- Increased workload when you return back to work at your home station.

- Did I mention long lines at the airport?

Living and Working Overseas

If you want to take business travel to the next level, you might consider living and working overseas.

Take a Selfie in Europe

Imagine spending your weekends or holidays taking in the panoramic view of the city of Paris from the top of the Eiffel Tower; stepping where battle-worn gladiators and 65,000 blood-thirsty Roman spectators had trodden in the ancient Coliseum in Rome; visiting the Alps in Switzerland, Austria, Italy or Germany to ski breathtaking slopes, picnic beside luminous lakes or tour enchanting villages and countryside; feeling the warm sand between your toes and the cool breeze through your hair (providing you have hair) on the spacious, lovely beaches of the French Riviera while time stands still as you relax at this European vacation spot; or feeling the excitement in the air while tourists gather to watch the royal guard and marching band dressed distinctively in tall black bearskin fur headgear, historic red coats and black pants nicely trimmed with red stripes marching proudly in step during the Changing of the Guard at Buckingham Palace.

Rather than spending an expensive and exhaustive family trip to see Disneyland's Sleeping Beauty Castle or ride the Matterhorn Bobsleds in America; living in Europe allows you to take your time on inexpensive day trips to walk through real castles, such as the luxurious Neuschwanstein Castle in Bavaria which Disney modeled their castle after; or take a breathtaking train ride to see the real Matterhorn mountain straddling the border between Switzerland and Italy.

Instead of dreading another long line of Black Friday bargain hunters and last minute Christmas shoppers pushing and shoving in city malls throughout the US; imagine friends and families laughing as they snuggle together seated at a table while feasting on bratwurst, gingerbread or other delicious treats and drinking cups of heartwarming Glühwein (warm red wine with spices, citrus fruits and sugar); or casually strolling through holiday lighting, decorations, holiday music, gifts, toys and the inviting smell of delicious food cooking at stalls and booths outside at a Christkindlesmarkt (Christmas market) under Germany's crisp, winter's night sky that sparkles with the twinkle of ol' Saint Nick's watchful eye. *Das ist wundervoll*! (That is wonderful!)

During Mardi Gras, you could rub shoulders among revelers adorned with beads in New Orleans; or you could celebrate Carnevale in Venice, Italy with partygoers, young and old, wearing colorful and elaborate costumes and masks of the 14th to 16th century era while strolling through the famous Piazza San Marco (Saint Mark's Square). You say you don't like crowds? Off in the distance, couples in lovers embrace are reclining in Venetian gondolas as they float their cares away across the calm, romantic waters of the Grand Canal.

Having lived and worked in Europe over 15 years, I've been able to see and do all of these things I just mentioned. It was easy and cheap because I lived and worked there; and so can you.

The advantages and disadvantages to living and working overseas are plentiful. Before we jump into some of those advantages and disadvantages, let's get a few definitions out of the way first.

Expatriates

Americans who relocate, temporarily or permanently, to foreign countries are called expatriates or expats for short. Expatriate comes from the two Latin words *ex* meaning "out of" and *patria* meaning "country" or "fatherland".

The term expatriate does not necessarily mean you are an "ex-patriot". A patriot is someone who loves and strongly supports or fights for their native country. An ex-patriot is simply someone who is the opposite of that definition; someone who no longer loves or supports their native country but instead has renounced their country.

"Expatriate" is not the same as "ex-patriot". Expatriates or expats still love and support their native country; they've just chosen to live and work temporarily or permanently in a foreign country. Whether or not a person still loves and supports their country is a personal patriotic choice; but the word expatriate is not the definition of that choice.

The US uses the term expatriate to classify non-federal employees living and working overseas, such as government contractors or employees of private companies living and working overseas. US government employees and Foreign Service employees are not considered expats.

The US Foreign Service is the part of the US Department of State that carries on US diplomatic functions in 265 overseas locations, called US diplomatic missions. You know many of these locations as US embassies and consulates where US diplomatic representation and services are performed by roughly 15,000 US professionals.

The difference between an expatriate and an immigrant is that immigrants always relocate to another country with the intent to take permanent residence in that foreign country. An expatriate's intention for relocating to another country is less concrete. Expats are either in that foreign nation only temporarily for work or education purposes; or expats could choose to remain there permanently but still retain their US citizenship.

The words emigrate and immigrate are two verbs describing different phases of the same process of becoming an immigrant. To emigrate means to leave a country to live in another foreign country permanently—it has to do with the exit part of the process of immigration. To immigrate means to enter a foreign country to live permanently after having left another country—it has to do with the entrance part of the process of immigration.

An immigrant and migrant is not the same thing either. Migrants are people who move from one place to another within the same country, such as an American living in California migrating to Colorado to live. Immigrants move between different countries.

The United Nations performs a variety of surveys on the world's population. In the UN report on immigrants, titled *International Migrants Stock Dataset in 2015*, 244 million people immigrated to another nation in 2015, an increase of 71 million people since 2000.

The US is not the only country that has expatriates or expats. Every country has expats—citizens of their own country living and working abroad in a foreign country.

The number of US expats living and working abroad is unclear because US censuses do not include Americans living abroad. Therefore, there is limited information as to the exact number of Americans living in foreign countries. However, delegates of the Association of Americans Resident Overseas (AARO) headquartered in Paris, an international non-partisan association with members in 46 countries, were told by State Department officials in 2015 they estimated roughly over 7 to 8 million Americans (excluding military) are living and working overseas in 160-plus countries. This is double the size of roughly 4 million Americans who were estimated living overseas in 1999.

Foreign Earned Income Exclusion for Expatriates

I've already mentioned one of the main advantages of living and working overseas—it's easier and cheaper to see and enjoy the sights of places like Europe or Asia while living there.

Another more profitable reason for Americans living and working overseas is the foreign earned income exclusion the IRS gives expats. This exclusion allows expats that are US citizens and file a US income tax return to exclude or reduce their taxable income.

How much income can be excluded?

It's an income exclusion that is adjusted annually for inflation. In 2014, expats could exclude $99,200 from their annual income. In 2015 and 2016, that exclusion amount rose to $100,800 and $101,300, respectively. That means if your salary from an overseas job was $90,300 in 2016, you could exclude all of your $90,300 when filing your income tax return. **Boom shakalaka**!

If you made $150,000 in 2016, you could exclude the maximum amount of $101,300 which means you only have to pay US taxes on $48,700. This is one of the main reasons why 7 to 8 million Americans have chosen to live and work overseas.

In addition to exclusion from tax on income earned overseas, the foreign earned income exclusion also allows expats to exclude or deduct a certain percentage of foreign housing expenses, or meals and overseas lodging provided by employers. This reduces your taxable income even further.

As I mentioned earlier, US government employees and Foreign Service workers are not considered expatriates. Therefore, US federal employees and Foreign Service employees living and working overseas are not allowed to use the foreign earned income exclusion when filing their taxes. However, these government employees and Foreign Service workers may receive some nontaxable allowances for overseas expenses; and may be eligible for tax deductions on some expenses that are greater than their nontaxable allowance. For Foreign Service employees, some of their allowances or deductions include expenses for travel, entertainment, gifts, and costs for official functions. These expenses are similar to the expenses of someone working for a private corporation on a business trip. After all, Foreign Service workers are on a business trip in a foreign country on behalf of their employer, the US Department of State—one very long business trip.

If you are interested in working overseas in the Foreign Service, here are a couple of websites to learn more about what they do, what are the requirements and tests, and how to apply for a Foreign Service job.

- https://careers.state.gov/work/foreign-service

- http://bit.ly/2dF14ao

In order for non-government employees and contractors to qualify for the foreign earned income exclusion, US citizens working overseas have to pass one of these two tests:

- **Bona fide resident test**: The expat was a bona fide resident of a foreign country for a full US tax year. A "bona fide resident" means you are residing or living in a foreign country, but your domicile (permanent residence) is still in the US.

- **Physical presence test**: The expat was outside the US for 330 days in any 12-month period. This means you can be in the US (such as a short vacation away from the foreign country) for no more than 35 days out of any 12-month period (365 days). For example, if you are in the US for 36 days while living and working in the foreign country in a 12-month period, you are automatically disqualified for the earned income exclusion.

Paying Income Tax to a Foreign Country

It's not all gravy when it comes to exemptions to income taxes while living and working overseas. Everything I mentioned so far has to do with US income taxes. The foreign country you are living and working in may also require you to pay income taxes.

The US has many tax treaties with foreign countries. Some of these treaties allow you to pay reduced or no income taxes to the foreign country. Without these treaties or if you do not fall within the qualifications of the treaty, you most likely will have to pay income tax to that foreign country.

Take Germany and Italy for instance. Those countries require US citizens living and working in their country to pay income taxes on income earned in their country. However, Germany and Italy have tax treaties with the US that exempts US military personnel and US government employees (not American contractors) from being taxed by their country. In order for US government contractors living and working in Germany or Italy to be exempt from that country's income tax, US contractors must qualify as "technical experts".

TESA

The criteria for meeting the technical expert status are defined in the Technical Expert Status Accreditation (TESA) agreement between the US and the foreign country. A technical expert under TESA is a US government contractor (not a US government employee who is automatically exempt from paying income taxes to Germany and Italy) who performs complex tasks of a technical-military or technical-scientific nature in support of US military forces in that foreign country. Administrative or blue-collar work would not qualify for the TESA accreditation.

TESA requirements vary slightly between Germany and Italy. Generally, the TESA criteria requires the person to have a degree, such as a bachelor's degree, a certain number of years of experience in a technical field, and be in a job considered essential for the operation and support of US military forces in that foreign country. The resume (written by the contractor) and the job description (written by the employer) also helps to identify the contractor occupying that position as technically qualified for TESA accreditation. Having a US government security clearance is not a requirement for TESA accreditation; therefore, you do not need a US security clearance to qualify for the TESA tax exclusion.

There are some conditions that can disqualify you from the income tax exclusion by the foreign country even though you previously met the TESA requirements. For example, if your status changes to a permanent resident of the foreign country, you can be subject to income tax by that foreign country.

Factors that identify you as a permanent resident of that foreign nation include marrying someone who is a citizen of that foreign country; your children are enrolled in that country's school system instead of an International School Service (ISS) or a US sponsored school (such as schools on US military installations) in that foreign country; owning property in that foreign country; or having an American spouse who is working in that country's local economy. All of these factors disqualify you for TESA status. Under these conditions, you would have to pay income tax to that foreign country.

How attached you become over time to that foreign country's lifestyle, people and culture can impact your income tax status while living and working overseas. Crossing the line in ways that negatively impact your tax status with that foreign country is like having a half-filled grocery cart with not one but two bad wheels at Walmart. Do you continue with the two bad wheels knowing the more you load the cart, the harder it will be to push it? Or do you empty the cart and start all over again with a new cart?

Many US government contractors who crossed the line chose to keep pushing that cart and ended up either returning to the US with a new foreign wife (or foreign husband) to avoid paying income taxes to the foreign country; or remaining in that foreign country and paying that country's income tax. Other US government contractors decided to empty and change their cart in order to avoid paying that country's income tax while remaining in that foreign country.

I've held US government contractor positions while living and working in foreign countries outside of the US; and was able to take advantage of both the US income tax exclusions under the foreign earned income exclusion law and exclusions from income tax of foreign countries under the TESA agreement I just explained. In my eyes, the advantages outweighed the disadvantages in those overseas locations (as long as I had a grocery cart with four good wheels).

The following is a quick overview of other advantages and disadvantages of living and working overseas:

Pros to Living and Working Overseas

- The US government agency or private company that hired you will pay for your flight tickets and other travel costs to your overseas location.

- The US government agency or private company will pay for the packing and shipping of your household goods and vehicle to and from the foreign country.

- Opportunity to have relatives and friends come visit you overseas for an experience of a lifetime.

- Getting paid housing allowance and cost-of-living allowances (COLA)—extra money your employer provides you on top of your salary to pay for housing and the costs of living in the overseas area.
- Some companies will pay for one or two vacation trips back to the US per year while you are living and working overseas.

- If working as a US government employee or government contractor, the military installation's Housing Office will provide you housing assistance. This office has a listing of homes for rent on the economy; and will help you with communicating with landlords and establishing the rental contract. The Housing Office will also provide you free loaner furniture (beds, couches, lamps, tables, etc.) and appliances (washers, dryers, stoves, refrigerators, etc.) to complete your home furnishings; as well as free delivery and pick-up services of these loaner items.

- The US government agency or private company will oftentimes pay for storage of household goods or a vehicle in the US if you plan to leave them in the US while you live overseas. If employers do not pay for this storage, you can deduct the first year's storage fees from your income tax as moving expenses for a new job.

- You can store your vehicle in the US and buy a cheap used car on the local economy of that foreign nation. This way you save wear and tear on your car in the US; and will have it available for you when you return to live in the US again.

- Your US dollar may be worth more or less depending on the exchange rate of that foreign nation. If your US dollars are worth more, you can buy food, gifts, souvenirs and other commodities for less money on the local economy.

- If you own a home in the US, you can rent out your home through a property management company so you can have another source of income to pay off your mortgage while you are living overseas.

- If you are a US government employee or government contractor, you will be allowed to purchase gas coupons that allow you to purchase gas for your vehicle at a reduced price on the local economy.

- If you are a US government employee or government contractor, you will be allowed to purchase value-added tax (VAT) exemption forms that allow you to purchase commodities on the local economy without having to pay that country's VAT tax on those products.

Cons to Living and Working Overseas

- You must obtain and maintain a current passport, work permit and possibly a visa depending on the country.

- This move will require a change of address to route your mail to your new address in the foreign country.

- Having to take your children out of the US school system and enroll them in a school within the International School Service (ISS) or in a school on a US military installation overseas. (The ISS is also a great job opportunity for teachers who want to work overseas with other international teachers.)

- Possibly having to learn the language spoken in that foreign country; and the challenge or difficulty in communicating with people in that country.

- Many foods you are accustomed to buying in US stores may not be available in the stores of foreign countries.

- Purchasing an international driver's license to allow you to drive in the foreign country; and finding an insurance company that insures your vehicle for driving on roads in foreign countries.
- Learning the road signs and rules of the road; driving on the left side of the road (in some countries such as the UK, Japan and Australia); taking that country's driver's exam; and converting

kilometers (KM) per hour to miles per hour in order to drive safely within the proper speed limit on the roads.

- Overseas areas, such as Europe, Asia and the Middle East use 220v power. Your electronic devices must have 110v/220v capability or you can bring or buy voltage converters that can convert the 220v power from outlets to 110v for your 110v devices. You'll also need to buy several adapters to convert the US power cord plug to the type of plug that works with outlet shapes used in foreign countries.

- Your smartphone may or may not work in these overseas locations depending on whether or not your mobile phone has the proper capabilities. Mobile phones typically use one of two types of radio systems: Code Division Multiple Access (CDMA) or Global System for Mobiles (GSM). The CDMA radio signal does not work with the GSM signal. In the United States, Sprint, Verizon and U.S. Cellular use CDMA; AT&T and T-Mobile use GSM. Most of the mobile phones used overseas are using the GSM radio signal.

- Voting must always be by mail-in ballot. If you don't have a problem with that, then this can be a pro instead of a con.

- You may need immunization shots based on the location of the foreign nation.

- Possibly the need to use a mail order pharmacy to receive your medications.

- The cost of shipping pets overseas. There may be other requirements before your pet is allowed to enter the foreign country, such as quarantine, an import permit, Blood Titer test, microchip or a pet passport.

- Greater vigilance may be required in some populated areas due to heightened awareness of terrorism.

The employer who hires you will assist you with many of the requirements listed in these pros and cons. For instance, your employer will oftentimes provide you an overseas mailing address beforehand so you can forward your mail to your new mailing address prior to departing the US. Employers typically provide their new employees with information on schools to enroll their children; housing information and housing assistance; vehicle registration and driving information; and other important information needed upon their arrival. Additionally, co-workers at their overseas job will offer assistance and information as well; and show them around the area to help them get settled in.

Resources for Finding Overseas Jobs and Living Overseas

If you'd like to try living and working temporarily in foreign countries, such as Germany, Italy, Greece, Belgium, Switzerland, Netherlands, Sweden, Spain, Turkey, UK, Australia, New Zealand, China, Japan, South Korea or South Africa; you can do so through a variety of ways.

Working as a US government employee, government contractor or employee of a corporation is just some of the ways of making that dream of living and working overseas a reality. You can also join an overseas volunteer program such as the Peace Corps; get on an internship or exchange program; attend an international career fair such as Global Careers Fair; or stay on the move internationally by trying yacht or cruise ship jobs.

In chapter 2, I go over US government employees and contractors, and how you can join that workforce. This will allow you to live and work overseas as either a US government employee or government contractor and take advantage of both the foreign earned income exclusion (to minimize your US income taxes) and possibly the TESA agreement so you don't have to pay income taxes to a foreign country, such as Germany or Italy.

You can find out about overseas jobs with private companies through online job boards in similar fashion to finding jobs in the US. In your profile on these job sites, you should also indicate which overseas countries you are willing to work in.

Following are some of the online job boards where you can find overseas jobs in the private sector:

- LinkedIn.com
  https://www.linkedin.com

- One Day One Job
  http://www.onedayonejob.com

- OverseasJobs.com
  http://www.overseasjobs.com

- InternationalJobs.com
  http://www.internationaljobs.com

- GoAbroad.com
  http://jobs.goabroad.com

- TransitionsAbroad.com
  http://www.transitionsabroad.com

- Peace Corps
  https://www.peacecorps.gov

- Global Careers Fair
  https://www.globalcareersfair.com

- Seek
  https://www.seek.com.au

- Expat Network
  https://www.expatnetwork.com

- Theguardianjobs
  https://jobs.theguardian.com

- Yacht Jobs
  http://www.yacrew.com

- All Cruise Jobs
  http://www.allcruisejobs.com

- Oil Jobs Overseas
  http://www.airswift/as/oil-jobs-overseas

- TeachAway
  https://www.teachaway.com/teaching-jobs-abroad

There are also many helpful online resources providing support groups and information on how to live and work overseas.

Following are some online resources about living and working overseas:

- U.S. Passports and International Travel
  https://travel.state.gov/content/passports/en/abroad.html

- TransitionsAbroad.com
  http://www.transitionsabroad.com

- GoAbroad.com
  http://www.goabroad.com

- Go Overseas
  https://www.gooverseas.com

- British Universities North America Club (BUNAC)
  http://www.bunac.org

- Easy Expat
  http://www.easyexpat.com

- Expats Abroad
  http://www.expats-abroad.com

- Expat Network
  https://www.expatnetwork.com

- ExpatWoman
  http://www.expatwoman.com

- American Citizens Abroad
  https://www.americanabroad.org

- Escape Artist
  http://www.escapeartist.com

- My World Abroad
  http://myworldabroad.com

- Alliance Abroad Group
  http://allianceabroad.com

- Moving Worlds
  https://movingworlds.org

- InterNations
  https://www.internations.org

Contractor Jobs in Austere, Danger/Hazard Overseas Areas

Not a Griswold's European Vacation

I talked about living and working overseas in safe, enjoyable overseas locations such as Europe where you can bring your family, pets and household goods, and invite friends and relatives to visit you there. The overseas locations I'm about to talk about next are not where you would find Chevy Chase and the Griswold family on one of their European vacations. We're talking about living and working in austere, danger/hazard overseas locations.

By "austere" I mean locations with extremely hot weather; isolation from your normal lifestyle of family, friends and community; minimum comforts and luxuries; and strict, rough, bare and simple living and working conditions. (Some of you are saying, *"That sounds like my life with my ex."*)

By "danger/hazard" I'm referring to places that either have the potential to be hostile to Americans or already are hostile to Americans depending on the area; places where there is a certain level risk to your life depending on the area (some of these locations are combat zones); places where there may be poor sanitation, diseases, poor drinking water (you might have to use bottled water) or poor air quality; and places that are unpaved (you might have to walk on dirt, gravel or mud walk paths and roads).

Most of these locations are primarily in the Middle East that has a US military presence there. These overseas countries include places such as Iraq, Afghanistan, Saudi Arabia, United Arab Emirates (UAE), Kuwait, Bahrain, Qatar, Oman, Egypt and Djibouti.

Defense Contractor Jobs in Austere, Danger/Hazard Areas

The majority of US civilians working in these locations are contractors; although a small handful is also government employees. Since these locations typically involve the US military, these contractors are usually US government contractors. More specifically, they are part of the Department of Defense (DoD) contractor workforce, and normally go by the name "defense contractors".

These defense contractors work for private corporations that provide equipment, services and personnel to the US government. I'll go into more details of the differences, advantages and disadvantages working as a government employee and government contractor in chapter 2. For now, let's talk about contractor jobs in these difficult overseas areas.

The majority of these defense contractors working at these locations are former military members who may have been deployed to these areas while in the military or have been deployed to similar areas with similar environmental, living and working conditions. However, you don't have to be a military veteran to work in these defense contracting jobs. Any US citizen is welcomed who has the experience, skills and qualifications needed in these areas.

American military and civilians are not the only nation present in these locations. Expats from other nations are also working at these locations, such as workers from Pakistan, India, and the Philippines. Oftentimes these locations have military members from other nations, such as British, French or Italian military forces deployed to these locations alongside US military forces. Some of these other nations allow family members and household goods of their military into these nations. For instance, the French military in Djibouti, a nation in Northeast Africa (Horn of Africa), allows their military's family members in this nation. US Armed Forces, government employees and contractors, on the other hand, are not allowed to bring their family members to this location.

Salaries and Benefits of Defense Contractors Working in Austere, Danger/Hazard Locations

Right about now you're thinking: *Why would I want to read about working in these areas? You just told me that it's "austere, dangerous and hazardous". I've been there, done that and "lost my tee-shirt" in my last marriage—I'm not looking for another austere, dangerous and hazardous environment to live in again.*

Before you go filing for a mental divorce on this subject, let's take a look at a few things first about working in these types of locations. Over the past two decades, contractor jobs in these austere, dangerous or hazardous locations have paid roughly $100,000 to $250,000 depending on the overseas location, experience, skill sets and salary negotiation skills of the contractor.

Don't forget, this is tax-free money up to $101,300 if earned in 2016 under the earned income exclusion for expats; and that tax exclusion increases each year. It's one thing to make $150,000 and have to give the IRS 30% or more in income taxes for that full amount. It's an entirely different thing making $150,000 and having the IRS tax you for only $48,700 of that $150,000 ($150,000 - $101,300 = $48,700). That's a whopping $101,300 you could earn without Uncle Sam touching a cent of it—it goes straight into your bank account.

Think about how much of your house mortgage, car payment or other bills you could pay off with $101,300 tax-free money. Think about how much you could put away for your children's college education with $101,300. Think about the places you could go or the things you could do with $101,300 tax-free money in the bank. Think about the amount of interest you could earn on an investment of $101,300. Now I ask you, *what's in your wallet* after a one-year gig like that?

Imagine how much money could be in your wallet if you worked 2, 3 or more years with that kind of income and tax exclusions? If you made $150,000 a year at one of these locations, you'll make more than $202,600 tax-free in year 2 and $303,900 tax-free in year 3. I say *"more than"* because your earned income tax exclusion will increase each year which means the IRS will allow you to exclude more than $101,300 each successive year from your income tax after the 2016 tax year.

Right now, thousands of defense contractors are doing just that across the globe—living and working in austere, danger/hazard locations for these reasons and more that I'm about to explain to you. Some defense contractors are content with making $110,000 or $120,000 for these locations; while other contractors will ask for and receive over $200,000 for these locations. Personally, I never accept less than $150,000 when going to these overseas locations. For most contractors negotiating their salary for these locations, it's about opportunity cost.

Opportunity Cost

Opportunity cost is an economics term that simply means a benefit, profit or value of something that you must give up in order to receive something else of benefit, profit or value.

The opportunity cost question contractors need to ask themselves is: Does the higher salary and company benefits (benefit, profit or value) I will receive for this overseas job outweigh the benefit, profit or value of my current status and location in America (or another safer country for our international readers) and the cost of living and working in an austere, danger/hazard overseas location?

That answer is different for each contractor. It depends on the price each US contractor chooses to put on their life in America that they're willing to give up temporarily to live and work in an austere, danger/hazard overseas location. That "price" will dictate what salary they are willing to accept for these overseas locations.

You already know what your comfortable and safe life in America is worth to you. So let's talk about the company benefits that come with the higher salaries that corporations are willing to pay you for these austere, danger/hazard overseas locations.

First, let's talk about a more important reason for living and working in these overseas areas. We've all seen the signs and bumper stickers: "Support Our Troops". One of the great ways of doing that is by taking a job in one of these locations alongside our US Armed Forces. If you're a vehicle or aircraft mechanic, a cook, nurse, heavy equipment operator, truck driver, trainer or instructor; your experience and skills are needed in these locations in support of our US military. If you work in law enforcement or security, construction, IT or telecommunications, finance, food service, housing management or waste management; you can support our troops in these places with your job experience. You can do all of these things in these austere, danger/hazard locations while being paid handsomely for your own personal sacrifice as a civilian who had a choice to stay home within the comforts and safety of the good ol' U.S. of A., but chose to live and work alongside our US military servicemen and servicewomen in these difficult places.

The US government and corporate employers of defense contractors realize the personal sacrifice these civilians are making—that's the main reason why their salaries are so high. Corporations provide a variety of paid vacations, called paid Rest and Relaxation (R&R); including paid travel expenses. Employers will pay for vacation days off and travel expenses to and from the danger/hazard location to the contractor's desired R&R location. This paid R&R may include airfare, hotel accommodations, local transportation, and a daily per diem for meals and incidentals.

These paid R&R benefits may be for one or more trips back to the US or another location of the contractor's choice for vacation time away from the austere, danger/hazard location. Other employers will provide 7 days of paid R&R after every 90 days (3 months) you work in a danger/hazard location. Instead of taking a 7-day vacation after 90 days, employers may allow the contractor to take 14 days of paid R&R after 6 months in the hazard/danger location.

Many defense contractors will use this vacation time to return home to enjoy some quality time with their families and friends; others arrange to meet their families in Europe or a Middle East city such as Dubai for a fun, enjoyable or romantic time with their loved ones; still others opt to take trips on their own to the country or island paradise of their choice.

As with private companies in the US, corporations pay all of the company benefits to you and your family members at home that I covered in the previous section when you accept a position in these austere, danger/hazard locations.

If it's not in writing, it never happened.

Make sure that whatever salary and benefits the employer has promised you, you negotiated with the recruiter or you expect to receive is put in writing in your contract offer letter. If it's not in writing, it never happened. If it's not in writing, the employer is not obligated to pay you or give you what you negotiated or what you thought you were going to receive. If it's not in writing, make the recruiter or employer put it in writing on your contract offer letter before you sign the offer letter.

These high salaries and great benefit packages are what keep defense contractors coming back for more. Many of these contractors work between 1 to 5 years at these locations; come back to the US; take some time off from work; then begin working in a US job again. Many defense contractors will work 1–2 years in one of these overseas locations; return back to the US to work for 1–3 years; and then return to the Middle East again to live and work for another 1–2 years.

Hardship Pay for Working in Auster, Danger/Hazard Locations

Another incentive corporations use to entice contractors to work in these austere, dangerous/hazardous locations is providing hardship pay. This is money the company will pay you on top of your salary for living and working in these overseas locations.

Hazard pay is a negotiable price. The amount of hardship pay companies give contractors can vary between $10,000 and $50,000 depending on if the employer factors the hazard pay into your total salary. When you ask for a higher 6-figure salary, your hazard pay will be fewer thousand dollars. If you ask for a lower 6-figure salary, you should ask for more in hazard pay.

When negotiating your salary for one of these austere, dangerous/hazardous locations, always ask for your hardship pay after you negotiate your salary. If you ask for hazardous duty pay while negotiating your salary, the recruiter will try to combine the hazardous duty pay with your salary to reach your desired salary. First make the recruiter pay you the salary you want for the job; and then make the recruiter pay you hazard duty pay on top of your desired salary compensation. Lastly, make sure your hazard pay is in writing on your contract offer letter before you sign it.

Completion Bonus for Working in Auster, Danger/Hazard Locations

The completion bonus is another incentive corporations use to get contractors to complete the number of months they agreed to fulfill in the austere, dangerous/hazardous location. As with the hazard pay, the completion bonus is negotiable and is typically in the thousands of dollars. After negotiating your salary and hazard pay with the recruiter, you should always ask for a completion bonus. You know what I'm going to say next: Get it in writing on your contract offer letter or it never happened.

There are a variety of reasons why contractors decide to leave the overseas area before completing their full time there. Some contractors will leave early because they feel unfairly treated by some (not all) of the US military as a result of the amount of money they are being paid for living and working in these locations while the military is making so much less. Have you watched how some dogs will chase their own tails? Well, that's sort of the way it is sometimes in the relationship between defense contractors and *some* US military members they're there to support in these locations. I say this because the majority of these defense contractors are former US military personnel who served their country faithfully while in the military. They've *been there and done that* in a military uniform in these austere, danger/hazard overseas locations. Now that they're out of the military in these same or similar locations— only for a higher salary as a government contractor—they feel unjustly ostracized by *some* US military members simply because of money.

Other contractors will leave early because of family situations back home in America. Sometimes, a family member's health or well-being requires the contractor to return to the US to help their family member.

Some contractors decide to depart the overseas location early because what the recruiter or employer told them about the overseas area or their job requirements in the overseas area did not turn out as they had expected.

Unlike the US military, if you want to leave that overseas area, you have the right to leave.

Using Leverage to Increase your Salary or Benefits for Austere, Danger/Hazard Overseas Locations

Both your salary and benefits are negotiable for these overseas locations. Again, you decide the premium (opportunity cost) for leaving a comfortable, safe life in America for a life in an austere, dangerous/hazardous location.

Obviously, your biggest leverage in asking what you want in salary and benefits negotiations is the fact that you will be working in an austere, danger/hazard location. There's no way your recruiter or employer can deny that; so negotiate confidently with that in mind.

Another source of leverage is the severity of the danger/hazard location. You have more leverage to ask for more money and benefits for a location where there is more hostility and higher risk of death than a location with mild hostility and a low risk of death.

Your knowledge, experience and skill sets can be used as leverage. This is about supply and demand. If your knowledge, experience and skill sets are highly desirable at that location, you have more leverage to ask for a higher salary or more benefits for that location.

Living Quarters, Food and Services for Defense Contractors Working in Austere, Danger/Hazard Overseas Locations

Depending on the location and threat conditions of the overseas area, defense contractors may be living in a villa housing complex outside of the military installation on the local economy provided specifically for contractors; living outside the military installation in homes or apartments that contractors can rent or employers pay for; living on a military installation in trailers that house 1–2 people per trailer; or living on a military installation in shared tents that house 30–50 people per tent.

When you are talking with a recruiter about working in these overseas locations, always ask what type of living quarters you will be provided for that location. It could mean the difference between sharing an apartment, condo or villa home with 2–4 people; sharing a trailer with another person; or sharing a tent with 30–50 people.

Places such as Iraq and Afghanistan typically require contractors to live and remain on the military installation. At these locations, contractors typically are not allowed outside the base, oftentimes referred to as outside the wire (barb wire). They only leave the base when their job requires them to perform their duties off-base. Places such as United Arab Emirates (UAE), Kuwait, Bahrain, Qatar, Oman and Djibouti allow contractors to either live outside the military installation or travel off-base.

The living quarters in these austere, danger/hazard overseas locations are typically non-negotiable because the US military commander that controls the US military and civilian workforce at these locations dictates if the US defense contractors are allowed to live on-base or off-base. Therefore, what you see is what you get in the housing arrangement; but at least there won't be any surprises when you arrive at your overseas location if you inquire about it ahead of time.

Living Outside the Military Installation in Auster, Danger/Hazard Locations

If you are living in a condo, villa, house or apartment on the local economy in these countries, you'll be able to buy food on the local economy and cook your meals in a kitchen at your residence. You will also be able to buy meals at restaurants on the local economy; eat free meals at the dining facility on the military installation; or purchase food from vendors on the military installation.

Voltage requirements outside of military installations in the Middle East are 220v just as in Europe and Asia. Therefore, your electronic devices must have 110v/220v capability or you can bring or buy voltage converters that can convert the 220v power from outlets to 110v for your 110v devices. You'll also need to buy several adapters to convert the US power cord plug to the type of plug that works with outlet shapes used in foreign countries. Military installations in the Middle East mainly use 110v power, but you'll also see 220v power on the installation.

Contractors living outside of military installations are either provided their own private vehicle that their employer pays for them to use or they will be provided bus transportation between their residence and the military installation. They can purchase gas for their vehicle either on the local economy or on the military installation.

Living in residences outside of military installations also allows you to have your own bedroom to yourself and use the utilities and appliances available in your residence. Although you may have to share one or two bathrooms with the other contractors assigned with you to that residence, you'll be able use a private shower, toilet and sink. This may not sound like much of a luxury until you consider how contractors live on a military installation.

Living Inside the Military Installation in Auster, Danger/Hazard Locations

Contractors and military members who live on military installations in either trailers shared with another person (sometimes contractors might be assigned a trailer room to themselves) or in 30-person or 50-person tents typically use shared shower stalls, toilets and sinks. Several small portable buildings about the size of a long trailer with shower stalls, toilets and sinks are set up in several places throughout on-base living quarters. The showers and sinks in each of these trailers can handle about 8–10 people at a time. That's not much room when there are hundreds of people getting up in the morning trying to get ready for work. There are 110v outlets installed at the sinks so you can use an electric shaver or other 110v devices.

Tent life may be new to some contractors and takes some getting used to if you haven't experienced this type of sleeping environment before. The large tents are usually set up on concrete floors. Bunk beds are used in these tents. You'll be provided free linen, blankets and pillows; and free laundry for these items. Most of the contractors who have been there for a while have already snagged all the lower bunks; so you'll most likely have to use a top bunk when you first arrive until a contractor vacates a lower bunk. There may be 110v outlets installed along the walls of the tent. Therefore, the prime real estate in these tents is a lower bunk next to the wall of the tent so that you can recharge your electronic devices.

Typically, there are not enough wall lockers to go around; so expect to store your luggage next to your bed. Bring locks to secure your luggage. The organization you work for may also have storage areas where you can store some of your gear.

There is lighting in these tents but all lights are turned off at a certain hour at night. It's pitch black in these tents when the lights are turned off; so bring a small flashlight and extra batteries with you to see your way into or out of the tent when the lights are turned off. Some contractors work at night and sleep during the day in these tents; so you'll have to keep the noise level down when entering these tents during the daytime.

If you are living in quarters on the military installation, you will be provided free meals within the dining facilities on the base that serve breakfast, lunch, brunch, dinner and midnight meals. You will also be able to buy meals from the available fast food vendors at that installation. You might be surprised to find several US fast food chains on some of these military installations, such as Burger King, Popeyes Chicken, Subway, Baskin Robbins and Anthony's Pizza. Depending on the threat condition of your overseas location, you may also be allowed to buy food at restaurants and stores outside the military installation on the local economy. Always ask for bottled drinking water when drinking water on the local economy.

Contractors living on the military installation are not provided their own vehicle. However, the military organization they are supporting on base may have vehicles they may be able to use to get around. There is also shuttle bus transportation provided throughout most areas on the military installation. Depending on the austere, danger/hazard overseas location, there are also taxis outside the military installation that can bring contractors into the local cities.

Many contractors and military personnel who live on military installations in these overseas location that allow them to venture off-base will use either one of the vehicles from their work (they are allowed to use these vehicles for off-base use) or take a taxi to venture off-base. They will drive to stores, restaurants, hotels, amusement or recreational areas, and other places of interest.

Many contractors who have a couple of days off from work will actually pay for a hotel room in the city during their days off to get away from "tent life" and enjoy the comfort and privacy of their own room, a decent shower, a real bed, and a more relaxing atmosphere.

When I was living on a military installation at one of these overseas locations, several defense contractors and I would oftentimes drive one of our work vehicles into town in the evening for a dinner together at a nice restaurant. During one Thanksgiving, several contractors and I drove off-base to the rental home that several defense contractors were living in; and we all enjoyed a home-cooked Thanksgiving dinner together at their rental home.

Dining Facility and Other Services on the Military Installation

The dining facilities on these military installations provide a wide variety of buffet style meals for free. Many of these dining facilities will provide a food selection that's just as good if not better than many of your favorite buffet restaurants in the US. The best part is you can eat as much as you want for free.

To help you work off those added pounds, these military installations have fitness centers and recreational areas where military personnel and civilians can exercise, play sports and stay in shape while living and working in these overseas locations. These fitness centers are similar to the fitness centers on US military installations in the US; with weightlifting and aerobic equipment; basketball or racquetball courts; swimming pools (sometimes); and baseball and football fields and jogging tracks.

Many of these military installations in the Middle East will have recreational or other services, such as money exchange, disbursement/cash cage or ATM machines; wireless access points; Moral, Welfare and Recreation (MWR) centers with board games or gaming devices, live music or bands, food and alcohol (alcohol use depends on the country), and trips to local area scenic or vacation spots (depending on the location); movie theaters that play many popular movies and provide popcorn for free; manicure, hair styling, haircuts and shaves shops; college classes to further your education; and laundry and postal services. Some of these services are free while other services charge a fee. There is usually a store, called the Army and Air Force Exchange Service (AAFES), at the military installation where you can buy toiletries, bedding, clothing, shoes, electronics, videos and music, snacks, footlockers and other consumer products. There is usually a chapel on the military installation where you can join others of like faith in religious services conducted at the chapel.

Although most of these countries in the Middle East are predominantly Muslim countries; and do not allow proselytizing people to another non-Muslim faith in their country; US military and civilian personnel are allowed to practice their own faith on the military installation or in the privacy of their own home off-base. So bring your religious books and other religious materials with you if you desire to do so. You can also load many religious books, music and other items on your electronic devices.

Staying Connected to Family and Friends While Deployed in Austere, Danger/Hazard Overseas Locations

You'll typically have Internet access to your family and friends in these overseas locations just as you do in the US; albeit the Internet speed and bandwidth may not be as great as you experience in the US. With Internet access, you'll be able to use email and the same social media sites you used in the US, such as Facebook, Twitter, LinkedIn, Pinterest, Tumblr or Instagram. You can also use an application, such as Skype, FaceTime, Facebook Video Chat or Google Hangouts, to make cheap Internet phone calls or enjoy some face time with family and friends in the US.

There are usually free Wi-Fi hotspots at different locations throughout the military installation for you to connect with family and friends online. Some of these Wi-Fi hotspot locations will have 110v outlets so you can charge your devices. There may also be a place on the military installation where you are allowed free use of online computers for a time limit. The time limit gives everyone a chance to get online with these computers.

If you live in a residence outside the military installation, your employer-provided quarters may already have Internet access available in the place where you are staying. The residence complex may also have recreational areas where free Wi-Fi is provided similar to hotels or apartment complexes in the US. Other contractors in rented homes or apartments may be able to purchase Internet access the same way you would for your residence in the US.

You'll also have the opportunity to connect with family and friends over a phone line. On the military installation, you'll have access to phone lines at your job. Both military and contractor personnel are allowed to use these work phones to make free morale calls back home to family and friends. Just as there will be places on-base where you are provided free computer use for Internet access; you'll be provided free phone calls at these locations as well for morale calls to family and friends.

Your smartphone may or may not work in these overseas locations depending on whether or not your mobile phone has the proper capabilities. Mobile phones typically use one of two types of radio systems: Code Division Multiple Access (CDMA) or Global System for Mobiles (GSM). The CDMA radio signal does not work with the GSM signal. In the United States, Sprint, Verizon and U.S. Cellular use CDMA; AT&T and T-Mobile use GSM. Most of the mobile phones used overseas are using the GSM radio signal.

Having a GSM phone alone may still not work in a particular overseas country because the GSM phone must support the frequencies used in that overseas location. Most of the mobile phones used in overseas locations use "quad band" or the specific frequency bands 850, 900, 1800 and 1900 in order to send and receive calls, texts and 3G and most 4G data.

To find out what frequencies are used in a particular overseas country, click on the following link: http://www.worldtimezone.com/gsm.html.

If you want to use your mobile phone overseas, check with your carrier to find out if your phone will work in the overseas locations you want to use your phone. You may have to buy another phone or switch to another carrier.

Another way to stay connected to family and friends while you are deployed at your overseas location is through good ol' snail mail—the post office. You'll be provided a mailing address at your overseas location. Family and friends will be able to send you cards and packages to your overseas mailing addresses. You'll also be able to send family and friends cards and packages through the post office on the military installation.

Medical, Training, Equipment and Other Requirements for Contractors Headed to Austere, Danger/Hazard Locations

Before defense contractors are allowed to deploy to austere, danger/hazard overseas locations, they must go through a standardized deployment process to pass a full physical and medical examination, and receive training and equipment for their overseas location.

There are three ways that defense contractors can be processed and cleared for overseas deployments in austere, danger/hazard locations:

1. **US government processing center:** Continental US (CONUS) Replacement Center (CRC) at Fort Bliss, Texas.

2. **Private company processing center:** US Training Center in Moyock, North Carolina.

3. **Employer-hosted processing:** Employers can pay for onsite trainers or medical personnel or send contractors to trainers or medical personnel in the local area.

Your employer will pay for (or reimburse you for) your travel costs to get you to the deployment processing center they have selected for you. Your employer usually pays for your lodging, meals and incidentals while you are at the processing center and while you are in transit to your final destination. Always make sure your employer reimburses you for the money you spend to accomplish these requirements.

You will need a credit card with several thousand dollars available because some of these expenses, such as airline tickets, hotels, rental car or food, are typically paid by you initially; and your employer will reimburse you for your expenses on a weekly basis while you are in transit to your final destination. Therefore, it is important for you to keep ALL of your receipts. Your employer will ask you to provide them copies of your receipts to properly reimburse you.

CONUS Replacement Center (CRC)

The US Army controls and manages the Continental US (CONUS) Replacement Center (CRC) that processes all military personnel, government employees and contractors for deployments to 38 theaters of operations in austere, danger/hazard overseas locations. The CRC operates 7 days a week including holidays; and processes over 400 people a week. The CRC is not used to process people for deployments to non-combative, non-danger/hazard overseas areas such as Europe or Asia.

In 2013 the Army consolidated multiple CRC centers in the US into a single CRC center located at Fort Bliss, Texas. Deployment processing at the CRC is a 7-day process that starts on a Friday and ends on a Friday for every person—military and civilian—who is preparing to deploy overseas in austere, danger/hazard overseas locations. Each person is expected to be deployment ready and catch their flight to their overseas location on that ending Friday.

What is it like trying to process 400 people a week at the CRC? Imagine being Viktor Navorski (played by actor Tom Hanks) stuck in the John F. Kennedy Airport terminal in the comedy-drama film *The Terminal*—only everyone (400 people) is stuck in the terminal together; and has to sit and stand together, eat and sleep together. Imagine everyone having to suffer through that for a week until their flight of freedom arrives on a Friday. (Some of you are saying, "*I don't have to imagine that. I was stuck in the airport during a snow storm.*") Well, that's kind of what it's like going through the CRC at Fort Bliss with over 400 other people.

During your one-week stay at Fort Bliss, you will be sitting, standing in line, sleeping and eating among 400 military and civilian personnel while you undergo training, equipping and examination for your deployment.

Lodging and Transportation at Fort Bliss, Texas

As a contractor, you will be required to sleep in the Army barracks on Fort Bliss during that week if your employer does not pay for you to stay in a hotel. These barracks are dorm style rooms where everyone sleeps on bunk beds in the same room. Men are separately from the women in different rooms. These barracks or billeting buildings come with common areas, such as a day room where you can sit and watch TV, laundry room, and storage areas. The open bay area where you sleep has wall lockers where you can lock up your gear. It is highly recommended that you lock up your gear because of theft that is common in these areas.

Certain items are prohibited in these barracks, such as firearms, knives (longer than three inches), ammunition, illegal drugs, alcohol, open flames (such as candles or incense) and heating devices (such as standalone heaters, hot plates and coffee pots).

When you are negotiating your salary and benefits with the recruiter, ask which processing center you will go through. If you are told that it will be at Fort Bliss, ask the recruiter to have the employer pay for your stay at a hotel and a rental car during your week of processing at Fort Bliss. If the employer agrees to provide you a hotel and rental car, make sure you get it in writing in your contract offer letter. This will allow you to stay in more comfortable and enjoyable accommodations. Although the CRC provides transportation to and from training and administrative events on the military post; you'll have the liberty to get around both at Fort Bliss and in the local area if you have a rental car. If you have a vehicle, make sure you get a vehicle permit during in-processing at Fort Bliss.

Meals at Fort Bliss, Texas

You will be provided meals at the Fort Bliss dining facility during breakfast, lunch and dinner for free (or you will be reimbursed by your employer if you are charged a fee for these meals). Ask your employer if they will pay for meals you purchase off post at restaurants in the local area.

Medical, Dental and Physical Examination Requirements for CRC Processing

Most if not all of your medical, dental and physical examinations will take place in your local area before you arrive at the CRC located at Fort Bliss, Texas because the CRC requires you to complete these requirements prior to your arrival.

The CRC requires the physicians examining you to complete certain forms that either the physician's office will fax to the CRC or complete online, or you or your employer will fax to the CRC. Your employer will provide either you or the physicians they've selected for you the required forms. Make sure the forms are filled out completely; and that you get copies of all the completed forms in case the forms do not make it to the CRC, are lost or are unreadable when faxed to the CRC.

Unless you're the type of person who enjoys sitting in bumper-to-bumper traffic jams or loves waiting endlessly for your number to be called at the DMV; you're going to want to get copies of those forms. Having copies will save you many hours of unnecessary pain waiting in long lines, panic attacks, energy and money at the CRC to provide the CRC examiners the completed forms that are missing or incomplete (did I mention there will be over 400 tired, irritable people there at the CRC?).

Lost, incomplete or missing forms could result in you being delayed beyond your Friday flight at the end of the week. That means you could be spending another week at the CRC sleeping on an Army bunk until the following Friday flight comes around. That also means you just missed out on one week's worth of a big tax-free paycheck for not being in your overseas location for that week.

Following is a list of medical and physical exams you must accomplish before your arrival at the CRC:

- **Physical exam:** Must be completed within 90 days of your CRC processing. The exam is good for 12 months once you are deployed. Get a copy of your completed physical exam forms (DD 2807 and 2808 or OF 178) and bring it with you to the CRC.

- **Audiology exam:** This hearing test must be completed within 90 days of your CRC processing. Get a copy of your completed audiology exam form (DD 2215) and bring it with you to the CRC.

- **Vision exam:** Vision prescriptions are good for 12 months. The CRC will also perform visual acuity tests on you. It is important for you to have an ample supply of eyeglasses and at least 180 days of contact lenses (if you use them) with you for your deployment. The CRC medical staff will ask you to show them your supply of eyeglasses and contacts. Most contractors are issued gas masks; therefore, ask your vision care provider if they can fit you for eyeglass inserts for use with gas masks. If they tilt their head to one side like your pet dog trying to figure out what you're talking about; you can order eyeglass inserts for gas masks online. Get a copy of your vision exam and bring it with you to the CRC.

- **Dental exam:** Your dental exam is good for 12 months. Have the dentist perform a complete checkup to include X-rays. If possible, request a copy of the X-rays. If you need any dental work, it must be accomplished prior to your CRC processing. Get a copy of your completed dental exam form (DD 2813) and bring it with you to the CRC.

- **Laboratory (blood and urine) tests:** The results of your lab work must be on printouts from the performing lab or clinic with dates. Handwritten lab results will not be accepted at the CRC; so make sure the results are in printout form. Get a copy of your completed lab work and bring it with you to the CRC.

Following are the basic lab work required for all contractors:

- **G6PD enzyme level:** One-time test only. This lab test can be drawn at the CRC medical site. Glucose-6-phosphate dehydrogenase (G6PD) is an important enzyme in your blood that provides proper red blood cell function to protect your body from harmful accumulated by-products while fighting infections or from taking certain medications.

- **Blood pressure:** One-time test only unless results show unacceptably high pressure. This test can be performed at the CRC medical site.

    Blood pressure is an important measure of heart health. If the contractor's blood pressure reads too high; the contractor can be retested the following day. If the contractor's blood pressure remains at an unacceptably high level after a retest, the contractor can be disqualified for deployment.

    For this reason, many contractors who tested with an unacceptably high blood pressure reading will take several aspirin the nights before their next retest in order to lower their blood pressure enough to pass the retest. Several studies have shown that taking aspirin at bedtime can lower blood pressure; however, taking aspirin in the morning had no effect on lowering blood pressure.

There are a lot of things contractors do prior to their blood pressure test to help their chances of passing this test. Some contractors will avoid caffeinated soda drinks, coffee or alcohol; avoid foods high in sodium, fats or cholesterol; and exercise more regularly.

I'm not Dr. Oz and this is not my prescription for your healthy heart. High blood pressure should be properly diagnosed and treated by your doctor. If you have high blood pressure or other signs of possible heart disease, see your physician.

If you are controlling your blood pressure with medication, make sure your physician annotates that in your physical exam form. Bring a 90–180 day supply of your blood pressure medications along with the same amount of other medications you may be taking such as cholesterol medication. The CRC may ask to see your supply of medications, so bring them with you. Make sure you set up your medication refills through a mail-order pharmacy before your arrival to the CRC.

- **(All contractors age 40 and over) Lipid panel test:** This lab test must be drawn within 12 months of CRC processing. A lipid panel is a panel of blood tests that are used as a broad medical screening for abnormalities in your body's lipids, such as cholesterol and triglycerides.

Cholesterol and triglycerides levels are important measures of heart health. High levels of bad cholesterol can produce plaques in artery walls that eventually block blood flow, resulting in heart attacks and strokes.

Triglycerides are a type of fat lipid in your blood. Your body converts unused calories in your body to triglycerides stored as fat cells to be used later for energy. When you eat more calories than you burn off, your body will produce a high level of stored fat cells. Excess triglycerides can lead to heart disease causing heart attacks and strokes. If the contractor's cholesterol or triglycerides levels are at an unacceptably high level, the contractor can be disqualified for deployment.

As a contractor, it is important for you to eat healthy and get plenty of exercise prior to taking the lipid panel test. This can increase your chances of having acceptable levels; allowing you to deploy to your overseas location.

If you are controlling your cholesterol with medication, make sure your physician annotates that in your physical exam form. Bring a 90–180 day supply of your cholesterol medications along with the same amount of other medications you may be taking such as blood pressure medication. The CRC may ask to see your supply of medications, so bring them with you. Make sure you set up your medication refills through a mail-order pharmacy before your arrival to the CRC.

- **Blood type:** One-time test only.

- **HIV test:** This lab test must be drawn within 120 days of CRC processing; and results must be negative. An oral HIV test is not accepted by the CRC.

- **DNA sample:** One-time test only. This lab test can be drawn at the CRC medical site.

- **(Females only) Pregnancy test:** This lab test must be tested within 30 days of CRC processing; and test results must be negative. This lab test can be drawn at the CRC medical site.

- **PPD testing (tuberculosis):** This lab test must be drawn within 90 days of CRC processing. A chest X-ray must be performed within 90 days of CRC processing; and test results must be negative.

- **Immunizations:** Your required immunizations depend on the location you are deploying to. Your employer will determine what shots you will need for your location. If you are a military veteran, you may have received many of these shots while in the military; and many of these shots may still be valid. If so, you can show your military shot record to the immunization clinic administering your shots.

  When I was going through this immunization examination along with several other defense contractors who were preparing for deployment to overseas contracting jobs, I showed the medical technician my military shot record. I was able to avoid about 8 of the 11 shots all of us contractors received. Those other poor slobs were stuck like pin cushions because they either did not have a shot record to prove they had these shots or they did not bring their shot record with them. So don't throw away your shot record after you leave the military.

  You may have also received these shots on a previous contractor deployment. Make sure you show these shot records to the immunization clinic.

  Once the medical technician verifies that the immunizations on your shot record are still valid, make sure they annotate those shots on your immunization form for CRC. You should also bring these military shot records or records from a previous contractor deployment with you to CRC. If in doubt, man up and take the shot. Better to have another pin stuck up your cushion than be held up at the CRC for a missing vaccination.

  Following are standard vaccinations required for all contractors deploying to these overseas locations:

  - **Adult Tetanus, Diphtheria, Pertussis (TDAP):** One dose every 10 years.

  - **Varicella (chickenpox):** Two shot series, 30 days apart.

- **(Korean Peninsula only) Smallpox:** One dose every 10 years. This shot may be administered at the CRC.

- **Measles, Mumps, Rubella (MMR):** Two shot series within lifetime.

- **Polio:** One immunization as an adult. For those deploying to Afghanistan or Pakistan, you must have an injectable polio vaccine within 12 months of your CRC processing.

- **Influenza:** Yearly vaccine. New influenza vaccines are usually distributed on September 1 of each year.

- **Hepatitis A:** Two shot series; first and second dose must be 180 days apart. If contractors have never received the Hepatitis A vaccine, contractors may still be able to deploy if they get the first shot and receive the second shot at their overseas location. Just nod your head and say, *"Yes, I'll get my other shot at my overseas location."*

- **Hepatitis B:** Three shot series; first and second dose must be 30 days apart. The third dose is 6 months after the first dose. If contractors have never received the Hepatitis B vaccine, contractors may still be able to deploy if they get the first shot and receive the second and third shots at their overseas location. Just nod your head and say, *"Yes, I'll get my other shots at my overseas location."*

- **Anthrax:** Five shot series with the first shot given at week 0, followed by shots given week 4, week 6, week 12 and week 18. Contractors may need to receive their first shot at the CRC medical site. If contractors have never received the anthrax vaccine, contractors may still be able to deploy if they get the first shot and receive the follow-on shots at their overseas location. Just nod your head and say, "*Yes, I'll get my other shots at my overseas location.*"

- **Typhoid:** Injectable dose within 2 years of CRC processing. Oral dose within 5 years of CRC processing.

- **(For high risk individuals only) Pneumococcal:** One dose of the PPV23 vaccine; then one time booster if 5 years or greater since first dose. High risk individuals are classified as adults ages 19–25 who smoke cigarettes, have chronic heart disease, congestive heart failure, hypertension, chronic lung disease to include chronic obstructive lung disease, emphysema and asthma.

All those shots will make you *Walk Like an Egyptian* pincushion when they're done with you.

CRC Training Requirements

All military and civilian personnel must complete some standard training in order to deploy to their austere, danger/hazard overseas location. There is also specialized training that certain people will receive based on their overseas location and job requirements. For instance, if your job is with law enforcement or security that requires the use of weapons; you may receive specialized training on weapons while the other contractors will not receive this training. Military and civilian personnel will not be allowed to deploy until they complete all of their required training—the CRC is very strict about this.

When you are at the CRC, you will complete this training in a classroom setting. Everyone will be split up into different training group sizes based on the size of the rooms. You will be provided instructors for some of the training. Other training will be through self-paced computer-based training (CBT) at your desk in the classroom. Make sure you bring your own laptop to complete the CBT online training at your desk. Some of this training will feel like death by a thousand PowerPoint slides. Just keep reminding yourself that it is only for a week.

Make sure you sign in and sign out on the class roster sheet to get credit for attending the class. When you have completed your instructor led training or your CBT training; initial and date the completion of the courses for that day on your Theater Specific Individual Readiness Training (TSIRT) requirements sheet; and have the instructor stamp or sign your form. This will ensure you get credit for completing those courses for that day.

If you finish your training earlier than other people in the class, you will be able to leave earlier for lunch, dinner or a longer break until the next class session begins.

As with medical and physical exam requirements, you may be allowed to complete some of these training requirements online before you arrive at the CRC. I highly recommend you complete as much of this training as possible while you are in the comfort and quietness of your own home rather than trying to complete all of these online training in classes at the CRC. This will save you several hours of classroom time that you can have off for the day.

Some of this CBT training is on the Army Knowledge Online (AKO) or the Joint Knowledge Online (JKO) websites. Ask your employer how you can access and complete some of this CBT training at home before your arrival at the CRC. If you complete any CBT training at home, make sure you print out your certificate of completion and bring it with you to the CRC.

Following is a list of training items you must accomplish before you are allowed to deploy to your overseas location:

- **Computer Based Training (CBT)**

    - Personnel Recovery-Isolated Personnel Report (ISOPREP): The ISOPREP report is used to positively identify you in case you get separated from your unit or captured by unfriendly or enemy forces in your overseas location. When friendly forces rescue you, they will use the ISOPREP report to make sure you are the right person they are helping or rescuing. You will need to provide two digital photos of yourself: one front-facing photo from a chest-up view; and one profile-view or side-view photo. Do not wear hats, sunglasses or prescription eyewear when taking these photos. For step-by-step instructions on completing the ISOPREP report, go to this link: http://bit.ly/2dTTMCN.

- U.S. Army Threat Awareness and Reporting Program (TARP)

- Operations Security Awareness Training (OPSEC)

- Sexual Harassment/Assault Response & Prevention (SHARP)

- Hot & Cold Weather Injury Prevention

- Combating Trafficking In Persons (CTIP) General Awareness Program

- Mild Traumatic Brain Injury (MTBI)—PTSD

- Pre-Deployment Health Assessment (PDHA)

- Country Specific Orient & Culture Awareness Training

- General Orders

- SERE 100.1 Code of Conduct

- DoD Cyber/Media Awareness Challenge/IA Training

- Cross Domain Violations (CDV) Brief

- Level 1 Antiterrorism Training

- Proper Handling of Islamic Religious Materials

- Discharge of Classified Information (DCI) Awareness Brief

In addition to the CBT training that may come with some instructor led training, you will also be given the following instructor training at the CRC:

- First Aid Training

- Improvised Explosive Device (IED) Awareness Training

"No Go" Rosters and Employer Communications at the CRC

The CRC will post "No Go" rosters indicating which people—military or civilian—the CRC will not allow to deploy to their overseas location. This No Go status could be for a variety of reasons, such as incomplete training, incomplete or missing medical, dental, vision or immunizations documentation.

It is important to find out WHY your name is on the No Go list because no one is going to come up to you and tell you why you are non-deployable. This requires some assertiveness on your part because if you don't take action to find out why your name is on that list, Friday will arrive and you won't be allowed to get on your plane to your overseas location.

If your name is on the No Go list, go to the CRC operations room or window and ask why your name is on the No Go list. If it has to do with documentation that you know you completed and submitted, find out which office is holding you up, whether it's the medical, dental or vision center or some other office. Get that office's contact information and location on Fort Bliss, and then contact that office or go to that office (this is another good reason for having a rental car). Bring that office a copy of the completed documentation they need from you.

Remember, you may only have 2 or 3 days left before your scheduled Friday flight takes off; so don't delay taking action on getting your name off of the No Go list. Otherwise, you may be staying another week at Fort Bliss for the next week's Friday flight out. Things may not seem so blissful at that point (sorry about the pun). Make sure you keep your employer in the loop on any roadblocks. You're employer has no doubt gone through a multitude of problems before with other contractors; and they may be able to offer you some assistance through this process.

Keep your employer abreast of your status at the CRC. Once you pass all of your requirements and are cleared to board your flight on Friday, let your employer know. This will start the clock on your payments for your overseas salary. When you arrive at your overseas location, let your employer know you've safely arrived.

Common Access Card (CAC)—Your Total Access Card

A Common Access Card (CAC) is a smart card used for multiple purposes for military personnel, DoD government employees and contractors. This card is used to identify the person that card was issued to; give access to physical buildings and controlled areas; provide access to DoD computer networks and systems; give defense contractors privileges to enter, use or shop in places such as dining facilities (DFAC) and Army and Air Force Exchange Service (AAFES) stores on military installations; and allow you to travel in and out of countries using the DoD Military Aircraft (MILAIR) transportation system between military installations worldwide without having to go through commercial airlines.

This card provides important and personal information about you and your access rights, such as expiration date, government affiliation, branch of service/agency, pay grade and rank, blood type, date of birth and Geneva Convention category. This card also contains a chip, like most credit cards, that stores your personal information and access information.

In short, you lose this card and you lose your access. That's a big problem when you lose this card in the US; it's an even bigger problem when you lose this card in your austere, danger/hazard overseas location; so guard your CAC card with your life.

To obtain your CAC card, your employer (who is your sponsor) must work with Trusted Agents (TAs) to initiate the process for enrolling you in the Trusted Associate Sponsorship System (TASS). Your employer must also initiate a background check on you that you must pass.

After the TA enrolls you in TASS, the TA will provide you a user ID and password that allows you to log into the TASS website. In TASS, you must complete the CAC application within 30 days of your initial login. The TA will review and approve your application submission and background check for CAC card approval.

Once the TA approves you to receive a CAC card, you must proceed to the nearest Real-Time Automated Personnel Identification Systems (RAPIDS) site. RAPIDS sites are offices that can be on a military installation or within your city, such as an Army, Air Force or Navy Reserve or Guard office. At the RAPIDS site, you will present them two forms of ID: a 6 to 8 digit number of your choice used as your Personal Identification Number (PIN); and your US government unclassified email address (your employer will help you obtain this email address). Once you provide these two items, the RAPIDS office will issue you your CAC card on the spot.

Some contractors are successful in getting their employer to initiate their CAC card process before they arrive at the CRC center in Fort Bliss. I highly recommend you attempt to get your employer to do this before you get to Fort Bliss, especially if you have a RAPIDS office near your home. This will be one less hassle for you to deal with while you are going through deployment processing and training at Fort Bliss.

To locate a RAPIDS office closest to your home, use the RAPIDS Site Locator at this link: http://bit.ly/1WOTfjZ.

It's not a show-stopper if you don't get your CAC card before your arrival at Fort Bliss. Your employer can set up your CAC enrollment; you can complete your CAC application and approval process while at the CRC; and then get your CAC card at the RAPIDS office on Fort Bliss. You must set up an appointment with the RAPIDS office at Fort Bliss. Here is the link for the contact information and appointment scheduler for the RAPIDS office at Fort Bliss: http://bit.ly/2e5YUOR.

Equipment Issued to You at the CRC

The Central Issue Facility (CIF) at the CRC will issue you the gear you will need for your austere, danger/hazard overseas location. The equipment issue process typically goes by fairly easy. Most contractors are issued standard gear, such as a helmet, chin strap, first aid kit, safety glasses, body armor, gas mask (the CRC will train you on the use of the gas mask) and two duffel bags to store and carry all of these items. As with training, you will be provided standard equipment given to all contractors; and there will be specialized equipment given to some contractors based on their location and job requirements.

To view a list of standard items contractors may be issued at the CRC, click at this link: http://bit.ly/2dYAA4T.

Based on the austere, danger/hazard location you are headed to, you will be issued standard gear for your protection and safety. Make sure you take your time fitting into the gear they give you at the CRC. Not only must this equipment provide you protection and safety; it must also fit comfortably. (I'd say you want to look good in this equipment too; but everyone just looks like one round green ninja turtle when wearing their helmet and body armor.) Don't accept any gear that does not fit properly; and ask for another size that fits well if the size they give you is wrong. Whatever changes you make to equipment, its size or quantity; make sure this is properly reflected in the hand receipt CIF personnel will make you sign for that equipment.

You are responsible for the return of all items listed on that hand receipt once your overseas deployment is completed. Upon your return to the US, you must return all of these items. When you return this equipment, if any item is not the same type, quantity or is missing that you signed for on your hand receipt, you will be responsible for paying for that item. So make sure what you see is what you sign for; and then make sure you secure that gear properly at all times so that it is not lost or stolen.

When you return from your deployment, some employers want you to send your equipment that you were issued at the CRC to them or some other location. If in doubt what you should do with your equipment, return your issued equipment yourself to the Central Issue Facility at the CRC in Fort Bliss, Texas where you received them.

Contractors will come up with creative ways to haul all of their necessary and desired gear to their deployed location. Some contractors will transfer some of their clothes or other items from their personal luggage over to their issued duffel bags; some will use one duffel bag and one personal luggage; others will put all of their gear in two large pieces of luggage. Some contractors will bring a folding luggage cart with wheels to carry these items along with their other luggage they have to tote around. If contractors already know what their address is at their overseas location, some of them mail some items to their deployed location. That way, they can carry a lighter load, and receive these items at their overseas location—assuming they pass all of their requirements at the CRC and are allowed to deploy. Other contractors have someone who will send them additional items; use online shopping to purchase additional items; or will buy items they need at their deployed location.

It's always best to bring as little as possible with you to your overseas location so that you carry as light a load as possible.

Then have a family member or friend send you the rest of the things you want or need when you get to your overseas location. You can also purchase items you want or need at your overseas location.

While in transit to your overseas location, and usually when you arrive at your overseas location, you might have to carry your gear across sand or gravel. This is fine for short distances but if you have to carry this gear a long way, too much gear will make your life miserable while traveling.

Flights to Your Overseas Locations

All military and DoD civilians (employees and contractors) processing through the CRC are provided transportation to their overseas location through the DoD Military Aircraft (MILAIR) transportation system. MILAIR uses the Biggs Army Airfield at Fort Bliss for its deploying military and civilians. The DoD MILAIR is similar to the Air Force Space-Available (Space-A) transportation system. MILAIR allows DoD to transport personnel and equipment between military installations in different countries worldwide without using the commercial airlines transportation system.

There are some exceptions to using MILAIR, such as cases where employers pay (or reimburse contractors) for their flight to their overseas location. If this is the case, contractors will use commercial airlines to reach their overseas location. It is also common for contractors to use a combination of MILAIR and commercial airlines to travel between the US and their overseas location.

Baggage Allowed for Your Flight to Your Overseas Location

When contractors are taking a MILAIR flight after completing their processing at the CRC, they must comply with the checked baggage requirements for their flight. These checked baggage requirements are similar to checked baggage requirements for commercial flights.

Following are the checked baggage requirements for military and civilian personnel using MILAIR for their flight:

- **Contractors:** 2 checked bags and 1 carry-on.
  - 70 pounds maximum weight allowed per checked bag.
  - 50 pounds maximum weight allowed for carry-on.

- **DoD and DA Civilians/LEP/Linguist:** 3 checked bags and 1 carry-on.
  - 70 pounds maximum weight allowed per checked bag.
  - 50 pounds maximum weight allowed for carry-on.

For more information on the CRC process at Fort Bliss, Texas and MILAIR, check the following links:

- http://bit.ly/2fcdjsB

- http://bit.ly/2e9eB7E

- http://bit.ly/2e2P5Sr

Thank You Sir, May I Have Another?

As I mentioned earlier, many contractors will redeploy to the same or different austere, danger/hazard overseas location after completing a previous assignment in one of those locations. The training they received at the CRC is good for one year only. After one year from their last CRC training, contractors must once again process through the CRC at Fort Bliss, Texas or an alternate CRC training center, such as at the US Training Center in Moyock, North Carolina in order to redeploy to an austere, danger/hazard overseas location.

US Training Center in Moyock, North Carolina

In the north-east corner of North Carolina near the border of Virginia and roughly 16 miles from the Atlantic coast, nestled in a quiet, isolated part of town sits 7,000 acres used for the United States Training Center. It is the largest privately-owned training center in the US. It has 54 tactical ranges, five ballistic houses, a variety of scenario facilities, four ship-boarding simulators, two airfields and three drop-zones, a three-mile tactical driving track, 25 classrooms, multiple explosive training ranges, a private training center, and accommodations and support activity centers for over 450 people.

The US Training Center was founded in 1997 by former Navy SEAL officer Erik Prince. The company's original name was Blackwater; then it was renamed XE Services in 2009; and then given its current name of Academi in 2011 after the company was acquired by a group of private investors in 2010.

The US Training Center provides training for law enforcement, logistics, close quarter training, security services and training for defense contractors headed to austere, danger/hazard overseas locations. They also provide basic handgun training for people at all levels of experience; and training retreat packages for corporations, whether it's small groups of people or an entire organization.

Since the Continental US Replacement Center (CRC) at Fort Bliss, Texas is oftentimes overwhelmed with processing personnel, the Department of Defense has partnered with other Alternate CRC centers, such as the US Training Center in Moyock, North Carolina.

The US Training Center at Moyock provides the same 1-week of training, equipment issue and documentation verification to clear contractors for deployments to these overseas locations. They also have the authority to deny any contractor the right to deploy if that contractor has not accomplished all of their requirements. All of their trainers are highly-skilled instructors, many of whom are veterans of US Special Operations Forces and US law enforcement agencies.

You must complete all of your preliminary requirements, such as medical, physical, dental exams and immunizations requirements before your arrival at the US Training Center just as with the CRC at Fort Bliss.

Lodging at the US Training Center

The US Training Center has about 59 semi-private rooms with a shared bathroom that sleeps two people per room. This lodging includes daily housekeeping; a communal kitchenette with refrigerator and microwave oven; coin-operated washers and dryers; fitness center with weight room; and recreation area with two large-screen TVs, movie rentals, computers, wireless Internet, vending machines, outdoor grills and picnic tables.

If your employer arranges for your training to take place at the US Training Center in Moyock instead of the CRC at Fort Bliss, your employer may authorize you to stay at a hotel in town and the use of a rental car. When I went through my defense contractor training at this US Training Center, my company allowed me to do this. I used my own credit card to pay for my hotel room and rental car; and my company reimbursed me for these expenses including gas, all meals and per diem for incidental expenses. This was the case not only for me, but all the contractors I was with from different companies that sent us to this training center. Since you'll have better accommodations, greater liberty and fewer people to contend with at the US Training Facility, I recommend you ask your employer if you can process through this training center in North Carolina instead of the CRC at Fort Bliss.

Meals at the US Training Center

The US Training Center has a large 12,000 square feet dining facility with buffet style food that can feed up to 1,200 people. Contractors pay for their meals and their employers reimburse them for these costs.

Since all of us contractors attending this US Training Center were staying in hotels and using rental cars; we typically would have breakfast at one of the local restaurants near our hotel in the morning; have lunch at the dining facility at the US Training Center; and then have dinner at a restaurant near our hotels in the evening.

Although you have greater liberty to eat what you want, when you want and where you want at the US Training Center, I would caution you to be careful of the types of food you eat that might increase your blood pressure or triglycerides levels.

For example, the following morning after other contractors and I arrived for our first day at the US Training Center, one of the first things our instructors did was have their medical team check our blood pressure.

"What? Nobody told me I was going to have my blood pressure checked at the US Training Facility!"

The contractors with unacceptably high blood pressure were told they would have to retest the following day. Any contractors whose blood pressure did not come down to acceptable levels would be disqualified for deployment. I was one of those contractors. Guess what happened when I heard that bit of news? My blood pressure went up even higher.

What I'm going to tell you next is not a recommended cure for high blood pressure. High blood pressure should be properly diagnosed and treated by your doctor. If you have high blood pressure or other signs of possible heart disease, see your physician.

As I mentioned earlier, many contractors will take several aspirin pills in the evening to lower their blood pressure when their levels tested too high at their training center. So several contractors and I who tested high on our blood pressure test decided to take several aspirins that evening and eat a very light, healthy meal that evening before our retest. We also ate this way for the rest of our week there, and worked out in our hotel's fitness room to maintain a good exercise program that week.

At the same time, several other contractors who passed their blood pressure test with flying colors that day celebrated with deliciously decadent hors d'oeuvres that make you wanna slap your mama; spicy hot wings dipped in ranch style dressing; fall-off-the-bone ribs that will make you fall off your chair; large multi-topping pizzas with extra cheese just daring you to try a slice; their favorite alcohol and sodas to wash it all down with; and deserts so delicious I swear I could hear it singing like the Right Said Fred band, "*I'm too sexy for your body*".

As delicious as all of this sound, these were all high calories, high carbohydrates, high fat, high sodium and high cholesterol meals and drinks they were enjoying.

Many of us contractors went out to dinner together to the same restaurants each evening; so it was tough watching them enjoy all of that delicious (but unhealthy) restaurant food while I and the other contractors with high blood pressure ate fish and vegetables and other light healthy meals. As much as I wanted to reach across that table and snatch one of those chicken wings like one of your pet dogs eyeing your food at the table, I resisted all temptation in hopes of passing my blood pressure retest.

The following day, I and most of the other contractors with excessively high blood pressure passed our retest. The next thing the medical staff at the US Training Center told us was they were going to perform a lipid panel test to check our cholesterol and triglycerides levels.

"What? Nobody told me I was going to have my triglycerides checked at the US Training Facility!"

When our blood work came back, guess which contractors had excessively high triglycerides? You guessed it—some of the contractors that had celebrated with those unhealthy meals at the restaurant with us. Unfortunately for them, you can't get rid of stored fat (triglycerides) by popping a few aspirin pills the way you can for high blood pressure. What ended up happening at the end of the week was that some of those contractors could not lower their unacceptably high triglycerides levels in time; and were disqualified for deployment at the end of the week. They were sent home while the rest of us caught our flights to our overseas locations.

What's the moral of this true story that sounds vaguely familiar to the fable about the race between *The Tortoise and the Hare* by the Ancient Greek storyteller Aesop? Make sure you wait until after you pass all of your medical examinations and other requirements that you are racing through before you *party like it's 1999*. It may mean the difference between you passing or failing the requirements to deploy to your overseas location.

Common Access Card (CAC)—Your Total Access Card

The US Training Center does not have a Real-Time Automated Personnel Identification Systems (RAPIDS) office. Therefore, you must obtain your CAC card before your arrival at the US Training Center.

The procedure for obtaining your CAC card is the same whether you are processing through the CRC at Fort Bliss or the US Training Center at North Carolina. I highly recommend you get your employer to assist you in getting your CAC card before you get to the US Training Center, especially if you have a RAPIDS office near your home.

To locate a RAPIDS office closest to your home, use the RAPIDS Site Locator at this link: http://bit.ly/1WOTfjZ.

For more information on the US Training Center at Moyock, North Carolina, check the following link: http://bit.ly/2eAhH81.

Baggage Allowed and Flights for Your Trip to Your Overseas Location

Your baggage weight and allowance on a commercial flight depends on the commercial airlines you use for your overseas trip. Most commercial airlines allow two checked bags and one carry-on. If you are using a MILAIR flight as part of your flight itinerary to your overseas location, you must abide by the MILAIR baggage allowance I discussed earlier for that MILAIR portion of your flight.

Your employer will arrange your flight to your overseas location after you've passed your training and other requirements at the US Training

Center. Depending on your overseas destination, your employer can arrange for MILAIR travel, a commercial flight or a combination of both for you.

There are no MILAR or commercial flights at the US Training Center. Therefore, you will have to drive to the location of your departure flight. After I was cleared to deploy through the US Training Center, I drove my rental car to my commercial airlines; dropped off my rental vehicle at the airport; and boarded my plane for my flight to my overseas location. It's that simple.

Be prepared for possible stops or layovers between your flights from the US to your final overseas destination. For instance, on my flight to my overseas location, my employer gave me a flight from the US that had a stop and overnight layover in Dubai, a popular city in the nation of the United Arab Emirates (UAE). My company reserved a hotel for me in Dubai. I took a taxi from the airport to my hotel; had dinner and breakfast there; and took a taxi back to the airport in the morning to finish my flight to my final destination. Although I paid for my taxi, hotel and meals, my company reimbursed me for these costs afterward.

Cleanup and Recovery after Hurricane Matthew

In 2016, North Carolina and other states on the East Coast were hit hard with Hurricane Matthew, the first Category 5 hurricane since Hurricane Felix in 2007. Hurricane Matthew caused many precious lives to be lost in Haiti, other parts of the Caribbean Islands and in the US. The hurricane's damage was estimated to be over $6.91 billion to the US overall. Although Matthew was downgraded to an extratropical cyclone by the time it hit North Carolina in October 9, it caused $1.5 billion worth of damage to North Carolina mainly due to widespread flooding. The US Training Center in Moyock, North Carolina also suffered damage during this time and had to close their business.

As North Carolina and other parts of the southeastern seaboard of the US recover and rebuild from the Hurricane Matthew aftermath; hopefully, we'll see the US Training Center reopen again too.

Employer-Hosted Training or Processing for Overseas Locations

We've already covered how employers can arrange and pay for your medical and physical examination requirements in your local area; and send you to training centers at other locations for deployment training. Employers can also pay for onsite trainers or medical personnel at the employer's location.

This type of training employers provide contractors is more specific to the type of job they will perform or the type of equipment they will use in their job at their overseas location. This type of training is not the same training contractors receive at the CRC or an alternate training center. Contractors must still attend training at one of those training centers to be authorized to deploy.

Employers can also have a medical team perform many of the medical or physical requirements at their location instead of having contractors accomplish these examinations at a medical facility in the contractor's local area.

When I accepted a position for job in an austere, danger/hazard overseas location, my new employer flew me from Colorado to their company on the East Coast for two weeks of training on specific communications equipment I would work on in my overseas area; and to complete all of my medical and physical examination requirements at my employer's building. My company paid for my flight, hotel, meals and per diem for incidentals during my two-week stay on the East Coast. They set up appointments for me and other defense contractors they hired to attend medical and dental facilities in their local area in addition to bringing in medical staff to their company building to complete other medical and immunization requirements. After completing these training and medical requirements, they sent all of us to a training center to complete our required deployment training.

Taking Care of Things Before You Leave for Your Training Center

You must have everything in your life ready for your extended absence the moment you arrive at the training center. After you complete all of your training center requirements and are approved to catch your flight to your overseas location, you won't have any time to go back home to take care of any personal belongings, responsibilities or issues.

It works to your advantage to have a family member or friend that will take care of some or all of these things, such a house, car, mail or bills, while you are in your overseas location. If you have someone to take care of these things, you don't have to worry about any of these things before your departure to the training center; unless of course a relative or friend wrecks your car while you're away, but that's another story.

The following is a quick overview of the things you may have to take care of before your arrival at the training center:

- **Important and necessary documents:** You must apply for or purchase documents, such as a passport, visa (depending on the country) and international driver's license well in advance of your departure to your training center.

- **Change of address:** Your employer will provide you your overseas address. Make sure you ask your employer for your new overseas address well in advance so that you can have all of your mail forwarded to your overseas address. If you fail to pass your requirements at the training center, you can always change back to your old address.

- **Your house in the US:** If you own a home, having a family member or friend to live in or watch over your home while you're away is a huge plus. You can also rent out your house through a property management company. This way, you can have another source of income to pay off your mortgage while you are living and working overseas. You still have to remove your household goods, put them in storage, and prep your home for rental use.

- **Your rental apartment or house in the US:** If you rent a home or apartment, having a family member or friend to live in or watch over your rental while you're away is again a huge plus. Otherwise, you may have to break your rental agreement; pay the break lease fee; and move out of your rental before you depart to your training center. During your salary and benefits negotiations with your recruiter, ask the recruiter to have your employer pay for your break lease fees.

- **Household goods:** If you don't have someone who can take care of your residence and household goods in the US, you will need to put these things in storage. In your salary and benefits negotiations with the recruiter, ask about the employer paying for the storage of your household goods including the costs to pack and move your household goods to storage.

- **Your vehicle:** If you don't have someone who can care for your vehicle while you're away, you can put it in storage. Once again, ask your employer if they will pay for storage of your vehicle along with household goods.

- **Utilities, services and rental equipment:** If you don't have a relative or friend who can do this for you, you'll need to coordinate the turn-off of your utilities and services and turn-in of any rental equipment before you leave for the training center.

- **Medications:** If you take prescription medication, you need to set up and use a mail order pharmacy to receive your medications while overseas. Talk with your primary care doctor about your plans to live and work overseas; and arrange a way to have your primary care doctor approve your follow-on prescriptions while you are in your overseas location.

Resources for Finding Defense Contractor Jobs in Austere, Danger/Hazard Locations

You can find out about jobs in these austere, danger/hazard locations through the same online job boards used for finding jobs in non-austere safer overseas locations, such as in Europe I listed earlier. In your profile on these online job sites, make sure you indicate which overseas countries you are willing to work in.

Here are some other job sites to consider for jobs in austere, danger/hazard overseas locations:

- Job Monkey
  http://www.jobmonkey.com/uniquejobs/civilian-contractor

- Private Military
  http://www.privatemilitary.org/private_forces.html

- Civilian Contractor Jobs
  http://www.civiliancontractorjobs.com

- Danger Zone Jobs
  http://www.dangerzonejobs.com/artman/publish/index.shtml

- FLUOR
  http://www.fluor.com/careers/logcap_iv_opportunities/pages/default.aspx

You should also put your desired overseas countries in your resume so that the applicant tracking system (ATS) recruiters use to filter resumes will key in on the countries you've indicated. For instance, you could put the following statement in your resume: *Willing to work in overseas countries such as Iraq, Afghanistan, Saudi Arabia, United Arab Emirates (UAE), Kuwait, Bahrain, Qatar, Oman, Egypt and Djibouti.*

CHAPTER TWO

US Government Employee and Contractor Workforce

Starting over is the opportunity to come back better than before.
Ryan Kahn

US Government Employees—Who We Are

Who is the US government employee or government contractor next door? I'm glad you asked. They're your sons and daughters, your fathers and mothers, your sisters and brothers, your in-laws, your college graduates and your military veterans. In short, they're people just like you and me.

US government employees, also referred to as federal employees or civil servants, are part of the US government called federal civil service that was established in 1871. They are civilians who work directly for and are paid by the US federal, state and local government. Besides the multitude of US government agencies and organizations where professionals work, the government employee workforce also includes the executive, legislative and judicial branches of government. Uniformed military services are not part of the civil service workforce.

US government agencies are considered primary companies with direct control over their government employees. Therefore, the IRS requires government agencies to withhold taxes from the earnings of government employees. Government agencies record employee earnings and withholdings on a W-2 tax form that is reported to the IRS.

By mid-year 2016, the Bureau of Labor Statistics reported there were 21.1 million total US government workers. Among this workforce, there are over 4 million federal, state and local government civilian employees, not counting civilians that work directly in the executive, legislative and judicial branches of the US government. On the other side of that government coin, you have over 10 million civilian government contractors who also work at the federal, state and local levels of our US government.

All of these government civilian employees and contractors are employed in over 500 US government departments and agencies both in the US and abroad in other countries. These government departments and agencies cover all areas of US governance. Areas such as transportation, telecommunications, health, education, agriculture, economy, finance, energy, commerce, postal service, drugs and alcohol, Peace Corps, labor, defense, veteran's affairs, homeland security, border patrol, science and international affairs. It's easy to see that a large portion of America's business sectors are made up of civilian government employees and government contractors. A complete listing of the US government departments and agencies and their contact information can be found at https://www.usa.gov/federal-agencies.

Military Veterans and Their Family Members as US Government Employees and Contractors

A large part of the US federal civilian employee and contractor workforce is former military members, in addition to spouses and children of active and retired military members. We all want to promote opportunities for our military and their family members after these brave men and women have served their country so well; and government employee and contractor job opportunities are avenues for the American public to give back to our military.

Former military members are oftentimes more willing and able to adapt to the restrictions placed upon civilians working in a government job or the changing working environment of the contractor world. After all, military members routinely change their tour of duty location every 2 to 5 years. They'll move to another state or another country, oftentimes bringing their family and household goods in tow with them; and begin working in a new military assignment for new bosses, new co-workers and new customers on a regular basis throughout their military career.

This "tour of duty" mentality was used by Reid Hoffman, the co-founder and executive chairman of LinkedIn, in his book, *The Alliance*, to explain a more realistic approach by employers and employees in accepting the fact that employment at one job, at one company, at one location isn't for life. According to Hoffman, the biggest lie that employers tell employees is that their employment relationship is for life like a family; and the biggest lie that employees tell employers is that their loyalty to the company is for life.

Working alongside our military as a defense contractor, I've witnessed on numerous occasions where military members served our country faithfully in a military uniform, and when it was time for them to leave the military, they simply changed clothing but not their job. In other words, they continued performing their same job in the government facility, but now they were performing these tasks as a government civilian employee or contractor instead of as a military member.

How is that possible? Because the same or similar job they were performing while serving in the military was also being performed by defense contractors or government civilian employees working alongside them. Upon their release from the military, these military veterans were immediately offered a civilian job—usually with an increase in pay—by a private company or a government agency in the same organization. It happens all the time.

I wish it would happen more often for our military veterans—**they deserve it!**

Naturally, the majority of people searching for jobs will not have the opportunity to land a job by simply transitioning from a military uniform to civilian attire while staying in the same workplace. Most of us have to go through the process of searching for a job. That's what this book is about. Read on and discover valuable information that will give you the success you need to transition to your next job.

The Department of Defense (DoD)

The Department of Defense (DoD) is the oldest and largest among the hundreds of agencies within the US government. It is charged with the responsibility of providing military forces (Army, Navy, Marines, Air Force, their respective reserve and guard components, and unified military commands) and to protect the security and interests of the United States.

The DoD also encompasses over 12 defense agencies such as the Defense Intelligence Agency (DIA), Defense Information Systems Agency (DISA), Missile Defense Agency (MDA), North American Aerospace Defense Command (NORAD), the Defense Logistics Agency (DLA), and the National Security Agency (NSA) that operates as part of the DoD while simultaneously reporting to the Director of National Intelligence.

Some agencies thought to be a part of the Department of Defense actually belong to other departments. For example, under the umbrella of the US intelligence community, you have the Federal Bureau of Investigation (FBI) that belongs to the US Department of Justice; and the Central Intelligence Agency (CIA) that is the only independent US intelligence agency reporting to the Director of National Intelligence.

Within the Department of Defense, thousands of defense contractors and government civilian employees support the responsibilities of DoD agencies and our nation's military both on US and foreign soil. These civilian employees and contractors supplement our military who are already "doing more with less" to accomplish the mission of national objectives and to preserve national security.

Life and the Working Environment within US Government Organizations

US government agencies and organizations can have similar office dynamics as in private businesses and corporations. There are policies and procedures in government organizations just as in private companies, such as dress code, codes of conduct, conflict of interests, sexual harassment, confidentiality and non-disclosure policies. Federal employees work a variety of work schedules; they can flex their hours; and can adjust their hours in similar fashion as in private businesses. Government organizations provide newcomer orientation briefings and on-the-job training either on-site or they may send employees to other locations for training. Government managers or supervisors provide performance evaluations similar to what you might experience in corporations. Government employees enjoy office parties and potlucks for holidays or special occasions, and team-building activities together as employees in private sectors.

If you are among the government employee or contractor workforce of a US government organization, especially the Department of Defense, you will be held accountable to higher standards than what you might expect in the private sector. Yes, you will encounter similar workplace standards in areas such as human relations policies, conflict of interests, dress codes, and other typical company regulations and policies. However, working within a DoD or other similar government agency holds the all-important charge of accomplishing national objectives and protecting national security. For this reason, you may be held accountable not only for your actions and behavior on the job but for your actions and behavior off the job. Things like your financial responsibility, friendships with people who are considered hostile or unfriendly to the US, and background checks into your personal life to determine your qualification for a security clearance.

For those of us with previous military experience, this is par for the course but for those with little familiarity with a DoD or other government organizations, these extra requirements may seem a bit daunting or too intrusive. Rest assured, many men and women have easily accepted and fulfilled these additional requirements for decades—and so can you.

Restrictions on What You Can Bring Into a US Government Agency

The working environment of a US government agency, such as a DoD agency, can place more limitations on what you can bring onto the premises. Electronic devices such as cameras, phones and other devices with camera capability, and personal laptops are typically prohibited items in DoD agencies. As a general rule, removable flash-type drives and other storage devices such as compact discs, USB thumb drives, memory sticks/cards and camera flash cards are typically not allowed on all DoD and other government agency computers.

Additionally, your personal networking equipment, such as a personal laptop from home or wireless device, is not allowed to connect to US government networks. Also not allowed is software—downloaded from the Internet or something you bring to work—on a government network that is not authorized for use.

Many of these government agencies have both military and civilian armed security forces as well as other security personnel. These security personnel are authorized to confiscate your electronic devices if those items are prohibited in the government agency.

Consequences of Violating US Government Agency Policies

Your computer use at a government agency comes with greater monitoring, scrutiny and consequences. When I was working as a network engineer at the Missile Defense Agency, one day while working in my office, in walked several people including security personnel. Next thing I see is one of my colleagues packing up his belongings and quietly being escorted out of the office.

Since everyone's computer activity was constantly monitored at that government agency, the agency's network security team discovered my colleague was accessing prohibited websites. Once the security team had gathered enough evidence of that person's repeated computer violations, he was fired on the spot and escorted from the building right there in front of all of us in that office.

Uncle Sam Wants You to work in his government agency, but Uncle Sam will also kick you to the curb in a heartbeat if you violate US government workplace policies.

Military Exercises at US Military Installations

As you might imagine, military scenario exercises is commonplace and routine for military members. What you might not know is that US government employees and contractors on military installations or government agencies may have to participate in those exercises at times along with the military.

No, I'm not talking about doing jumping jacks, running a couple of miles with a backpack or wearing a gas mask. The military exercises I'm referring to involve scenarios where the military installation pretends it is experiencing different emergency situations. These practice scenarios could be a terrorist attack, a fire or explosion where personnel are injured, or inspectors walking around asking people questions. These impromptu questions from inspectors will test a person's knowledge on basic security policies or procedures everyone on the military installation received training on and are expected to know.

Some of these exercises on military installations are the same type of standard drills performed by many private companies. For instance, people in buildings of private corporations might be required to participate in a fire drill where everyone will leave the building and gather together outside in a predesignated location in an open parking lot or elsewhere.

There is also intruder or threat drills where the military installation pretends it is undergoing a security incident or threatening attack. In these types of exercises, you may be required to remain in your building and not go outside during certain timeframes. If you are caught outside your building during these exercise timeframes, you could be tagged as an "exercise player" and have to pretend you were injured and be required to go through a triage line for medical treatment. Sometimes when you are caught outside during an exercise, the evaluators can make you participate as a captured civilian that is being held hostage by an imaginary intruder until you are released. Try explaining that one to your boss. There goes your lunch break.

Would you like to become a part of these government civilian employees and contractors supporting our nation's goals alongside our military at home in the US and abroad in foreign countries? You can. Before you take the plunge in joining the ranks of government professionals, you have to decide if you want to become a US federal employee or a US government contractor. Let's take a look at US government employees first.

The Office of Personnel Management (OPM)

All of the US federal, state and local government civilian employees are managed by the Office of Personnel Management (OPM). The OPM provides the following services to the government's civilian workforce:

- Recruits civilian candidates for government jobs by managing the government job announcements at the USAJOBS.gov website.

- Establishes and manages the standards used in the government recruitment and hiring process.

- Performs background investigations and maintains security clearances required for government jobs.

- Manages and controls the merit system used in promotions within the government civilian employee workforce.

- Manages and distributes benefits, such as health insurance and retirement pensions, offered to government employees and their families.

- Provides training and development programs to the government employee workforce.

Salaries of US Government Employees

Salaries for government employees are strictly regulated under multiple government pay systems. These pay systems consists of the Federal Wage System (FWS) for blue-collar employees, the General Schedule (GS) for white-collar employees, Senior Executive System (SES) for Executive-level employees, the Foreign Service Schedule (FS) for employees working in US embassies, consulates and other diplomatic missions worldwide, and other alternative pay systems. To learn more about these pay systems and their salary pay rates available to all US government employees, go to http://bit.ly/2e7g6XM on the Office of Personnel Management (OPM) website.

Each of these government pay systems are based on fulfilling certain requirements for each pay category and are normally non-negotiable rates of pay. These requirements include a resume and documented qualifications, such as certifications and degrees, skill level, years of experience, and length of government employment.

The goal of these pay systems is to establish *equal pay for equal work* regardless of race, ethnicity, gender, age, religion or salary negotiation skills.

This is what differentiates the US government's pay system, which is non-negotiable, from private company pay systems which are negotiable contracts. Salaries in the private sector do not give equal pay for equal work because each person negotiates their salaries. Some workers in the private sector will negotiate a lower or higher salary than another worker doing the same job in the same company because of their salary negotiation skills.

The General Schedule (GS) Pay System

Roughly 60 percent of all US government agencies use the General Schedule (GS) pay system; making the GS schedule the most used pay system by federal, state and local agencies. Government employees paid under the GS schedule use the W-4 and W-2 tax forms for filing their IRS income tax returns.

Base Pay and Locality Pay in the GS Pay System

The US government uses data from the Bureau of Labor Statistics, which is a government agency under the US Department of Labor, to set pay rates under the GS system.

The GS pay system is made up of two parts:

1. The salary part called base pay.

2. A locality pay adjustment.

Base pay is adjusted locally for the cost of living in the particular location where the government employee is working. For instance, a GS-12 employee in San Francisco would have a higher base pay than a GS-12 employee living in Colorado Springs because it is more expensive to live in San Francisco than it is in Colorado Springs.

Locality pay covers 47 locality pay areas that is adjusted annually for changes in the economy and is based on BLS surveys. It's the locality pay that increases the base pay depending on the location. For instance, the 2016 annual locality payment for Colorado Springs, Colorado is 14.52 percent. The 2016 annual locality payment for the cities of San Jose, San Francisco and Oakland in California is 35.75 percent.

To view the GS Locality Pay Tables for all locations in the US, click this link: http://bit.ly/1YqUsNJ.

Cost of Living Allowance (COLA) in the GS Pay System

The US government uses a non-taxable allowance called Cost of Living Allowance (COLA) to supplement the base pay for US government employees who work outside the Continental United States (CONUS) in non-foreign areas and foreign areas. The non-foreign COLA areas are Alaska, Hawaii, Guam and the Northern Mariana Islands, Puerto Rico and the US Virgin Islands. The foreign COLA areas are non-CONUS and non-US areas, such as Canada, South America, Europe, Asia or the Middle East.

The added COLA amount can increase GS pay rates 4 to 60 percent higher than the GS pay rates used within the Continental US. This is one of the popular reasons for working as a US government employee overseas.

The following are examples of the 2016 COLA rates for non-foreign areas:

- Anchorage, Alaska: 5.31 percent
- Honolulu, Hawaii: 12.05 percent
- Puerto Rico: 4.08 percent
- US Virgin Islands: 13.70 percent

To view all COLA rates for all non-foreign areas where US government employees are living and working, click this link: http://bit.ly/2eWJf6a.

The following are examples of the 2016 COLA rates for foreign areas:

- Buenos Aires, Argentina: 30 percent
- Sydney, Australia: 35 percent
- Nassau, Bahamas: 42 percent
- Brussels, Belgium: 25 percent

- Bermuda, Bermuda: 60 percent
- Rio de Janeiro, Brazil: 25 percent
- Toronto, Canada: 25 percent
- Beijing, China: 25 percent
- Havana, Cuba: 20 percent
- Prague, Czech Republic: 10 percent
- Copenhagen, Denmark: 42 percent
- Paris, France: 50 percent
- Kaiserslautern/Stuttgart/Wiesbaden, Germany: 15 percent
- Iraklion (Crete), Greece: 10 percent
- New Delhi, India: 5 percent
- Dublin, Ireland: 30 percent
- Tel Aviv, Israel: 25 percent
- Rome, Italy: 30 percent
- Tokyo City, Japan: 50 percent
- Osan Air Base, Korea: 25 percent
- Amsterdam, Netherlands: 20 percent
- Oslo, Norway: 50 percent
- Madrid, Spain: 15 percent
- Stockholm, Sweden: 50 percent
- Geneva, Switzerland: 60 percent
- London, UK: 50 percent

To view all COLA rates for foreign areas (foreign countries) where US government employees are living and working, click this link: https://aoprals.state.gov/Web920/cola.asp.

Special Pay Rates for US Government Jobs

The Office of Personnel Management allows provisions to the GS pay system that allows government agencies to recruit and retain top talent in hard-to-fill positions, such as professionals in the scientific, technical and medical fields. Other reasons for using special pay rates are the remoteness of the working location and undesirability of working conditions or the type of work involved. These special pay rates allow agencies to increase salaries within the GS pay system apart from the locality pay adjustment or the COLA allowance.

As with other government policies and regulations that have loopholes, the special pay rates provide a loophole to the requirements for pay grade progression within the GS pay system. Many US government jobs in overseas locations will provide a higher GS grade than would normally be given for a position within the Continental US (CONUS) without having to fulfill the education requirements of the GS pay system. These special pay rates can work to your advantage if you are the adventurous type who would enjoy the opportunity of working outside of CONUS in places like Alaska, Hawaii, Canada, South America, Europe, Asia or the Middle East.

To explain how the special pay rates work, consider the pay grade requirements of a government employee working under the GS pay system. According to the *General Schedule Qualifications Standards*, the government employee must possess the following college degrees from accredited institutions for continued promotion through the pay grade levels.

- **To qualify for a GS-5 pay grade**, the government employee must possess a bachelor's degree.

- **To qualify for a GS-7 grade**, the employee must have one full year of graduate level education or superior academic achievement (class standing, such as being in the upper third of the graduating class; GPA, such as 3.0 or higher or 3.5 or better; and membership in a national scholastic honor society, such as Alpha Beta Gamma or Pi Delta Phi).

- **To qualify for a GS-9 grade**, the employee must have a master's degree or two full years of higher level graduate education leading to a master's degree.

- **To qualify for a GS-11 grade or higher**, the government employee must have a Ph.D. or equivalent doctoral degree or 3 full years of higher level graduate education leading to a Ph.D. or equivalent doctoral degree.

Want to know how people working as government employees under the GS pay system are getting around the education requirements for GS pay grades, particularly the requirements for a master's degree or Ph.D.? They're taking advantage of the special pay rates provision by working overseas in places like South America, Europe, Asia and the Middle East.

It's common to find government employees without a master's degree or Ph.D. working in GS-9 and above pay grades in overseas locations due to the special pay rates provision. The US government is willing to waive those higher degree requirements to recruit and retain people to work in those overseas locations.

Not every American wants to move outside of the comforts and safety of the good ol' U.S. of A. to live and work in a foreign country. The US government realizes that too. What is one American's dream (to get paid for living and working overseas) is another American's nightmare. Therefore, the federal government applies the special pay rates provision to many government positions overseas, in addition to increasing the employee's salary with a COLA allowance, to entice Americans to live and work in these overseas locations.

I've spent over 15 years living and working overseas both while serving in the US Air Force and as a civilian contractor working for US corporate companies. During my time in Europe, I've met and worked with many US government employees that did not have a Ph.D. that were working in government GS-12 positions. In fact, the majority of GS-12 employees I've met in Europe did not have a master's degree. Since the US government needed to fill those overseas positions, the government waived the requirements for higher education for these individuals willing to live and work in Europe. The US government credited the knowledge, experience and skill sets these individuals possessed toward the education requirements for those higher GS pay grades.

This happens all the time for US government jobs overseas.

Military Veterans Working Overseas as US Government Employees

One of the benefits for our US military members serving in many of these overseas locations is having the opportunity to take advantage of these special pay rates when they leave the military. A large portion of US government employees working overseas are military veterans.

Instead of returning back to the US after their military service is up, many service members opt to remain in their overseas location to live and work as a US government civilian employee or contractor. Some veterans remain overseas because they are married to one of the local nationals of that foreign country. Others do it because they've grown to enjoy the people, culture, food and sights of the country where they served while in the military.

The Office of Personnel Management also has offices on military installations at many of these overseas locations, making it easier for overseas military members leaving the military to join the ranks of civil service employees in the same overseas location or other overseas locations of their choice.

Grade Level and Step Level in the GS Pay System

The **base pay** portion of the GS system is calculated based on two factors:

1. Grade level

2. Step level

The Grade Level

There are 15 grade levels from GS-1 (the lowest level) to GS-15 (the highest level) used for employees in professional, technical, administrative and clerical positions. The higher your grade level in the GS system, the higher your salary or **base pay** is.

The following Table 2-1 explains how these pay grade levels translate to a government employee's qualifying career progression, education or training which includes their job responsibilities, experience and certifications.

Table 2-1 *Qualifications for grade progression GS pay system*

Grade	Qualifying Career and Education
GS-1	No college degree required. Normally used for someone with no high school diploma.
GS-2	No college degree required. Normally used for someone with a high school diploma or equivalent.
GS-3	1 academic year above high school. Usually for internships or student jobs.
GS-4	2 academic years above high school or an associate's degree. Usually for internships or student jobs.
GS-5	4 academic years above high school or a bachelor's degree. Typically entry-level positions.
GS-6	4 academic years above high school or a bachelor's degree. Typically entry-level positions.
GS-7	Bachelor's degree or 1 academic year of graduate education. Typically entry-level positions.
GS-8	Bachelor's degree or 1 academic year of graduate education. Mid-level positions.
GS-9	Master's degree or 2 academic years of progressively higher level graduate education leading to a master's degree. Mid-level positions.
GS-10	Master's degree or 2 academic years of progressively higher level graduate education leading to a master's degree. Mid-level positions.
GS-11	Ph.D. or equivalent doctoral degree. Mid-level positions.
GS-12	Ph.D. or equivalent doctoral degree. Mid-level positions.
GS-13	Ph.D. or equivalent doctoral degree. Top-level supervisory positions.

GS-14	Ph.D. or equivalent doctoral degree. Top-level supervisory positions.
GS-15	Ph.D. or equivalent doctoral degree. Top-level supervisory positions.

This list may seem a bit intimidating as you move up in the GS grades. First of all, you can get around the higher education requirements, such as a master's degree or Ph.D., by accepting government jobs in overseas locations as I mentioned earlier. Secondly, this list is not set in stone for all career fields. For instance, government employees working in clerical and administrative support positions do not require any college education throughout their GS pay grade progression.

A government employee in a technical position would normally need a bachelor's degree to work as a GS-5; but a government employee working in clerical and admin support position would not need any degree for a GS-6 or above pay grade. This means government clerks with no degrees could be making considerably more money than other government employees with bachelors or master's degrees, such as civil engineers, nuclear engineers, chemical engineers or network engineers.

This is Uncle Sam's idea of ***equal pay for equal work*** under the US government pay system.

This is where I drop the mic and walk away.

To see the complete list of qualifications requirements for each career field under the US government General Schedule pay system, go to http://bit.ly/2dK8Eza on the OPM website.

The Step Level

The GS schedule also uses 10 step levels, Step 1 (the lowest level) through Step 10 (the highest level), to identify a government employee's career tenure for automatic promotional pay increases. Each step within the same grade level is approximately a 3 percent increase of the federal employee's **base pay**. In order to receive the automatic step from one level to the next within the same grade level, the government employee simply has to remain in that GS pay step for the required timeframe. These steps are not based on the federal employee's qualifying responsibilities, experience, certifications or education as with the grade level progression.

Following is a list of the amount of time government employees must wait in their current GS pay step in order to step to the next pay level within their GS grade.

- **Step 1 to Step 2:** Wait 52 weeks of civil service in Step 1.

- **Step 2 to Step 3:** Wait 52 weeks of civil service in Step 2.

- **Step 3 to Step 4:** Wait 52 weeks of civil service in Step 3.

- **Step 4 to Step 5:** Wait 104 weeks of civil service in Step 4.

- **Step 5 to Step 6:** Wait 104 weeks of civil service in Step 5.

- **Step 6 to Step 7:** Wait 104 weeks of civil service in Step 6.

- **Step 7 to Step 8:** Wait 156 weeks of civil service in Step 7.

- **Step 8 to Step 9:** Wait 156 weeks of civil service in Step 8.

- **Step 9 to Step 10:** Wait 156 weeks of civil service in Step 9.

The Grade-Step Level Matrix in the GS Pay System

The grade-step levels are used in a matrix to determine an employee's base pay. This matrix allows a government employee to increase their salary two different ways: either through a change in their grade level or an increase in their step level.

To explain how this matrix works, see the following Table 2-2. This table shows how the grade-step levels work together as a matrix for pay grades GS-1, GS-7 and GS-15 to give you an idea of how the grade-step levels work together.

Table 2-2 *Portion of the 2016 grade-step salary table for federal employees*

Grade	Step1	Step2	Step3	Step4	Step5
GS-1	$18,343	$18,956	$19,566	$20,173	$20,783
GS-7	$35,009	$36,176	$37,343	$38,510	$39,677
GS-15	$102,646	$106,068	$109,490	$112,912	$116,334

Grade	Step6	Step7	Step8	Step9	Step10
GS-1	$21,140	$21,743	$22,351	$22,375	$22,941
GS-7	$40,844	$42,011	$43,178	$44,345	$45,512
GS-15	$119,756	$123,178	$126,600	$130,022	$133,444

As shown in this grade-step matrix chart, if a government employee held a GS-7 grade and is in step 9 of their government career, their base pay would be $44,345. That base pay amount of $44,345 would be adjusted (increased) with either the locality pay adjustment for where the government employee lives and works in the Continental US or their COLA allowance for living and working outside of the Continental US. You can view the complete 2016 GS pay schedule at http://bit.ly/1rsGa1V on the OPM website.

Negotiating Your Salary in the GS Pay System

Although the pay grade levels and career step levels are standardized salary rates, you have one window of opportunity to negotiate a better salary in the government GS pay system. It is when you are offered the job by the government agency's HR department after the hiring manger selected you for the job.

Although you can't do much to negotiate the pay grade level, you might be able to negotiate what career step level you should come in at. For instance, if you are offered a GS-7 pay grade with a Step 7, you could give the HR specialist a counter-offer asking for a GS-7 pay grade with a Step

8, 9 or 10. Just be ready to justify your reasons why you should receive the higher step level.

Conversion of the GS Pay System to the National Security Personnel System (NSPS) and the Acquisition Demonstration Project (AcqDemo) Pay Systems

By now, some of you who are experienced working under the General Schedule pay system are rolling your eyes about my discussion about the GS system because of the government's attempts to convert the GS pay system to other pay systems.

These other pay systems are the National Security Personnel System (NSPS) pay system, and more recently the Acquisition Workforce Personnel Demonstration Project (AcqDemo) pay system.

Did you ever watch that *"Rabbit Season, Duck Season"* cartoon with Elmer Fudd, Bugs Bunny and Daffy Duck (you can watch the cartoon on *YouTube* at this link: http://bit.ly/2dhRQQd), or the Abbott and Costello comedy skit about *"Who's On First"* (you can watch the skit on *YouTube* at this link: http://bit.ly/1fJKVMX)? If you have, well that's how it's been with the US government converting the GS pay system to the NSPS and AcqDemo pay systems—confusion among the masses.

National Security Personnel System (NSPS)

The US government felt the 15 grades and 10 steps of the General Schedule (GS) pay system were too cumbersome and not flexible enough for managers to properly establish pay levels for government employees. (Did I mention the government's MO is layers of bureaucracy?) Therefore, Congress created the National Security Personnel System (NSPS); and in 2006 NSPS replaced the GS pay system for the Department of Defense (DoD).

One of the main goals of the NSPS pay system was to retain and reward high quality people in government jobs. To reach that goal, the NSPS was designed as a **pay-for-performance** system that recognized an employee's performance with an increase in pay level. Instead of automatic raises in pay for each step under the GS pay system, government employees now had to earn those raises by their performance under the NSPS system. Managers were given greater flexibility in rewarding performance with pay.

However, this greater flexible system came at a heavy price to managers who had to spend more time documenting employee performance and managing compensations (raises and bonuses) for that performance. This extra burden incurred by management was due to the fact that the NSPS system no longer included the automatic step pay increases of the GS pay system.

The NSPS was poorly received by both management and government employees, and was overwhelmingly unpopular and controversial immediately after implementation.

Management didn't like the NSPS system because of the increased cost to managers for the time-consuming effort to manage the documentation of employee performance and the compensation for that performance. This negative cost of time and effort quickly outweighed the management flexibility benefits of the NSPS system.

One outcry about the NSPS pay-for-performance system that came from government employees was that this system showed favoritism and inequalities. An analysis by the American Federation of Government Employees (AFGE), an American labor union showed that white government employees were receiving, on average, higher performance ratings resulting in more salary increases and bonuses than government employees of other races and ethnicities. Further analysis also showed that, depending on what government agency within the Department of Defense you worked for, you could receive more or less raises and bonuses based off of better or worse appraisals from the managers within that agency.

As a result, in 2009 (only 3 years after NSPS was first implemented), NSPS was repealed and the government converted back to the GS pay system for all DoD employees by 2012.

As you could imagine, the US government employee workforce during these times was in a state of controversy and confusion—like Elmer Fudd trying to figure out if it was rabbit season or duck season; and like Lou Costello, they didn't know if they were on first base or second base.

Currently, you'll find many US government job openings are advertised as GS positions. However, that's about to change . . . again.

Where's that Elmer Fudd shotgun when you need it?

Acquisition Workforce Personnel Demonstration Project (AcqDemo)

In 2015, Congress mandated another stab at changing and improving the GS pay system with another pay system. The government chose to first demonstrate the worthiness of this new pay system through experimentation, and called the demonstration the Acquisition Workforce Personnel Demonstration Project (AcqDemo).

AcqDemo is not new to the scene of US government pay systems. It was first created by Congress under the National Defense Authorization Act (NDA) back in 1996 to provide managers greater **control** in managing their civilian workforce, and was called the Acquisition Demonstration Project back then.

As its name implies, AcqDemo is a demonstration or experiment; or to put it more accurately, a *live* experiment currently being tested today. It is not approved for widespread use by Congress; however, participants are already undergoing the AcqDemo experiment that was originally running until September 30, 2017. The AcqDemo project's termination date has now been extended to 2020 by Congress in the National Defense Authorization Act.

One group of participants is 13,000 non-bargaining government civilian employees at the Air Force Material Command that were selected to transition from the GS pay system to the AcqDemo pay system by June 2016.

So how do people feel about the AcqDemo pay system? Many government employees and the AFGE, the American labor union that forced the US government to repeal the NSPS system, view the new AcqDemo pay system with skepticism, believing that AcqDemo is just the same old NSPS system with the same flaws but rebranded with a new name.

The US government states the AcqDemo pay system is not a pay-for-performance system as the failed NSPS system. Although there is now less paperwork involved to document employee performance, managers still have the flexibility and control over the raises and bonuses given to government employees based on their performance just as in the NSPS system.

Perhaps Lou Costello would describe the AcqDemo pay system this way: Instead of figuring out *who's* on first base or *what's* on second base, the US government decided to throw the ball to third base. (By the way, the third baseman's name is "*I don't know*".)

The good news is that the new AcqDemo pay system includes a more simplified process that streamlines and speeds up the hiring process of job candidates seeking employment in the US government sector.

Under the AcqDemo pay system, the 15 GS pay grades are consolidated into only 4 categories called broadbands; and the 22 occupational families in the GS system are consolidated down to just 3 occupational families.

The 3 occupational families of the AcqDemo pay system are:

1. **Business Management and Technical Management:** Examples are budget analysts, electrical engineers and IT professionals.

2. **Technical Management Support:** Examples are computer operators, engineering technicians and library technicians.

3. **Administration Support:** Examples are secretaries, accounting technicians and procurement specialists.

The 4 categories (broadbands) of the AcqDemo pay system are used among the 3 occupational families as follows:

Business and Technical Management Professional (NH)

- **Broadband I:** Covers the former GS-1 through GS-4 pay grades. Salaries in this broadband are $17,803–$31,871.

- **Broadband II:** Covers the former GS-5 through GS-11 pay grades. Salaries in this broadband are $27,431–$65,371.

- **Broadband III:** Covers the former GS-12 to GS-13 pay grades. Salaries in this broadband are $60,274–$93,175.

- **Broadband IV:** Covers the former GS-14 to GS-15 pay grades. Salaries in this broadband are $84,697–$129,517.

Technical Management Support (NJ)

- **Broadband I**: Covers the former GS-1 through GS-4 pay grades. Salaries in this broadband are $17,803–$31,871.

- **Broadband II:** Covers the former GS-5 through GS-8 pay grades. Salaries in this broadband are $27,431–$48,917.

- **Broadband III:** Covers the former GS-9 to GS-11 pay grades. Salaries in this broadband are $41,563–$65,371.

- **Broadband IV:** Covers the former GS-12 to GS-13 pay grades. Salaries in this broadband are $60,274–$93,175.

Administrative Support (NK)

- **Broadband I:** Covers the former GS-1 through GS-4 pay grades. Salaries in this broadband are $17,803–$31,871.

- **Broadband II:** Covers the former GS-5 through GS-7 pay grades. Salaries in this broadband are $27,431–$44,176.

- **Broadband III:** Covers the former GS-8 through GS-10 pay grades. Salaries in this broadband are $37,631–$59,505.

Company Benefits for US Government Employees

Government employees enjoy company benefits that are just as good if not better than many private companies. The government offers their employees health insurance (medical, dental, vision); pay for holidays, vacations, maternity leave, sick days, paid time off (PTO) and overtime pay; reimbursement of expenses, such as education, certifications and work-related travel, accommodations and meals; and retirement plans, such as the Federal Employees Retirement System (FERS) and the Civil Service Retirement System (CSRS). You can learn more about the benefits available to all US government employees at https://www.usa.gov/benefits-for-federal-employees on the USA.gov website.

The Civil Service Retirement System (CSRS)

The Civil Service Retirement System (CSRS) retirement plan consists of only a pension plan with no Social Security. This retirement plan can be used only by government employees who participated in this plan prior to 1987. Since participants of the CSRS retirement plan do not pay Social Security taxes for their wages, they do not receive Social Security benefits when they reach the qualifying age for Social Security. This is no different than other state and local government agencies that allow their employees to opt out of participation in the Social Security retirement program.

The Federal Employees Retirement System (FERS)

The FERS retirement plan was created by Congress in 1986 and consists of a pension, a Thrift Savings Plan and Social Security. The pension plan under FERS is called the Basic Benefit Plan to which federal employees contribute a percentage of their paycheck. Their contributions actually help pay the pensions of currently retired federal employees. After you retire from federal service, your pension will also be paid from contributions of currently working federal employees. The amount you receive from the Basic Benefit Plan is similar to that of the Social Security plan. In other words, your pension allotments are determined by the number of years worked in civil service and your highest three earning years. Currently, the minimum retirement age for federal employees under the FERS plan is 57 years of age.

To our brave men and women who served in the US Armed Forces, the US government's retirement plan provides the unique opportunity to use their time in military service toward the minimum retirement age of 57 under the FERS plan. However, Uncle Sam does not provide that opportunity for free. You've heard the saying: *freedom is not free*. Well, retirement from the US government civil service isn't free either.

To receive FERS credit, military veterans who served after 1956 must pay what's called a deposit in order to use their military service toward their federal employee retirement plan. This deposit amounts to a percentage of the military veteran's last basic pay when they were in the military.

Military veterans that are receiving military retirement pay cannot use any of their military service as credit towards their FERS retirement computation. The exception to this rule is military retirees that fall in one of the two following categories:

- The veteran is receiving retirement pay due to a service-connected disability either incurred in combat with an enemy of the US or caused by an instrumentality of war and incurred in the line of duty during a period of war.

- The veteran falls under the provision of Chapter 1223 Title 10, U.S.C. (pertaining to retirement from a reserve component of the Armed Forces).

There is still a way for military veterans receiving military retirement pay to have their time in the military credited toward their civil service employment under the FERS retirement plan. Retired veterans must waive their military retirement pay and pay the post-1956 deposit requirement if they want to apply their time in service to the FERS retirement plan. For details about crediting military service for the FERS or CSRS retirement plans, go to http://bit.ly/2dRyGmV on the OPM website.

The Thrift Savings Plan

The government Thrift Savings Plan is a 401(k) retirement plan; and the US government contributes 1.0 percent of your base pay to this plan. This plan operates as tax-free contributions similar to many 401(k) plans offered by private companies. If the federal employee adds more money than the minimum requirement to this 401(k), the government will match that contribution up to a maximum percentage.

The Application Process for US Government Employee Jobs

Welcome to Jurassic Park

As I guide you through the jungle of red tape wrapped around the axle of the US government employee job application process, I might as well introduce you to this section by saying, "*Welcome to Jurassic Park.*"

Ask any survivors of the US government application process and they'll probably respond with that deer in the headlight look and start to shake uncontrollably. Then they'll make a mad dash into the woods while screaming at the top of their lungs like the blonde-haired Lex Murphy, the young girl in the 1993 *Jurassic Park* film. That was her response when she first encountered the sofa-wide jaws and sharp fangs of the Tyrannosaurus Rex tearing open the jeep, like a can of tuna, where she and her little brother were hiding in.

As you enter the job-hunting jungle of the government's application process, crawling your way through the slush and muddied trail where prehistoric raptors work in paired hunting parties to devour job-hunting candidates' applications, resumes, documentations, time and effort; you'll soon feel more like the prey being hunted than the job hunter. Only the strong survive that process and live to talk about it.

What Doesn't Kill You Makes You Stronger

Don't get me wrong. My goal is not to discourage you from trying to seek a job with the US government. I'm preparing you for the journey you are about to embark on should you choose the career path of a US government employee. This journey requires an understanding of how the government's job application process works, and the patience and fortitude to persevere through this process. What doesn't kill you in the process will make you stronger.

It's not that the US government is intentionally trying to make their application process as difficult as climbing Mount Everest. They're just being... well, *the government.*

The government's modus operandi is layers of bureaucracy, and that is reflected in the way they process job applications. It's important to understand this because, compared to the application processes of private companies, the government's application process will make you feel like you just joined a Cirque du Soleil performance as you try to jump through all the hoops the government demands from job-seeking candidates submitting their applications online.

The jury is still out on whether or not the AcqDemo project, the new pay system currently being tested to replace the General Schedule (GS) pay system, will streamline the government hiring process enough for us to see a significant reduction in the time it takes to hire candidates for government positions. Until a quicker, more efficient job application process is in place, job seekers will have to endure the government's current job application process.

It requires a lot more stamina and patience to continue through the US government's online application process to the end. There are a lot more requirements, questionnaires and documentation you must provide to government agencies than you normally would to private companies for a job.

Most government agencies try to fill their open positions within 80 days or less from the date the job opening was posted. However, the waiting periods for multi-level reviews of multiple candidate applications and other required documents by government agencies can take several months compared to private companies that may only take weeks—all of that before you are considered for a job interview at the government agency.

The USAJOBS and Other Websites for US Government Jobs

All US government jobs are posted online in job announcements on a variety of websites. The official website for searching and applying for government jobs is at USAJOBS using the link https://usajobs.gov/. Normally, you have to create an account and profile on the website to apply for open positions the same way you have to for other online job boards.

At the USAJOBS homepage, there are only two main search windows displayed: a **Keywords** search and a **Location** search window. The Keywords search window allows you to locate US government jobs by job title, skills, agency or other keywords. The Location search window allows you to locate US government jobs in the US or other countries, such as Italy, Germany, United Kingdom, Japan or South Korea. It's that simple. The search results will provide you a long list of open job opportunities to choose from. Just click on the job title in the list to learn more about the job and the application requirements.

Job announcements on these websites for US federal, state and local government positions typically include the following:

- The job title for the position.

- Number of vacancies for that particular position.

- Salary range for the position.

- Series & Grade stating the pay grade level for the position.

- Location of the job site.

- Open Period showing the date when the job announcement was first opened. The agency will accept applications during the open period.

- Closed Period showing the date when the job announcement is closed. The agency will no longer accept applications after the closed period.

- Announcement Number used as a tracking or reference number for the open job.

- The US government department, such as the Department of Defense.

- The agency within the government department, such as the Missile Defense Agency which is an agency within the Department of Defense.

- A summary of the government agency that is seeking candidates for the open job. This information explains what the mission of the agency is.

- Position or work schedule info, such as full-time.

- Who may apply, such as internal candidates only or open to all external candidates.

- The job description outlining the responsibilities of the position.

- Other pertinent information, such as whether or not travel or a security clearance is required for the position.

To search and apply for US federal, state and local government jobs, try some of the following websites:

- USAJOBS
  https://usajobs.gov/

- USAJOBS Resource Center
  https://help.usajobs.gov/index.php/Main_Page

- Feds Hire Vets
  http://www.fedshirevets.gov/

- America Jobs
  http://www.americajobs.com/

- USA.GOV
  http://www.usa.gov/Citizen/Topics/Government-Jobs.shtml

- US Postal Jobs
  http://bit.ly/2eaXDGK

- Army Civilian Service
  https://armycivilianservice.usajobs.gov/

- Army Civilian Service
  http://armycivilianservice.com/

- Air Force Civilian Jobs
  http://www.afciviliancareers.com/

- Air Force Civilian Jobs
  http://www.afpc.af.mil/

- Navy Civilian Jobs
  http://www.secnav.navy.mil/donhr/Pages/Default.aspx

- Navy Civilian Jobs
  https://don.usajobs.gov/

Knowledge, Skills and Abilities (KSA) Questionnaire

Your application for a US government job is processed by the human resources (HR) department of each government agency. Your application submission includes an occupational questionnaire about your knowledge, skills and abilities (KSAs) as it relates to the responsibilities of the open position. Each government agency will tailor the KSA questionnaire to fit the responsibilities of their open job. Therefore, each KSA questionnaire is different for each federal, state and local agency's job opening just as each job description is different for each private company's job opening.

You are required to type out your narrative answers to each KSA question in the online application process. This gives each candidate the opportunity to briefly address each KSA in their own words using their best examples to increase their chances for success in the selection process. If you need to leave the online application to work on your KSA answers, you can save your work in the application and return to it later when you are ready to resume.

I recommend you type your narrative answers to the questionnaire on Microsoft Word or other type of document first. Do not rush through this process. Take the time you need to formulate your words carefully because not only are your answers being reviewed, your spelling and how you structure your sentences are also scrutinized. Use the spell checker when you're done with all of your answers on Word. Then copy and paste your answers to the online questionnaire.

As you can imagine, writing out narrative answers to KSA questionnaires can be time-consuming and burdensome for both the candidates who have to answer these questions as well as for HR personnel and hiring managers who have to review these narratives. In an effort to streamline this process, President Obama signed an Executive Order in 2010 to remove the KSA questionnaire from the initial screening of candidates for federal jobs.

As a result, what you will find today is that some agencies removed the KSA questionnaire entirely from their online application process; some agencies moved the questionnaire towards the end of the screening process; and other agencies simply kept the questionnaire at the start of the online application process. In other words, not every agency is rowing in the same direction in this government love boat. Government agencies basically move the KSA questionnaire around to their liking—to the front, middle or back of the hiring process—similar to a magician or con artist playing the shell game by swapping three shells around to disguise the location of the single bean or pea underneath one of the shells. Your guess is as good as mine as to where the KSA bean will be for each job announcement.

Resumes for US Government Employee Jobs

Resumes for government jobs should include work histories that are a lot longer than what might normally be written for private company jobs. Longer and more descriptive work histories provide greater depth about your knowledge, skills, abilities and experience in the workforce. Having a resume that is 5–7 pages long increases your chances of being selected for further screening and an interview than a resume that is 1–2 pages long.

Another tip that will increase your chances for success in the government selection process is filling your resume with keywords and phrases showing knowledge, skills and abilities that match or reflect the KSA requirements and job description found in the job announcement. Whether your resume is being screened by the Office of Personnel Management's automated Assessment Decision Tool (ADT) or by actual people, such as HR specialists or hiring managers, both screening methods will compare your knowledge, skills and abilities in your resume and on your KSA questionnaire with the knowledge, skills and abilities requirements and job description found in the job announcement.

Many websites posting US government jobs, such as USAJOBS.gov, have resume builder applications that will walk you through the resume writing process step-by-step, and creates your resume in the proper format for viewing by agencies. You have the option to either upload your resume to the online application page or let the resume builder help you build your resume. I recommend you use the automated resume builder when available to ensure your resume contains all the necessary information and is in the proper format.

The Validity Coefficient—the Threshold for Your Selection

After you complete the online job application and KSA occupational questionnaire, your application along with your resume and supporting documentation are compared to your narrative responses to the questionnaire. This comparison produces a numeric rating between 0.0 and 1.0 called a **validity coefficient** which represents a score of how well your background matches the knowledge, skills and abilities (KSA) requirements for the open position.

Table 2-3 depicts the way the validity coefficient value is used to determine your technical fit for the job opening. Most government agencies will consider applicants for further review whose validity rating is 3.0 or higher.

Table 2-3 *Validity coefficient values for evaluating candidates*

Validity Coefficient Value	Usefulness for the Job
.35 to 1.0	Very useful
.21 to .35	Likely to be useful
.11 to .21	Probably useful
.11 or below	Unlikely to be useful

Candidate applications with a validity rating reaching the threshold value determined by the agency, such as 3.0, are passed to a panel, such as a 3-member panel, that will then rate each candidate's KSA factors in relation to the job description requirements. Candidate applications below 3.0 may be rejected. If the agency does not receive any applications rated 3.0 or higher, they may consider applicants with ratings lower than 3.0. Length of experience is considered when they need a tie-breaker between similar candidate qualifications.

This process will produce a list of the best to the least best candidates for the job. This list is forwarded to a selection official, also known as the hiring manager, for final decision on which candidates should be interviewed for the job.

The US Government's Assessment Decision Tool (ADT)

Since government agencies oftentimes receive large volumes of applications for open jobs, many agencies will use an automated system called the Assessment Decision Tool (ADT) to screen job applications. The OPM's automated ADT system is a glorified version of the Applicant Tracking System (ATS) that many corporations and staffing agencies use to identify, screen, sort and categorize tens of thousands of resumes for available job openings in the private sector.

Government agencies have the freedom and flexibility to adjust their assessment tools used for candidates depending on the number of applications they expect to receive; the timeframe they have to find a candidate for the job; and their resources, such as budget and manning for their candidate selection process.

After the government agency inputs their requirements for their open job into the ADT system, it produces a comprehensive report detailing customized assessment strategy methods. These assessment strategies summarize competencies of the job and provide match criteria and information for each assessment method that can be used in the hiring process for their open position.

The Waiting Period and Status after Submitting Your Application for US Government Employee Jobs

Because the US government's selection process is much more layered and time-consuming than the hiring process of private companies, you can expect the waiting period for a response to your application to be a lot longer with government agencies. Depending on how many applications are being processed, it could take anywhere from one month to several months from the time you submitted your application for a job announcement to the time you are notified that the hiring manager wants to interview you.

Patience is definitely a virtue when applying for US government jobs. Your best bet is to apply for multiple government positions. This way you'll have several irons in the fire at the same time while you wait on responses from government agencies.

The government agency's HR department will notify you of your application progress using the online application website. You can check the status of your application by logging into your account at USAJOBS.gov, and then clicking on the "Application Status" link in the side menu. The Application Status page will provide status on when your application was received; when your application passed the initial review by panel members; when your application was forwarded to the selecting official; and when your application was rejected during the review process. You will be contacted by the agency's HR department if the hiring manager wants to interview you or if you were hired for the job.

If you have not received any feedback on your job application from the government agency, via online status, phone call or email after 20 to 30 days from applying online for a job, you can contact the government agency for status of your application. The contact number for the HR specialist handling that job opening will be posted with the job announcement. The agency will ask you for the job announcement reference number of the open position to locate the status of your job application.

US Government Contractors—Who We Are

US government contractors are civilians who work for and are paid by private companies, such as Boeing, Northrup Grumman, Lockheed Martin or a staffing agency that provides personnel, equipment and services to US government departments and agencies. Exceptions to this definition of contractors would be independent contractors who are self-employed individuals that do not rely on an outside company or staffing agency.

There are over 10 million civilian government contractors who work at the federal, state and local levels of our US government. It's common to see government contractors working alongside government employees and military personnel in the over 500 US government departments and agencies throughout the US and in overseas locations.

The government agency where the contractor works would be considered the primary company with the business need. However, the government contractor is employed by a private company (the secondary company) to meet the business need of the government agency. The government agency does not have direct control over the government contractor. The private company that pays the government contractor's salary and benefits has direct control over the contractor. Therefore, the IRS requires the contractor's employer—not the government agency—to withhold taxes from the contractor's earnings if the contractor is working under a W-2 tax form. Otherwise, contractors must track, record and withhold their own taxes for the IRS if they are using either a 1099 or Corp-to-Corp tax form.

Salaries of US Government Contractors

Unlike US government employees who have clearly defined and regulated pay scales, salaries for government contractors are individual, negotiable contracts between the contractor and a private company or staffing agency. The contractor's salary is based on the government agency's budgeted salary range for that position, documented qualifications (resume, certifications, degrees, skill level and years of experience), interview performance and the candidate's salary negotiation skills.

If your resume looks strong, you knocked it out of the park in your interview, and you know how to negotiate your salary; it is possible for you to obtain a salary $5,000 to $20,000 per year more than your peers—contractors or federal employees—who are working in the exact same or similar position as you in the same government agency.

Because of the disparity between salaries among contractors, contractors normally do not reveal their salary to their colleagues they work with—be it other contractors or government employees. The private company or staffing agency the contractor works for also discourages sharing salary information among co-workers. Ignorance is bliss until you find out what your co-worker is making for doing the same job as you.

Imagine working alongside someone who is doing the same job as you at work, knowing that person is making $20,000 more than you for the same job. How would that make you feel? Would it make you feel jealous, angry, animosity, spiteful, insignificant, unappreciated, cheated, some of the above or all of the above? Would you try to ask for a raise because of your co-worker's higher salary? When you tell your boss or company you want a raise because your co-worker is making $20,000 more than you, how do you suppose your boss or company would respond to your knowledge of your co-worker's salary? Would you tell other people at work doing the same job as you about the higher salary your co-worker is making; and would you start asking other co-workers what they're making for the same job? If the co-worker who is making $20,000 more than you for doing the same job as you needed your help at work, would you still be as friendly and willing to help that person as you were before knowing about their higher salary?

All of these feelings, reactions and responses are very real occurrences among co-workers when they find out each other's salary. When co-workers share their salary information, someone always wins and someone always loses in that conversation. If you're on the losing end of that conversation, how you handle the realization that you're making less—perhaps a lot less—than your colleague for the same position depends on the type of person you are and how your co-worker's higher salary makes you feel.

Now put those higher salaried shoes on your own feet.

How do you think your co-worker would feel if they knew you made $20,000 more than them for doing the exact same or similar job? Get the point?

Some people can handle that salary information better than others. Some people can't handle or accept the fact that you are making more money than them. That's when problems can occur in your workplace. That is why it's always best not to reveal your salary to another colleague at work or ask about another co-worker's salary.

It's also true that employers do not want their employees to know about each other's salaries because employers know everyone's negotiated salary is different. This gives the employer a certain level of knowledge, power and control over the salary negotiation process for each individual worker. If the worker lacks the knowledge and experience in salary negotiations, the employer has the advantage over the worker in setting their salary. The employer can get the worker to accept a lower salary than another co-worker for the same job without the person knowing what money they're missing out on. This saves the company money. If the worker is knowledgeable and experienced in salary negotiations, the worker can have greater advantage over the employer in setting their salary, knowing they can ask for more money.

In private business sectors, everyone negotiates their salary. It's the same way for the salaries of government contractors. Those who **know** how to negotiate their salary; understand the **power** of leverage in negotiations; and can **control** the negotiation process come out with higher salaries than other people in the same job who have not learned and developed these skills. In chapter 7, I'll take you through the process of salary negotiations to increase your advantage over employers in getting top dollar for your skill sets.

The Application Process for US Government Contractor Jobs

Welcome to Disneyland Park

Compared to the *Jurassic Park* government employee job application process, the job application process for government contractors is like *Disneyland Park* (minus the expensive entrance fees).

The government contractor's entire hiring process is done through a private company or staffing agency. The people that interview and select the contractor for the government job are either from the private company that will pay the government contractor's salary or from other non-government corporations (such as contractors of another company that also work in the government agency). The contractor does not interact with the HR department or other government employees of the agency during the contractor's job application, salary negotiations, interview and selection processes. Therefore, the government contractor does not experience the months of delays and red tape associated with the government hiring process.

Contractors find government contractor jobs through the same online job websites as job-seekers in search of non-government private sector jobs, such as Monster.com, Indeed.com or CareerBuilder.com. Government jobs can also be found on the career links of a private company's website. You can apply for a specific government contractor job found on these sites or you can upload your resume to these job search websites so recruiters can contact you for government jobs that are currently available or will come available in the future.

As you might imagine, some government contractor jobs require you to either have a security clearance or be able to get one. In chapter 3, I go over security clearances and how people obtain them.

To Be or Not to Be
a US Government Employee or Contractor

So which should you choose: a government employee job or government contractor position?

That answer comes down to your personal preference. Both job types have advantages and disadvantages to consider.

Government contractor salaries are typically higher than that of government employees for the same or similar jobs because contractors can negotiate their salaries. One contractor can make more money than another contractor or government employee without any of their colleagues knowing about their higher salary.

Government employees, on the other hand, don't have to negotiate their salaries; therefore, one government employee can't make a higher salary than another employee based on their salary negotiation skills. Salary ranges are set in stone under the GS pay system. Everyone—government employee and contractor—basically know what each government employee's salary is based on their GS grade and how many years they've been in that grade level.

A government employee's job and career can be more stable and secure with less risk than contractor jobs. Remember, government employees work directly for and are paid by their government agency. These government employees are not competing with other government agencies or private companies for their jobs. A government employee's only real competition comes during their job application process when they are initially competing with other candidates for the government position. After they're hired, they don't ever have to worry about losing their job to a contractor of a corporation or staffing agency.

However, government civil service jobs are not an ironclad security blanket. We've all seen through the downturn of the economy and the US government sequestration process that many government employees can lose their jobs unexpectedly too.

US Government Contracts with Private Companies

Private companies and contractors are always in competition with one another through a government contract bidding process for available contractor slots and required services within the government agency.

When a corporation wins the contract to provide personnel, services and equipment to support a government agency, it doesn't mean that company is given a 10- to 20-year contract where you can hang your hat for many years while you pay down your mortgage and save for your children's education. Many of these business contracts between the US government and private companies start out as a 1- or 2-year trial period. The government contract might be a 5-year contract, but the trial period may only be for 1 to 2 years.

After this trial period, the government agency will evaluate if they are satisfied with the personnel, equipment and services that the corporation brought to the agency. If the agency is satisfied with the company after the trial period, the agency will then either extend the existing contract or create a new contract for perhaps 3 or 5 years with this company. If this process sounds vaguely familiar to you, you probably follow sports because this process is similar to the contracts of professional sports athletes. As with professional athletes, the government contract can be either extended or a new contract written.

After the extended or new contract is created, the government agency will re-evaluate the company again over the length of that new contract period to determine if they still want to keep the company or open up those positions and services through the contractor bidding process again. This contract rotation can occur several times for companies providing contractor personnel and services to government agencies.

For companies offering personnel, equipment and services, this government contract merry-go-round could happen every 1–3 years until the government agency is satisfied with the contract deliverables of a company; at which time the agency will provide a somewhat longer contract (5 to 8 years) to that company.

When Another Company Wins the US Government Contract

What typically happens when another corporation wins the contract is that the government agency will require the new company to retain a small percentage of the existing contractors from the previous company that lost the contract. This provides a degree of stability for the government agency's operations during this transition to new personnel, equipment and services.

The rest of the contractors who didn't get selected to stay on board with the new company are out of a job.

It is very common for gainfully employed contractors to be sitting pretty in a good government contract job with a great salary one year; only to be sitting on pins and needles the next year, not knowing if they'll still have that job to feed their family, pay their mortgage, and so on. Pins and needles, that is, until the government agency announces which company was selected after the bidding process.

If their company won the bid or if they are selected to stay onboard with the new company that won the bid, contractors can exchange those pins and needles for pillows and cushions to sit on. If their company lost the bid or they were not selected to join the new company that won the bid, they'll get up that following morning; look themselves in the bathroom mirror and say, *"Let the depression begin."*

You know how every year just before the regular season of NFL football; nearly one thousand NFL players will lose their jobs during roster cuts? Or how every Major League Baseball team will start off with 55–65 players during spring training; and then cut 30–40 players before regular season to get their number down to 25 players on the active roster? Do you remember how millions of people watched the 2016 USA Women's Gymnastics Olympic trials; and waited breathlessly as gymnastics coach Martha Karolyi deliberated on the final cuts; and then announced the five women who would call themselves the *Final Five* and go on to win gold medals at the 2016 Rio Olympics?

Well, that's kind of what it's like during the government contract bidding process among corporations. Only difference being that in government contracts, not only do certain players (contractors) get cut (fired); the entire team (corporation) gets cut (fired). You could argue that another difference is that professional athletes stand to lose millions when cut while contractors lose only thousands of dollars. However, being cut or released (fired) from a team (company) hurts the same no matter if its millions of dollars lost, thousands of dollars lost, or Olympic medals lost.

I was working as a network engineer at the North American Aerospace Defense Command (NORAD), a government agency in Colorado Springs, Colorado, when NORAD decided to open their NORAD contract for bidding between private companies. Several companies bid for the contract. I and hundreds of other people worked for the incumbent company at the time. Unfortunately, my company lost the contract. This meant a new company was coming in that would select which of us would stay and which ones would lose their jobs. Fortunately, instead of being cut from the roster, the new company offered me the opportunity to join their team.

The only private company free from the NORAD contract bidding process is Santa Claus and his reindeers. NORAD may be able to track Santa's progress and services during the Christmas holiday, but NORAD can't touch Santa's contract.

When a new company wins the bid for the government agency's contract, what typically happens is the new company will inform all the contractors of the former company which contractors were cut from the roster, so to speak. Then, the management and HR crew of the new company will have a group meeting with all of the contractors they want to keep. In that meeting, the new company leaders will tell the contractors about their new company and give them a pep talk about doing great things together for the government agency. In that meeting, they will also ask each contractor to provide them their previous employment information, such as their job title, the office they worked in, and their salary.

The new company wants this information, especially the salary information, from the contractors so they can determine what salary to offer each contractor in their job offer letter they will send to each contractor they want to keep.

Here's where I'm going to share with you another little secret employers don't want you to know.

Although it's a dirty little secret, it's not a government secret so don't worry. The amount that each contractor writes down as their former salary is the salary the new company typically will pay the contractor. The secret is that some contractors know this and some contractors don't. Knowledge is power, and power is control.

So what do you think many of the contractors who knew this secret did? Wait for it . . . yep, they wrote down a salary that was higher than what they actually made with their previous employer. Did the new company pay them that higher rate? Yes.

Regardless if you think this is right or wrong, ethical or unethical, the fact is the new company paid those contractors the higher salary that they stated they were making. I'm providing you this information to give you knowledge and insight on what takes place during this transfer of power and control from one private company to another in a government agency. Let your conscience be your guide concerning what you will do with that knowledge.

Job Opportunities for Contractors during the Government Agency Bidding Process

The government contract bidding process can result in many people losing their jobs. It also presents the opportunity for many people to find new jobs. Every time a government agency opens a bid to private companies for their agency contract, there is a mad dash by many companies, large and small, that want a piece of that government pie.

These government contracts can be worth anywhere from tens or hundreds of millions of dollars to billions of dollars in revenue to these corporations, depending on the size, scope and requirements of the government agency. After all, the government is the world's largest consumer of products and services.

During the bidding process, a variety of companies will compete, oftentimes in group partnerships, for the government contract. As each company prepares to compete for the contract, they must find people who can fill those contract positions. As part of the government bidding process, these competing companies are required to have candidates lined up and ready to start working if they win the contract.

If your resume is posted on one of the many online job search websites, you may receive an email or phone call from a recruiter offering you one of these contract positions. When these recruiters start calling, the important thing to realize is that the private company looking for people to fill these positions **has not won the contract**. They are simply looking for people—sometimes hundreds of people—who are willing to sign up for the potential of being offered a position with that company **IF**—not **when**—they win the government contract. In other words, this contact from the recruiter is not about an actual job you can interview for right now. It's about a future job **IF** the company wins the contract.

If you are considering signing up for this *future* job opportunity, ask the recruiter when the government agency will make a decision on the winning company. This way you'll know how long you will have to wait before that future job becomes a reality.

This future job opportunity will benefit only the private company—*not you*—on the front end; however, it has the potential of benefiting you on the back end if the company wins the contract. You're basically doing the company a favor in exchange for a possible future job opportunity that is not guaranteed to you. You're allowing that company to use your resume as part of the pool of people they are trying to gather together for a future possibility of winning the government contract. The company can only return the favor to you—with a job—if they win the contract in the end.

Since there is no guarantee of a job under these circumstances, you don't want to discontinue your job search with other recruiters and other avenues if you agree to allow the recruiter to represent you for this future job opportunity.

The recruiter will most likely try to get you to sign a letter of intent agreement stating you will not let another company competing for this government contract to use you and your resume for this bidding process. This is similar to the exclusive rights agreement some recruiters want you to sign. I'll go into more detail about the exclusive rights agreement in chapter 6.

If the company already won the contract, then you can treat this job opportunity like any other actual job position that needs to be filled immediately by an employer. When the company wins the contract, they will be eager to fill those open government contractor positions in order start impressing the government agency with the much needed personnel to fulfill the requirements of the contract.

The Choice is Yours

In spite of all the instability within the government contractor workforce, contractors continue to adapt and prosper within the changing environments of US government agency contracts—and so can you.

So the question you should ask yourself is this: *Do I want the higher salary with less job security and more risk that comes with a contractor career; or do I want the lower salary with seemingly more* *job security and less risk that comes with a government employee career?*

Only you, and perhaps your significant other, can answer that question.

Don't forget that government civil service employees can quit their job and become government contractors any time they want, and vice versa. This happens all the time as well.

It's all up to you. The choice is yours.

CHAPTER THREE

Security Clearances and Training

To keep your secret is wisdom; to expect others to keep it is folly.
William Samuel Johnson

What Are US Government Security Clearances

A security clearance is our United States government's method of ensuring a US citizen passes certain requirements and criteria before considering that individual trustworthy, reliable, loyal to the United States, and eligible to access certain levels of classified information.

Security clearances are granted, controlled and owned by the US government. Security clearances are not granted to non-US citizens, although rare exceptions are made for people who possess superior skill sets sought after by our government.

Having a security clearance does not automatically authorize you access to classified information; you must also have what is called a "need to know". In other words, your position and job responsibilities must dictate that you have access to that specific classified area, information or equipment to perform your job; otherwise, you will not be allowed access to that area, information or equipment any more than a person who does not possess a clearance. Each clearance determines your degree of access to classified information.

There are three levels of security clearances:

1. **Confidential clearance:** When something is classified as Confidential, its unauthorized access or disclosure could cause ***damage*** to US national security.

2. **Secret clearance:** When something is classified as Secret, its unauthorized access or disclosure could cause ***serious damage*** to our national security.

3. **Top Secret (TS) clearance:** Something classified as Top Secret could cause ***exceptionally grave damage*** to our national security if accessed by or disclosed to an unauthorized person.

There are other terms that people mistake for a security clearance that are merely categories of classified information, such as COSMIC Top Secret (CTS). COSMIC is a category of classified information used with a Top Secret security clearance. The term COSMIC denotes one of the four categories of sensitive information shared among NATO allies; COSMIC being the highest of the four categories.

Another common misconception people have is thinking that the Sensitive Compartmented Information (SCI) and the Single Scope Background Investigation (SSBI) are security clearances. They are not security clearances.

Sensitive Compartmented Information (SCI)

Sensitive Compartmented Information (SCI) is a type of classified intelligence information used by military personnel, government employees and contractors. Individuals are given SCI access based on "need to know" responsibilities that require them to have access to critical and sensitive intelligence information or processes to perform their duties. The Director of National Intelligence has overall control of SCI information.

The sensitive SCI information is called "compartmented" because SCI information is subdivided into different compartments or control systems to give the government greater management and control over the information or processes people are allowed to access.

The classified information in SCI is considered more critical and sensitive than Top Secret information. That is why most people who are being considered for a TS/SCI must take a polygraph test.

Single Scope Background Investigation (SSBI)

Single Scope Background Investigation (SSBI) is the background investigation used for military personnel, government employees and contractors who require a Top Secret clearance, Q access or access to SCI information. Q access is the Department of Energy's equivalent to the Department of Defense's Top Secret clearance.

The "Single Scope" in the SSBI background investigation refers to how far is the scope or reach of the investigation. The investigation's scope goes back as far as 10 years or up to the age of 18 years of age. However, the scope of the SSBI investigation can be expanded or contracted as needed. People with a Top Secret clearance who do not have a TS/SCI typically have a TS/SSBI.

When Are Security Clearances Needed

Many of the jobs in the Department of Defense and other government departments require security clearances such as a Secret or Top Secret clearance. The type of job you perform will determine if you need a clearance or not. For instance, if you are involved with IT networks in a US government agency, such as a DoD agency, chances are very likely you will need and possess a security clearance to perform your job.

Your security clearance is good for jobs that require a clearance equal to or less than your clearance level. For example, if you possess a Top Secret clearance, you are allowed to work in jobs that require a Top Secret, Secret or Confidential clearance. If you possess a Secret clearance, you are allowed to work in jobs that require a Secret or Confidential clearance, but not in jobs requiring a Top Secret or higher clearance.

How Long Are Security Clearances Valid

Security clearances are valid for a certain number of years before you must resubmit another clearance questionnaire application and be reinvestigated to renew your clearance.

Once you obtain a clearance, it is not good for life—each clearance is valid for a specific number of years before it is either renewed or expired. Confidential clearances are typically good for 15 years before they must be renewed; Secret clearances are good for 10 years; and Top Secret clearances are good for 5 years.

Each security clearance has a certain status as follows:

- **Active:** Your clearance is considered "**active**" when you are using your unexpired clearance to work in your current job.

- **Current but Inactive:** If you are not using your clearance for a job you are currently working in, but your clearance has not expired, your clearance is considered "**current**" but "**inactive**".

- **Expired:** Your security clearance is "**expired**" when it has reached its respective length of term before you renewed it or re-activated it. In this case, you have to complete the Electronic Questionnaires for Investigations Processing (e-QIP) application and background investigation again to obtain a clearance.

The moment you leave a job where you were using your security clearance, the Security Manager responsible for your clearance will place your clearance in the inactive status using the Joint Personnel Adjudication System (JPAS), the DoD record system for security clearances. You have 24 months (2 years) from the time your clearance is placed in the inactive status to re-activate your clearance by working in another job that requires your security clearance. As long as your inactive clearance is within the 24 month window, and your clearance has not reached its expiration date, your clearance is considered "current" but "inactive". As long as your inactive clearance remains current (within 24 months) and is still within its normal expiration date, it can be re-activated again for use in another job requiring that security clearance.

If your security clearance remains inactive beyond 24 months, your clearance is no longer considered current; and is automatically expired. This is the case even if your clearance did not reach its normal expiration date. Once your clearance is declared expired due to lack of active use within 24 months, you will have to complete the e-QIP questionnaire and go through the background investigation again as if you were requesting a security clearance for the first time—called "initial". Therefore, if you plan to keep and reuse your "current" but "inactive" security clearance for future US government jobs, you must find a government job that will re-activate your clearance within 24 months of your clearance's inactive status. That government job can be either a government employee or government contractor position.

Obtaining a US Government Security Clearance

But how does a person obtain a security clearance?

The first thing you should know is that there is no training involved in getting your security clearance, nor is there a test you have to take. However, you do have to fill out an extensive online questionnaire and undergo a thorough background investigation to assess and verify the information in your completed questionnaire.

You cannot initiate or apply for a security clearance. You have to be sponsored by a private company or government agency that requires you to have one. The Security Manager or Facility Security Officer (FSO) is the person who initiates the request for your security clearance. This Security Manager or FSO can be an employee of a corporation or government agency. The Security Manager uses JPAS, the DoD record system for security clearances, to make a request for security clearances up to Top Secret.

Joint Personnel Adjudication System (JPAS)

The Joint Personnel Adjudication System (JPAS) is also the system government agencies or private companies, including staffing agencies, can use to check the status of your existing security clearance for a job opportunity that requires a clearance.

To check your clearance status, the JPAS system requires your social security number and date of birth. Oftentimes, when you are seeking work in a government agency through a corporate recruiter, staffing agency recruiter or a government agency recruiter, that recruiter will ask you for your social security number and date of birth to verify the status of your existing security clearance. This is a perfectly normal procedure—they cannot verify your security clearance in JPAS without your social security number and date of birth.

However, you should always guard your social security number. Be careful when someone, such as a recruiter, asks you for your social security number and date of birth. Someone impersonating as a recruiter could be trying to steal your identity and use your personal information fraudulently. Don't believe every recruiter who emails you or cold-calls you about a job opportunity with the US government; and then asks for your social security number or date of birth to verify the status of your existing clearance in JPAS. The person could be a con artist trying to steal your personal information to open credit cards or other accounts in your name.

Applying for a Security Clearance

If you've never held a security clearance before, and the job you are seeking requires you to possess one, the Security Manager of the corporation (for government contractors) or the US government agency (for federal employees) that hires you will start the process of obtaining you a clearance at the security level required for your new position.

The Security Manager will provide you an online link to a secure website containing a questionnaire form, called an Electronic Questionnaires for Investigations Processing (e-QIP), which is managed by the Office of Personnel Management (OPM). The e-QIP form replaced the old hardcopy forms SF-86 and SF-85P used up until 2003 for background investigations for government positions.

The e-QIP questionnaire will ask you a multitude of questions that seem to go on forever.

Your answers to all of these questions help determine your qualifications and fitness for a security clearance.

You'll be asked personal questions related to your financial responsibility, mental health, meetings with people or groups, associations and friendships with groups, affiliations, and people that are either of foreign nations or considered potentially hostile or unfriendly to the US.

You are asked questions about prior clearances and investigations; your work history and military service; your criminal records, alcohol related incidents and court actions; and other personal life events, such as where you lived, your family background and history, and places you visited or vacationed over a span of several years.

You will have to provide details about every member of your family—living and deceased; their full names, birth dates, addresses and citizenship; their relationships with other people who may be potentially hostile or unfriendly to the US; and places they may have visited in other countries.

The higher your security clearance, the more years of your life you have to cover when answering these questions. An initial or first-time security clearance typically requires questions covering more years of your life than an existing clearance renewal. For instance, a first-time Secret clearance may require you to go back the last 7–10 years of your life, and then only 5 years for a renewal. A Top Secret clearance may require you to answer questions covering the last 15 years of your life.

You can complete the e-QIP questionnaire using your personal computer at home. Since there are so many questions, some of which require you to dig out old records or contact other people to find the answers, you are allowed a sufficient amount of days to accomplish this electronic form.

Obtaining your security clearance will require other actions for you to complete, such as submitting your fingerprints (typically performed at a law enforcement building—an out-of-pocket expense that will be reimbursed back to you by your employer); be interviewed by an investigator; or take a polygraph test (for higher level clearances). Additionally, once you are hired, almost all DoD and other government jobs require you to take a drug test. Your employer will pay for this test too.

If you think applying for a security clearance may be even a remote possibility in your career future, you should start now to collect these types of information that will be asked of you later in life—it will make this process a lot easier for you down the road.

Once you complete the e-QIP application questionnaire, your Security Manger uses JPAS to send your completed e-QIP application and clearance level request to the centralized DoD Central Adjudication Facility (DoDCAF)—of which the Defense Industrial Security Clearance Office (DISCO) is a part—or a separate DoD Central Adjudication Facility (CAF) for review and processing.

After DISCO or DoDCAF completes its review of your e-QIP application, they will forward your clearance application to the Office of Personnel Management (OPM). The OPM office conducts the background investigation. An investigator will be assigned to perform a background check to investigate the records, people and places you mentioned in your online questionnaire. You can even expect the investigator to contact the people you mentioned in your questionnaire. The investigator will inquire about your character, behavior and other areas that will either validate or invalidate your eligibility for a security clearance.

If something in your answers raises a red flag to investigators, they will contact you to obtain further information on that particular subject from you. For instance, if you are married to someone who currently holds or held a citizenship in a foreign country, this could raise a red flag to investigators.

Once OPM completes its background investigation on you, they will forward their findings back to DISCO or DoDCAF who will either grant you or deny you a clearance based on the investigation results.

The length of time it takes to get your security clearance, from the time you complete your online questionnaire form to your clearance being adjudicated and granted, could be 4 to 8 months depending on the type of clearance you are applying for; your answers (missing, incorrect or red flags), the investigation period; and any backlog in clearance applications that need adjudicating before your clearance can be looked at.

Interim Security Clearance—Your Foot in the Door

So if it takes 4–8 months to obtain a security clearance, how can you possibly expect a job-hunter to wait this long when there are bills to be paid?

A common practice is to grant someone what is called an "**interim**" security clearance or "interim eligibility".

Once you are hired and you completed your online clearance questionnaire, DISCO or DoDCAF will complete their minimum investigation requirements on you—typically completed within a few days to a few weeks—to award you an interim clearance. This interim clearance will allow you to work in the government agency without allowing you access to classified areas, equipment and information.

The interim clearance will allow you to go through your government agency's newcomer orientation process; meet your new managers, supervisors, colleagues and clients; get your desk, computer and phone set up; and start performing work that is not classified (referred to as unclassified).

Yes, you are limited in what you can do; and at times you may have to be escorted by someone to get from one place to another; but be thankful and congratulate yourself because you now have your foot in the door. You're earning a paycheck and you're well on your way to doing great things for our nation while you wait for the completion of your clearance adjudication process.

Security Clearance Adjudication—the Final Decision

The security clearance review, background investigation and approval process is called the **adjudication** process. Once this adjudication process is completed and a decision is made to either allow or deny you a security clearance, the final judgment is considered "adjudicated". Your Security Manager will inform you when your clearance is fully adjudicated and whether or not you were granted your clearance.

Getting Employers to Submit You for a Security Clearance

So you don't have a security clearance but you want to get one so you can work in jobs that require a security clearance. Since companies are the ones who have to initiate submitting you for a security clearance, what can you do to get a company to submit you for a security clearance?

First of all, you have to make it known to employers that you are interested in working for a US government agency that requires a security clearance.

There are several ways you can do this.

One way is to apply for US government employee jobs on the USAJOBS or other online job search websites I listed earlier. The government job you apply for must be one that requires a security clearance, such as IT, security, warehouse or some administration jobs.

Security Clearances and Training

Another way is by applying for defense contractor jobs in austere, danger/hazard overseas locations. Although there are a large number of defense contractors working in these areas, their numbers are quite small compared to the rest of the American workforce that live and work outside of those areas. Therefore, the demand for workers in these difficult areas is oftentimes higher than the supply of workers willing to work at these locations. That means employers are more willing to pay for getting a security clearance in the hands of qualified people who are willing to live and work in these overseas areas. Once again, the overseas job you are applying for must be in a career field that requires a security clearance.

A third way of attracting employers to consider you for a security clearance is making it known in your resume that you are interested in obtaining a security clearance. You can put a statement in your resume that indicates you are willing and able to pass a security clearance. This will let employers know that you are not only willing to go through the tedious process of getting a security clearance; you are also certain your background history is clean enough to pass an exhaustive background investigation to obtain a security clearance. This will give employers some assurance that their investment in you for a security clearance will not be wasted. The statement you can put in your resume can be the following: "I am willing and able to obtain a security clearance."

By including the key phrase "security clearance" in this statement, the automated Applicant Tracking System (ATS) recruiters use to search for, collect and filter thousands of online resumes from different Internet job search and social media websites will key in on those words for recruiters performing resume searches containing those words. Recruiters include the key phrase "security clearance" when they are looking to place people in US government jobs. In chapter 5, I go over in great detail how recruiters use the ATS system; and how you can use this knowledge to increase your chances of getting your resume noticed and selected by recruiters.

Job-Hunting Advantages of Having a Security Clearance

The administrative processing and subsequent background check for a security clearance costs thousands of dollars; and the higher your security clearance, the greater the cost. These costs are paid for by the corporation or government agency that hires you for the position.

This presents a unique advantage to job-hunters—who already possess a clearance—over job-hunters who don't have a clearance. Having a security clearance makes you a more desirable candidate than non-cleared professionals to companies seeking people with clearances to fill government job openings. When possible, companies would rather hire candidates who already possess a clearance, in order save money, than to shell out all that cash to perform the necessary background check.

The background check doesn't guarantee the candidate will receive a clearance after the investigation is completed—and companies know this. The candidate could fail the background check. If that happens, the company's investment will go down the drain—they don't get that invested money back. Therefore, when several job-hunters are applying for a US government position requiring a security clearance, the candidates who already have their clearance are usually the ones who get the job. Consider it one of the benefits of having gone through the lengthy process of obtaining your clearance.

The law of supply and demand also works in your favor when it comes to having a security clearance. There are fewer job-seekers with clearances than those without clearances. This means the demand for cleared job-seekers is greater than the supply of cleared job-seekers. The pool of competition among people with security clearances looking for government jobs requiring a clearance is a lot smaller. All of this increases your chances and odds of getting hired more quickly and easily for contractor jobs for a government agency.

Military Veterans and Security Clearances

Many military veterans who were recently discharged from the military oftentimes benefit from having a security clearance while in the military because their clearances will carry over from the military to a civilian job in a US government agency.

There are many men and women in the military who have gone through the thorough background investigation process to qualify for and hold security clearances. When they leave the military, they still have these current but inactive clearances on file which can be re-activated for jobs in government agencies requiring such clearances.

This is one of the benefits afforded our US military veterans who held a security clearance while serving in the military. It gives them an added advantage when competing for defense contracting and federal employee jobs requiring a security clearance. This is a unique qualification many of our nation's military possess along with their other professional skill sets that help position them for success when they leave the military.

If you've never served in the military, don't lose heart when it comes to getting a security clearance. I've worked alongside many people in US government agencies that have never been in the military and either held a security clearance or had an interim clearance as they waited on their adjudication process for their security clearance.

Using Your Security Clearance

After you are approved for a security clearance, you will be provided a security badge that allows you access to certain levels of classified areas, information and equipment based on your clearance level. Having your security clearance allows you to complete the full requirements of your job.

Clearance badges are usually attached to lanyards that are worn around your neck; and are clearly visible so everyone in the government facility can easily identify if you have proper security authorization when you are around classified areas, information or equipment.

Perhaps you've seen people around town wearing their work badge attached to a lanyard while taking a break for lunch, filling up their tank at the gas station or shopping in a store. For many, that piece of plastic hanging from their neck is their badge of pride; a status symbol of having made it somewhere in life; a feeling of belonging, importance or authority. That's all well and good. I congratulate you—I see ya'.

But for those of us who have a security clearance, displaying your clearance badge outside of your work facility is a no-no that is not allowed by US government agencies. Your security clearance badge is your access card, your pass to enter and access classified areas and information. Displaying your security clearance badge offsite in public is not only an inappropriate way to satisfy your ego; it identifies your level of clearance and places you at risk of being targeted by those who seek to gain unauthorized access to US government facilities, equipment and information.

After your clearance is granted, you should always maintain a copy of your clearance information and the contact information of your current or last Security Manager. When you decide to move on from this government job to another job that requires a security clearance, your new Security Manager will need your clearance information to transfer your security clearance to your new employer.

Security Training, Testing and Certification Requirements

Although obtaining a US security clearance does not involve any training or tests, this does not mean there are no security training, testing and certification requirements for those of us who work as a US government contractor or federal employee. There are actually more security training, testing and certification requirements in US government jobs, particularly government IT jobs, than there are in the private sector.

Hardly a week goes by where you don't hear or read of yet another report of an individual opening an innocent-looking email attachment with a Trojan Horse virus; a hacker breaking into a network and harming or stealing valuable business and personal information; someone working on the inside of an organization stealing information off the network; or someone whose credit card or personal information was stolen. We're all constantly on our guard when we're online more than ever and rightfully so. Institutions that we thought were protected and well insulated from cyberattack appear to be just as vulnerable as the rest of us consumers using our home or mobile computing devices.

A 2015 Time article, titled *Data Breach Tracker: All the Major Companies That Have Been Hacked*, stated that a reported data breach occurs almost on a weekly basis. Over the past few years, hackers have breached data networks of brand name companies, such as Sony, Home Depot, Target, EBay, JP Morgan to name a few.

In 2014, correspondent Scott Pelley of *60 Minutes* gave a television interview of FBI Director James Comey at the command center of the FBI headquarters in Washington. During this interview, director Comey said *"There are two kinds of big companies in the US. There are those who've been hacked by the Chinese and those who don't know they've been hacked by the Chinese."*

It would be naive of us to think the Chinese government is the only entity trying to hack into our US computer network systems. Today, you can expect hackers to come from many sources both within and outside the US.

Nothing seems off limits for these hackers and cyber attackers. Although banks, such as Europay, MasterCard and Visa, have developed the EMV, the credit card chip technology initialed after those companies, to reduce the theft of credit card information; hackers, cybercriminals and spying governments are still roaming free across the Internet looking for their next target.

An October 2014 Gallup poll showed that the crime Americans worry about the most is having their credit card information used at stores stolen by computer hackers (69%); followed by fears of having their computer or smartphone hacked (62%). This is in stark comparison to Americans participating in this poll who feared having their homes burglarized (45%); having their car stolen (42%); getting mugged (31%); being sexually assaulted (18%); or getting murdered (18%).

No one is safe from cybercrimes, including me. I also received those unwelcomed letters from both a private corporation and US government agency telling me my personal information was compromised in their network data breach by hackers. Healthcare, banking, credit bureaus, online dating sites, social media sites, and yes, US government networks have all been hacked.

US government networks are just as vulnerable as private companies and individual consumers. The Heritage Foundation is a research and education think tank whose primary audiences are members of Congress; key congressional staff members; policymakers in the executive branch; the nation's news media; and the academic and policy communities. In Issue Brief#4488 on Cyber Security by The Heritage Foundation, an article titled *Continued Federal Cyber Breaches in 2015* by Research Assistant Riley Walters reported the following US government agencies were hacked in either 2014 or 2015:

- Department of Health and Human Services (HHS, August 2014)

- White House (October 2014)

- National Oceanic and Atmospheric Agency (NOAA, November 2014)

- United States Postal Service (USPS, November 2014)

- Department of State (November 2014)

- Federal Aviation Administration (FAA, April 2015)

- Department of Defense (DoD, April 2015)

- St. Louis Federal Reserve (May 2015)

- Internal Revenue Service (IRS, May 2015)

- US Army Web site (June 2015)

- Office of Personnel Management (OPM, June 2015)—yes, this is the office that controls your security clearance information.

- Census Bureau (July 2015)

- Pentagon (August 2015)

Security Training and Testing

Education on network security is one of the ways US government agencies are combating cybercrimes. If you choose to work at a US government agency, you can expect to receive online security tips; security alerts and bulletins; and security training while at work on a regular basis that the government agency uses to educate its personnel on network security threats.

The computer-based training (CBT) you'll receive at a government agency can be completed on your computer at your work desk for convenience. This security CBT training is embedded with tests on the material you read that you must pass in order to receive credit for completing the training.

If you plan to work at a US Department of Defense organization, you will be required to complete further security training and certification that you might not have to at other government agencies. Because of increased cyberattacks, DoD agencies now make it mandatory for all its workers—military and civilian—whose responsibilities involve information assurance (IA) to have some type of professional security certification and ongoing security training. Testing for one of these required security certifications are completed off-site at one of your local certification testing centers.

Information assurance involves the protection of the integrity, availability, authenticity, non-repudiation and confidentiality of user data by identifying, controlling and managing the risks involved with using, processing, storing and transmitting information over IT networks.

To help combat the increasing threat of cyberattacks, the Department of Defense issued DoD 8570.01-M *Information Assurance Workforce Improvement Program* in 2005 that provided guidance and procedures for the training, certification and management of the DoD workforce—both military and civilian—whose responsibilities involve IA.

What evolved from this directive are DoD approved baseline security certifications for certain categories and levels of IA, such as Information Assurance Technical (IAT) levels I, II and III; Information Assurance Management (IAM) levels I, II and III; and Information Assurance System Architect and Engineer (IASAE) levels I, II and III. For instance, for those working in IT, the junior and senior engineers follow the IAT tract; IT managers follow the IAM tract; and IT architects and professionals involved with advanced levels of security, such as encryption devices or secure software development, follow the IASAE tract.

As cyberattacks evolved and increased over the years, the DoD also responded to these changes. On August 11, 2015, representatives of the DoD replaced DoD 8570.01-M with updated DoD 8140.01, *Cyberspace Workforce Management* to expand upon the existing policies and assigned responsibilities for managing the DoD cyberspace workforce.

I can see your eyes glaze over, so let's move on.

Security Certification Through Computing Technology Industry Association (CompTIA) Security+

For most government professionals involved with information assurance, only the Computing Technology Industry Association (CompTIA) Security+ baseline certification is required along with continuing education (CE) in security.

CompTIA is a non-profit trade association that provides vendor-neutral IT certifications accredited by the American National Standards Institute. Other DoD approved security certifications, such as the Certified Information Systems Security Professional (CISSP) or the Certified Secure Software Lifecycle Professional (CSSLP), can be obtained from the International Information Systems Security Certification Consortium or (ISC)², another non-profit organization that specializes in information security education and certifications.

Although the CompTIA Security+ certification, a lifetime certification, was once all that was needed for security qualifications for an IT job in a DoD organization, DoD 8570.01-M changed all of that. As of January 1, 2011, the Department of Defense no longer recognizes the CompTIA Security+ certification as a lifetime certification and requires people to go through ongoing education in security best practices.

In response to the DoD's new view of their lifetime certifications, CompTIA changed the status of their Security+ certification. Today, a CompTIA Security+ certification dated after December 31, 2010 is good for only 3 years from the certification date; and you are automatically enrolled in the CompTIA Continuing Education (CE) Program. Lifetime CompTIA certifications earned prior to January 1, 2011 still have a good-for-life (GFL) status and do not expire. CompTIA CE program participants must also pay an annual fee to remain in the CE program.

CompTIA Continuing Education (CE) Program

Government workers with one of these CompTIA GFL certifications must manually enroll in the CompTIA Continuing Education (CE) program if they want to work in a DoD organization. You can still be hired for a position in a DoD organization without possessing one of these IA security baseline certifications, but you must be certified within 6 months of being hired.

The CompTIA CE program ensures your security training is an ongoing process as directed by DoD 8570.01-M. Once you are enrolled into the CompTIA CE program, and your Security+ certification has reached its 3 year limit, you will be required to obtain further security training from your choice of a variety of sources each year.

You might also be able to fulfill the CE requirement by retaking and passing the Security+ exam again before its 3-year expiration date, but this may require permission from CompTIA first.

The following list is some options for completing ongoing CompTIA CE training:

- Earn a new certification or recertify in a CompTIA or non-CompTIA certification

- Work experience related to security

- Attend a security Webinar

- Attend a security conference

- Complete a security training course

- Complete a college course related to security

- Complete a workshop on security

- Teach a course on security

- Create instructional materials or publish an article or book, white paper, blog or post on security

Company Reimbursement for CompTIA CE Fees

Since the security certifications and the CompTIA CE program all cost money, contractors should ask their employer to reimburse them for these certification and training requirements. If you are a contractor negotiating your salary and benefits with a staffing agency or private company for a contractor job with a US government agency, ask about their education and certification reimbursement benefits. The CompTIA Security+ certification, annual CompTIA CE fees and ongoing CE training is an out-of-pocket expense that you must complete to maintain your job in a DoD organization. Make the recruiter include reimbursement for these certifications and annual CE fees in your contract agreement. When the recruiter agrees, make sure this reimbursement is included in writing in your offer letter. If it's not in writing, it never happened.

As for US government employees, each government agency has a different way of processing training reimbursements for their federal employees. Government employees must check with their local organization on reimbursements for their out-of-pocket expenses for the Security+ certification and the annual CompTIA CE fees.

Advantages of Security Certification for Job-Hunters

This entire security certification requirement may seem like an extra burden to many people. However, having the CompTIA Security+ certification alone places you at an advantage over other job-hunting candidates searching for work in US government agencies who do not have this certification. Keeping your Security+ certification current through the CompTIA continuing education program ensures you will be a more desirable candidate for future government jobs over other job seekers who either no longer have a current Security+ or who do not have a Security+ certification at all.

CHAPTER FOUR

Corporate Employee and Contractor Workforce

Go confidently in the direction of your dreams.
Live the life you have imagined.
Henry David Thoreau

Who We Are

Apart from the US federal employee and government contractor, we have the corporate employee and contractor workforce. You already know them as your first responders, healthcare providers, grocery store clerks, teachers, coaches, programmers, engineers, accountants, consultants, entrepreneurs, building contractors, mechanics, service providers, self-employed, home business, small and big businesses, non-profits, for-profits and a myriad of other non-public, non-government ventures that touch the fabric of everyday life in American society. They too can be your sons and daughters, your fathers and mothers, your sisters and brothers, your in-laws, your college graduates, and your military veterans. As a collective whole, we call them the private or commercial sector; and they are roughly 4 times the size of the US government labor force.

The US Bureau of Labor Statistics reported a 159 million total civilian labor force in mid-year 2016; and this figure is well on its way to a BLS projected growth of 164.4 million by 2020. If you are already in the private sector or are thinking of joining our ranks, then this book is for you too.

Corporate Employee—Who We Are

Corporate or private company employees are civilians who work for and are paid by non-government, non-staffing agency, private companies that own—or their shareholders own—that company's business. In other words, the paychecks and company benefits of these employees come directly from that business company, not from a US government agency or a staffing agency.

These employees are what William H. Whyte, who first coined the term "groupthink" in *Fortune* magazine in 1952, introduced to the twentieth century public as *The Organization Man* in his 1956 bestseller book by the same name that sold over two million copies. These employees are often referred to as "permanent", "full-time", "company" employees, and "company man" or "company woman".

Their salaries are individual, negotiable contracts between the employee and the private business. Their salaries are based on the company's budgeted salary range for that position, documented qualifications (resume, certifications, degrees, skill level and years of experience), interview performance, and salary negotiation skills.

Corporate Contractor—Who We Are

Corporate or private company contractors, on the other hand, are not considered as one of the full-time or company employees of a business (the primary company). They fall into either an independent contractor or dependent contractor role.

Independent Contractors

Independent contractors in the private sector are self-employed contractors providing products and/or services to individuals, groups, organizations and companies. They may receive payment from these clients or customers but they sign their own paychecks because they own their own business and they are their own boss. Consequently, independent contractors must track, record and withhold their own taxes for the IRS.

Dependent Contractors

Dependent contractors in the private sector are not self-employed. They work for a company or staffing agency that pays them their wages. If the dependent contractor is working under a W-2 tax form, the company or staffing agency will track, record and withhold taxes from their earnings for the IRS. If the dependent contractor is working under other tax forms, such as a 1099 or Corp-to-Corp tax form, they must track, record and withhold their own taxes for the IRS, just as independent contractors.

The remainder of our focus in this chapter will be on company employees and these dependent contractors that we'll simply call contractors. This group of non-company employees is oftentimes referred to as "contractor", "consultant", "freelancer" or "temporary" (temps) workers.

The name contractor is not a title given to only low or medium wage earners. Contractors include top managers and professionals, such as lawyers, doctors, Chief Executive Officers (CEOs) and Chief Financial Officers (CFOs). These contractors are called *supertemps* by Jody Greenstone Miller and Matt Miller in a Harvard Business Review article titled *The Rise of the Supertemp*.

Job-Hoppers and Jumpers

Many contractors are also humorously referred to as "jumpers". A jumper is a caricature taken from the 2008 film *Jumper* that was based on the 1992 science fiction novel written by Steven Gould that used the same title; telling the story of an individual who could jump from place to place through teleportation. In this context, a jumper is a term used to depict a contractor who moves from one job to another; in other words, a job-hopper.

In the *2016 Job Seeker Nation Study*, an annual report produced by Jobvite Inc., a software and recruiting corporation known for its surveys into social recruitment, between 34 and 35 percent of the 2,305 participants (aged 18+) in the 2016 survey reported they changed jobs after 1-5 years. Among this job-hopping group, those who are more likely to job-hop every 1-3 years are Millennials (ages 18-29) at 42 percent, 55 percent are millennial women and 31 percent are single people.

In their *2015 Recruiter Nation Survey*, Jobvite reported 30 percent of job seekers job-hopped every 1-3 years; 29 percent job-hopped every 4-6 years; 15 percent job-hopped every 7-10 years; and only 14 percent job-hopped every 10+ years.

It is clear that job-hopping is here to stay, and is popular across all industries in both public and private sectors.

Contractors are Free Agents

Contractors are what Daniel H. Pink, the former chief speechwriter for Vice President Al Gore, classified as part of the *Free Agent Nation* and expounded upon in his book by the same name in 2001. And like the free agents of your favorite professional football, basketball or baseball team, these free agent contractors roam more freely and more often from one company to the next with the opportunity of gaining more experience and making more money than their company employee counterparts.

Although the IRS views most people in the film industry (actors, crew members and other people working on a film production) and professional athletes, coaches and staff of professional sports teams as employees instead of independent contractors; these people also move from one job to the next, one film to the next, and one team to the next just like contractors.

And yet, we call actors and professional athletes *free agents* who work through other agents in controlling multi-million dollar contracts they want for the film or team they play in. Why? Because in practice, most actors and professional athletes move from one job to the next just like any other contractor. Their normal career pattern is to move from one job to the next. One year they're gainfully employed on a film or team; the next year they're unemployed without a film or team to speak of; and hopefully, the next time you see them, they're in another film or on another team again.

Wade Phillips, the National Football League (NFL) defensive coordinator for the 2016 Super Bowl 50 Champions, the Denver Broncos, was out of work in 2014. He was let go by the Houston Texans in 2013; he was a free agent looking for work. In 2015, he was hired as the defensive coordinator of what became one of the best defenses in NFL history during the 2015 regular season; and he was named the Assistant Coach of the Year in 2016.

Phillips started his NFL career with the Denver Broncos and made his rounds through five other teams—Buffalo Bills, Dallas Cowboys, New Orleans Saints, Atlanta Falcons and the Houston Texans—before he made his way back to Broncos Country in his coaching job. He's changed jobs more times than many contractors today. While being interviewed by reporters after the Broncos Super Bowl 50 win against the Carolina Panthers, Wade said, "*It was really special going from unemployed to winning the Super Bowl.*"

Such is the life of free agent contractors that job-hop.

I learned this lesson early in my career after leaving the military and accepting my first job with a large corporation for a spattering $42,000 annual salary. I thought I would try being a "company man" who would stay with this company and increase my salary as I was recognized and promoted for my work.

After three years working for the company, I was promoted and they increased my salary to $52,000 a year—a $10,000 increase in my starting salary. In my fourth year with this company, I was told that since the company had just acquired another company, there would be no raises given that year.

That was when I realized that being a company man was the slow path to increasing my salary; so I decided to jump on the free agent bandwagon and job-hop.

By the end of that fourth year, I was working for another company for an annual salary of $85,000. This was a $33,000 a year increase in my previous $52,000 salary just by job-hopping!

What I've learned since then and the years that followed was that you can gain a lot more ground in increasing your experience and salary by job-hopping than you ever could by being a lifelong company employee.

Today, because of all the knowledge, experience and certifications I've gained by job-hopping, I can now command a six-figure salary in my career. That's the power of being a free agent contractor who job-hops.

Contractors in the Corporate World

Contractors in the private sector may provide the same or similar services as a company's full-time employees, but they work for and are paid by a secondary company that has a business relationship with the parent or primary business company—the client.

If you've worked in the contractor workforce for any length of time, you know it is common practice for a single secondary company or multiple subcontractor companies to work in partnership with one primary company, referred to simply as the prime. These secondary companies can be either smaller or larger than the parent or prime company.

Besides your typical secondary company, such as Boeing, SAIC or Verizon, that can provide personnel, services and equipment to a prime company; secondary companies can also be staffing agencies whose sole purpose is to provide personnel for secondary or primary company clients.

Fortunately for contractors, there seems to be no end in sight of staffing agencies—also known as recruiting agencies or temp agencies—whose sole mission and purpose is to locate and provide qualified candidates as full-time company employees or contractors to businesses in both the public and private sectors.

Commercial contractors can be working either full-time (in terms of hours worked just like company employees) or part-time; and their salaries are negotiated in similar fashion as company employees. The main difference in salary negotiations of contractors and company employees is that contractors, who usually work directly for and are paid by a secondary company such as a staffing agency or subcontracting company, negotiate their hourly rate or salary with the secondary company instead of with the primary business company client as company employee hires would do.

Private Companies, Businesses and Organizations

Something both private company employees and commercial contractors enjoy over federal employees and government contractors is less security constraints. This is a huge benefit to workers in the private sector unbeknownst to them unless they've experienced working in a US government organization, particularly in a Department of Defense agency.

The DoD and other government departments typically have more layers of security than the private sector. Many of these government agencies are on military installations or in restricted locations that require many checkpoints and other security measures before you even get to the building you work in. Once you're in the government building, the security checkpoints and other security measures only increase. You thought Maxwell Smart, a.k.a. Agent 86 played by actor Don Adams, had a lot of doors to go through during the opening of each *Get Smart* TV show. That was child's play compared to some security checkpoints you have to go through in an actual DoD facility today.

In contrast, individuals working for a private company have more freedom and less security than government agencies. Accessing the building of a private company may only require you to simply drive up to the building, get out of your vehicle and walk in the open door.

People working in private sectors aren't held to the higher standards of accountability with their offsite lifestyles because the security clearance requirements of a US government job do not exist in the private sector. In the private sector, you may still be required to undergo drug testing, reference checks and a minor background check, but nothing as extensive as the requirements to obtain a US government security clearance.

Private companies are also more lax than government agencies in terms of what you can bring onto the organization's premises. Whereas cameras, smartphones and other devices with camera capability, a thumb drive or personal laptops may be prohibited in a government facility; these items are regularly allowed in the private business environment.

Regardless if you choose the path of a full-time company employee or contractor in the private sector; if you have a strong resume; your interview skills put smiles on the faces of the people in the interview room; and you know how to negotiate your salary; it is possible for you to secure an hourly rate or annual salary that is $5,000 to $20,000 per year more than your peers who are working in a same or similar position as you. I've done this too as a contractor working in the private sector; and so can you.

As in government jobs, it is taboo to talk about your salaries with your colleagues in the private sector. Both your employer and colleagues understand how demoralizing it could be to know someone working alongside you doing the same job as you is making 10–20 grand more than you. It would undermine the mutual respect, rapport and cohesiveness that businesses strive to develop and maintain amongst their co-workers.

So the next time you are tempted to casually discuss salaries amongst your colleagues, remind yourself of this one fact: one of you is going to come out on the short end of that conversation. The person on the short end of the stick is going to feel less appreciated and more agitated and dissatisfied while working alongside the person who is making more money. Bottom line is you are doing yourself and your colleagues a disservice by discussing salaries—it's all fun and games until someone gets hurt.

Time To Choose

So should you become a "company man" or "company woman"; or should you opt to become a contractor in the private sector?

As with the government sector, it just comes down to personal preference. The beauty of it is you can swap back and forth between the two at any time in your career.

As with US federal workers and government contractors, many believe that company employee positions are more stable than contractor positions. I would have to agree.

But as Daniel H. Pink, Jody Greenstone Miller and Matt Miller have stated, contractors have a huge advantage over permanent company employees when it comes to the freedom to move from one job to the next, oftentimes with increased knowledge, experience and skill sets, better resume portfolios and higher salaries with each move.

Unlike government contractors in the public sector whose contract is at the mercy of the government bidding process, contractors in the private sector are more in control of their own contracts; and typically sign a contract to work for a set amount of months or one to two years at the most for a negotiated hourly rate or salary.

These corporate contracts oftentimes come with future opportunities with the company client. In other words, the contractor could be offered a permanent position with the primary company as a full-time company employee or the contractor can have his or her contract extended for more months by the company. If the contractor wants neither, the contractor can simply move on to their next job opportunity or take several months off for a well-deserved extended vacation or enjoy other life interests before returning to the job market.

As flattering or secure as an offer for a permanent company position or an extended contract may seem, I oftentimes opted to say my goodbyes and take an extended vacation off from work. This allows me to return to the job market fully rested, relaxed and rejuvenated. This time off also gives me time to come back to work with more certifications (the best time to get certified is when you're not working); a stronger resume; more ideas and creativity (like writing this book); and greater energy and enthusiasm on the job and in my personal life. All of this can equate to a higher salary waiting for me at my next job after a well-rested vacation.

That's the power and beauty of being a contractor. That's also the opposite definition of job *burnout*.

This is not to say being a company employee is without its benefits. Being a tenured company man or company woman has its advantages too. In addition to the greater stability and less risk of working as a company employee, many company professionals enjoy the full benefits offered by their company, such as health and dental benefits, a growing 401K, stock options, and other company perks given to keep you as their employee.

True, these company benefits are a definite plus for working as their employee, but something also to consider is the fact that many of today's staffing agencies are now powerful enough to offer many benefits and investment options to their contractor workforce. Staffing agencies may also provide contractors certain perks; and the primary company client will oftentimes provide some of the same company perks—such as free food onsite and at restaurants or company-paid fees for team outings—to contractors that company employees are enjoying.

CHAPTER FIVE

The Perfect Resume

Simplicity is the ultimate sophistication.
Leonardo da Vinci

Resume + Recruiter = Job Interview

The word resume comes from French origin meaning *summarized* or *summary*. The first resume was used by the Renaissance Man himself, Leonardo da Vinci, in 1482 when he wrote a letter to Ludovico Sforza, Duke of Milan, Italy. In his letter, Leonardo promoted his many talents, the things he could achieve in the field of engineering and his ability to paint. He passed his job interview, was hired for the job and Leonardo had a successful career from 1482 to 1499 working for his employer, the Duke of Milan, while living in Castello Sforzesco (Sforza castle). The Renaissance Man's letter is what we call a CV or resume today.

The Curriculum Vitae (CV) and Resume

A curriculum vitae (CV) comes from a Latin expression meaning *the course of my life*. CVs are similar to resumes; however, CVs are used mainly within academia or medical circles. Resumes are typically used for positions in industry, non-profit, for-profit or the public and private sectors. Although a CV traditionally uses greater detail than a resume, it is normally shorter than a resume.

The resume gets you the interview, not the job.

Whether you use a CV or resume, their main purpose is the same: to provide a document that represents your background, knowledge and education, credentials, experience level and skill sets in order to get you an interview. Notice I did not say its purpose is to get you a job because that is not its main purpose. The CV's or resume's purpose is to get you an interview for a job; and how well you perform in the interview will determine whether or not you get that job. The resume that most job seekers submit is used in the screening or decision-making process by a potential employer, hiring manager, humans relations (HR) department or staffing agency to determine if you should be granted an interview for a job.

You'll find endless books and online articles and tips on how you should write your resume. You also have the option of writing your resume yourself or having a professional resume writing service do it for you. Regardless if you choose to write your own resume or have someone else write it for you, your resume along with thousands of other resumes submitted on Internet job search websites has to get the attention of countless recruiters reviewing thousands of online resumes.

How Recruiters Review Your Resume

The goal in submitting your resume is to capture and hold the reader's attention long enough for them to consider you a possible candidate for positions they are trying to fill. Rather than waste your time with yet another *how to write a resume* piece, let's approach this goal from the angle of seeing what happens after you submit your resume online. More specifically, let's go over how your resume on Internet job boards is being reviewed by recruiters because they are the majority of the doorkeepers to the all-important job interview. Whether it's a staffing agency recruiter, a company human resources recruiter or hiring manager reviewing your resume; if they don't like your resume, you're not getting a call or email about the job opening, let alone an invitation to a job interview—it's that simple.

I'm going to demystify the mystery of what it takes to not only get your resume noticed by recruiters but also how to captivate and hold their attention the way Leonardo's letter held the attention of the Duke of Milan.

Make Recruiters Search for You Instead of You Searching for the Job

I always average between 7–15 recruiters that contact me each day by phone and email the first two weeks after I upload or update my resume on Internet job search websites. I get so many calls about job opportunities from recruiters that I have to turn my phone off or else I get overwhelmed by all these recruiters calling me each day. I no longer have to look for jobs by attending job fairs, searching for jobs online, asking businesses if they have any openings or other job-hunting activities. Why? Because the jobs always come looking for me. I just sit back, relax and let the recruiters contact me each time I'm searching for a new job.

If this was only a one-time deal or a sporadic hit-or-miss occurrence each time I uploaded or updated my resume, you could right me off as someone whose ego is greater than his insight. However, the fact is this happens EVERY TIME I upload or update my resume on job search websites. This isn't luck or an unexplained phenomenon. I planned it to work that way. Now I'm going to show you how this can work for you too.

Would you like to know the secret to sitting back and letting the jobs find you every time you're job hunting? What you're about to learn in this chapter is going to change your way of thinking about what makes your resume attractive to a recruiter. This information is going to help you determine if your resumes are doing their job on all those job search websites where you posted them. By "doing their job", I mean getting the attention of recruiters in order to get you the job interviews you want and deserve. So let's begin by seeing how recruiters view our resumes.

The Ladders Study on How Recruiters Review Your Resume

In 2012, TheLadders, an online job search service, conducted a formal, quantitative 10-week study of 30 professional recruiters using eye tracking technology to evaluate how recruiters treated online resumes. The study, called *Eye Tracking Online Metacognition: Cognitive Complexity and Recruiter Decision Making*, evaluated how long recruiters spent reviewing online resumes; how they processed the information in resumes; and the process recruiters used to review online social media profiles of candidates to determine their fit for a job opportunity.

Eye tracking technology is not a new science. Studies of eye movement were conducted in the 1800s. For instance, in 1879, French ophthalmologist Louis Emile Javal used eye tracking to discover that reading—such as this book you're reading—does not involve smooth eye movement across each line, but rather a series of different lengths of jerky movements (called saccades) between short stops (called fixations) across each line.

6 seconds

Before the recruiter eye tracking study performed by TheLadders in 2012, it was believed that recruiters spent an average of 4 to 5 minutes on each online resume they reviewed. The study revealed that the actual amount of time a recruiter spends reviewing each online resume is only 6 seconds. This is not a typo. Your online resume is reviewed by every recruiter for only **6 seconds** before they decide to either keep or toss your resume.

Within this 6-second window, recruiters tend to follow a consistent visual path starting at the top and working their way down. The more organized the resume is, the easier it is for recruiters to review it in that 6-second window before they make a yes/no decision on a candidate's potential for an interview.

The Perfect Resume

As the actor Samuel L. Jackson might ask, *"Now tell me, what's in your resume?"*

The consistent visual path recruiters are looking for in your resume in that 6-second window translates to a resume that has a clear, organized visual hierarchy of groups of related and pertinent information in your resume regarding your background, knowledge and education, credentials, experience level and skill sets. For instance, your resume could have the following hierarchy of titles representing groups of related, pertinent information under these titles that I use in my own resume:

- **Full name, phone number, email address and mailing address** (Nothing more.)

- **Objective** (Optional. If you are targeting several positions, use a simple one sentence stating what type of jobs you are seeking. If you are targeting a specific job, ensure the objective states that position.)

- **Certifications** (More is better—get certified on a regular basis. If you completed only one of multiple exams required for a particular certification, include that exam you passed.)

- **Security Clearance** (Optional. Include this if you have a clearance and you are seeking a US government job.)

- **Education** (Degree earned and name of college. GPA or membership in a national scholastic honor society, such as Alpha Beta Gamma, is optional; nothing more.)

- **Applications/Software Experience** (Software, operating systems, GUIs, computer skills, etc.)

- **Equipment Experience** (Include equipment applicable to your target job.)

- **Summary of Qualifications** (Brief bullet points highlighting your overall skill sets.)

- **Work Experience** (Start with your current or last job. Always list the company name first; followed by your job title on the second line; followed by the date of employment on the third line.)

If you can list related, pertinent information under these types of hierarchy of titles in a concise, simple, easy-to-read fashion, chances are the recruiters reading your online resume will make it to your current and previous job title and company in your Work Experience section in that 6-seconds window. In the words of Leonardo da Vinci: *Simplicity is the ultimate sophistication.*

The recruiter's 80-20 percent rule.

TheLadders eye tracking study revealed that recruiters spent **80 percent** of their 6-seconds resume review gazing at the following six items on your resume:

1. Name

2. Education

3. Current job title and company

4. Current position start and end dates

5. Previous job title and company

6. Previous position start and end dates

How Recruiters Use the Applicant Tracking System (ATS) to Find You

The reason recruiters spend so much time on these six areas is because of the Applicant Tracking System (ATS). The ATS system recruiters use will automatically present this list of six items first to recruiters.

Most companies, especially large companies and staffing agencies, use a computerized ATS system to search, collect, filter and sort, organize, process, store and manage thousands of online resumes and candidate information from different Internet job search and social media websites. This makes it quicker and easier for recruiters reviewing resumes to locate, select, track and communicate with the best candidates or the top 10 candidates that meet the requirements for job openings they are trying to fill. There are a variety of ATS software produced by different vendors, such as iCIMS Recruit, Newton, Workable, Gild, BambooHR and Taleo.

The ATS system uses a resume optimization technique similar to Search Engine Optimization (SEO) algorithms found in search engines such as Google or Amazon. Employers will also use SEO software to seek and filter out candidate profiles on LinkedIn.

The ATS system does not present a candidate's resume in the same sequence in which your resume was written. Instead, ATS systems collect and organize resume information in a database, and then presents that information to a recruiter's computer screen in a certain order. That order is those six items I just listed for you.

With the help of the ATS system, recruiters have already made their yes/no decision about your fitness for a job opportunity they're trying to fill within 6 seconds. Never mind about the recruiter reading through your entire long-winded Work Experience section. They will have already made their decision to pursue you as a possible candidate for a job opening or reject your resume before getting past your second most current job history.

If they give your resume a yes in 6 seconds, that's when the recruiter will consider reading the rest of the more lengthy Work Experience section in your resume. A yes in 6 seconds also means the recruiter will be giving you a call or sending you an email or text, depending on your contact information provided in your resume.

This is why you should not include distractions in your resume, such as unnecessary or unprofessional words, formats, photos, images, icons or those irresistible emojis. All of these things are only eating into your 6 seconds of fame and fortune with recruiters.

This advice coincides with a 2013 survey of 2,076 hiring managers and human resource professionals by Harris Interactive on behalf of CareerBuilder. This survey revealed that these participants who are directly responsible for hiring you would automatically dismiss your resume if it had typos (58%); didn't include your skill sets (35%); an excessive amount of wording from the job posting (32%); inappropriate email address (31%); didn't include exact dates of employment (27%); used decorative paper (22%); and included a photo (13%).

I can cover all six of the items that recruiters focus on the most, including that list of hierarchical titles representing groups of related and pertinent information within 3 pages of my resume. However, my resume is 7 pages long. So what's in the other four pages of my resume? Those remaining four pages are my long-winded Work Experience section.

The Key to Getting a "Yes" from a Recruiter for Your Resume

The key is to get the recruiter to say yes to your resume within the first 2 or 3 pages of your resume. Once they're hooked, they'll read the rest of your resume. When talking with recruiters, I've never had a recruiter mention to me that my 7-page resume was too long. I have had many recruiters tell me that they've read my entire resume and that they were impressed with what they saw. The reason they read my entire resume is because I got a "yes" from them after the 6 seconds it took them to cover key areas in the first 2–3 pages of my resume.

I know many people have been taught that a resume should not be any longer than 2 pages, but that's the old school of thought. In today's digital world with a computerized ATS system that quickly processes thousands of resumes, it's ok to have a 7-page or 10-page resume. What you need to know is that whether your resume is 2 pages or 20 pages long, recruiters that view resumes online are going to use an automated ATS system that is going to pick your resume out among hundreds, if not thousands, of other resumes. In fact, a longer resume will provide the ATS system with more information that will increase your chances of matching the job description of an opening. Then the recruiter is going to spend roughly 6 seconds in reviewing your resume; and those precious 6 seconds translates to about 2 to 3 pages of your resume. Therefore, what you have in those first 2 to 3 pages of your resume is critical to getting a call from recruiters about job opportunities.

So how do you maximize the white space of an 8.5 inch by 11 inch sheet of writing paper (hardcopy or softcopy) with the most efficient use of words under the hierarchy of headings I just described? You must use a format and keywords and phrases in your resume that will get the attention of the ATS system that recruiters use.

It's the ATS system that matches keywords and phrases in your resume with the job description of the job opening the recruiter is trying to fill. When the ATS system finds a matching resume, it will present the recruiter that list of six items from that resume.

The recruiter's 20 percent—Keywords and Phrases.

TheLadders eye tracking study revealed that recruiters spent the remaining **20 percent** of their 6-seconds resume review scanning matching keywords and phrases in your resume.

The ATS System Looks for Keywords and Phrases in Resumes

These ATS systems will look for keywords and phrases in online resumes that match important keywords and phrases in job descriptions of online job openings provided by Internet job search and social media websites. The more the keywords and phrases in your online resume match those important keywords and phrases in the job description, the greater your chances of the ATS system picking your resume out of tens, if not hundreds, of other resumes for a particular job opening.

You could be the best person for the job but if your resume does not have the matching keywords or phrases, your resume won't even be selected as a possible candidate for the position by the ATS system. So if you found a job you're interested in on an Internet job board, make sure you update your resume with the same important keywords and phrases used in the posted job description. If the job description wants a person who is *"experienced in"* certain areas, and you have that experience, include those keywords and phrases reflecting your experience in those areas in your resume. If the job description is looking for a professional who is *"knowledgeable of"* or has a *"functional understanding of"* various subjects, and you possess knowledge and understanding about any of those subjects, include those important keywords and phrases reflecting your knowledge in those areas.

Make the jobs search for you.

But what if you're like me. I never search for jobs on these online job boards. As I mentioned, I just upload my resume and wait for the recruiters to contact me for jobs that match my online resume. I make the jobs search for me; I don't search for the jobs.

To do this, you must ensure your online resume has enough keywords and phrases to match important keywords and phrases used in **multiple** job descriptions. The best way to do this is by first reviewing important keywords and phrases used in several job descriptions at various online job search websites. **Then ask yourself this question:** *Are those keywords or phrases in all of these job descriptions something I know or do in my career?* If it is something you know or do, then put those same keywords and phrases in your resume.

Allow me to use my own career field in IT as an example to explain this further. Let's say several job descriptions in IT reveal employers are looking for people who are knowledgeable of and/or have experience related to keywords or key phrases, such as "IT", "network engineering", "network design", "experienced in troubleshooting", "created network designs in Visio", "Cisco routers", "Juniper routers", "Alcatel-Lucent switches", "ASA firewalls", "Palo Alto firewalls", "Riverbed WAN optimizers" or "F5 load balancers".

Then what I should do is ensure all of these keywords and phrases are in my resume under the appropriate hierarchy of headings I explained earlier. This is true of certifications, especially in the IT field where employers are always looking for IT certified professionals, such as Cisco CCNA, CCNP, CCIE, Juniper JNCIA, Microsoft MCP, CompTIA Security+, F5 TMOS Administration or Riverbed RCSA.

Additionally, make sure you use both the full spelling and the acronyms of words. For instance, instead of just putting "CCNP" on your resume, put "Cisco Certified Network Professional" and its acronym "CCNP" in your resume. The reason for this is because recruiters will set up the ATS system to search for resumes with the full spelling of the word (Cisco Certified Network Professional), the acronym (CCNP) or both. You don't know which the recruiter will ask the ATS system to search for in resumes; therefore, it is always better to put both the full spelling and acronym of words in your resume.

The more certifications you can pass and include in your resume along with important keywords and phrases, the more you will be able to sit back and let the jobs (the ATS systems) find you.

Using this method, I always average between 7–15 recruiters that contact me each day by phone and email the first two weeks after I upload or update my resume on Internet job search websites.

It's not necessarily because I'm the best candidate for all of these positions that recruiters are contacting me to fill. It's because I understand the system—the ATS system that is. This is not cheating the system; it is having an understanding of how the system works and making the system work for you. This is the same approach website developers use to get their webpages noticed by SEO search engines, such as Google or Bing. Self-publishers of books also use this technique to get their books noticed by SEO software on book publishing and distribution websites such as Amazon, Barnes & Noble Nook or Kobo.

What the ATS System Doesn't Like in Resumes

ATS systems can also be a bit picky in terms of format and function that can work against online resumes that are actually a good match for a job description. For instance, if you upload a resume in PDF format, the ATS system will automatically reject your resume. If an item is out of place on your resume, such as your employment date placed before the company title, the ATS system will automatically reject your resume. The ATS system will reject your resume under these conditions because it thinks your resume has a low relevance ranking, regardless if you have the matching keywords and phrases in your resume and are a perfect match for the job.

ATS systems use database fields that the ATS tries to fill with information it picks out from your resume. If the ATS system does not recognize the information in your resume, it will not populate its fields correctly or completely. These improperly filled or incomplete fields could be the deciding factor on whether the ATS system either selects your resume as a possible candidate match for an open position the recruiter is trying to fill (or a specific job you submitted your resume for) or rejects it altogether. This is another reason why you should not use photos, images, icons, emojis or tables in your resume. It may seem creative or attractive to you, but it increases the potential of causing your resume to be rejected and bypassed because the automated ATS system does not read graphics and can become confused by tables or misinterpret the contents in those tables.

Making Your Resume Stand Out to Recruiters and Hiring Managers

We've talked about how to make your resume stand out to machines—the ATS system. I showed you how you have only 6 seconds to get a recruiter's attention once the ATS system spits out your resume in front of their computer screen. We covered ways you can get the recruiter to say yes to your resume in those 6 seconds.

It's the well-organized easy-to-read resume with keywords and phrases that gets the attention of the ATS system and the recruiter. This will get you the phone call or email from the recruiter. However, it's the "**results**", "**impact**" and "**action verbs**" of your accomplishments at past jobs that get the attention of the employer's *hiring manager*. It's the hiring manager that decides to interview you and hire you, not the ATS system or the recruiter.

Now suppose the recruiter has said yes to several resumes including yours. Suppose also that the recruiter has submitted your resume along with those other resumes to the hiring manager. Key words and phrases will not help you at this point. Those key words and phrases did their job concerning the ATS system. Now you need something else to make your resume stand out in the eyes of a human being—the hiring manager. What your resume needs is positive impact statements and action verbs to make your resume stand out among the other candidate's resumes sitting in front of the hiring manager's eyes.

Using Positive Impact to Make Your Resume Stand Out

In addition to using keywords and phrases throughout your resume, you also need to use the Work History section of your resume to show the recruiter, and more importantly the employer's hiring manager, reviewing your resume how your contributions at work had a direct **positive impact** on the company or workplace where you worked. Just showing what actions you took, what tasks and assignments you completed or what projects you accomplished in your resume is not enough. You need to show the positive **results** and **impact** of your actions.

By "results and impact" I mean you need to show the hiring manager how what you did at previous workplaces saved time, energy, money; improved processes, documentation and drawings; met critical deadlines and shortened delivery times; increased productivity and revenue; satisfied customers and stakeholders; educated and trained personnel; troubleshot and repaired critical components that restored or allowed continued service to customers and the mission; and awards, recognition and promotions received from company leadership for outstanding work.

In other words, the Work History section is the area in your resume that convinces the employer that they can expect a return on their investment in you. That's what will set you apart from other candidates that have similar keywords, phrases, skill sets and qualifications in their resume as you.

To help explain what I mean by using results and impact in your resume's Work History section, here are a few examples used in resumes for IT jobs. The positive results and impact portion is in **bold** print.

- *Designed replacement of end-of-life Cisco 6506 Access switches with stacked 3750X switches having more robust failover in power and Supervisor control and **increased capability for expansion of port density and PoE support, supporting the future growth of Missile Defense Agency (MDA) services and personnel.***

- *Coordinated the Return Material Authorization (RMA) of 21 each 6506-E switches to Cisco for a two-for-one deal that **provided the MDA 42 each 3750X switches free of charge that saved the MDA $603K.***

- *Trained new engineers on MDA engineering processes and created a consolidated document of all IT engineering processes to successfully complete projects—**received the Joint Research and Development Contract (JRDC) Recognition Pin for outstanding contribution to the MDA IT engineering department.***

- *Created 80 Visio network drawings of Missile Defense Agency enterprise LAN, MAN, and WAN networks. These end-to-end network drawings show loop-back devices (patch panels, modems, ATM nodes, SONET mux's, etc.), POC phone numbers, and tech data to properly set test equipment for troubleshooting. **These detailed end-to-end drawings made analysis and troubleshooting of vital MDA circuits easier for engineers and technicians.***

- *Wrote a Device Commands quick reference document that provided information, commands, and troubleshooting tips and scenarios using the Cisco Adaptive Security Appliance (ASA), G2 Sidewinder firewall, and Bluecoat Proxy devices, and distributed this 44-page document to all 561 Network Operation Squadron (NOS) personnel to **aid them in troubleshooting and resolving network problems to 60 Air Force bases in the Continental US (CONUS) and the Pacific.***

- *Created various network diagrams in Visio used for briefing Headquarters NORAD-US NORTHCOM (N-NC) senior leadership (civilian and military) and for providing accurate snapshots of classified and unclassified N-NC networks. **These network drawings in Visio are now being used for analyzing and troubleshooting the N-NC networks by Network Operations Engineers and other departments within the N-NC; for compliance with the DISA STIG*** configurations; and for inspections such as the DISA Command Cyber Readiness Inspection (CCRI).

- Received Boeing award for research, design, procurement, and installation of network solutions that **expanded the ability to connect more network resources (current and future) to various Boeing GPS Development and Sustainment laboratories.**

- Created several engineering drawings for the Boeing Security Manager that **resulted in Boeing being certified in the International Organization for Standardization (ISO) 9001 that opened more multi-million dollar contracts for Boeing.**

- Within 3 months of arrival at DISA-CONUS, wrote 16 Standard Operating Procedures (SOPs) to instruct Network Controllers and Tier II Analysts on configuration, installation, and operation procedures. **These SOPs directly helped DISA-CONUS at Scott AFB pass their first SIPRNet Accreditation Inspection with 0 discrepancies out of 343 items. As a result, was nominated for the Verizon Excellence Award by the Verizon CONUS Area Regional Manager.**

- Wrote a 42-page Network Controller Training Plan consisting of 443 training tasks on classified and unclassified networks. **This training plan provided qualification training, ensuring both SIPRNet and NIPRNet outages were quickly troubleshot and restored, resulting in network availability rates at or near 100%—end result: Satisfied Customers! Received a Verizon VIP cash bonus award for this training plan.**

- *Developed solution to transition from legacy satellite systems—Regency Net (RN) and Flaming Arrow Net-Europe (FAN-E)—to the Secure Mobile Anti-Jam Reliable Tactical Terminal (SMART-T) and Milstar satellite system at 15 telecommunications sites throughout Europe. Through talking papers and briefings, personally convinced Joint Chiefs of Staff, EUCOM, and USAFE General Officer panel to support this transition idea, **resulting in a one-time savings of $15 Million and $239,000 annually.***

- ***Saved $27,000 annually for commercial leased lines** through Department of Defense communications upgrades by installing, activating, and testing the IDNX90, Cisco router, and associated cabling and connections to support increased bandwidth needs for voice, video and data circuits.*

Action Verbs to Make Your Resume Stand Out

Notice how most of these impact statements above start with **action verbs**, such as *designed, coordinated, trained, created, wrote, developed* and *saved*. Each of these action verbs describe an attribute you possess as part of your skill sets that makes you productive in the workplace. Putting the action verb at the front of the sentence immediately tells the hiring manger what specific ability you possess and exhibited at work that produced the impactful result in your workplace.

If you need a little help on thinking of some action verbs for your resume, try these links:

- http://muse.cm/1kCnKEh

- https://www.livecareer.com/quintessential/action-skills

Attributes that Make You Stand Out to Hiring Managers

All of these action verbs and the impactful results reveal attributes employers seek in job candidates. Employers seek candidates with attributes, such as leadership skills, ability to work in a team environment, communications skills, problem-solving skills, strong work ethic, initiative, analytical and quantitative skills, flexibility and adaptability, and technical skills. Action verbs and impactful results in your resume's Work History section paints a picture of the attributes you possess that make you successful in your career.

The National Association of Colleges and Employers (NACE) is a nonprofit professional association comprised of 5,200 college career services practitioners and more than 3,000 human resources (HR) professionals that conduct research focused on the careers, hiring outlook, job search and salaries of college graduates and the employers that hire them. In the *Job Outlook 2016: Attributes Employers Want to See on New College Graduates' Resumes*, a job outlook survey conducted by NACE, 201 NACE employer members participating in the survey provided the following insight into what attributes employers seek the most on a candidate's resume.

- Leadership—80.1%
- Ability to work in a team—78.9%
- Communication skills (written)—70.2%
- Problem-solving skills—70.2%
- Communication skills (verbal)—68.9%
- Strong work ethic—68.9%
- Initiative—65.8%
- Analytical/quantitative skills—62.7%
- Flexibility/adaptability—60.9%
- Technical skills—59.6%
- Interpersonal skills (relates well to others)—58.4%
- Computer skills—55.3%
- Detail-oriented—52.8%

- Organizational ability—48.4%
- Friendly/outgoing personality—35.4%
- Strategic planning skills—26.7%
- Creativity—23.6%
- Tactfulness—20.5%
- Entrepreneurial skills/risk-taker—18.6%

Have a Professional Write Your Resume

Some people struggle with trying to organize their thoughts on paper to produce a 6-second hierarchical picture of your background, knowledge and education, credentials, experience level and skill sets, and a Work Experience section that shows action verbs with impactful results that recruiters and hiring managers seek in resumes. If you are one of those people, you should consider having a professional resume writing service create a professionally prepared resume for you.

According to TheLadders eye tracking study, *"professional resumes had less data, were evenly formatted and were described as "clearer""* than resumes written by the job seekers themselves. In TheLadders study, the Likert scale, the most commonly used response survey scale named after its inventor, psychologist Rensis Likert, was used to determine how recruiters responded to different resumes. Recruiters gave self-written resumes an average rating of 3.9 versus 6.2 for professionally written resumes on a Likert scale of 1 to 7, with 7 being the easiest to read resumes. You've heard of the old saying, *"a happy wife makes a happy life."* Well, a happy recruiter (happy about your easy-to-read resume) will make your job search life happier with better results (more recruiters and hiring managers contacting you about interviews for jobs). You can read the full copy of the TheLadders recruiter eye tracking study at http://bit.ly/1ddZeSN.

To get the best results out of your resumes, this recruiter eye tracking study should be required reading by anyone submitting their own self-written resumes on Internet job search websites.

If you're wondering why little to no attention is being given to the subject of a cover letter, it's because recruiters that review your online resume give very little attention to it these days. In the *2015 Recruiter Nation Survey*, an annual report produced by Jobvite, 1,404 recruiting and human resources professionals spanning several industries were surveyed. 63 percent of the recruiters that participated in the 2015 survey ranked the importance of a cover letter either a 1 or 2 on a scale of 1–5, with 5 being very important.

Internet Job Search Websites

Online job search websites allow you to submit your resume for current and future job openings in US government and private sectors. On these sites, you can create customized job alerts that can send you emails or text messages when new job opportunities come available on these websites. These Internet job boards allow government agencies, private companies or staffing agencies to view your resume and contact you directly about job openings they are trying to fill.

Here are some websites where you can find out about US government civilian employee jobs:

- USAJOBS
  https://usajobs.gov/

- USAJOBS Resource Center
  https://help.usajobs.gov/index.php/Main_Page

- Feds Hire Vets
  http://www.fedshirevets.gov/

- America Jobs
  http://www.americajobs.com/

- USA.GOV
  http://www.usa.gov/Citizen/Topics/Government-Jobs.shtml

- US Postal Jobs
  http://bit.ly/2eaXDGK

- Army Civilian Service
  https://armycivilianservice.usajobs.gov/

- Army Civilian Service
  http://armycivilianservice.com/

- Air Force Civilian Jobs
  http://www.afciviliancareers.com/

- Air Force Civilian Jobs
  http://www.afpc.af.mil/

- Navy Civilian Jobs
  http://www.secnav.navy.mil/donhr/Pages/Default.aspx

- Navy Civilian Jobs
  https://don.usajobs.gov/

Corporate and US government contracting jobs can be found at the following Internet job boards:

- Go to the website of the private company you are interested in working for and click on that company's Career link.

- Monster (for our United States readers)
  http://www.monster.com/

- Monster (for our international readers)
  http://www.monster.co.uk/geo/siteselection

- ClearedJobs
  http://clearedjobs.net/

- CareerBuilder
  http://www.careerbuilder.com/

- Indeed
  http://www.indeed.com/

- ClearanceJobs
  https://www.clearancejobs.com/

Update Your Resume Online To Attract Recruiters

Once you submit your resume on one of these online job boards, your job is not over. There is something you need to do besides uploading a well-written resume to get the attention of recruiters at these sites. With the exception of some online job boards that request you not resubmit your resume for the same job, you need to update your resume on these online job boards on a regular basis. This does not mean you have to edit or improve your resume. You need to perform an update on the website that is hosting your resume so that your resume appears recent to recruiters searching for the most recent resumes. You can do this by either uploading the same resume again or saving your resume again on the job search website.

Just as job seekers can search for jobs that were posted in the last week, last 30 days or last 60 days on Internet job search websites, recruiters search for resumes based on date filters using the ATS system.

Every time you update and save something in your resume on Internet job boards, that action automatically resets the clock on your resume back to day-one on the online job board. Recruiters know that job-seekers will oftentimes leave their resume in the "searchable" setting on Internet job boards, instead of turning off the public viewing setting on their resume, long after job-seekers have found a job. This clutters online job boards with resumes of people who are no longer seeking jobs; and recruiters' attempts to contact these people are a fruitless waste of time, energy and money. Therefore, recruiters will sort their resume searches by date, giving the most recently updated resumes their highest attention.

By uploading your resume once on a job board and then leaving it there for months on end without any updates, you have basically taken your online resume out of circulation by removing it out of every recruiter's search criteria of the most recent resumes. No wonder you're not getting any more calls or emails from recruiters the way you were the first couple of weeks after you initially uploaded your resume.

Since recruiters always search for the most recent resumes posted or updated on these websites, you need to update your resume on all of these Internet job boards at least once a week (if you need a job immediately) or once a month (if you are taking your time looking for work).

This advice is backed up by years of personal experience with recruiters. Every time I update my resume on Internet job search websites, I get in the range of 7–15 recruiters contacting me by phone or email every day for the first 2–3 weeks. That number drops to 1–7 recruiters contacting me every day after three weeks from my last online resume update. Immediately after I update my online resume again, 7–15 recruiters begin contacting me each day again. Many of these recruiters will mention to me that they noticed I recently updated my resume. That tells you recruiters are performing resume searches based on the date the resumes were last updated in addition to searches based on key words and phrases.

How Social Media Affects Your Job Opportunities

In the *2015 Recruiter Nation Survey,* an annual report produced by Jobvite, the 1,404 recruiting and human resources professionals who completed the survey revealed that the majority of recruiters (92% of recruiters surveyed) are joining the social media bandwagon when it comes to locating candidates for job openings. In fact, of all the recruiting areas recruiters plan to increase their investments—areas such as employee referrals, campus recruiting, Internet job boards and outside agencies—for finding and selecting candidates for job interviews, social media was at the top of their list of investments (50%) according to the Jobvite report.

Recruiters dig deep into your social media posts to determine what type of person you really are; your potential for being a good fit in the business culture and job opportunities they are trying to fill; and how well you will represent either the company that hires you or the staffing agency that recommends you. Get the picture? In other words, your posts on social media sites are your pre-screening process by recruiters, hiring managers and HR reps in determining if they should even consider contacting you for that all-important job interview you are seeking.

The following list shows the percentage of this crop of social media savvy HR and staffing agency recruiters that are using social media sites in their recruiting process as reported in the Jobvite survey:

- LinkedIn—87%
  https://www.linkedin.com/

- Facebook—55%
  https://www.facebook.com/

- Twitter—47%
  https://twitter.com/

- YouTube—21%
  https://www.youtube.com/

- Google+—14%
  https://plus.google.com/

- Instagram—13%
  https://www.instagram.com/

- Snapchat—3%
  https://www.snapchat.com

So what are recruiters looking for when they review your profile on social media sites?

To answer that question, here are staffing agency and company HR recruiter's recommendations to job-hunting candidates on the use of social media as reported in the 2015 Jobvite Recruiter Nation Survey:

Do these things on social media:

- Volunteering, professional or social engagement work (76 percent of recruiters surveyed view this positively).

- Appropriate engagement with current events (47 percent of recruiters surveyed view this positively, while 52 percent view it neutrally).

- Good spelling and grammar in your posts (72 percent of recruiters surveyed view poor spelling and grammar negatively). This reflects a 2013 survey of 2,076 hiring managers and human resource professionals by Harris Interactive on behalf of CareerBuilder revealing that 58 percent of these participants—people directly responsible for hiring you—would automatically dismiss resumes that have typos.

Don't do these things on social media:

- Alcohol consumption or marijuana usage (54 percent of recruiters surveyed view alcohol negatively, and 75 percent view marijuana negatively). Although marijuana is legal in some states, all US government agencies prohibit the use of marijuana in addition to illegal drugs. If there is evidence proving your use of marijuana, such as on social media sites, you will be fired from your job at the government agency.

- Selfies (Although 72 percent of recruiters surveyed view selfies neutrally, 25 percent of recruiters view them negatively). Must be the 25 percent haters. But seriously, I would just caution you about posting selfies showing you consuming alcohol, using marijuana or anything else that would reflect negatively upon you in the recruiter's and hiring manager's decision-making process in determining whether or not to contact you about job opportunities and interviews.

- For those seeking jobs in communications or marketing, don't delete your social media profiles. 33 percent of recruiters surveyed viewed limited social media presence negatively for people in these communications or marketing fields.

In June of 2016, Microsoft announced that it was acquiring LinkedIn, the professional networking site that boasts a membership of over 433 million users and over $3 billion revenue. What this $26.2 billion all-cash deal between Microsoft and LinkedIn means to you as a job-seeker, if you are one of those LinkedIn members, is that your LinkedIn profile will become even more accessible to hiring managers and HR personnel in the workplace. That's welcomed good news for you if the people viewing your profile like what they see. It can cost you a job interview if hiring managers and HR personnel see things they don't like in your LinkedIn profile.

Once Microsoft's ecosystem of over one billion customers are connected to LinkedIn's over 433 million users, that 87 percent majority of HR department and staffing agency recruiters that Jobvite reported are reviewing candidate profiles on LinkedIn is about to morph exponentially into a much larger audience. Microsoft plans to synergize LinkedIn with Microsoft's products, such as Outlook, Calendar, Office, Windows and other Microsoft apps, making your LinkedIn profile even more accessible by not only recruiters but hiring managers, interviewers, co-workers, all levels of management, anyone and everyone who has access to Microsoft products on their computer at work or home.

Pulling up your LinkedIn page in the workplace will become as commonplace as pulling up a Microsoft Word document. When an employer is considering interviewing you for a job opening, they'll not only use Microsoft software to calendar your potential interview appointment for the hiring manager and each interview team member scheduled to interview you, they'll use Microsoft software to include the link to your LinkedIn page so all interviewers can view your profile before interviewing you.

Resume Reality Check

Is your online resume not getting you the phone calls or emails from recruiters that you want? If your resume is not getting noticed on Internet job search sites, ask yourself the following questions:

- Is my resume written in an organized, hierarchical and easy-to-read format? If not, rewrite your resume to make it more ATS-friendly and recruiter-friendly. If you need help writing your resume, consider having your resume written by a professional resume writer.

- In the first 6 seconds of reading my resume, does my resume provide enough information for a recruiter to make an informed yes/no decision in my favor? If not, rewrite your resume using the tips previously mentioned in this chapter or have a professional resume writing service rewrite your resume.

- Are there enough keywords and phrases in my resume to match the important keywords and phrases in a specific job description (for a specific job you're applying for online) or multiple job descriptions (if you want the jobs to find you)? The computerized ATS system will select the best resumes based on the inclusion of keywords and phrases in resumes that match important keywords and phrases in the job description.

- Am I using the wrong format, such as a PDF document instead of a Word document, or placing items out of order (such as placing my employment date before the company name) when I upload my resume to online job boards? The ATS system will reject resumes in PDF format. The ATS system will also leave your work history blank when the date of employment is placed before the company name. This may cause the ATS system to bypass your resume due to lack of work history relevance.

- Are there any, pictures, images, tables or unnecessary information in my resume? If so, get rid of those distractions. Those images and tables could cause the ATS system to reject your resume; and are only making it harder for recruiters to read your resume in their 6-second reviewing timeframe.

- Am I updating my resume at least every two weeks on Internet job boards? If not, do so and set up a reminder to yourself to perform this simple task that will help get your resume noticed by more recruiters that are searching for resumes based on the date the resume was last updated.

- Did I make my resume "public" on the online job search website so that employers and staffing agencies can view my resume? Check your profile or resume section of the online job search website to ensure you have allowed your resume to be viewed by the public. Just as with social media sites where you can make your posts public or private, you can make your resume public or private on Internet job boards. The resume private setting can be used after you've been hired, when you do not want recruiters to keep contacting you about job opportunities. Just remember to set public viewing back on when you are job-hunting again.

- Do my social media posts show poor spelling, alcohol or marijuana use, or place me in some other negative light to recruiters, hiring managers or HR personnel? If so, it's time to clean up your social media posts (or readjust your privacy settings on those social media sites).

CHAPTER SIX

Dealing with Recruiters

If opportunity doesn't knock, build a door.
Milton Berle

Staffing Agencies

For those of us job-hunters in search of available job openings, some ways to get our foot in the door are through company career websites, job fairs, professional networking and external staffing agencies. Sometimes staffing personnel come looking for us to work in an open position.

There are both internal and external staffing offices. Internal recruitment offices use company employees, such as the human resource (HR) department of the company, to recruit employees from within the company, through promotions or position changes. Oftentimes, companies will use internal recruitment first to fill available slots, but if that is unsuccessful, companies will seek help from external recruitment agencies to find candidates for the job. Staffing agencies are external recruitment companies whose main purpose is to connect business needs with qualified personnel who can meet those needs.

Although you will encounter staffing agencies that will do their utmost to connect you to a client (private company or US government agency with the job opening), it's important to realize that whether you are dealing with an internal recruiter of a company or an external staffing agency, they both work for the employer (company client), not for you (the job-hunter).

This does not mean you cannot have a meaningful, professional, repeat relationship with a recruiter of a staffing agency who is helping you land a job. It just means the staffing agency's bread is being buttered by the employer, not you. Therefore, your relationship with a staffing agency recruiter is similar to the relationship a person who is looking to buy a home has with a real estate agent who is representing the seller of the home, not the buyer of the home.

The company client—not the staffing agency—is also the one who is ultimately providing your salary. If you get hired for a job through a staffing agency, the company paying your salary and benefits could be either the staffing agency or the private company client (or US government agency) the staffing agency connected you with. Whichever way you collect our paycheck, the money is originating from the employer with the job opening, not the staffing agency.

The Recruiters

When a staffing agency initially contacts you, the person communicating with you is usually a recruiter. Recruiters are the first line staffing personnel who make the initial contact with potential job-hunting candidates. Recruiters have various job titles, such as Executive Search Consultant, Professional Recruiter, Staffing Consultant, Recruiter, Sourcing Agent, Technical Recruiter, Senior Talent Delivery Strategist, Tech Rep or Recruiting Partner.

There are a plethora of recruiters in today's job market. That surplus of recruiters, both locally and out-of-state, allows you to be selective on which recruiters you want to work with, especially once you learn how to make recruiters seek you out for job openings and not the other way around. Although staffing agency recruiters are working for the employer, stick with recruiters that make you feel as though they are working for you and avoid the rest.

Retained and Contingency Recruiters

Recruiters operate in one of two categories with company clients: retained or contingency.

Retained Recruiters

Recruiters working on a retained basis with a company client means the company is giving that recruiter exclusive rights to fill their job openings. The company client will not accept resumes from their internal (HR) recruiters, other staffing agencies, candidate applications submitted directly to the employer's career website, or any other channels the employer can get resumes. The company client may even have the retained recruiter on an annual contract basis.

Retained recruiters may seem more personable and patient than contingency recruiters because they don't have to compete with other staffing agencies for the employer's available positions. They will take more time to ensure the candidate is the best fit for the employer.

When employers use retained recruiters, it typically means the recruiter's staffing agency has developed a long-standing, trusted relationship with the company. It's an expensive relationship though because employers pay up to 50 percent of a candidate's projected first annual salary to retained recruiters. However, the employer is confident that this staffing agency can find them the quality professionals they're looking for. Because of this expense, employers typically use retained recruiters for more experienced or senior positions instead of junior positions to get a greater return on their investment.

When the employer needs to fill a position, the retained recruiter may present between 3 to 10 candidate resumes, along with each candidate's salary expectation, to the employer to choose from to interview.

When the retained recruiter asks for your permission to submit your resume to an employer, your resume may actually be one of several resumes the recruiter is submitting to the employer for the same job opening. This is important to know because, although the recruiter and the employer may have agreed to your desired salary, if your skill sets and qualifications are similar to the other candidates the employer is interviewing for the same job, the employer may select the candidate with the lower salary. This way, the employer saves money by hiring the candidate with the lower salary resulting in a lower commission for the retained recruiter.

It's good to be able to ask for more, but sometimes less is more, especially when you are competing with other candidates with similar skill sets and qualifications as you for the same position.

Contingency Recruiters

When a recruiter works on a contingency basis with a company, this means the recruiter is competing with other staffing agencies; the employer's internal (HR) department; applications submitted directly to the employer's career website by job-hunting candidates; and from other channels the employer is willing to accept resumes.

Contingency recruiters operate on a "no win, no fee" or "no cure, no pay" basis with employers. This means contingency recruiters only get paid a commission if their candidate is hired by the employer. Their commission is typically between 10–25 percent of the candidate's projected first annual salary.

As with retained recruiters, when the contingency recruiter asks for your permission to submit your resume to an employer, your resume is actually one of several resumes the recruiter may be submitting to the employer for the same job opening.

You can tell when recruiters are working under a contingency basis with an employer when you receive multiple calls or emails from several recruiters of different staffing agencies about the same job opening. It's basically first come, first served—the recruiter who can get the best resumes in the hands of the employer first will get those resumes looked at first. That's why there is such a rush of recruiters trying to reach out to you about the same job. Their rush job makes contingency recruiters appear less personable and less patient than retained recruiters. They simply do not have the luxury of time and exclusivity that retained recruiters have to find the right candidate for available job opportunities.

Recruiter Alliances

The life of a contingency recruiter can be a dog-eat-dog world with so many recruiters competing for the same job-seeking candidates and available job openings. So instead of going it alone, some recruiting agencies have learned over time that there is safety—and commissions—in numbers. Like wolf packs that instinctively hunt their prey in groups, these headhunters hunt in packs to increase their chances of success in getting a commission. These recruiters have learned to headhunt together through recruiter networks or alliances; and when their teamwork results in a commission, they will share the profits 50–50.

These contingency recruiters will form into networks or alliances in order to share job listings and potential job-hunting candidates. This allows them to spread a wider net in finding open jobs and candidates to fill those jobs. By sharing knowledge about open jobs and candidates amongst themselves, they are applying the principle of **knowledge is power**, and **power is control**. Like the rest of the animal kingdom, these recruiters have learned to adapt to their working environment in a way that enables them to control more of that competitive recruitment environment.

The Recruiter's Commission

Employers pay a commission fee or flat rate to staffing agencies for finding professionals to fill available positions. Although we speak of the commission as being a recruiter's commission, the recruiter actually receives only a percentage of the commission that the employer pays to the staffing agency.

For retained recruiters, the commission paid to staffing agencies by employers is typically between 40–50 percent of the candidate's first annual salary. For example, if your negotiated annual salary is $80K a year, the employer will pay the staffing agency $40K at a 50 percent commission rate. If your negotiated annual salary is $120K a year, the employer will pay the staffing agency $60K at a 50 percent commission rate.

For contingency recruiters, the commission paid to staffing agencies by employers is typically between 10–25 percent of the candidate's first annual salary. For example, if your negotiated annual salary is $80K a year, the employer will pay the staffing agency $20K at a 25 percent commission rate. If your negotiated annual salary is $120K a year, the employer will pay the staffing agency $30K at a 25 percent commission rate.

Staffing agencies understand that if you don't get hired, they don't get paid. It is in the staffing agency's best interest to provide you the best service possible in helping you land that job you're looking for; and the higher your salary is, the greater their commission.

Some recruiter commissions are structured on the number of candidates they can place in job openings, and not necessarily on the quality of candidates placed in those positions. This leads some recruiters to behave more like headhunters than professional recruiters in their pursuit of greater commission compensation. For this reason, you need to be smart about the recruiter you are dealing with.

Since staffing agencies are being paid by employers, there is no reason for you to pay staffing agencies for their service in helping you find a job. So avoid those agencies that require you to pay them a fee for assisting you in your job search. Employers may also pay staffing agencies based on the contractor's hourly billings for the duration of the contract. Some staffing agencies are paid a fee by companies regardless if the candidate is hired or not, such as staffing agencies with exclusive rights with a corporation to find candidates for that company.

The Recruiter's Knowledge and Experience in Your Career Field

Just because a recruiter is contacting you about an available position, it does not mean they are very knowledgeable or experienced in your line of work. Some recruiters may have previously worked in your profession who can converse with you on various subjects about your line of work. Other recruiters are not from your career background or have very little knowledge or experience in your career field.

Be patient with recruiters when they begin asking you questions related to the job description of the open position because many of these recruiters don't have any idea about the details of your type of work. They just know that these items are on the job description, so they're trying to verify how good of a match you would be for that available position.

The ATS system has already picked your resume out of a crowded field of online resumes, so the recruiter knows you are a potential fit for the job. The recruiter's initial questions are their final screening process to determine if they should submit you for the available position. So the more you can "help the recruiter help you" by making the recruiter feel comfortable with your answers, the more convinced they will be that you're the right person for the job.

Be Wary of a Recruiter's Request for Your Resume

Make sure the recruiter wants to submit your resume for a specific job at a specific location. Some recruiters may just be gathering resumes to spam them or throw them out there like bait on a fishing line, a process called speculatively (on spec), to any and every company seeking personnel with your skill sets. Unless you want your resume to go out to multiple companies in a shotgun approach, it's best to avoid these types of recruiters.

To ensure a recruiter has a legitimate, specific job opening they are trying to fill, ask the recruiter to provide you the information in the following list. If the recruiter will not provide you this information, do not provide the recruiter your resume; do not sign any forms; and do not give the recruiter any exclusive rights to represent you or submit your resume. If the recruiter is hesitant in giving you the information below, you can either choose not to work with that recruiter (something I normally do) or you can proceed with extreme caution while dealing with that recruiter.

- **Name of the company client with the job opening:** Having the company name allows you to do a little research online at the company's website and search engines (such as Google) to learn the company's business, history, mission statement, financial status, top brass and department leaders, etc. This information will also be useful during the interview process.

  Some recruiters are a bit hesitant to provide you the name of the company because they do not want you to bypass them and submit your resume directly to the company's website. That's understandable; recruiters are trying to make a living just like you. If the recruiter does not provide you the name of the company, it is up to you to decide at that point whether or not you want to continue with the recruiter. If the recruiter provides the other information below, I'll oftentimes cut the recruiter some slack and continue working with the recruiter.

- **Location of the company client:** I always ask for the city and address of the company so I can determine if the location of the job is within my desired commute between home and the worksite.

- **Job description:** The job description is the real deciding factor on whether or not you would be interested in working in that position. The job description not only tells you what the job responsibilities entail, it also identifies areas you might want to review and brush up on for the potential interview if you're interested in the job. If the recruiter does not have a copy of the job description, they can get a copy from the employer. So ask the recruiter to get you a copy of the job description before you hand over your resume.

- **The industry of the client company:** If you work in a career that spans multiple industries, such as IT, finance, supply and warehouse or management, you want to know which industry the position is in. You may be inclined to work in some of these industries but not all of them for one reason or another.

The following items are additional information you might consider asking the recruiter to provide you before giving the recruiter a copy of your resume:

- What is the contract structure? Is this a full-time company employee position, a contractor position or a contract-to-hire position? If it is a contract position, how long is the contract?

- Is this position an exempt or non-exempt position?

- Is this position a salaried or hourly position?

- Who is the primary (prime) company in this contract? When the company client is in a primary-secondary company relationship with another company, it's good to know if the company with the job opening is the prime company or the secondary (sub) company.

- What work shift is this position? Is this a straight day job, or is there swing shifts or night shifts involved? If so, that may end your desire to work there.

- How much travel is involved with this position?

- The names of the people that will interviewer you.

The Good, the Bad and the Ugly Recruiter

When it comes to recruiters, you can expect *the good, the bad,* and *the ugly* to come calling. If you've dealt with as many staffing agency recruiters and account managers as I have, you know there are good recruiters, bad recruiters and the ugly recruiters just as there are in other lines of work. Here are a few types of staffing agency recruiters or account managers that will eventually contact you during your job search.

Big Brother and Big Sister Recruiters (The Good)

I have my own unofficial name I've come to give this type of recruiter after dealing with them over the years: big brother (for a male recruiter) and big sister (for a female recruiter). Just as you can talk with your big brother or big sister about things you normally cannot or do not want to talk about with your parents; you can talk to your recruiter about things that you normally cannot talk about or do not want to talk about with the parent company—the corporation or the US government agency with the job opening.

What things? Things like your salary and benefits for starters. You've probably heard that it is bad form to talk about salary or other company benefits when you are in a job interview. This is true because the people who are interviewing you are "the parents" so to speak. The people interviewing you are part of the corporation that will make the final decision to hire you. Talking about money and benefits with them in the interview has always been taboo; and engaging in a conversation with them about these things sheds a negative light on you during the interview.

So how can you help a brother out? You talk to your big brother or big sister—the staffing agency recruiter—about these things. That's one of the reasons why recruiters are there: to discuss with you all the things that would be considered inappropriate for you to talk about with interviewers in the job interview.

And like a big brother or big sister, you can be quite frank and upfront in your conversations—online or on the phone—with recruiters about important compensatory aspects of that job opportunity, such as salary and benefits (medical, dental and vision benefits, 401K, education/certification reimbursement, paid vacation and time off, perks, etc.). These are things you want to hammer out with the staffing agency recruiter before your job interview with the employer.

The staffing agency is the one you want to negotiate your salary and benefits with. The interviewers are the people who decide if they hire you for the job. You do not want to engage the interviewers directly about your salary and benefits.

"But isn't the company client the one who is ultimately providing the money to pay me through the staffing agency?" you may ask. Yes, but once you negotiate and establish *with the recruiter* what your desired hourly rate or salary will be, the staffing agency's account manager (if they don't already know) will check with the employer to get approval of the hourly rate or salary you want.

This process is similarly played out among players in professional sports. The pro athletes do not haggle with their team's coaches, management staff or ownership about their millions of dollars they want to be paid. The players talk to their agent and their agent deals with their team ownership. What agents are to these professional athletes in money matters with the team ownership, recruiters are to job-seekers; only the company ownership of your team may be paying you through the recruiter's staffing agency.

Once the staffing agency recruiter agrees to pay your desired compensation; that means the employer agrees to pay you that same amount through the staffing agency—that is, if you pass the interview and get hired. This may seem like you're putting the cart before the horse—negotiating your salary and benefits before you are interviewed—but that's how the system works with staffing agency recruiters.

If you are working directly with an employer instead of through a staffing agency, you would typically go through the interview process first; and if you pass the interview, you would discuss your salary and benefits afterward.

Once the staffing agency recruiter has determined you are a good fit for an available job opportunity, you will negotiate your salary and benefits with the recruiter or the staffing agency's account manager. After you and the recruiter agrees to your desired compensation, the recruiter will either continue working with you in getting you a job interview or the recruiter will hand you off to their staffing agency accounting manager who will set up your job interview with the business client.

When the recruiter hands you off to the account manager, you may not hear from the recruiter any more at that point; and you will be dealing with the account manager from that point on.

Recruiters (or account managers) play another important role—the big brother or big sister role I mentioned—after they set up an interview for you with the company client. Recruiters will oftentimes provide you guidance on how you should prepare for the interview, such as good grooming tips and proper interview attire; questions about the company or the job you should prepare ahead of time; and how to conduct yourself during an interview, such as greeting, enthusiasm, posture and taboos.

On the day of your interview, some staffing agency recruiters or account managers will meet you at the employer's facility where you will be interviewed; introduce you to the interviewer; and send you on your way with their vote of confidence—just like a big brother or big sister would do.

If you are happy with the help you received from a staffing agency, it's always a good idea to keep the contact information of the recruiter who initially contacted you from that agency. Most of us in jobs do not intend to stay in the same workplace forever, so a good recruiter becomes a valuable part of your networking portfolio just as previous colleagues you've work with in the past.

Headhunter Recruiters (The Bad)

The unofficial, unflattering name most people in search of jobs know recruiters by is headhunter. Some recruiters may have earned themselves that name by coming across as a bit primitive in their practices of hunting for candidates to fill vacant positions. If your email inbox or voicemail are filled with numerous recruiter messages, you sometimes might feel as if you're the prey being hunted.

Dealing with Recruiters

The key to working with headhunters is to "keep your head" (pun intended) when dealing with staffing agency recruiters and account managers. It's important to understand that many recruiters are in tough competition with other recruiters in the hunt for candidates who can fill an available position. For many of them, their job is a constant race to see who can get that candidate first before they are beaten out by other competing recruiters. It's good to have thick skin when dealing with recruiters or account managers because some of their practices may offend you if you're not used to their aggressive recruiting style.

Keep in mind that your relationship with staffing agents is a business relationship first and foremost; friendship is optional. You might not like some of the ways staffing agents conduct their business, but as long as you see them as a business process or a means to an end, which is locating jobs that result in you being interviewed and hired for a job, you won't take their behavior personal. This will help your job search go a lot smoother for you.

Some recruiters who email you will have someone else's name other than yours in their message. Other recruiters will send you multiple copies of the same job opening. That's because they're juggling so many candidates to win over a commission, they don't slow down enough to realize they got your name mixed up with someone else or that they already sent you that email. Just remember: *To err is human; to forgive is divine*. If the job interests you, reply back to the recruiter and let them know your correct name.

Some recruiters submit your resume but were told by the employer that several key interview team members are out of the office for an extended period of time. As a result, the employer has put the interview process on hold until those key people return. That's the good part. The bad part is the recruiter does not contact you to let you know there will be a delay in the decision on interviewing you for the job. Again, this oversight is typically due to the recruiter juggling so many candidates at the same time, they're forgetting simple details such as contacting candidates and letting them know about the delay.

Rejection and delay is a normal part of the job search process. Everyone has to go through it from candidates running for the US presidential office to candidates in search of work in the most menial of jobs. Sometimes there is a delay in the employer's resume review process, so getting feedback from the recruiter or account manager is necessary. If in doubt about the status of your resume submission, contact the recruiter who submitted you to the employer. I've contacted staffing agents in the past for feedback about my resume submission, only to find out from the staffing agent that the hiring manager or one of the key people on the interview team is out of town on a business or personal trip; and the staffing agent was waiting for their return.

Dr. Jekyll and Mr. Hyde Recruiters (The Ugly)

Dealing with staffing agency recruiters and account managers can oftentimes make you feel like you're dealing with Dr. Jekyll and Mr. Hyde from the popular novella written by the famous Scottish novelist, Robert Louis Stevenson. The reason I say this is because many of the staffing agents you will deal with have a Jekyll and Hyde personality when it comes to their behavior either "before and after" you send them a copy of your resume or "before and after" your job interview.

You've been hit by a smooth criminal.

Oftentimes, staffing agents will act like the friendly Dr. Henry Jekyll during your initial contact and while negotiating your salary. When you give them a copy of your resume to pass on to an employer to see if the hiring manger is interested in interviewing you—then comes the eternal silence. No word or feedback from the staffing agent about what happened after they submitted your resume to the employer. They just disappear into the night, never to be seen or heard from again. If you've used staffing agencies for any length of time in your job searches, you've probably met the evil Mr. Hyde who stole away into the night's darkness with your resume after you provided the friendly Dr. Jekyll your resume during the day.

If Michael Jackson were to explain what just happened to you, he'd sing, *"You've been hit by a smooth criminal."*

The same is true concerning job interviews. Oftentimes, before a scheduled job interview, staffing agency recruiters or account managers act like the polished, polite and professional Dr. Henry Jekyll. They're friendly, interested and communicative with you throughout the job search process right up to your job interview.

After you complete the job interview, these same staffing agents act as if they drank down Dr. Jekyll's potion that turned them into the evil Mr. Hyde. Their behavior changes opposite to the way they were before the interview. After the interview, they transform into this unrecognizable, unprofessional, unsociable and uncaring person who will not communicate with you to provide you feedback about the results of your interview. They don't bother to respond back to you to provide you any input from the hiring manager as to how you did—good or bad.

Here's the harsh reality of the strange behavior of staffing agency recruiters and account managers after submitting your resume or after your job interview. If the hiring manager wants to interview you or if the hiring manager who interviewed you tells the staffing agent you were selected for the job, you can be certain the staffing agent is going to contact you immediately with the good news. After all, your good news is their good news. It means they might or will get a commission from your first year's salary. In other words, the friendly Dr. Jekyll will be in touch with you just as soon as he or she gets the good news from the hiring manager.

However, if the hiring manager notifies the staffing agent that they do not want to interview you or, if after you were interviewed, you were not selected, that bad news is like drinking Dr. Jekyll's serum of misery to some staffing agents. They could hardly swallow that medicine, and now they have to get you to swallow it too. As with so many other candidates they've submitted resumes or set up interviews for in the past, instead of giving you the courtesy of a phone call or email informing you of the bad news, something else sinister takes place within these staffing agents.

That serum of rejection from the hiring manager begins to take over their moral compass and character. They begin to choke and writhe in pain, like Dr. Jekyll transforming into the hideous Mr. Hyde, over the idea of having to call yet another candidate AGAIN and give them the bad news that they weren't selected for the job.

As the staffing agent tries to reach for the phone or keyboard to notify you, their fingers become knotted and twisted with the angry and depressing thoughts of losing another valuable commission that slipped through their helpless fingers. Now they are too paralyzed to call you as if stricken with the worst stages of arthritis. Their face begins to twitch and tighten, and their lips and tongue become numb as if they just came out of a dentist's chair. They feel as if their teeth are now protruding hideously from their mouth like Jerry Lewis' teeth in *The Nutty Professor* film. They become that awkward and clumsy professor, unable to communicate the bad news to yet another job-hunting candidate.

On top of all of this, your bad news is their bad news—they won't be getting a commission off of your salary after all. As a result, these headhunters move your head from the asset column to the expendable column on their ledger of candidate head collections. In short, the evil Mr. Hyde has taken over their mind, emotions, conduct and character; and they **consciously chose** to not contact you rather than give you the courtesy of a phone call or email letting you know you were not selected for the job.

Not all recruiters or account managers have the grit to go through the arduous task of calling or emailing every job candidate to give them the bad news every time hiring managers decide to pass over these candidates after reviewing their resume or after interviewing them. Whether it's your resume or your job interview being passed over by the hiring manager; some staffing agent recruiters and account managers just aren't able to do the right thing in the end by contacting you with the bad news. They've already moved on to their next candidate, expecting you to get the message by their silence.

Again, this is where you need to keep your head and be thick skinned because not all staffing agents act in a professional manner by providing you feedback. Although I think this headhunter conduct of not providing you feedback on the employer's decision is highly unprofessional, I'm not ignorant of the fact that for so many of these headhunters, job candidates are just a numbers game. The more candidate heads these headhunters can capture, the greater their chances for getting a commission through one of them. They're simply playing the odds.

Therefore, when a week has passed after the staffing agent has given your resume to the employer or after you completed your job interview with the employer, you should contact the staffing agent and ask for feedback. Otherwise, you might as well accept their silence as meaning the employer has passed over you after reviewing your resume or interviewing you. You should move on to the next staffing agent too. In either case, if the answer is no from the employer, you need to learn to move on with your head held high (no pun intended) and continue your job search with another staffing agent.

Regardless of your experiences with staffing agencies or the names you give recruiters, learn to accept the job search process for what it is and make the process work for you, not against you.

Requests from Recruiters for Your Exclusive Rights Agreement

In most cases, employers will accept candidate resumes from multiple external staffing agencies. To prevent the employer from being overwhelmed by too many resumes from multiple staffing agencies, the employer may limit the number of resumes it will accept from each staffing agency, such as limiting each staffing agency to a maximum of three resumes.

In response to this limit, some staffing agency recruiters try to get a prospective candidate to sign or acknowledge a simple exclusive rights agreement, also known as a "right to represent" or "non-compete" agreement. This agreement states the candidate gives the recruiter the exclusive right to submit their resume to the employer. This prevents the candidate in search of work from trying to submit their resume to the same employer through multiple staffing agencies or through the employer's career website. Typically, it's a contingency recruiter who will use this method with candidates whose resume they want to have sole control over with an employer. Contingency recruiters do this in an attempt to gain an added advantage over other recruiters who try to submit you and other candidates for the same open position.

Perhaps you've seen this type of agreement come through an email request from a recruiter after you've agreed to have them submit your resume for a position. The recruiter sends you the email requesting you to acknowledging that you agree to them submitting you for that position. If you concur or electronically sign the agreement, you are giving the recruiter some assurance in writing that you will not attempt to have another recruiter or staffing agency submit your resume for the same job twice.

When you give a recruiter exclusive rights to be the only recruiter who can submit you for a particular job opening, do you know what you've done? You've just given your **power** and **control** over that job opportunity into the hands of that recruiter, a complete stranger who calls or emails you out of the blue.

Am I saying this is a problem?

I'm saying this agreement benefits only the recruiter, not *you*. What proof do you have that there really is a job opening when you sign that agreement? What guarantees do you have that the recruiter will submit your resume to the client company? Would you sign an agreement with a salesman for a house or car without fully knowing what you're signing? Of course you wouldn't. The fact is the exclusive rights agreement promises or guarantees you nothing while the recruiter gets everything—

complete control—over you and your resume concerning this job opportunity.

By signing the exclusive rights agreement, you are essentially stating you are providing a service to the recruiter. That service is that you are giving the recruiter the sole right to make a commission profit off of you that amounts to 10–25 percent of your projected first year's salary with the new employer. If your first year's annual salary is $90K, that salary means you have agreed to give that recruiter the sole right to receive a $22,500 commission (at a 25% commission rate) off of you. Now how much are you charging that recruiter for that service you are providing them that is potentially worth $22,500 in their pocket? Nothing! If you ask me, job-seeking candidates should be charging recruiters at least $1,000 for providing recruiters this service. Knowledge is power, and power is control.

If you've seen one of these exclusive rights agreements from a recruiter, you'll notice that the agreement does not say the recruiter will submit your resume immediately to the employer. It does not say the recruiter has to submit your resume at all. All it guarantees is that you cannot let any other recruiter submit you for this job opening. It also guarantees that you cannot submit your resume to the employer's career website for the job.

When you sign that exclusive rights agreement, don't be surprised if that friendly Dr. Jekyll turns into the evil Mr. Hyde and you don't hear from that recruiter again. It happens to many job-seeking candidates all the time. If it happens to you, just remember: *You've been hit by a smooth criminal.*

It's not that the exclusive rights agreement is a scam. It is the fact that the exclusive rights agreement doesn't benefit *you*. It benefits only the recruiter. More bad things can potentially happen to you than good when you sign an exclusive rights agreement.

What about if you have a long-term business relationship with a recruiter you enjoy using for finding jobs? Should you sign an exclusive rights agreement with them? Chances are if you and a recruiter have established a trusting business relationship, then the recruiter shouldn't need to ask you for an exclusive rights agreement.

However, if you're going to relinquish the control you have over a particular job opportunity, here is some advice you can use to limit the control you give to the recruiter:

- Negotiate your salary for this job with the recruiter before you sign the exclusive rights agreement. This way, you have more leverage in asking for whatever amount you want for that job. If the recruiter wants that exclusive rights from you, they have to first be willing to ensure you get the hourly rate or annual salary you want. Otherwise, they don't get exclusive rights to submit you for that job.

- Make the recruiter provide you a full job description of the available position before you sign the exclusive rights agreement. Some unscrupulous recruiters actually do not have an open position from a company client they are seeking to fill. They just want to collect your resume along with other resumes to use in future job openings. Therefore, follow these next two pieces of advice.

- Make sure the exclusive rights agreement includes the name of the company client; the job title; the amount of compensation you negotiated with the recruiter; and the city in which the company client is located. This limits the range of control in which the recruiter can use you and your resume for what is hopefully a real job opening.

- Make the recruiter include a statement in the exclusive rights agreement that limits the timeframe the recruiter can use you and your resume for this available position. For example, the statement should say that the recruiter is allowed to use the exclusive rights for one week or two weeks only from a specific date in the agreement.

This time limit you set in the agreement does three things:

1. **It de-escalates a conflict between two recruiters submitting your resume for the same job opening.**

If an employer receives your resume from two or more recruiters, the employer has to decide which recruiter receives the commission if the employer decides to hire you. The recruiter with the right to represent you usually wins. The employer is more inclined to pay the commission to the recruiter who has the exclusive rights agreement with you.

However, if the exclusive rights agreement has a time limit that is expired, the employer can work with the recruiter you choose to represent you; and pay that recruiter the commission fee if you are hired. This allows you to move forward with another recruiter of your choice when the time limit is expired with the recruiter who has your exclusive rights.

2. **You force the recruiter to submit your resume immediately for the job.**

This strategy prevents the recruiter from holding on to your resume while the recruiter submits another candidate, perhaps for less salary than your desired compensation, for the same position. If the other candidate doesn't get selected for the job, no problem for the recruiter—they have you in their hip pocket. They can submit your resume next or after whoever is their second or third choice. If the first or second candidate gets hired for the job, they can collect their commission and drop your resume in the trash. Then they can inform you (or not) that you weren't accepted for the job.

The important thing to realize is that once you sign the exclusive rights agreement with the recruiter, you don't automatically become the recruiter's first choice to submit to the employer. You could actually become the recruiter's last choice—their safety net. The recruiter knows no one else can submit you for this position, so the recruiter can submit other potential candidates before you. The recruiter knows they will not lose you to another recruiter if they plan to submit other candidates before you for that available position. It's all about knowledge, power and control.

3. **It prevents the recruiter from using your resume 6 months to a year or later without your permission.**

If that recruiter turns out to be an evil Mr. Hyde who you never hear from again, that recruiter can still submit your resume for future jobs with that employer without you ever being aware of it. If there is no company listed on the agreement, the recruiter can submit your resume to other companies looking for someone in your line of work.

With that signed agreement, the recruiter can basically hold your resume and job search effort hostage. No other recruiter can use your resume for future jobs with that company or possibly other companies. The employer has to honor your agreement with that sole recruiter.

What if that employer or other employers do not like doing business with that recruiter that has your signed exclusive rights agreement? Well, do you remember that mystery woman that was always trying to kill Jake Blues (played by John Belushi) in *The Blues Brothers* film? Yeah, you guessed it. That blacklisted recruiter is the mystery woman. If that recruiter is an evil Mr. Hyde, they will constantly show up with your resume, sabotaging and killing your chances to be considered for future jobs with employers. There goes your mission from God.

- Type the agreement yourself. This way you—not the recruiter—spell out the terms of the agreement. This will give you greater control over the terms of the agreement. You can type out the agreement on a Word document, attach it to an email, and send it back to the recruiter for their signature. Ta da!

The following example on the next page is a temporary exclusive rights agreement. This is something you can type yourself using the suggestions I just outlined, and email it to a recruiter you plan to give exclusive rights to. This will give the recruiter *limited control* over you and your resume as they solely represent you to a client company that has an open position.

Concerning you and the recruiter signing this agreement, email this agreement **UNSIGNED** to the recruiter first. In the email, tell the recruiter they must sign the agreement first. Once they sign the agreement and email it back to you, you can sign it and email a copy back to them with both of your signatures on the agreement.

Do not provide the recruiter a copy of your resume until after they sign this agreement.

Temporary Exclusive Rights Agreement

January 9, 2017

This temporary exclusive rights agreement is only between [your full name] (*Candidate*) *and* [recruiter's full name] (*Recruiter*) *at* [staffing agency name] (*Staffing Agency*).

This temporary exclusive rights agreement will end and become **null and void after January 17, 2017.**

I, [your full name] (*Candidate*), *agree to be solely represented by* [staffing agency name] (*Staffing Agency*) *only for the conditions stated below*:

- **Staffing Agency Name / Website:** [staffing agency name] / [staffing agency website]

- **Staffing Agency Recruiter Name:** [recruiter's full name]

- **Staffing Agency Recruiter Contact Info:** [recruiter's phone number] / [recruiter work email address]

- **Company Client Name:** [company name]

- **Company Client Location:** [company city and state]

- **Job Title of Available Position:** [job title]

- **Salary Negotiated between** [your full name] **(Candidate) and** [recruiter full name] **(Recruiter) at** [staffing agency name] **(Staffing Agency):** [$ annual salary or $ hourly rate]

- *I am willing to provide professional references **after** the job interview with the company client.*

- *I am willing to provide a copy of my resume **after** the [staffing agency name] representative shown below signs this agreement.*

This temporary exclusive rights agreement is null and void if both parties (Candidate and Staffing Agency representative) do not sign this agreement below, and if both parties (Candidate and Staffing Agency representative) do not have a copy of this signed agreement:

[Your Signature]   [Recruiter Signature]
[Your Printed Name]   [Recruiter Printed Name]
[Your Email Address]   [Recruiter Email Address]
[Your Phone Number]   [Recruiter Phone Number]

****

Notice this exclusive rights agreement gives the recruiter only 7 working days (from January 9–17) as the length of time this exclusive rights agreement is valid. Some recruiters will argue that they need more time than a week because the employer is the one to decide where candidates fall in the interview line of candidates. Essentially, what the recruiter is telling you is that there are other candidates that will be interviewed before you. What the recruiter won't tell you is that they could be one submitting other candidates ahead of you.

Regardless if that recruiter or a different recruiter is submitting candidates before you, the recruiter is telling you your place in the interview line is not first when they ask you for more time in the agreement. Your place in that interview line could be last. That's why the recruiter is asking for more time to get you an interview. While you're waiting out that extra time, the hiring manager could make their hiring decision on another candidate well before they reach you.

Don't forget, employers normally allow recruiters to submit 2–3 resumes for the open position. You are just one of several candidates that recruiter wants to or plans to submit to the employer. If the recruiter can get you on an "extended" exclusive rights agreement, they can submit other candidates ahead of you, knowing that no other recruiter can submit you for that same job.

Signing an exclusive rights agreement for a recruiter should be done in a quid pro quo fashion. In other words, if you are going to give the recruiter this huge favor and advantage, giving them first place and making them top priority among all other recruiters, the recruiter needs to do the same for you. The recruiter needs to make you and your resume first place and top priority among all other job-seeking candidates in getting you an interview with the hiring manager.

By signing the exclusive rights agreement, you are positioning that recruiter and their staffing agency to make tens of thousands of dollars off of you. Where's your return on your investment? You should get something in return for that guarantee you are giving that recruiter and their staffing agency. The recruiter and their staffing agency needs to do everything in their power to ensure you get into an interview that first week before all other candidates in exchange for you ensuring that recruiter has exclusive rights to submit you for an interview.

If that recruiter and their staffing agency can't get you into the first week of interviews among that competition between recruiters, you're working with the wrong recruiter and staffing agency. They're like empty calories. Their words taste so sweet but their actions don't benefit you at all. Get rid of them. Find yourself a recruiter and staffing agency that will work for you; not make you work for them.

Bottom line, if you want to maintain control over your job search process instead of relinquishing complete control to a recruiter, you must put that recruiter on a short lease when it comes to an exclusive rights agreement. Now that you have this knowledge, take the power and control out of the hands of the recruiter and place it firmly back in your own hands.

Well, I think that recruiter horse has been thoroughly beaten to death; so let's move on.

Submitting Multiple Resumes for the Same Job Opening

All of this advice about exclusive rights agreements with recruiters should not be interpreted to mean you should submit your resume through multiple recruiters for the same job opening. Don't let this knowledge corrupt your own power and control over the job search process.

In all fairness to recruiters, don't try to submit your resume through multiple recruiters for the same job opening. It isn't fair to all recruiters involved; it isn't fair to the company client with the job opening; and you would be doing a disservice to the integrity of all job-seeking candidates who are trying to conduct their business fairly with recruiters and employers.

Once you submit your resume through one recruiter for a particular job opening, don't try to submit another resume through the employer's career website or through another recruiter for the same job again.

Employers notice when you try to submit your resume through multiple recruiters for the same job they are trying to fill. This activity sheds negative light on both you and all staffing agencies that submitted your resume for the same job.

Everyone ends up looking bad when multiple recruiters give your resume to an employer for the same job. You look bad in front of the employer because it shows that you are trying to work the system by going behind the backs of multiple recruiters for the same job. This makes you look untrustworthy in front of the employer. This reason alone could give hiring managers reason to cross your name off their list of people they would consider hiring. The staffing agencies look bad because they all submitted a resume on the same candidate who obviously cannot be trusted. Unfortunately, this reflects poorly on the recruiter's ability to weed out undesirable candidates and identify quality candidates.

In this case, everyone loses. The candidate whose resume gets rejected by the employer loses. The staffing agency recruiters lose because they are out of a commission and may not be welcomed again by the employer. And the employer loses because they still have an open position to fill.

Although it may seem tempting when you have several recruiters contacting you about the same job opportunity, select only one recruiter you like for that particular job opening. Kindly tell all other recruiters that you are already working with a recruiter for that job opportunity. Tell them you would be willing to consider other opportunities from them (because getting hired for that job is not a sure thing).

Recruiters are more likely to contact you again for other available positions knowing that you were upfront with them about working with another recruiter for an open position. They know they can trust you to tell other recruiters the same thing when they submit you for an open position in the future.

The same goes for submitting your resume through the employer's company website versus through a recruiter—choose one or the other but not both. By submitting your resume through both of these channels, you become less desirable to hiring managers because your actions suggest you show no regard for the recruiter's source of income—their finder's fee or commission. Despite the bad rap recruiters get as headhunters, employers know recruiters are people too with families to feed and care for, and bills to pay. After all, aren't those the same type of reasons why you're looking for a job?

Don't Show All Your Cards to Recruiters

When a recruiter asks you if you have any interviews or job offers on the table, don't reveal this information to the recruiter. Recruiters are only asking for this information so they can decide if they want to submit your resume to an employer. If you tell them you do have an interview or job offer, the recruiter will put off submitting your resume to an employer. No recruiter wants to submit a resume on a candidate only to have to tell the employer that the candidate was hired by another employer. They would rather pass up on you and submit another candidate for the job who they know they have a chance with.

You don't have to tell the recruiter you have an interview lined up or a job offer on the table if it is for a different job than the one the recruiter is offering you. Put on your poker face and tell the recruiter you've talked with other recruiters but there isn't anything on the table—interview or job offer. This way, you maintain control of the recruiter; and not the other way around.

Requests from Recruiters to Visit Their Office

Some recruiters in your local area will ask you to come to their office to visit with them first before they consider submitting your resume to employers. This visit to the recruiter's office transfers control from the job-seeking candidate to the recruiter.

The first rule of office politics is: whenever you have someone visit another person's office, the person that office belongs to is always the person in **control**. Simply by entering their office, their den, their lair, you relinquish control of your job search to the recruiter. You've started the process of jumping through their hoops instead of making the recruiter jump through your hoops.

It's an elimination process.

The second important thing to know about visiting the recruiter's office is: this visit is not a selection process; it's an elimination process. The recruiter is not asking you to come to their office to see if they should select you for the job. They're asking you to come to their office to decide if they should eliminate you from the pool of candidates they are considering for the open position.

Sure, the recruiter will tell you they want you to come to their office because they like to build relationships with their job-seeking candidates or that they like to have a face to a name. That's just a ploy to get you to come into their office. Their main goal to get you into their office is to decide whether or not they like you enough above other candidates to submit you for the open position.

Once you enter the recruiter's office, they will immediately make an assessment of you based on their subjective judgment on whether or not they should submit you to an employer. Chances are, by the time you are done shaking hands and saying your goodbyes to the recruiter, they've already made up their mind to either submit you to a potential employer or never contact you again. They won't tell you that while you're in their office, but they've already made their decision.

How do you know if the recruiter already made their decision not to submit you for an open position after visiting their office? When you don't hear from that recruiter again concerning that job opening, that's when you know they made their decision while you were in their office.

What's interesting about your visit to the recruiter's office is that the recruiter won't ask you the type of questions the employer's hiring manager and interview team will ask you to determine your fitness for the job. The recruiter will simply ask you the same basic questions that other recruiters ask you over the phone, such as *"Why are you looking for work?"* or *"How long did you work in your last job?"*

The problem with this approach is that the recruiter has already made the decision not to hire you when that control should be in the hands of the hiring manager. The hiring manager and his or her interview team should be the ones who should review your resume; interview you; and then make the decision to hire you or not. The recruiter who invites you to their office can make that decision themselves by simply not submitting your resume to the employer after you visit them—all without you being asked one technical question about your job.

That's what I mean when I say the recruiter's estimation of you while you visit their office is a subjective judgment decision to not submit you for an interview with the employer. Their decision is not based on any job-related questions or your fitness, skill sets or ability to perform the job. They just looked you up and down and decided you're not the person they want to submit to the employer.

All the recruiter had to go on in making their decision not to submit you for the open position are the way you talk, the way you look or how old you look, the way you dress, your hair style, your skin color, and so forth.

Do you really want to give that much control over to that recruiter?

If you want to maintain control of your job search process, tell the recruiter that you don't visit recruiter's offices until recruiters first schedule you for an interview with employers first. This way you force the recruiter to submit your resume to the hiring manager based on what is in your resume and the salary you're asking for the position; not based on how they subjectively judge you in person.

Don't worry about the recruiter passing up on you for not coming to their office. Most recruiters don't ask you to jump through this hoop anyway; so you're not missing out on anything by passing up on that recruiter and working with the multitude of other recruiters in your local area who don't ask you to go to their office before submitting your resume to employers. Chances are there are several other recruiters who will contact you for the same job opening anyway; and they won't ask you to come to their office first so they can look you up and down before deciding to submit your resume to the employer.

Requests from Recruiters for Your Personal Information

It cannot be emphasized enough that we all must guard our personal information. Providing personal information, such as your birth date, social security number, financial account information or passwords to people requesting this information over the phone, via email or social media, or in person can result in loss of your money; theft of your identity; and thieves opening fraudulent accounts in your name that can damage your credit rating or financial standing.

When it comes to having recruiters submit your resume for job openings, you'll find there are rare times when you have to cough up some of your personal information. For "legitimate recruiters" of "legitimate staffing agencies", asking for some of your personal information is a routine part of the job search process.

In the discussion about US government security clearances in chapter 3, I talked about how recruiters will ask you for your social security number and date of birth to verify the status of your existing security clearance in the Joint Personnel Adjudication System (JPAS), the DoD record system for security clearances. Under these circumstances, you are obviously seeking a US government job that requires a government security clearance that you already possess. The security department of staffing agencies has access to the JPAS system; and they must verify the status of your existing security clearance before submitting you for the government job that requires your security clearance.

Other than this scenario, there should be no other justifiable reason for providing your full social security number and full date of birth to a recruiter.

However, it is your responsibility to make sure the person on the other end of the phone or email is a legitimate recruiter from a legitimate staffing agency, and not someone trying to steal your personal information. After you have verified that the recruiter is legit, you can provide your social security number and date of birth for the sole purpose of verifying your security clearance.

If you do provide this personal information to a recruiter, you should not provide this information via email or a text message. Unsecure email and text messaging can be easily intercepted by online thieves who will be able to steal your personal information in transit. If you are providing your personal information to a recruiter over the phone, make sure there is no one in earshot of your conversation that might be able to copy down your personal information during your conversation with the recruiter.

Another case where recruiters might ask you for your personal information is when the employer with the open position requires staffing agencies to use a unique identifier in order to submit candidates for their available positions. This unique identifier uses a format that includes the **birth month and day only** (without the birth year) of the job-seeking candidate. In some cases, the employer also wants staffing agencies to include the **last four numbers of the candidate's social security number** (not the full social security number). If a recruiter is asking for more than this information, such as asking for your birth year or your full social security number, you are probably being scammed. Hang up the phone on that recruiter or delete that email from the recruiter.

This requirement for your birth month and day only or last four of your social security number is not something the staffing agency recruiter is making up. It is a requirement from the employer with the open position. The staffing agency is simply following the rules laid out by the employer.

Employers use a vendor management system (VMS), an Internet-enabled Web-based application that allows businesses (company clients; not staffing agencies) to manage and procure staffing services for their business. There are a variety of VMS application software on the market that company clients can purchase and use.

The bottom line is it is the employer with the open position—not the staffing agency—that configures their VMS application to ask for the information that staffing agencies are asking you to provide them. Staffing agencies must input candidate information in these VMS systems, owned by the employer, in order to submit candidates for positions.

As with providing personal information to verify security clearances with the JPAS system, it is your responsibility to always ensure the recruiter and the staffing agency are legitimate before you provide them your personal information for the VMS system.

Of course, if you still feel uncomfortable with providing your personal information to a recruiter, you should tell the recruiter you prefer not to provide any of your personal information. Let the recruiter know that you would be willing to work with them on available positions from employers that don't require your personal information in order for the recruiter to submit you for the job. After all, most employers do not require staffing agencies to obtain your personal information before submitting you for their open positions. This way, the recruiter can come back to you with those available jobs from employers that don't require your personal information for the VMS system.

If the recruiter decides to pass on you completely, at least you walk away with the confidence and assurance of knowing you did not disclose any of your personal information to a complete stranger asking you for this information over the phone or via email. There are plenty of other jobs out there and corporations and staffing agency recruiters for you to work with. You don't have to compromise your gut feelings about inquiries into your personal information.

Requests from Recruiters for Your Job References

Eventually, HR personnel and staffing agency recruiters get around to asking you for your job references. Some staffing agency recruiters ask for your references at the front end of your conversations before submitting your resume to the employer's hiring manager. Some recruiters will ask for your references once they have secured an interview for you with the employer. Other recruiters will ask for your references after the interview or after you were selected for the job by the hiring manager.

In 2015, SkillSurvey, a leading provider of hiring solutions and software for businesses to enable them to effectively recruit, hire and manage employees, conducted a survey of 300 professionals across business, healthcare and higher education who are involved with the hiring process to determine the importance of checking the references of job-hunting candidates. Here are some of the findings from their survey:

- 70% of the people surveyed said they check references on every job candidate.

- Reference checking increases with more senior positions.

- 62% of recruiters perform reference checks on job candidates compared to 36% of reference checks performed by hiring managers.

- 86% of employers stated that reference checks is one of the most important steps in the hiring process.

- As to why they conduct reference checks, 63% of those surveyed said it helps them hire better employees; 61% said it is part of their interviewing process; and 59% said it helps to avoid bad hires.

- When compared to other methods of identifying the right candidate for the job, 77% of those surveyed said reference checking is second only to a background screening; 55% placed reference checks ahead of skills assessment to do the job; and placed reference checks ahead of behavioral based assessment (39%) and personality assessments (33%) to determine a candidates cultural fitness for the job.

Never take a request for your references lightly. References are part of the commerce of the job hunting economy. Treat your references like you treat your money—you should expect something in return for giving your references to recruiters. I'm not talking about a 12-piece bucket of chicken from Colonel Sanders. You should only give your references to recruiters as a quid pro quo; an exchange for them to do something for you. Notice I said "do" something for you; not "promise" something or in hopes they will do something for you. In other words, do not give your references to anyone just because they ask you. Your references are much too valuable for you to provide them to every Tom, Dick and Mary recruiter who asks you for them.

Your references aren't a bunch of names and contact information. References are people. If you picked your references wisely, these are people waiting in the wings to give a glowing review about you to the people contacting them on your behalf. Glowing reviews, that is, for the first two or three callers. But once those calls keep coming in non-stop, you will soon wear out your welcome with your references.

That's to be expected when you consider all the questions hiring managers, HR personnel and staffing agency recruiters pepper your references with. How would you like it if you constantly received multiple calls out of the blue from complete strangers calling you and asking you multiple questions as if you were the one interviewing for the job instead of your friend? You'd get pretty tired of these calls after a while too.

Use your references as leverage to get recruiters to do what you want them to do for you. Oftentimes, when a recruiter asks me for my references, I'll tell them I don't provide my references until after I've completed the job interview. This does two things. First, it forces the recruiter to submit my resume to the employer and get me a job interview. Secondly, it prevents a ton of recruiters from constantly badgering my references with phone calls and emails asking them a bunch of questions about my fitness for work.

Here are some things you should get from the recruiter before handing over that all-important list of references:

- **The job description:** You need to see the job description first to determine if the job is even a good fit for your skill sets. No use handing over your references for a job you don't plan to pursue.

The job description will also help you with preparation for the job interview if you decide you want to interview for this position. In chapter 8, I go over how you can use the job description to help prepare you for a successful job interview.

- **The location (city) of the job's worksite:** As with the job description, if you have no desire to work in the city where that job is located, there is no reason for you to provide your references to the recruiter.

- **A negotiated salary:** Don't hand over your references before you negotiate your salary and benefits with the recruiter. If the job does not pay the type of salary or benefits you're looking for, there's no reason to give your references to the recruiter.

- **A job interview first:** This is the most important reason for withholding your references from the recruiter. Use your references as leverage to get the recruiter to submit your resume to the employer and get you that all-important interview. No job interview; no references.

I've gotten recruiters to provide me all of these things I listed, including a job interview, before I gave them my references. This is what I mean by quid pro quo. Once the recruiter gives me what I want, I'll give them the references they want.

So what type of questions are hiring managers, HR personnel and staffing agency recruiters asking your references?

To answer this question, the following list shows some typical questions hiring managers, HR personnel and staffing agency recruiters ask your references (managers or co-workers):

- What are [job candidate's] skills, strengths or strongest attributes?

- What are [job candidate's] weaknesses or areas needing improvement?

- In what areas will [job candidate] need additional training, coaching or support?

- What is [job candidate] like to work with in the office?

- How would you describe [job candidate's] interpersonal skills?

- How did [job candidate] get along with other people?

- What was [job candidate's] personality or character like in the workplace?

- How well does [job candidate] work in a team environment?

- What were [job candidate's] duties in their position?

- How would [job candidate] best be managed by the manager?

- Did [job candidate] have any discipline problems?

- How was [job candidate's] punctuality and attendance?

- What would you say motivated [job candidate] the most?

- How far do you see [job candidate] growing professionally?

- Why did [job candidate] leave their job in your workplace?

- What was [job candidate's] work performance like?

- What kind of work ethic did [job candidate] have?

- What was [job candidate's] biggest accomplishment?

- Did [job candidate] work from this start date to this end date while working in your company?

- Would you rehire or recommend [job candidate] for rehire?

How to Manage Your Job References

There's a right way and a wrong way in handling your job references. Here's an overview of some dos and don'ts concerning managing your references.

Do this with your references:

- **Gather at least 5 references.** Most recruiters and hiring managers ask for 2–3 professional references—people who worked with you in past jobs. They do not want references of family, friends or people from your social network. Oftentimes, you will be asked to provide at least your last two managers as references. Therefore, you should collect reference information from your last 2–3 managers, supervisors or team leads.

    Obviously, you should not provide any manager, supervisor or team lead references when you are currently working with those leaders; and you don't want them to know you're looking for work elsewhere. It's been said that the best time to look for work is while you still have a job. A call from a recruiter to one of your managers in your current job might result in you having to look for work while unemployed.

- **Include the full name, job title, email address and phone number of your references.** Some hiring managers, HR personnel and staffing agency recruiters prefer to communicate with your references via email while others want to call them. Having both the email address and phone number of your references helps reduce delays in contacting your references.

- **Ask your co-worker, colleague or managers first before using them as your reference—always.** Never assume someone will automatically be a reference, especially a good reference, for you just because you worked with them. It's important you get their permission first before subjecting them to the 10–15 questions recruiters or HR personnel will be asking them about you.

    It's equally important to get some assurance from them that they will be a "good" reference by asking them a simple question such as, *"Can I count on you to give me a favorable reference?"* If they have to pause or hesitate to answer, you might want to skip them and try asking another co-worker.

    Oftentimes, that reference will provide you their personal email or phone number so that reference can respond to email or phone call inquiries outside of work. In many workplaces, the manager works alongside people who are your references. Most references prefer to not have their manager hearing this phone conversation they're having with your recruiter about you.

- **Provide your reference with a copy of your resume or at least the portion of your resume when you both worked together.** This way, your reference has something to remind them about your performance. They can use that information as reminders and examples when answering questions from the recruiter.

- **Let your references know you are in the job market, and someone might be contacting them.** This way, your references are not caught off guard when they are contacted. This is also a good time to provide your references with a copy of your resume or an excerpt of the portion of your resume when you both worked together.

- **Update your reference list as you move on from one job to the next.** A reference older than 10 years is too old, unless of course if you've been working in the same job for the past 10 years. If you've been working in multiple jobs over the past 10 years, get references in your most recent jobs.

Don't do this with your references:

- **Include your references in your resume.** That's like posting your credit card information on social media—they can use it anytime they want; and believe me, recruiter's will. Your references will become inundated with email and phone call inquiries. That's the quickest way to turn your dream references into your worst nightmare. Additionally, no need to appear like Captain Obvious by including a statement in your resume that you can provide references upon request. Recruiters and employers already know that.

- **Use friends or social network who have not worked with you as references.** The person calling your references wants to talk to someone who has worked with you so that they can ask questions related to your work performance, character and work ethic on the job, strengths and weaknesses in the workplace, and other work-related questions.

- **Provide your references before you've had a chance to review the job description.** Never give your references until you've seen the full job description and decide to move forward with that job opportunity. Once you have the job description, you'll know if the job is even worth pursuing. If it is not what you're looking for, no need to trouble your references over a job opportunity you're not going to pursue.

- **Provide your references before you've negotiated your salary for the open position.** Never give references until you know what the hourly rate or annual salary you can get for the job. It's possible the job might pay below what you're willing to accept. If that's the case, no need in subjecting your references to inquiries for a low-paying job that you have no plans on accepting.

- **Provide your references before you know where the job is located or other details about the job.** Never give your references until you know the location of the job site. There are going to be many jobs you won't accept after you find out it's in another state or in a city outside of your desired commute. If the job is not located in your desired areas, no need to provide the recruiter with your list of references.

    Other details you might want to know about the job before giving the recruiter your references are the working hours (the job may be a swing shift, night shift or rotating shift); how much travel is involved (some jobs require you 25%, 50% or 75% travel); or exempt or non-exempt position.

- **(Optional) Provide your references before you have an interview scheduled or before you completed the job interview.** As I mentioned, you should get something in return for your references. Oftentimes, I'll use my references as leverage to force the recruiter to get me the job interview. When the recruiter asks me for my references, I tell them I don't provide my resumes until after the job interview because I don't want to stress out my references by too many contacts from recruiters. Sure, this is taking a risk, but it's a risk I'm willing to accept. No risk, no reward.

Some recruiters will not attempt to schedule me with an interview with the employer without my references. I've also had many recruiters agree to wait until after the job interview to collect my references. My rule of thumb concerning references is this: protect your references and do not give them until after the staffing agent has arranged an interview for you.

What about if you are a reference for someone else and a recruiter emails you questions about your friend's work performance, character and other traits? If you provide written answers, make sure you save your answers. There's a good chance you'll be asked those same questions again by another recruiter. This will save you time in responding to their questions again. You can also use these responses for other co-workers who are using you as their reference.

CHAPTER SEVEN
Negotiating Your Salary

You have to learn the rules of the game.
And then you have to play better than anyone else.
Albert Einstein

Few things can invigorate and supercharge your career more than to negotiate the highest salary you've ever received for a job. In contrast, few things can take the wind out of your career sails more than starting a new job knowing you are being paid a salary much lower than what you know you're worth. The way to increase your chances of negotiating a higher salary each time you look for work is by learning the rules of the game; and then playing better than anyone else. In this chapter, I'm going to teach you how to do that.

Before we do a deep dive into this section on negotiating your salary and benefits, let's go over three key rules right from the start:

1. **If it's not in writing, it never happened.** In other words, whatever salary and benefits you negotiate and agree upon with staffing agencies, hiring managers or HR representatives; you must get it in writing in order for it to become legally binding by law.

2. **The best time to increase your salary** is when you are job-hunting.

3. ***YOU*** decide what your annual salary is going to be for each job; not the employer, not the staffing agency, not any company.

If it's Not in Writing, it Never Happened

That's right; I'm playing this record again because it's especially important as we enter this chapter on negotiating your salary and benefits.

We're going to go over a variety of ways to increase your salary during negotiations. You're about to learn how to play this game of salary negotiations better than recruiters, hiring managers and HR personnel. However, none of this advice will do you any good if you don't get it in writing afterward. Don't let all your hard work in learning and applying these lessons be in vain.

Make sure that whatever salary and benefits the employer has promised you; or you negotiated with the recruiter; or you expect to receive is put in writing in your contract offer letter. If it's not in writing, it never happened. If it's not in writing, the employer is not obligated to pay you or give you what you negotiated for or what you thought you were going to receive. If it's not in writing, make the recruiter or employer put it in writing on your contract offer letter before you sign the offer letter.

The Best Time to Increase Your Salary is When You're Job Hunting

I've gone over this subject in chapter 1 when I stated *your highest raise is the salary you negotiate.* The best time to increase your salary is during your search for a new job. That's good news if you are currently looking for a new job. It's a much better time than asking for salary raises after you have the job. Why? Because you can make more money at the start of a job than you can by asking for more money in raises after you've been working in that job. The time to increase your salary to where you want it to be at is not after you are in that job. The best time to increase your salary is while you negotiate your salary for that job before you sign the offer letter.

The quickest way to increase your salary for a job is to start off by asking for the highest possible salary when you are first hired for that position. This strategy works better than accepting that job at a lower salary; and then expecting to receive annual raises to increase your salary to the level you'd like it to be at.

You Decide What Your Salary Is

Before the ink is dry on your signature on a job offer letter signifying your acceptance of a specific hourly rate or annual salary for a new job, the decision to pay you that amount of compensation was made by *you*, not the employer.

Just because a hiring manager, human resources (HR) rep or staffing agency recruiter or account manager tells you what they are offering you for a particular job; that does not mean you have to acquiesce to accepting that offer without a contested response. When it comes to your annual income that a company will pay you for a position in that company, you have carte blanche to negotiate with them for more money however way you see fit.

Ultimately, you have the power to say **NO** to any compensation—hourly rate or annual salary—that is being offered to you for a job. You have the leverage of saying no and walking away from any job offer if the money is not at the right figure you want it to be at for that job opportunity you are considering. Sure, saying no to a job offer runs the risk of the employer, hiring manager, HR rep or staffing agent recruiter or account manager withdrawing the job offer from you. So what; it doesn't diminish the fact that you can say no to any salary offer and give them a counter-offer asking for more money. You have the power to walk away from any job offer that does not meet your salary requirements. That power no one can ever take away from you.

You are not committing a business mistake or a job-hunting faux pas by not accepting the hourly rate or annual salary someone is offering you for a job. It is your right and responsibility to say no to a salary offer; to negotiate a better salary for yourself and your family; to ask for more money; and to let a company know you will walk away from their offer if it doesn't meet your desired compensation.

It's important that you understand this fundamental principle of salary negotiations before we go any further because what follows in this chapter is predicated on the fact that you have the power and the right to negotiate your desired hourly rate or annual salary. Your future employers, hiring managers, HR reps and staffing agency recruiters and account managers already know and understand this principle. Now it's time for you to embrace this truth too.

I mentioned in the opening chapter of this book that life is a competition; and the person with the right technique wins in that competition. I also said that whether you are building a relationship, building a business, building a nation or building your career; **knowledge, power** and **control** will give you the upper hand and leverage for success in every endeavor in life. This game of wits, this competition of salary negotiations you will engage in with recruiters, HR reps and hiring managers is a game of knowledge, power and control. The one who knows the rules of the game and can apply that knowledge with proper technique will have the greatest power and control over the negotiation process—and will come out the winner. I'm not talking about control to win at the counter of a National Car Rental agency; I'm talking about winning at the salary negotiations table.

Much of what you're about to learn in this chapter is going to give you knowledge, power and control over the salary negotiation process in order to help you increase your salary in your next job search. That's good news when you plan to move on to your next job. That's even better news if you're already on the move in the job search process.

Now that you have these three key rules under your job-hunting ninja belt, let's get started.

There are several ways that conversations about your salary get started with recruiters and account managers of staffing agencies and hiring managers of companies. Sometimes the recruiter or account manager of the staffing agency or hiring manager of a company will initiate discussions about salary first. Other times, job-hunting candidates start the conversation rolling about salary.

We'll cover these salary negotiation conversations between staffing agencies and job-hunting candidates in this chapter. Hiring managers or other interviewers may also try to engage in salary negotiations with you during your job interview. I'll go over how you should respond to those hiring manager and interviewer salary questions when I cover interviews in chapter 9.

Salary Negotiations Initiated by Recruiters

Before a staffing agency recruiter attempts to arrange an interview for you with a corporation or US government client, the recruiter will oftentimes attempt to establish your desired hourly rate or annual salary for the position before submitting your resume to the employer.

When it comes to talking about money with recruiters or account managers of staffing agencies, throw out whatever you've learned or were told concerning not discussing salary in a job interview. Talking about money with a recruiter or account manager of a staffing agency is not a job interview. It is a conversation you are having with a staffing agency outside the realm of the job interview. Your discussion about both salary and company benefits, such as health and dental insurance, is perfectly acceptable and expected of you by staffing agencies.

When the Recruiter Asks You What is Your Salary Expectation

It is very common for recruiters to initiate salary negotiations with you by asking you one of these simple questions:

"What is your salary expectation?"

"What is your desired compensation?"

Your salary expectation or desired compensation is the amount of money apart from the benefits package you want to be paid once you are hired. Your salary expectation or compensation is in addition to the standard benefits, such as medical or dental benefits, offered by the staffing agency, private company or US government agency. This dollar amount can be expressed either as an hourly rate or an annual salary.

You may have not realized it but the moment the recruiter mentions your salary expectation or desired compensation, you officially enter into salary negotiations with that recruiter for the job they are hoping to fill with you. That's the moment you need to put on your game face because the amount you agree to—following their simple question about compensation—is what is going to be written in your job offer letter and become your permanent wages for the length of your contract for that job.

Again, now is the time for you to talk about these things with the recruiter—your big brother or big sister. You should not discuss your salary with the hiring manager or other interviewers during your job interview.

If you're not sure what hourly rate or annual salary you should ask for as compensation for a job opportunity, you can ask the recruiter what is the compensation range for this job opportunity. It never hurts to ask the recruiter about the hourly rate or annual salary for the job if you don't know. I've asked recruiters this question many times to get a feel for what the job market is paying for positions in my local area.

When I want to make sure I don't ask for a salary that's so high that I price myself out of the market, I'll ask the recruiter, *"What is the rate the employer is paying for this job because I'd like to stay within the employer's range?"* I've asked this question many times; and recruiters have always been willing to tell me the employer's range if they know it.

Just make sure you decide ahead of time the minimum amount of compensation—hourly rate or annual salary—you are willing to accept. This way you do not short sell yourself in the moment, agreeing to take less money than you normally would, had you had the time to think it over carefully.

You can also find out salary information for different job markets at online salary websites, such as salary.com, glassdoor.com and payscale.com.

A Specific Compensation is better than a Salary Range

Whenever a recruiter asks you for your salary expectation during a phone or email conversation, do not give a range to the recruiter. If your answer is: *"My salary expectation is between $80K and $85K per year"*; in all likelihood, the recruiter will set your salary at $80K/year—not $82K/year or $85K/year as you had hoped. Trust me on this one; I've had this happen to me several times when I gave recruiters a salary range.

Some recruiters would rather err on the side of caution—by choosing the lower salary for you—to increase your likelihood of being hired, especially if they know there are other candidates in the mix with similar skill sets and qualifications as you. The recruiter knows that the higher your annual salary is, the higher their commission is. However, the recruiter also knows that they work for the employer; and if you don't get hired, they don't get paid a commission.

The lesson here though is that you must ask for exactly what you want to be paid. Don't leave it up to the recruiter to decide what to pay you within a certain range because that leaves the door open for the recruiter to choose the lowest amount in your range. This lower salary will become concrete in your job offer letter after you successfully pass your interview and are hired for the job.

So if you want $85K/year, **ask for $85K**! Don't beat around the bush by giving what you think is an acceptable salary range to the recruiter, hoping the recruiter is going to pick toward the higher range. They won't. You may be sadly disappointed like I was many times after giving recruiters a salary range. If you want $100K/year, **ask for $100K**; if you want $120K/year, **ask for $120K**. Just make sure your skill sets can back up your desired salary expectation.

Be direct when asking for the salary you want. I've always been direct with staffing agency recruiters or account managers by telling them the six figure annual salary I want to be paid for an open position; and most times, they would agree to pay me that amount.

Of course, asking for more money comes with a measure of risk. Don't forget you are competing with other candidates who may be willing to accept less for that available position. Your resume could be one of several resumes the recruiter is submitting to the employer for that same position, in addition to possibly 10–15 other staffing agency recruiters submitting resumes for that same position. The higher you set your salary, the higher the risk of the employer hiring a less costly candidate. It's a balancing act between supply and demand in the job-hunting ecosystem.

Here's your strategy in that job-hunting ecosystem: You have to ask for as high a salary as possible while managing and minimizing the risk of being overlooked by the employer because candidates with similar skill sets and qualifications as you are asking for less. However, with greater risk comes greater reward.

The world is filled with people who became successful, rich and famous because they accepted and chose the greater risk instead of settling for the path of least resistance.

It never ceases to amaze me wherever I've worked; there were always people in my workplace that were smarter and more experienced than me who were making less money than me. It's all because of how each of us negotiated our salaries. They chose to play it safe by asking for less money either because of lack of knowledge about their worth or fear of not being hired for the job. I chose to take the risk and asked for a higher amount during salary negotiations. This lopsided salary difference in the workplace happens all the time based on each person's awareness of their monetary worth and their technique in salary negotiation skills.

When the Recruiter Tells You What the Salary Is

If the recruiter already knows what the employer is willing to pay for the job opening, the recruiter may initiate salary negotiations with you by telling you upfront what the hourly rate or annual salary is for the job opportunity. If that happens, you simply have to decide if that salary is the amount you're looking for in your next job. If it is in your acceptable salary range, let the recruiter know you accept their stated salary and are willing to move forward toward submitting your resume to the employer in hopes of securing a job interview.

However, if the quoted salary is below your desired compensation, you can refuse the compensation quoted by the recruiter and ask for more money right on the spot; or you can decline the job opportunity. If you ask for more money, the recruiter now has to decide if they or the employer are willing to pay you the higher compensation you asked for; or decline your counter-offer and move on to other candidates their ATS system has identified for this job opportunity.

If the recruiter quotes an hourly range (such as $39/hour to $41/hour) or a salary range (such as $80K/year to $85K/year) to you for a job opportunity, you should immediately ask for the higher range ($41/hour or $85K/year, respectively). Why? Because of two reasons:

1. You're a free agent.

2. The recruiter would not have mentioned that higher end of the salary range if they or the employer were not willing to pay that amount for the position.

As a free agent negotiating your own salary, you have greater freedom and control to ask for a higher salary. So negotiate; only do it in a way that works to your advantage, not the recruiter's advantage. Do what free agents do which is ask for more money, not less.

As a free agent, you have the right to take advantage of every opportunity the recruiter gives you to come out on top in the negotiation process. If the recruiter gives you a salary range, always ask for the high end of the range as your desired salary. You have nothing to lose and everything to gain by asking for the higher compensation range quoted by the recruiter.

Salary Negotiations Initiated by Job Candidates

You can choose to initiate salary negotiation discussions with a staffing agency recruiter or account manager when communicating over email, text or by phone. I prefer to do this by email instead of by phone because email conversations are more impersonal conversations than talking on the phone. I can be more direct with the recruiter via email than I normally am over the phone.

Here's how I go about initiating the salary negotiation conversation with a staffing agency recruiter:

When I am contacted by a staffing agency recruiter, I first ask for the job description if it is not included in their email or if they contacted me by phone. Once the staffing agent emails me the job description, I can decide if I should ask for a compensation that is below a predetermined dollar amount or above that predetermined amount based on the responsibilities listed for the job. Only you know what that dollar amount is. My predetermined dollar amount is $100K/year. If I'm corresponding via email, I can take my time thinking about what salary I want for this particular job above or below $100K without the recruiter breathing down my neck over the phone.

Oftentimes, when I ask the recruiter for the job description via email, the recruiter responds by not providing me the job description. Instead, the recruiter requests I call them to discuss the position further over the phone.

When that happens, try these three tips to get the job description you want from the recruiter:

1. **Give the recruiter the silent treatment:** When the recruiter doesn't want to give me the job description, I don't call the recruiter or respond to their email reply. I just wait a day or two without saying anything to the recruiter. What happens over this waiting period is the recruiter gets the message from my silence that I will only deal with them until they send me the job description. They usually end up emailing me the full job description after a couple of days have passed. Once I have the job description—Bingo! Now I can make my decision about my salary.

   "*What if the recruiter decides to flip the script and gives me the silent treatment?*" you ask. You have one of two choices. You can give in and call the recruiter to discuss the job further or you can walk away from that recruiter.

   I always choose the latter because: (1) there are plenty of other recruiters out there; so I don't have to come groveling to any recruiter for the job description. I can get the job description from another recruiter; and (2) I want to see the job description first before I go any further in conversations with any recruiter. This saves me the hassle of having to go through all the questions recruiters like to ask job-hunting candidates. This is a waste of my time if the job description turns out to be something I'm not interested in.

2. **Ask for the job description again:** This leaves no question in the recruiter's mind what you want. Email the recruiter again and tell them you prefer not to move forward in discussions until after you've had a chance to review the job description. Then give them the silent treatment again until they send you the job description.

3. **Call the recruiter:** This doesn't mean the recruiter will give you the job description. It just means you are now playing by the

recruiter's rules instead of your own rules. The recruiter basically wants to find out more about you before they decide whether or not to provide you the job description. Bottom line is the recruiter is now in control, not you.

Once I have the job description and I've decided what salary I want for the position, that's when I will initiate salary negotiations with the recruiter. I will email the recruiter back and I will either tell them what hourly rate or annual salary I want for the job, or I can ask them what hourly rate the employer is willing to pay for the position.

Telling the Recruiter What Salary You Want

If you choose to tell the recruiter what hourly rate or annual salary you want for the job, **always try to ask for more than what you made at your last job**. This way, you continue to increase your salary with each new job. Remember: the best time to increase your salary is when negotiating your salary for a new job.

As I stated earlier, initiating salary negotiations by telling the recruiter what compensation you want for the job opening always comes with some risks. The first risk is that the price you're asking may be too high for the job. If that's the case, the recruiter may decide to pass on you. On the other hand, the recruiter may attempt to continue the salary negotiation conversation with you by simply telling you that your asking price is above or outside the range of the employer's budget. In other words, the recruiter may have told you the asking price is too high, but they did not tell you *goodbye*. That means the recruiter still wants to negotiate your salary with you in order to come to a dollar amount that everyone—you, the recruiter and the employer—can agree upon.

Another risk in telling the recruiter what salary you want is you might actually be asking for **less** than what the employer is willing to pay for the position. In this case, you sold yourself short; and the recruiter and employer will be happy to oblige you. In most cases, the recruiter will make your lower salary request your contract salary if you are hired for the job. In some cases, the recruiter will tell you that the employer is offering a higher salary than what you're asking. The recruiter is revealing this information to you because they feel confident you're a good fit for the job; and they know your higher annual salary translates to them receiving a higher commission on your first year's annual salary.

If you like the job opportunity and are willing to lower your desired compensation, then tell the recruiter you are willing to stay within the budget of the employer. Then ask the recruiter what the employer is willing to pay for the job. All of this conversation is a normal form of salary negotiations between job-hunting candidates and recruiters.

Asking the Recruiter What Salary the Employer is Willing to Pay

Sometimes, your safer bet is to initiate salary negotiations by simply asking the recruiter what the employer is paying for the position. I will oftentimes do this when I'm not certain what the employer is willing to pay for the job; and I don't want to miss out on the employer's higher salary offering. When I've asked this question with past recruiters, I've been happily surprised many times to find out the employer was willing to pay a higher salary than I was planning on asking for the job.

As I'm writing this piece right now, I just happened to be having an email conversation with a staffing agency recruiter about a job opportunity at the same time—*in real-time*. A couple of days ago, I asked this recruiter to send me the job description just as I'm advising you to do. I just received the job description from the recruiter a couple of minutes ago.

Based on what I see in the responsibilities for this job, I've decided I want to ask the recruiter for a 6-figure salary. However, I'm not sure if I should ask for a higher or lower 6-figure salary. I decided to go with a lower 6-figure salary for the job to be safe.

Since I'm in the middle of writing this section on initiating the salary negotiations, I thought I'd try a little experiment. Instead of telling the recruiter what salary I want for the job, I'm going to ask the recruiter what the employer is paying for this job.

I emailed the recruiter right this moment asking her what the employer was willing to pay for the position.

A couple of minutes have passed . . .

The recruiter emailed me back just now and said, "*The client (employer)* asked us *(staffing agency)* to not disqualify anyone based on pay. So whatever rate you think is fair for you at this point in your career we can consider.*"

Hallelujah! At this point I emailed the recruiter back telling her the higher 6-figure salary I wanted.

I'm waiting again for her response . . .

Boom!—I just got an email from the recruiter saying, "*I believe this rate would work.*"

That's what you call a successful salary negotiation. No fuss, no mess. Just *show me the money*. You can do this too. Initiate the salary negotiations with your next recruiter and see what happens. You too can be pleasantly surprised at what your future employer is willing to pay you for your next job if you just ask for more.

Ask For More Money

This simple, brief conversation about monetary compensation you will have with recruiters will take less than 5 minutes to communicate but it is one of the most critical components of money matters decisions you will ever make in your life should you be hired for the job.

Do you want to continue being paid the same wage throughout your career or are you looking to increase your salary with each new job? If you're like most of us in the workforce, you want to increase your knowledge, experience and **salary** with each new job.

Give yourself permission to ask for more money.

So do yourself a favor and ask for more money when you can. Give yourself permission to ask for more. You're not being greedy; you're just being a smart, informed and confident job-hunter. You understand the risks and you're willing to take them to increase your quality of life.

Whether you are asking for a raise, negotiating salary over the phone or email, or responding to a job offer letter; don't believe the hype from recruiters, HR reps or hiring managers telling you that you have to justify your request for more money. Recruiters, HR reps and hiring managers use this tactic of making you justify your worth to **control** and manipulate you during the salary negotiation process.

Their goal is to keep you at the salary they want to pay you; not at the salary you deserve. They're not looking out for your interests; they're looking out for their company's interests.

There's only one time you have to justify your worth to your employer. It is when you've been working for your employer throughout the year. You are justifying your worth each time during your annual or bi-annual evaluations or through other regularly scheduled reporting mechanisms, such as weekly or monthly activity reports on the work you've performed for the company. In other words, you are already providing the company evidence of your worth through these means if you've worked for that company six months to a year.

Supervisors and managers in US government agencies and corporations typically ask their workers (employees and contractors) to provide them "bullets" on their performance at the end of each evaluation period, whether it is on a bi-monthly or annual basis. This is standard procedure in many workplaces. Even US military members of each branch of service provide bullet points about their performance to their supervisors at the end of each evaluation year.

This is what recruiters, HR reps and hiring managers don't want you to know: **you don't have to justify or prove anything!**

You—not the recruiter, HR rep or hiring manager—ultimately decide what you're worth. When a recruiter, HR rep or hiring manager challenges your request for more money, it just means that recruiter's, HR rep's or hiring manager's company can't afford you or are not willing to pay you what you're worth. It doesn't mean other companies can't afford you or aren't willing to pay you what you're worth. If they don't want to give you the salary you want for the job, move on to other companies that are willing to pay you what you know you're worth.

Don't take the bait of justifying your worth. Once you try to play their game of justifying the increase in your salary, you transfer the power and control of your worth from your hands into their hands. You allow them to be the judge of your worth rather than you being the judge of your own worth. The good news is they're not the ones in control. You control the value of your skill sets and you control the salary negotiation process for the value you bring to that workplace.

THE ART OF SALARY NEGOTIATION

In 2016, Von Miller, an outside linebacker for the Denver Broncos, became the highest-paid non-quarterback player in NFL history. Do you know why? Because he asked for more. However, Miller's employer was not willing to pay him more; and tried to get him to justify his worth. Miller did not play into the hands of his employer by trying to justify his worth. Miller knew his worth. Instead of giving control of his worth into the hands of his employer, Miller stuck by his guns and kept that control in his own hands. It was the art of negotiation in full display before the eyes of all the public.

This, my friend, is the art of negotiation.

In 2015, free-agent Ben Zobrist, a Major League Baseball player, agreed to a $56 million contract for four years with the Chicago Cubs baseball team. Do you know why? Because he asked for more. That decision led to another great event in his life. On November 2, 2016, Zobrist was named the MVP in the Chicago Cubs 8-to-6 win over the Cleveland Indians in the World Series; a historic event that ended the 108-year title drought for the Cubs. After he received his MVP trophy, he was handed the keys to a new car. That's what I call a payday!

When I was working as a network engineer at the Missile Defense Agency (MDA) in Colorado Springs, Colorado, an MDA colleague of mine interviewed for an IT team lead position—a potential promotion—in another section of the MDA. The recruiter of the private company he worked for offered him a minor raise in pay should he be hired for the new position. He was very upset about the salary his company planned to pay him for the higher position but he felt there was nothing he could do about it.

When he revealed to me the salary his company was offering him for his new position, I told him what I'm telling you: ***Ask for more***!

He couldn't believe I was telling him to ask for more. Although he was upset at how little his salary increase would be; he thought that if he asked for more money, his company would disapprove of his assertiveness or worse, not want to keep him. He gave me excuse after excuse why it's a bad idea to ask for more money.

My colleague was suffering from what many working people suffer from. I call it the **Oliver syndrome**. I'm referring to Oliver Twist, the orphan boy in the Charles Dickens novel by the same name.

Oliver is one of many orphans depicted in mid-19th century London where poor child labor laws trapped so many children slaving away in workhouses with little food and meager comforts given in return for their hard labor. Oliver drew the longest straw in the lot among the hungry boys to see who would ask for more gruel porridge. Oliver sheepishly approached his hard taskmasters and asked that famous line, "*Please sir, I want some more*", and then runs for his life from the punishment that ensues.

Like Oliver, so many people fear asking for more wages for their hard work, fearing the worse if they ask recruiters or their employers for more.

I told my colleague that he's the free agent in control of his desired salary, not his company; and that he sets his salary rate, not his company. *"That's how we contractors roll"*, I told him. It took me a couple of days but I finally convinced him to ask for more. I coached him to tell his company that if they don't give him the salary he wants, he'll find another company to pay him that amount after he is chosen for that new position.

Now, instead of sheepishly asking for more like Oliver, my co-worker demanded his company pay him the amount he wanted or else he would find another company that would pay him his desired salary. My colleague came back later beaming with pride and joy because his company agreed to pay him the higher amount he asked for, not the amount they wanted to pay him. I congratulated him on his successful salary negotiations with his company and said, *"Welcome to my world."* He was hired for the lead position at the salary he wanted, and the rest is history. (I'm still waiting on him to pay me for that little bit of career advice.)

There's a whole new world of higher salaries waiting for you too if you will only learn to ask for more. This is how contractors successfully negotiate their contract salaries with companies and staffing agencies all the time. While you're in the job market looking of your next job, tell yourself you are worth the increase in your annual income, and this is the time to make that dream a reality.

The old cliché **"*If you don't ask, you'll never have*"** is true concerning your response to a recruiter about your salary expectations. So don't sell yourself short in this seemingly inconspicuous, short-lived salary negotiating process with a recruiter—ask for more.

Staffing agencies oftentimes have an idea what the client—the corporation or US government agency—is willing to pay for their open positions. When you ask for more, the recruiters can let you know if what you are asking for is too high of an amount. If you are willing to accept less, that's when you should let the staffing agency know you are willing to accept less, but not beforehand. In other words, don't show all your cards until you have to. If you try this advice, you will be pleasantly surprised, as my colleague at the Missile Defense Agency, to discover more often than not that staffing agencies and employers are willing to pay you the amount you asked for. I've done this numerous times as a contractor in both US government and private job sectors; and so can you.

Asking For More with Multiple Recruiters

Along the same lines of initiating salary negotiations with recruiters and asking for more is the advantage of having more than one recruiter contact you about the same job opportunity. Since there are so many recruiters vying for candidates to fill the same job openings, you'll undoubtedly receive phone calls or emails from different recruiters for the same job. This presents a unique opportunity for job-hunting candidates wanting to increase their asking salary or hourly rate for their next job.

The goal here is to experiment with asking for more when you have multiple recruiters offering you the same job. If you are not used to asking for more, what you will gain from this technique will be an eye-opener lesson on just how much employers are willing to pay for positions they need to fill.

First, start with one recruiter and ask that recruiter for the information I suggested you get from them—the job description, worksite location, etc. It's best to do this via email instead of by phone so you'll have time to look over the information without the recruiter breathing down your neck.

Once you decide you are interested in the job description and want to go after the opportunity, select a salary or hourly rate that is higher than all your previous jobs. Ask for more than you normally would ask for the job. Ask the highest salary or hourly rate that you're able to stomach. Stretch yourself by taking a risk in asking for more. Then email the recruiter back; tell them you're interested in the job; and tell them the salary or hourly rate you want for the available position.

Usually, the recruiter will email you back saying your desired compensation is either fine or too high. If the recruiter tells you your asking price is fine, that means the employer may be paying even more than what you asked. At this point, it would be difficult to ask the recruiter for more because you already set your asking price. Whether the recruiter tells you your asking price are fine or too high, put your email conversation with the recruiter on hold and follow this next advice.

This is where the other recruiter that is offering the same position comes into the picture.

If the first recruiter told you your desired compensation is fine, select a new salary or hourly rate that is above what the first recruiter said they would be willing to pay you. Again, stretch yourself by taking a risk in asking for more. Then email the second recruiter telling them you're interested in the job and tell them the next highest salary or hourly rate you want for the available position. If the second recruiter agrees to pay you this new higher compensation, go with the second recruiter in seeking that job opportunity.

If the second recruiter tells you that your new higher compensation is too high, you have two choices. The first choice is to ask the second recruiter how much the employer is willing to pay for this position. If the second recruiter quotes a salary or hourly range that is higher than the first recruiter, you should tell the second recruiter you are willing to accept that amount and continue pursuing that job opportunity with the second recruiter. The second choice is to go back to the first recruiter, who said your desired compensation is fine, and tell the first recruiter you are willing to accept that amount and continue pursuing that job opportunity with the first recruiter.

The bottom line is you want to push the envelope as far as possible to edge of that salary negotiating table to see just how much higher you can increase your salary with your next job.

"**What about the recruiter that was dissed?**" you ask. This is nothing personal, it's just business. You're not in a love relationship with recruiters; you're in a business relationship with them. This may seem a bit harsh to some, but the reality of it is this: if the recruiter found another candidate they were certain they had a better chance of getting a commission from than you for this job opportunity, the recruiter would not hesitate to kick you to the curb. The recruiter would tell you the same thing I'm telling you: *It's nothing personal, it's just business.*

Here's some advice for those tender hearts out there that are brokenhearted over the recruiter that was kicked to the curb. Email the recruiter you passed over for another recruiter and respectfully let that recruiter know you're going to pass on this job opportunity with them.

For those not-so tenderhearted folks out there, email the recruiter you plan to pass over for another recruiter who is willing to pay you more. Tell that recruiter that another recruiter has offered you more money for the position. Tell the recruiter the salary or hourly rate the other recruiter is willing to pay you but do not reveal the recruiter's name or staffing agency. Then tell the recruiter that if they are willing to beat the other recruiter's offer, you will swap over to them. The highest bidder wins.

It's nothing personal, it's just business.

Salary Negotiations Based on Other Factors

There are other factors that staffing agency recruiters, HR reps and hiring managers will try to weigh in during salary negotiations to manipulate and control the negotiations. I'm here to demystify these factors.

College Degrees versus Experience and Certifications

The notion that you must have a master's degree or a Ph.D. to obtain a 6-figure salary is just not true in various industries. I'm living proof of that.

I only hold a bachelor's degree and yet I can easily make a 6-figure salary. Why? It's not because of my degree. It has more to do with my experience, certifications and my ability to negotiate my salary than it does with my degree.

Employers are willing to pay 6-figure salaries to professionals who possess a certain amount of knowledge, skill and experience, and who have certain types of certifications regardless of their degrees.

What's interesting and somewhat amusing to me is the fact that employers are willing to pay large salaries to professionals for different reasons. Take my own career field in IT for example. I've worked with IT professionals who had a bachelor's degree as I did but who only had lower level IT certifications, such as the Cisco Certified Network Associate (CCNA) certification, that were making a 6-figure salary as I who had several higher level certifications, such as the Cisco Certified Network Professional (CCNP) certification.

"How is that possible?" you ask.

They had the IT experience and skill that the employer wanted them to have for the job the employer wanted them to do. I, on the other hand, may have had less experience than these more experienced IT professionals, but I held more and higher level IT certifications than my more experienced colleagues. Therefore, I too was being paid a 6-figure salary because I had the IT certifications along with my experience the employer wanted me to have to do the job they wanted me to do.

I've also worked with IT professionals who had neither a bachelor's degree nor higher level certifications but still were making a 6-figure salary.

What was their secret? Again, they had the experience and skill the employer was looking for in the person they needed on their team.

I'm not knocking higher education. What I'm revealing to you about various industries is that it oftentimes takes more than higher education to make a 6-figure salary—it takes experience and certifications. The more experience and certifications you can get under your belt, the more valuable you will become to employers, regardless if you hold an undergraduate, graduate, Ph.D. or none of the above. For many employers, value is not measured in higher level education; it's measured in experience and certifications. The more valuable you become to employers, the more money you can ask for during salary negotiations.

The Salary "Depends on Experience" Statement

Oftentimes in job postings, you will notice the salary is DOE (depending on experience). Some recruiters will email you or tell you over the phone that the salary for the open position depends on experience.

Translation: The salary is negotiable just like all other negotiable salaries.

When you hear the phrase "salary depends on experience" or see the initials "DOE", you might think that you have to go through an interview first before your salary can be determined. You don't. You should always negotiate your salary with the staffing agency recruiter before you are interviewed.

The experience you have listed on your resume helps support the hourly rate or annual salary you want for the open position. After all, the recruiter wouldn't be contacting you if they didn't already decide you have the potential experience to fill the position. That in itself is leverage you have in negotiating your salary with the recruiter.

How well you think your experience matches up with the job description is also leverage you use in asking for the salary amount you want for the job. (This is why it is important to get the recruiter to provide you the full job description.)

So what does DOE mean?

It means you have to convince the recruiter your experience justifies your desired compensation; and your desired compensation has to fall within what the employer is willing to pay for their open position.

"Wait, what about that fancy 'I don't have to justify my worth to anyone' speech you just gave me?" you ask in astonishment.

That speech still stands. This is not about experience. This is about you negotiating a salary you are willing to live with for this job. If the job does not pay what you're willing to work for, you have the power and control to refuse the job, regardless of your level of experience. The reality of this situation is that your salary is not based on experience even though they advertise the job this way. Your salary is based on how well you negotiate your salary.

You've probably heard the saying that when a married couple decides to divorce, there are always three sides to their story: his story; her story; and the truth. DOE salary figures have three sides too: the recruiter's figure; your figure; and the figure the employer is willing to pay. The key with DOE salaries is to find the figure that all sides can agree upon—you, the recruiter and the client company. If they can't agree with your asking price, then it's time finalize that divorce by walking away from that job opportunity.

When the salary is dependent on experience; no one knows your experience better than you—not the recruiter nor the employer. That means you have leverage in negotiating your salary based on the value ***you***—not the recruiter, HR rep or hiring manager—place on your experience. All you have to do is believe in yourself—your experience.

You tell them what your experience is worth; they don't tell you what you're worth. If you know your level of experience is worth a certain amount of salary in your chosen career field, stick by your guns and ask for that desired hourly rate or annual salary for the value you can bring to that job. That's how you convince the recruiter your experience justifies your desired compensation—by your confidence in your experience and the salary you want for that experience; nothing more.

The bottom line is you decide—not the recruiter or employer—how much money it will take to get you to accept the job opportunity. You are the one in control here; not the recruiter or employer. That includes jobs where salaries depend on experience. Plan ahead of time the salary range you are willing to accept for a particular job and stick with that salary range regardless if the salary is DOE or not.

The recruiter most likely already has a salary range they are willing to submit a candidate for this DOE job opportunity. The recruiter wants to know if you fit within the window of their acceptable salary range. At the same time, you obviously have a target compensation you would like this job to come in at. You don't want to waste your time talking with a recruiter about a job that doesn't pay what you're looking for in salary. Therefore, the best thing to do is break the ice early with the recruiter by initiating salary negotiations.

You can start off the salary negotiations by telling the recruiter what you're looking for in compensation for the available DOE job opportunity. This will immediately let the recruiter know if your salary expectation fits within what the employer is willing to pay for this position.

If the recruiter tells you they are willing to pay your requested amount, you're good to go. You can proceed with having the recruiter submit your resume to the employer.

If the recruiter tells you your desired compensation is over the client's range, and you are willing to lower your salary quote, tell the recruiter you are willing to negotiate down. Just be prepared ahead of time on how much lower you are willing to negotiate down. This way you don't compromise beyond the limits of what you want to make for your next job. Then ask the recruiter what is the range the employer is willing to pay for the position. This will tell you what the salary ceiling is for the position. Then ask for the ceiling amount if you are willing to accept that salary amount.

HR, Hiring Managers and Staffing Agencies that Ask for Your Salary History

Some HR departments, hiring managers and staffing agencies might ask you what your salary from your last job was or from your last three jobs were. It's important to understand why they would ask this question because your answer can impact your salary negotiations; your opportunity to interview with a company; and your chances of being hired for the job. Answering this question always gives HR reps, hiring managers and staffing agencies greater leverage and control over you in your salary negotiations, interview opportunities and hiring for jobs.

Why HR Departments and Hiring Managers Ask for Your Salary History

HR reps and hiring managers work directly for their company, not for staffing agencies. It's this company client that is ultimately paying your salary, not the staffing agency. Even if a staffing agency is paying you wages, that money is originating from the company client—not the staffing agency—that hired you for the job.

HR departments and hiring managers ask for your salary history for several reasons, all of which are in the interest of their company, not for your interest or a staffing agency's interest. The company's HR and hiring manager want to know if your past salaries are higher or lower than what they are willing to pay you. If you provide them your past salary history, especially your most recent salary, they now have a baseline figure on your financial fitness for their available position.

If your previous salaries are below what the company originally planned to pay for this open position, they can now offer you a lower salary closer to what you made at your last jobs without you knowing they were willing to offer you more money for the job. After all, why should they offer a much higher salary when you were willing to accept a much lower salary in the past? Their reasoning about you salary history may not be what you wanted but that's their thinking anyway. This is playing hard ball. Only thing is, you're the ball. Although your lower salary history increases your chances of being interviewed and hired, you will be receiving a much lower salary than what the company was willing to pay for this position.

If your salary history is higher than what they originally planned to pay for this open position, they can make a quick decision on whether you are still worth interviewing, hiring and paying the higher salary; or pass over you for cheaper candidates. Your chances of being interviewed, hired or receiving your higher salary decreases with the number of candidates they get with similar qualifications as you seeking this job opportunity who are asking for less money.

Sharing your salary history before, during or after your job interview can also influence the hiring manager's decision to hire you. If an HR rep or hiring manager asks you this salary history question before interviewing you, and you answer it, they now have the option of either denying or granting you an interview based on your financial fitness for the job. If they ask this question during or after your job interview, their decision to match or beat your past salaries can be influenced by how well you performed in your interview.

In some cases, revealing your salary history could also work in your favor, particularly when your salary is upwards of $100K/year. Once you break the $100K/year salary barrier in your career, you naturally do not want to go backwards and accept a position that pays less than $100K. If you share your salary history showing you have made over $100K, it announces to the employer that they've got to pay you over $100K. If the employer's budget allows a $100K+ salary for that position, you can more easily request compensation over $100K during salary negotiations with the staffing agency recruiter or the company's HR rep.

Why Staffing Agencies Ask for Your Salary History

The motive of recruiters and account managers of staffing agencies for asking you about your previous salaries is slightly different than HR departments or hiring managers of company clients. The staffing agency could be asking for your salary history on behalf of an employer who requested the staffing agency get that information for them. Staffing agencies can also ask for this information to make their own decisions about job-hunting candidates.

Although staffing agencies technically work for company clients instead of for you, their commission is based on how much salary you will make in your first year with the client. Before recruiters can receive a commission, they have to get their candidate hired. Therefore, staffing agencies are not only concerned about how your previous salaries compare with what the employer is offering for the job; they have a personal interest in getting you hired so they can get paid. Recruiters know that the higher your first year's salary, the larger the commission they will receive.

Staffing agencies typically provide more than one candidate resume to companies looking for people to interview. If the staffing agency knows the past salaries of several candidates, they can be more selective on which resumes they will submit to companies for interviews by comparing each candidate's past salaries.

Like HR and hiring managers, if your past salaries are lower than what the employer is offering for the open position, staffing agencies can leverage your past salary information by offering you a salary that is lower than the company client's salary limit without you knowing it. This way the staffing agency makes you appear more attractive than other job-hunting candidates to a company; and hopefully, your lower salary influences the employer to hire you instead of other candidates.

So how should you respond when HR reps, hiring managers and staffing agencies ask for your salary history?

You have the right to not give them your salary history. This is your personal information and you can do with it as you please. Could that result in these people denying you a job opportunity if you refuse to provide past salaries? Absolutely, that's their right too. If this gives you pause for thought, and you choose to provide this information to people asking for it, I respect your decision. Just remember how your salary information will be used by these organizations if you provide them your salary history.

It really comes down to how much ***control*** you want over your salary information regardless of the consequences; and how comfortable you are with giving your salary history to these organizations. If you plan to stick by your guns and ask for the salary you want regardless of what you made in the past, then giving your salary information out or keeping that information private simply comes down to your personal preference. You can choose either option depending on how you want to interact with a certain HR reps, hiring managers or staffing agencies.

"What if they deny me the job opportunity because I refuse to provide them my salary history?" you ask. So what—there are plenty of other recruiters out there trying to contact you for the same or other job opportunities. Most of these other recruiters won't ask you for your salary history for the same job that another recruiter might be asking you to give.

Personally, I don't bother giving out my salary information to recruiters when they ask for it. I prefer to use the more direct and bullheaded approach when it comes to HR reps, hiring managers or staffing agencies asking me about my past salaries. I tell them I don't give out my salary history. I choose to control my salary information even if it means them refusing to consider me for an interview or the job. I prefer not to give these people that much leverage when it comes to paying me the salary I want. If they don't want to play, I'll take my marbles elsewhere and find someone who wants to play by my rules.

That's the beauty of being a free agent negotiating your own salary under your own terms.

I have made one exception to withholding my salary history. During one particular job search, I negotiated a six-figure salary with a staffing agency that they agreed to pay me should I be hired for the job. Afterward, this staffing agency asked for my salary history. Since they already agreed to pay me what I wanted, I showed them the courtesy of providing them my salary history. There was no way for the staffing agency or the company client to use my salary information as leverage to lower my salary because the staffing agency already agreed to pay me a six-figure salary I wanted. That's the reason I was doing business with this staffing agency in the first place. After my job interview with the company client, I was hired for the position. I got paid my requested salary and the staffing agency recruiter got a hefty commission. Everyone won in that situation.

Many of us who follow sports were watching the drama play out between Von Miller, the MVP of Super Bowl 50, and his team's organization, the Denver Broncos who won Super Bowl 50 against the Carolina Panthers. Miller, who was a key reason the Broncos won that Super Bowl, was now trying to win big in the post-season during his contract negotiations with the Broncos organization. Each side tried to gain the upper hand in negotiations by trying to gain more leverage than the other party. Miller chose to stick by his guns by telling the Broncos organization he would take his marbles elsewhere and not play NFL football for them in the 2016 NFL season under their franchise tag if the Broncos organization didn't play by his rules and pay him what he wanted. What is the result of his hardheaded determination? He is now the highest paid non-quarterback player in the history of the NFL with a whopping $114.5 million for a 6-year contract.

No, I'm not suggesting you'll walk away with millions if you take my more direct and bullheaded approach to the salary history question. I *am* suggesting that good things can eventually happen when sticking by your guns and playing by your own rules when it comes to negotiating your salary.

Converting Between Annual Salary and Hourly Rate

Below are two formulas for converting between annual salary and hourly rate to help you understand and determine the salary and its corresponding hourly rate you desire to be paid for an available position.

Converting Annual Salary to Hourly Rate

- **Divide the annual salary by 26 (weeks)**
  The answer will provide your pay period. A pay period is equal to two weeks of work or 80 hours. For example, if your desired salary is $100K per year: $100,000 divided by 26 equals $3,846.15 for 80 hours of work.

- **Divide the pay period by 2 (weeks)**
  The answer will provide your pay for one work week or 40 hours. For example, if the pay period is $3,846.15 per 80 hours: $3,846.15 divided by 2 equals $1,923.08 for 40 hours of work.

- **Divide the work week by 5 (days)**
  The answer will provide your pay for one work day or 8 hours. For example, if one work week is $1,923.08 per 40 hours: $1,923.08 divided by 5 equals $384.62 for 8 hours of work.

- **Divide the work day by 8 (hours)**
  The answer will provide the hourly rate for the given annual salary. For example, if the work day is $384.62 per 8 hours: $384.62 divided by 8 equals $48.08 per hour. $48.08 is the hourly rate for a $100K/year salary.

Converting Hourly Rate to Annual Salary

- **Multiply the hourly rate by 8 (hours)**
  The answer will provide your hourly rate for one work day or 8 hours. For example, if the work day is $48.08 per hour per hour: $48.08 multiplied by 8 equals $384.62 per 8 hours of work.

- **Multiply the work day by 5 (days)**
  The answer will provide your pay for one work week or 40 hours. For example, if the work day is $384.62 per 8 hours: $384.62 multiplied by 5 equals $1,923.08 per 40 hours of work.

- **Multiply one work week by 2 (weeks)**
  The answer will provide your pay period. A pay period is equal to two weeks of work or 80 hours. For example, if one work week is $1,923.08 per 40 hours: $1,923.08 multiplied by 2 equals $3,846.15 per 80 hours of work.

- **Multiply the pay period by 26 (weeks)**
  The answer will provide your annual salary for a given hourly rate. For example, if the pay period is $3,846.15 per 80 hours: $3,846.15 multiplied by 26 equals $100K per 26 weeks. $100K is the annual salary for a $48.08 hourly rate.

Table 7-1 is an annual salary-to-hourly rate conversion chart for quick reference. You can use this chart whenever recruiters, HR personnel or hiring managers ask you for your salary expectation or desired compensation.

Whenever I'm speaking with a recruiter, I always have this chart handy because I know at some point in our conversation the subject of my desired compensation will come up. I normally give the recruiter the hourly rate rounded up because recruiters usually like you to give them an hourly rate instead of an annual salary.

Table 7-1 *Annual salary-to-hourly rate conversion chart*

Annual Salary	Hourly Rate
$60K / Year	$28.85 / Hour
$65K / Year	$31.25 / Hour
$70K / Year	$33.65 / Hour
$75K / Year	$36.00 / Hour
$80K / Year	$38.46 / Hour
$85K / Year	$40.87 / Hour
$90K / Year	$43.27 / Hour
$95K / Year	$45.67 / Hour
$100K / Year	$48.08 / Hour
$105K / Year	$50.48 / Hour
$110K / Year	$52.88 / Hour
$115K / Year	$55.29 / Hour
$120K / Year	$57.70 / Hour
$125K / Year	$60.10 / Hour
$130K / Year	$62.50 / Hour
$135K / Year	$64.90 / Hour
$140K / Year	$67.31 / Hour
$145K / Year	$69.71 / Hour
$150K / Year	$72.12 / Hour

It's All Fun and Games until Someone Gets Hurt

Since contractors normally do not reveal their salaries to their colleagues they work with, employers can take advantage of *the silence of the lambs* to slay another job-hunter during salary negotiations.

If truth be told, corporations and staffing agencies prefer you remain in the dark about the maximum salary they're willing to pay you. They're better off paying you a salary well under budget, especially when you think you're being paid well enough for your position. All parties are happy. You're a happy camper because you're employed with what you consider is a descent salary; the staffing agency is happy because they got a decent commission out of the deal; and the employer is happy because they got you for a lot less than they were actually willing to pay you. (*If you don't ask, you'll never have.*)

Happy, that is, until you have that unsanctioned conversation with your fellow contractor about their salary. Ignorance is bliss until you find out what your co-worker is making for doing the same job as you.

Negotiating Relocation Benefits

Sometimes, getting the job or salary you want may require you to move to another city or state or country. This is called relocation or simply "relo". Before you accept the new position, you have to weigh your decision about relocating to the new job location in terms of "opportunity cost".

As I mentioned in chapter 1, opportunity cost is an economics term that simply means a benefit, profit or value of something that you must give up in order to receive something else of benefit, profit or value.

The opportunity cost question you need to ask yourself is: Does the new job, location, salary and company benefits (benefit, profit or value) outweigh the benefit, profit or value of my current status and location; and the cost of my time, energy and expenses to relocate to this new location?

Before you can answer this question fully to yourself, you must know what relocation benefits, if any, the new employer is willing to give you for moving to the new job location.

What are Relocation Benefits

Relocation benefits are what the new employer is willing to pay you or give you to help you with your relocation move and the expenses you will incur during that move, such a such as packing and moving of household goods, storage, travel expenses and temporary lodging costs.

There are as many types of relocation packages as there are boxes of cereals in a grocery store; and each company is different when it comes to relocation benefits. Most companies that offer relocation packages will provide more benefits for senior employees than for junior employees; some companies provide relocation assistance for certain company employees only; and some companies won't offer any relocation benefits at all.

The employer's relocation package could consist of reimbursements to you for some or all of the out-of-pocket expenses you incurred while moving to the new location and getting established in your new residence. The relocation package could be a simple lump sum amount the new employer gives you to spend however you see fit to relocate. Other companies will provide you housing in their local area until you find a place of your own. Still other companies may provide job search assistance for your spouse or help in selling your old house.

If you are at the top of the relocation food chain, such as a relocation move for Google employees, you could be provided the options of a cash lump sum, corporate housing, packing/unpacking and moving benefits or a combination of these. If you're at the bottom of this food chain, you'll be lucky if you get a *McDonald's Happy Meal*.

Income Tax Exemptions for Job Relocations

Uncle Sam helps job-hunters who relocate for a job by giving them a tax deduction for their moving expenses (moving costs, storage, etc.) if the relocation relates to starting a new job or a job transfer for their new employer.

To qualify for this IRS deduction, the distance between your old home and the new job location must be more than 50 miles. Additionally, you must work full-time for the new company for a minimum of 39 weeks during the first 12 months of being hired.

On the flip side of this tax coin, the money you receive for a relocation move is fully taxable by the IRS as part of your annual earnings. Your new employer is required to report this relocation dollar amount to the IRS at the end of the tax year.

Either the IRS or your new employer may require you to verify your expenses with your receipts. Therefore, it is important you obtain and keep all your receipts for every relocation expense.

For a complete explanation of the IRS rules on deducting your taxes for relocation, see IRS Publication 521 at http://bit.ly/2dtPqMj.

So when is the best time to negotiate relocation benefits?

The same time you negotiate your salary. The same rules apply for company benefits, including relocation benefits, as for salary increases—if you don't ask, you can't have.

In order to save money, some companies won't offer you any relocation assistance unless you ask for it or negotiate it while negotiating your salary. The key is to *ask* for it if a new job requires you to relocate.

If you're using a staffing agency recruiter, you can bring up the subject of relocation benefits anytime in your conversation just as with talking about your salary. If you are in a job interview, you should never bring up the subject of relocation benefits just as it is taboo to ask about salary and other benefits in a job interview.

If you're dealing directly with your potential new employer, you must wait until you have been selected for the job to initiate a conversation about salary and benefits, including relocation benefits. If your new employer provides you an offer letter for the job; that is the perfect time discuss a relocation package either with the hiring manager or the company's HR department that sent you the offer letter. When the employer agrees to pay for your relocation expenses, make sure they put it in your offer letter. You know what I'm going to say next: *if it's not in writing, it never happened.*

Since relocation packages vary with every company, make sure you ask for as much as you can from the start. Let the company tell you what they won't pay or give you in your relocation request.

Here are some ideas for what you can ask for when negotiating your relocation benefits with your new employer:

- A lump sum payment that pays for 30–90 days of expenses for temporary housing for you and your family to find a home to move in.

- One or two employer-paid trips (including airfare, hotel, meals and a rental car) to the new location for house-hunting purposes, checking out schools for children, etc.

- Company-paid temporary housing in a hotel, condo, apartment or home for 30–90 days for you and your family to find a home to move in.

- Company-paid movers to pack and move your household goods; and deliver and unpack your household goods once you find your new residence. Make sure this benefit includes both packing/unpacking and moving.

- Storage fees for your household goods until you find a home to move into.

- A cash stipend used to pay for miscellaneous expenses, such as food, gas for your car, laundry, etc. during your move. If the terms of your relocation package allows, you can even use this money towards the down payment of your new home, apartment or other costs.

- Paying the "break lease" fee for leaving an apartment or rental home before the end of the lease.

- Job search assistance for a spouse.

- Childcare assistance.

- Home sale and home buying services, such as paying the closing costs and/or commissions when your old home sells and/or when you purchase your new home; or compensation for your losses on the home sale.

- Shipment of a vehicle.

The bottom line is you must be able to weigh the opportunity cost of your salary and benefits including your relocation package against the cost of your relocation move to your new job. If the numbers weigh in favor of the move, go for it. If it doesn't, let the staffing agency recruiter, hiring manager or HR department know that the relocation package isn't enough to get you to move. Many companies are flexible on what's included in a relo package, and may be willing to provide you what you request if they really want you for the job.

So how do you tell recruiters and employers what you want for the relocation move?

First, make sure you let them know you like the job and you want to work for the new employer. Once you've shown your interest in the job, let them know the moving expenses are too much for your finances right now. Then give them a counter-offer of what relocation package would get you to take that position.

If they accept your counter-offer, or at least meet some of your terms to your satisfaction, you can proceed with the move. If they don't agree to your relocation terms, you have the option of trying to make the move at your own expense; ask for a higher salary to offset the moving expenses; or deny the offer.

How much higher salary should you ask for if the company denies your relo request?

You should ask for enough of an after-tax increase in salary that would be equal to your estimated costs for the move. This may sound risky asking for a higher salary to offset the cost of the relocation, but think of the risk you are taking if you do not have the resources to pay for the move. The important thing is you are in control of your decision to relocate or deny the job opportunity based on the opportunity cost.

To help you convince the person who will approve your request for relocation benefits, do some research into the costs of your move. List all of your expenses for the move. Spread the costs out for 60–90 days which is a reasonable timeframe required for finding a new home. Then provide this information to the recruiter or someone in the company who can get that information to the person who approves relocation requests.

Lastly, make sure whatever relocation agreements or approvals you receive from your new employer are put in writing. Everything your employer agreed to provide you for your relocation must be in your job offer letter and signed by the employer; otherwise, **it never happened**. You can say all you want that the employer agreed to pay the closing costs on your old or new house, but unless it's in writing, your employer is not obligated to pay those costs.

CHAPTER EIGHT
Interview Preparation and Tips

I will prepare and some day my chance will come.
Abraham Lincoln

As with many things in life, preparation is one of the keys to success. Preparation is the action behind the belief that one day, some day your chance will come to put that preparation to use. Without it, all plans, great and small, can fail. No matter how educated, gifted, talented, smart, experienced or resourceful you are—***you need preparation***. This is also true when it comes to your next job interview.

You've researched the career paths—US government agencies and private companies—and have made your selection of the job sector you will pursue. You've uploaded your resume on Internet job search websites and talked with recruiters. You've negotiated your salary with a recruiter and they submitted your resume to the employer. You beat out most of the competition from other staffing agencies, resumes and candidates; and the employer would like to interview you.

Now you have an appointment for a job interview in the next couple of days—***Congratulations***!

Everything you've done up to this point was for that job interview, but the competition doesn't end here. You are still in competition with other candidates during the interview process; and as with many job openings, only one person is going to get the job. So now is not the time to sit back, rest on one's laurels and wait for the day of your interview to arrive.

There's work to be done—it's called **pre-interview preparation**.

Carli Lloyd is the professional midfielder soccer player and co-captain of the US women's national soccer team; scoring the famous three goal hat trick within 16 minutes in that final match against Japan that won the 2015 FIFA Women's World Cup championship among 23 other international teams. She is also a two-time Olympic gold medalist and the 2015 FIFA Player of the Year. When it comes to preparation, Lloyd said, *"The harder you work and the more prepared you are for something, you're going to be able to persevere through anything."*

The same is true when it comes to preparing for your job interview.

Start With a Thank You

If you had a staffing agency help you get that job interview, your first order of business should be to thank your staffing agency recruiter or account manager for setting up your interview. In the excitement of being notified that the hiring manager wants to interview you, don't forget to take the time to thank the staffing agent that set up that all-important job interview for you. Show the staffing agent you are a classy professional by expressing your appreciation for their efforts thus far. This can be done by a simple thank you to the staffing agent over the phone following them giving you the good news about an interview or you can send a thank you email or text to the agent if you've been communicating online.

First Impressions Are Lasting Impressions

The job interview is all about making a good impression on the hiring manager and your interviewers. It starts with your first impression upon your arrival at the interview and continues throughout your interview to your last impression at the end of your job interview.

The old saying *first impressions are lasting impressions* is perhaps never more repetitively impactful in your adult life than with job interviews. The first impression you display at your job interview could mean the difference between you owning a home or losing one; paying off your debt or watching the bills pile up; having it or losing it; only dreaming it or actually living it; starting over or going under—**impactful**. Only you know just how impactful your next job interview is to you, to your loved ones and your place and status in life.

The job interview as a whole is the first and perhaps only opportunity you have to make a good enough impression on those interviewing you to influence them to either hire you for the job or invite you back for a second interview.

I'm going to help you in your preparation to make as good of an impression as you can. That's what this chapter is about.

Give Yourself Time to Prepare for the Job Interview

With preparation comes familiarity and a renewed level of normalcy in the thing prepared that produces better results, greater confidence and comfortability when you move from preparation to application. Therefore, you want to be as prepared as you possibly can before you go into the job interview so that what you are experiencing during the interview feels as familiar and normal as possible to you. This will make you feel more confident and comfortable throughout the interview process. However, preparation takes time.

Here in chapter 8, we're going to take the time to ensure you have all the information you need to know before an upcoming job interview; what you should research ahead of time; how to make a good impression with your hiring manager and other interviewers in the room; how you should dress for success; and what you should be prepared to say. This information will help you cover all the important key areas that will give you the greatest chances for success in your next interview.

In chapter 9, I'll go over all the details you need to know about the dynamics of job interviews when you are actually in the room with the interviewers; how to conduct yourself and respond in the interview to make the best impression; what things you should focus on and talk about; and what the interviewers are looking for in your answers.

I've been down this road many times and have learned what it takes to be prepared for job interviews. I'm completely confident and comfortable every time I go into a job interview because I've learned the secrets to preparing well for interviews. Now I'm going to show you how to do the same thing in these next two chapters. So rest easy; you're in good hands. (Sorry if that sounded like an Allstate commercial.)

After the staffing agency recruiter or account manager informs you that the hiring manager wants to interview you, they will ask you when you can come in for an interview (if it is an in-person interview), or when can you be interviewed over the phone. You should tell them you can interview in 2–3 days. This will allow you sufficient time for preparation, researching and planning for this interview. You should also provide a specific timeframe that fits into your work schedule (if you are employed) or personal schedule. If time is not a factor for you, you can tell the staffing agency that you will accept whatever time fits in best for the interviewer's schedule.

Do not ask for a week or more before you are ready to interview. Waiting this long will make the interviewers think you are either not interested in the job or are interviewing for other jobs before them; both of which will reflect poorly on you.

Sometimes the interviewers are under a tight interview schedule because of the number of candidates they are interviewing or due to their work priorities. In this case, the interviewers will provide you dates and times for your interview, and you simply have to pick one of those appointments.

Once you've given the staffing agency recruiter or account manager your desired interview date and time, the staffing agency will forward your requested interview appointment to the employer. If there are any conflicts in schedules, the staffing agency will let you know.

If all parties can make it to your interview appointment, the staffing agency will send you a confirmation email. This email usually includes the names of some or all of your interviewers; the address of the interview location (if it is an in-person interview) or the phone number to call (if it is a phone interview); and the scheduled date and time all parties have agreed to be present for your interview.

The following list is the key areas you should focus on when preparing for your upcoming interview:

- Appearance and attire

- The company client

- The interviewers

- The job description

- Your resume for the interview

- Certification's and experience's place in interviews

- Education's place among successful people

- Arrival at your interview

- Introductions in your interview

- Interview questions and answers

- Questions to ask the interviewers and closure

- Role playing interviews

Appearance and Attire for Job Interviews

What better way to start off our discussion about first impressions than with appearance and attire; but first a reality check.

Many employers prefer to have their first interview with you over the phone instead of in person. If this is the case, the staffing agent will let you know, and you will not have to concern yourself with this section on appearance and attire for that interview.

However, if the interviewers like how you answered their questions over the phone, they're going to either hire you for the job or they are going to ask you to come in for a second in-person interview. If the latter is true and the hiring manager wants you to come in for an in-person interview; then that's when this section will matter to you most.

How Your Appearance and Attire Makes an Impression

Whether you are asked to come in for an in-person interview once, twice or three times, you should always dress as professional in your second and third interviews as you would for the first. If you are dressed appropriately, this will start your interview off on the right foot. What you are wearing is the first thing your interviewers will notice when you arrive for the interview. Your appearance will form their first of many first impressions of you within seconds of your first meeting.

The staffing agency recruiter or account manager who submitted your resume may also be meeting you for the first time at the employer's facility. If you are dressed unprofessionally, the staffing agency may be hesitant about submitting your resume for other positions in the future if you do not pass this interview. After all, the way you are dressed not only affects the employer's impression of you, your attire is a reflection on the staffing agency's ability to find quality professionals who can dress appropriately for job interviews.

If you've been to a lot of job interviews as I have, it's not long before you notice that every time you show up for the interview looking your best in your professional-looking business suit or outfit, the interviewers are always wearing the typical casual dress people normally wear to work. If you work in the IT industry as I do, you know the look: khaki pants; worn buttonless short sleeve shirt or casual button-down long sleeve shirt with the tails hanging out; and shoes that look a bit worse for the wear.

If you've felt a bit overdressed sitting there in that room in your suit while they all get to wear casuals; just remember one thing about that interview: it *is* all about you, not the interviewers. They've all been through what you're going through in the interview process and they got the job. They were working that morning long before you arrived for your scheduled interview; and they have to keep working long after you leave. In other words, they earned the right to wear those casuals. What they're doing now, sitting across from you in their casuals, is taking time out of their busy day to focus solely on you. You're the one looking for the job; it's all about you, so enjoy the attention they're giving you despite their busy work schedule.

Your interviewers will appreciate the fact that you took your interview seriously enough to dress appropriately for the occasion, just like they had to when they were interviewed for their jobs in that company. Your appropriate response in dressing well for this job opportunity is another good first impression, even though your interviewers appear to be underdressed for the occasion. After you are hired, you'll be back to wearing the same casuals as the rest of your interviewers.

How to Dress for Visits to Recruiter Offices

When the staffing agency is in your local area, the recruiter may ask you to come in to their office first before they arrange an interview between you and the company client. Typically, you wouldn't wear a suit and tie for these meet-and-greet recruiter interviews as you would for a job interview with the company client. However, this visit at the recruiter's office is still an interview—a pre-screening interview.

The recruiter is asking you to come to their office because they want to see your personal appearance and how you present and conduct yourself.

From the time you enter the staffing agency's door and shake the recruiter's hand until you say your goodbyes in departing; the recruiter will be evaluating your appearance and their own comfort level in introducing you to potential employers.

Based on how you look and act in this introductory meeting, the recruiter will make their final decision on whether they should submit your resume to the employer or not. Therefore, dress appropriately in a business casual outfit to these meetings with recruiters. You can use some of the guidelines I provide in this section to pick out certain colors and materials in your outfit that are just as appropriate for the recruiter meeting as they are for your actual job interview.

If I decide to visit the recruiter at their office, I'll ask the recruiter if they'd like me to come in dressed in business casual or the suit I'll wear to the interview. This way, I'll know for certain how I should dress for this visit.

Prepare Your Attire Ahead of Time for the Job Interview

Once you have an appointment for an interview, one of the first things you should do is go over your business attire you plan to wear to the job interview. This is important because you may discover your business suit, outfit, skirt, shirt, blouse or shoes need cleaning, mending or replacing.

The cleaners can press and clean your clothes faster than their normal service but you'll have to pay a little extra for that. However, this still may take a day or two, hopefully in time before your interview.

Mending your clothes or shopping for something new also takes time. You do not want to be scrambling to accomplish these things the day of your interview when you're trying everything on. If you need to buy a business suit or business outfit, ask the salesperson at the clothing store for advice in picking out a conservative business suit or business outfit for a job interview. They'll be able to point you in the right direction—part of their job is to help make you look good for the right occasion.

Do yourself a favor and have a clean and pressed outfit set aside and ready for any job interview. Cover it in a plastic garment bag and hang it in your closet to keep it protected and free of lint or dust. You can purchase garment bags for as low as $6–$12 online or at your local shopping center.

Although I have several suits, I always have one suit with a clean white shirt that I only use for job interviews, covered in a garment bag hanging in my closet. The day before my interview, I pull my suit out of the garment bag; pick out a tie, belt, socks and shoes; and try everything on once as a final check to make sure all of my clothing is ready to wear the following day of my interview.

Conservative is king.

When it comes to your selection and fashion of outfits, conservative is king for job interviews. You are attending a business function, not a night out on the town or a party. Therefore, your choice of colors, material, fashion and fit in your attire should reflect this business event.

There may also be organizations in your local area that provide assistance to job-seekers with their job interview attire. For example, in my city of Denver, Colorado, there is the *Dress For Success Denver* organization that helps provide women with a network of support, professional attire and development tools to give them the greatest chance to succeed and thrive in the workplace.

I've provided you a list of conservative dress for both men and women who are preparing for their next job interviews. These colors, materials, fashion and fit are tried and true conservative choices used in every industry for job interviews. You can't go wrong with these guidelines.

Recommendations for Men's Appearance and Attire for an Upcoming Job Interview:

- **Suit:** Well-fitting, clean and pressed two-piece single-buttoned business suit with matching jacket and pants made of natural fibers such as wool; in conservative colors, such as dark navy blue or charcoal (dark gray). Do not mix colors or materials in the jacket and pants. No missing buttons, lint or smell of smoke.

- **Shirt:** Clean, pressed (or ironed yourself) long-sleeved button-down shirt in white or light blue solid color or conservative stripes. No stains around the collar or missing buttons. [For recruiter meetings: other conservative colors are acceptable.]

- **Tie:** Conservatively designed silk tie that coordinates with your suit color. Avoid bow ties, flashy ties meant for parties or night clubs, and fashion extremes such as character ties.

- **Shoes:** Cleaned and polished conservative shoes in black, dark brown or cordovan (burgundy) matching the color of your belt. Shoes can be lace-up or slip-on business shoes.

- **Belt:** Conservative belt in black, dark brown or cordovan (burgundy) matching the color of your shoes.

- **Socks:** Conservative dark single-colored socks that coordinates with, and is equal to or darker than, your pants color. The socks color should not be lighter in color than your pants. Avoid multi-colored socks with different patterns.

- **Hair and Facial:** Hair should be clean, well-kept and cut if needed. Avoid extreme or unnatural-looking hair colors during the interview. Facial hair, such as beards or mustaches, should be neatly trimmed or cleanly shaven (no stubble look). This doesn't mean you can't ever grow the stubble look or a full beard; you should wait until after you are hired to do that (contractors and employees do this all the time). Clip visible nose hairs. You can purchase an electric nose clipper at your local shopping center. No hats.

- **Mouth:** Brush your teeth and don't eat after you have brushed; otherwise, brush your teeth again. Have fresh breath (breath mints or sprays can help in this area). Don't smoke right before your interview. No gum, candy or other objects in your mouth during the interview.

- **Hands:** Clean hands; fingernails cleaned and trimmed to short length. No gloves.

- **Tattoos:** Conceal visible tattoos if possible.

- **Fragrance:** Little to no fragrance, such as cologne, after shave lotion or hair scents. Wear deodorant. Avoid smoking while in your suit to prevent the smell of smoke when in the interview room.

- **Watch or jewelry:** Conservative, nice watch (if you choose to wear one). A finger ring is acceptable, such as wedding, engagement or school rings. Other than wedding and engagement rings, the ring should be conservative, not flashy. Avoid wearing stackable rings, midi rings or multiple rings on several fingers. Avoid necklaces, bracelets and leather wraps. Avoid jewelry with political, religious or designs or insignia representing a movement or lobby. No visible body piercings.

- **Accessories:** Clean and conservative notebook, portfolio or slim briefcase (for holding unfolded resumes, notepad and writing pen). The portfolio or briefcase should coordinate with the color of your shoes. No pictures promoting your favorite sports team, movie or other images on the notebook or carrying device. No backpacks or other book bags. The interviewers normally have their own copy of your resume they received from the recruiter; therefore, a simple small notebook or portfolio should do if you need to bring these things. No need to bring documents showing your previous work unless you are told to do so before the interview.

Recommendations for Women's Appearance and Attire for an Upcoming Job Interview:

- **Suit, Dress or Skirt:** Well-fitting, clean and pressed pant suit, skirted suit or, as a last choice, a dress and blouse under a blazer or jacket. Pant suit, skirted suit or dress should be made of natural fibers such as wool or wool blend; in conservative colors, such as dark navy blue or charcoal (dark gray). Other less used but acceptable colors is neutral colors, such as beige, brown or possibly dark red or burgundy. Jacket can be 1 or 2-button. Do not mix colors or materials in the jacket/blazer and pants. If using a jacket over a dress, ensure colors match well with each other. No missing buttons, lint or smell of smoke. Dress or skirt should be of moderate length, not above the knee.

- **Blouse:** Clean, pressed (or ironed yourself) long sleeve blouse made of cotton or silk in white or another light color such as pastel. [For recruiter meetings: other conservative colors are acceptable.] Avoid low cut or sheer blouses. No stains around the collar or missing buttons. No camisole tops.

- **Hosiery:** Clean in neutral color such as tan or sheer black. Avoid white nylons. No runs or holes.

- **Shoes:** Cleaned and polished, conservative, moderate height heels or pumps (1–1 ½ inch) or flats in black, dark brown or cordovan (burgundy) matching the color of your belt.

- **Belt:** If used, should be conservative in black, dark brown or cordovan (burgundy) matching the color of your shoes.

- **Hair and Facial:** Hair should be clean, conservative and worn in a comfortable fashion, yet a polished, stylish look that's free of frizz and flyaways. Wrapped sleek-looking ponytail or bun, top not or French twist are acceptable. Avoid hair styles that cover your face or eyes during the interview. Avoid extreme or unnatural-looking hair colors during the interview. Makeup should accentuate your facial features and make you feel confident and comfortable without overdoing it or going to extremes, such as in a runway fashion show. Avoid using eyeshadow, smoky eye, double wing, cut crease or cat's eye makeup to an interview (save that look for your night out on the town). Clip visible nose hairs. You can purchase an electric nose clipper at your local shopping center. No hats.

- **Mouth:** Brush your teeth and don't eat after you have brushed; otherwise, brush your teeth again. Have fresh breath (breath mints or sprays can help in this area). Don't smoke right before your interview. No gum, candy or other objects in your mouth during the interview.

- **Hands:** Clean hands with fingernails cleaned, unchipped and well-manicured. Nail polish, if used, should be a conservative neutral shade, such as sheer, taupe, beige, mild pink or clear nail polish. Avoid nail art, sparkles, neons and stripes nail polish for the interview. No gloves.

- **Tattoos:** Conceal visible tattoos if possible.

- **Fragrance:** Little to no fragrance, such as perfume, lotions or moisturizers, creams, hair spray or scents. Wear deodorant. Avoid smoking while in your outfit to prevent the smell of smoke when in the interview room.

- **Watch or jewelry:** Conservative, nice watch (if you choose to wear one). Small, simple, conservative earrings or studs in gold, silver, pearl or diamond are acceptable. Avoid big hoops, dangling or whimsical motif earrings. A finger ring is acceptable, such as wedding, engagement or school rings. Other than wedding and engagement rings, the ring should be conservative, not flashy. Avoid wearing stackable rings, midi rings or multiple rings on several fingers. A conservative, thin necklace in gold, silver, pearl, or small pendant are acceptable. Avoid layered or large necklaces and large pendants. Avoid bracelets, bangles and leather wraps. Avoid jewelry with political, religious or designs or insignia representing a movement or lobby. No visible body piercings.

- **Accessories:** Clean, conservative, professional-looking notebook, portfolio or slim briefcase (for holding unfolded resumes, notepad and writing pen). The portfolio or briefcase should coordinate with the color of your shoes. Avoid bringing a purse. No pictures promoting your favorite sports team, movie or other images on the notebook or carrying device. No backpacks or other book bags. The interviewers normally have their own copy of your resume they received from the recruiter; therefore, a simple small notebook or portfolio should do if you need to bring these things. No need to bring documents showing your previous work unless you are told to do so before the interview.

Research the Company Client

In my chapter 6 discussion about recruiters, I spoke about the importance of getting the name of the company client where the recruiter wants to submit your resume, as well as getting the company address. Once you know the name of the company, you can perform a thorough online search of the company's website in addition to other information about the company on Internet search engines, such as Google, Yahoo! or Bing; or on social media sites, such as Facebook or LinkedIn.

Now that you have that company information, it's time to use that information to your advantage in preparation for your job interview. Review the following information on the company's website, social media and other online sites in preparation for your interview with that company:

- **Company's purpose and mission statement:** Familiarize yourself with what the US government agency or private company does for a living. If the company's home page does not provide this information, look in the *"About Us"*, *"Who We Are"* or *"What We Do"* sections of the company website.

  During your interview introductions, the person leading the interview will oftentimes tell you about their company as well as how the team you'll be on (if you get hired) fit into the company picture. However, you should always have a good understanding of the company's purpose, mission and goals before you go into the interview.

- **Company history and latest news:** Read about when, where and how the company was created; growth (in personnel, locations, acquisitions and annual revenue) over the years; and most recent news. This company information is usually found in the *"About Us"*, *"Who We Are"* or *"News & Events"* sections of the company website.

  When it's your turn to ask the recruiters questions or provide closing comments at the end of your interview, this is a good time to share what you know about the company in your closing conversation. Share your knowledge of recent news or other states where this company operates to show the interviewers your research and interest in their company. This will make another good impression on your interviewers because it shows you were interested enough in their company to research the company.

I usually jot down some notes about the company on a piece of paper that I bring with me to the interview. At the end of the job interview, when they ask me if I have any questions, I'll reference these notes during my closing comments.

- **Company posts and reviews:** There are other places you can look to learn about a company besides the company's own website. Today, many companies are posting their profiles on social media sites, such has LinkedIn and Facebook. If you type in the company's name using an online search engine, such as Google, Bing or Yahoo!, you can find a wealth of information about companies. There are also websites that provide reviews of companies by their employees or former employees, such as Glassdoor (glassdoor.com), Jobeehive (jobeehive.com), RateMyEmployer (ratemyemployer.ca), Kununu (kununu.com), JobAdviser (jobadviser.com.au) and TheJobCrowd (thejobcrowd.co.uk).

  You can get a better picture of the company's employees, facilities, on and off campus activities, working environment and culture by viewing the posts and pictures on these sites.

  Before one of my scheduled job interviews, I used a search engine to find information about the company and discovered the company was losing money and was recently acquired by another company. This company, which was once the headquarters, was now being run by another company that was downsizing their IT departments and personnel and moving their headquarters to another state. These were important events about the company that my staffing agency recruiter did not inform me about. However, I learned about these events before my interview because I had done my research on the company.

- **Company leadership:** Review the top brass—company President, Chief Executive Officer (CEO), Chief Financial Officer (CFO) and department leaders, especially leadership in your

Interview Preparation and Tips

department (if you know the name of the department you could be working in). Once you are hired, you will no doubt hear these names again or possibly get a visit from them while you're at work. This information is usually found in the "*About Us*" or "*Who We Are*" sections of the company website.

- **Company address:** You can verify the company address the recruiter gave you with the address on the company website. If the company's home page does not provide the company address, look in the "*Contact Us*" section of the company website.

    If the recruiter gave you the company name but not the address, looking up the company's name with an online search engine is a good way to find the address.

    Rest assured, once you have secured an in-person interview with the company, the staffing agency recruiter or company HR rep will ensure you have the company's address.

    Having the company's address, particularly knowing what city the company is located in, will help you decide if the company's location is within your desired commute. I've refused many job opportunities from recruiters simply because I did not want to drive so far through congested traffic to the city where the job site was located.

    If you are willing to commute to where the employer's company is located, and you are asked to come in for an in-person interview, the company's address will help you determine how long it will take you to drive, take a bus, train or subway to your interview from your home on time.

- **The interviewers.** Oftentimes the staffing agency recruiter or account manager will provide the names of one, some or all of the people who will be your interviewers along with the location, date and time of your scheduled interview. If the recruiter or account manager does not provide you any names of the people interviewing you, ask the recruiter or account manager to get you the names of your interviewers.

Just as you would research the employer's company, research what you can about your interviewers on social media sites, such as Facebook or LinkedIn. This will provide you valuable information about the interviewer's technical background, work history, as well as their personal interests. This information will be extremely helpful in you establishing a rapport quickly with the interviewers by showing them you are not only interested in them enough to look them up online but that you also have common interests.

This information about your interviewers will allow you to connect with them while they consider your "cultural fitness" for the job. Your cultural fitness determines your ability to fit in and work well with the members of your new team. Culturally fitness involves your appearance, personality, enthusiasm, interests, sincerity and attitude that's on display while you are answering your interviewer's questions. Your cultural fitness also involves your social skills, oftentimes referred to as soft skills.

Rarely do interviewers select a candidate for the job based solely on their "technical fit". Technical fitness is your experience, knowledge and understanding of the job that's on display when you answer technical questions.

Interviewers always take into account how well they think the candidate can fit in socially with their group, their team when considering the candidate for the job. This is your cultural fit.

By researching the interviewer's social media posts, you can find out what things the interviewers are interested in; their hobbies, favorite sports or sports teams; and their recreations or places they've visited or vacationed.

By bringing up things your interviewers are interested in, you enable the interviewers to see you more as someone they can connect with and get along with at work instead of just another distant "candidate" with no social connection. This social connection will help influence and convince your interviewers that you would make a good cultural fit on their team because of the things you have in common.

So when is the best time to mention things you have in common with the interviewers? Bring these things up at the beginning of your interview during the introductions when you are asked to tell the interviewers about yourself.

After the hiring manager or other person leading the interview introduces everyone and tells you about their company, he or she will then ask you to tell them about yourself. When the interviewer says to you, "*Tell us a little bit about yourself*", the interviewer is not simply asking you to tell them about your technical background. They are actually asking you to tell them a little something about your personal background too.

Some candidates think being asked to tell the interviewers about themselves means to go through this long-winded timeline of their past job history. This is not what the hiring manager or the interviewers are looking for when they ask you to tell them about yourself.

What the interviewers are looking for are two things:

1. Your technical fit.

2. Your cultural fit.

The way you should tell the interviewers about yourself is through the lens of your technical fitness in fulfilling the requirements outlined in the job description and your cultural fitness to interact well with your new team members. We'll cover these two areas in greater detail later in this and the next chapter.

Research the Job Description

Another piece of information I mentioned you need to get from the recruiter is the job description showing the responsibilities the person in that available position will perform.

First of all, the job description will reveal if you are capable of working, or whether you even want to work, in a job with the requirements listed in the description. The description should give you enough information to make your decision on whether or not to move forward with the recruiter in submitting your resume to the employer.

Oftentimes, a recruiter will email you a small portion of the job description when they first contact you. If the description is too short for you to make an informed decision, you should ask the recruiter to send you the full job description. I've asked recruiters many times to email me a longer job description which they have done for me.

Employers Don't Expect You to Know Everything in the Job Description

Don't be intimidated by everything you see in the job description. Rarely is a person capable of knowing or doing everything in most job descriptions.

The question you should ask yourself is: *Can I do most things in the job description and would I enjoy learning the rest of the things I don't know?*

If your answer is yes, you should go for it and allow the recruiter to submit your resume to the employer.

Very few people know everything employers list in their job descriptions. Take my field in IT for example. No one knows everything about the ever-growing IT technology explosion. Someone who knows a little something about the spell-bounding exponential growth of technology is Gordon Moore. Moore's Law is named after Dr. Gordon E.

Moore, the co-founder of Intel Corporation and Fairchild Semiconductor. In 1965, Moore stated that the number of components (transistors) per integrated circuit (IC) would double every year; and in 1975, he updated his prediction by saying these micro-components would double every two years. Moore was right in his observations and predictions.

In today's fast-paced growth of technology, you are not going to know every concept, device, network, application and configuration out there. Nobody is that smart, and nobody has the time, energy or money to learn everything. US government agencies and corporations know that too. What US government agencies and corporations want is someone who would be a good fit—*technically* and *culturally*—on their team; someone who knows or can do the majority—*not all*—of the items on the job description; and is willing to learn the things they don't know.

The Job Description Reveals What Subjects the Interviewers Will Ask Questions About

The second reason for asking for the job description is it reveals the subjects the employer's interviewers will be asking you questions about. The job description is like a summary or overview of the type of questions that will be on a test in school.

If you've decided to let the recruiter submit your resume for the job opening, review the job description carefully and identify areas that are your strong points; areas that you are weak in; and areas you don't know. Focus your review on areas you are familiar with first. Brush up on those subjects; reviewing and familiarizing yourself with those subjects. Once you've completed that review, research and learn as much as you can about areas in the job description that you have little or no familiarity with.

Your Resume for the Job Interview

Your Resume Review Ensures Your Interviewers Have the Latest Version of Your Resume

Before you even give the recruiter a copy of your resume to pass on to the hiring manager, you should always check your resume one last time for editing. This is your one last chance to make sure your potential interviewers see only what you want them to see in your resume. Your resume may have been sitting on online job boards for quite some time; and it may have been a while since you last looked at your resume. So give it one last look before handing it over to the recruiter.

In your interview, you will not only be tested on your knowledge and experience about the items in the job description, you may also be asked questions about items that are in your resume, such as equipment, processes, technologies, protocols, applications, certifications or previous job experience. Actually, anything you put in your resume is free game for interviewers to ask you questions about if they want to.

This should be an important reminder to you that you should only put items in your resume that you can confirm and talk about in an interview. There's nothing worse than having an interviewer point out a specific item in your resume and then start asking you questions about it when the only answer you can give them is the deer in the headlights look. So make sure you trim your resume accordingly for the job you are interviewing for.

Your Resume Review Ensures You Are Prepared to Talk About Your Resume

Sometimes, interviewers will ask you questions about certain sections of your resume. A good review of your resume before the interview will help you talk confidently about the Work History section of your resume if the interviewers ask you questions about some of your past work.

When recruiters ask you about previous jobs you worked at, use that as an opportunity to toot your own horn about yourself. I'm talking about making yourself stand out among the other candidates those interviewers plan to interview for that same job. Your next source of income is on the line in this interview, so this is not the time to be bashful, humble or shy—talk about yourself.

The proper way to toot your own horn about yourself is by telling the interviewers the same things I mentioned you needed to have in your resume in Chapter 5. Briefly tell the interviewers how your contributions at that former job resulted in positive impacts for the company, workplace or customers.

By reviewing your resume for things you did at previous jobs, you will be able to more quickly and easily remember and point out the things you accomplished and how your actions produced results and positive impacts on the job.

When the interviewer asks you about past work, answer in a way that shows the interviewer how what you did at that previous workplace saved time, energy, money; improved processes, documentation and drawings; met critical deadlines and shortened delivery times; increased productivity and revenue; satisfied customers and stakeholders; educated and trained personnel; or troubleshot and repaired critical network components that restored or allowed continued service to customers and the mission.

Certification's and Experience's Place in Job Interviews

In my discussion on negotiating your salary in chapter 7, I debunked the idea that employers only pay high salaries to people with higher education. Employers are willing to pay 6-figure salaries to professionals who possess a certain amount of knowledge, skill sets and experience, and who have certain types of certifications regardless of their degrees.

The same is true when it comes to your job interview.

Other than checking off a box for some positions requiring a degree, it is certifications that rule supreme over college degrees for many job interviews. As someone who works in the IT industry, it never ceases to amaze me how impressed and fascinated recruiters and interviewers are with the IT certifications on my resume instead of the degrees on my resume. Not once over the years have I ever had a recruiter or interviewer say to me, "*That's a really nice degree you have there*" or "*Your degree is really something to behold.*"

In many career fields, certifications trump a degree, and experience trump a degree and certifications.

Here's the difference between a degree, a certification and experience to employers:

- **A degree** just tells an employer you have the mental capacity for the job.

- **A certification** tells an employer you have the knowledge for the job.

- **Experience** tells an employer you can do the job.

It's amazing how much we invest in our education with so little return on that investment. You spend all that time, energy, money, sweat and tears over years of sitting on hard school chairs; handwriting or typing instructor notes until your fingers were numb; burning the midnight oil reading books, researching online and writing papers; buying expensive textbooks on a thin budget; taking classes on subjects you would never have taken if they weren't required; overcoming fear and trepidation while cutting your teeth on giving oral presentations; and dissecting every partition of your gray matter for answers to tests, midterms and finals.

Once that sheepskin is hanging prominently on your wall and given its proper place on your resume, what response do you get from recruiters

Interview Preparation and Tips

and interviewers for all that hard work? Wait for it . . . crickets. Nada, nothing, not a peep.

What you will hear often from recruiters or interviewers is, "*I noticed you have your* [fill in the blank] *certification*" or "*Your certifications are pretty impressive.*" That's because, when it comes to many jobs, your certifications say more about your technical fit for most of these jobs than a college degree.

In addition to certifications giving you more leverage in asking for higher pay during salary negotiations, having multiple certifications on your resume will immediately get the attention of recruiters and employers.

How many certifications should you have? I say as many as your budget, time and interests will allow. The more certifications you have on your resume, the more you will stand out among your peers in the eyes of your interviewers before you even step into that interview room.

If you completed only one or two of multiple exams required for a particular certification, include the exams you passed in your resume even though you don't have the certification yet. This shows your interviewers you are taking the initiative to improve your skills; something interviewers, bosses and employers desire in their employees.

If this information is discouraging to you right now because you have little to no certifications, don't despair. Fortunately, your interview is not based solely on your certifications, but also on your experience and skillsets you've highlighted in your resume; your ability to answer technical questions; and your cultural fit in the company.

Here's more good news for you: getting certified is not a one-time deal for one interview; it should be a continuous goal throughout your entire career. The longer you are in your career, the more certifications you should be racking up along with your experience and skills. Take the time to get certified.

Take this for what it's worth: having certifications and experience is more important than having higher or advanced degrees when it comes to many job interviews.

Angela Duckworth earned her Ph.D. at the University of Pennsylvania where she is now the associate professor of psychology. She has been an advisor to the White House, the World Bank, Fortune 500 companies and to NFL and NBA professional sports teams. In 2013, Dr. Duckworth gave a TED talk on TED.com, a nonprofit organization that shares ideas about technology, entertainment and design (TED) worldwide. Her talk was titled *Grit: The power of passion and perseverance*, and it is also the title of her 2016 New York Times Best Seller book.

Dr. Duckworth and her team conducted extensive research across all levels of academia to find out the single factor that produces success. Her study revealed that *"one characteristic emerged as a significant predictor of success; and it wasn't social intelligence, it wasn't good looks, physical health, and it wasn't IQ. It was* **grit**.*"*

Duckworth defines grit as *"passion and perseverance for very long-term goals"*.

Because of this passion, drive and determination that Dr. Duckworth calls grit, it is also possible to have great success in life without higher education. If you think it's ludicrous to suggest you can become very successful in your career and obtain higher salaries without higher education, try convincing these following people otherwise.

Bill Gates, whose estimated net worth of $82.9 billion in 2016 made him the richest person in the world, entered Harvard University in 1973. While at Harvard, he created the Microsoft Company in 1975, and later dropped out of Harvard in 1976 at the age of 21 to focus on his company. In June 2007, 31 years after dropping out of Harvard, Bill Gates was given an honorary doctorate of Laws degree from Harvard. Gates told the crowd who witnessed his honorary degree, *"I'll be changing my job next year, and it will be nice to finally have a college degree on my resume."*

Mark Zuckerberg's high school years were spent at the Academy of Phillips Exeter, a boarding school in Exeter, New Hampshire where he graduated in 2002. In that same year he entered Harvard where he started his Facebook project and dropped out of Harvard in his sophomore year, only two years in the Ivy League, to concentrate on his Facebook social media project. Zuckerberg's 2016 estimated net worth was $51.4 billion making him the 6th richest person in the world at the time.

American businessman Larry Ellison, cofounder and CEO of Oracle Corporation studied at the University of Illinois at Urbana-Campaign for two years before dropping out of that college; and attended the University of Chicago but dropped out of that college after one term. In 1977, he founded Software Development Laboratories (SDL) with two other partners; later renamed it Relational Software Inc. in 1979; and then renamed it again to Oracle Systems Corporation in 1982. Ellison's 2016 estimated net worth was $49.5 billion making Ellison the 7th wealthiest person in the world at the time.

Entrepreneur Elon Musk, the founder of Tesla and SpaceX, started his college education at Queen's University in Canada at age 19, but in 1992 he transferred to the University of Pennsylvania where, in 1995, he earned bachelor's degrees in economics and physics at age 24. In that same year, he entered Stanford University where he planned to pursue a Ph.D. in energy physics but dropped out of Stanford two days later to launch his first company, Zip2 Corporation. Musk's 2016 estimated net worth was $11.2 billion.

Michael Dell, founder and CEO of Dell Inc., a leading seller of personal computers (PCs), entered the University of Texas in 1983 but dropped out of college in his first year at the age of 19 to focus on his new company called PC's Limited which he operated out of a condominium. His newly formed company made $6 million in sales in its first year. When he incorporated his company in 1987, he renamed it Dell Computer Corporation and sales increased to $159 million at the end of 1988. Dell never looked back at returning to college since then. Dell's 2016 estimated net worth was $20.5 billion.

IT entrepreneur and inventor **Steve Jobs**, the cofounder and CEO of Apple Computers with Steve Wozniak and cofounder and CEO of Pixar Animation Studios, began his college education in 1971 taking a freshman English class and attending lectures at Stanford while still a senior at his Homestead High School. Jobs entered Reed College in Portland, Oregon in 1972 but due to lack of funds by his parents who were paying for his education, Jobs dropped out of college after only six months. In 1976 at the age of 21, Jobs started Apple Computer with Wozniak in Jobs' family garage. At the time of his death in 2011, Steve Jobs' net worth was roughly $10.2 billion.

Besides having brilliant minds who chose to pursue their passion instead of higher education, the one common denominator in this previous list of some of the most successful and wealthiest people in the world are that they are all college dropouts; and only Elon Musk earned a bachelor's degree; while Bill Gates was given an honorary degree.

In his commencement speech to the 2005 graduating class at Stanford, Steve Jobs said, "*Your time is limited, so don't waste it living someone else's life. Don't be trapped by the dogma, which is living with the results of other people's thinking. Don't let the noise of other's opinions drown out your own inner voice. And most important, have the courage to follow your heart and intuition. They somehow already know what you truly want to become. Everything else is secondary.*"

Steve Jobs told his audience that by dropping out of college, he could stop taking the required classes that he was not interested in. It freed him to take only classes that piqued his interest. In his final words to this 2005 graduating class at Stanford, Jobs encouraged them to "**Stay hungry, stay foolish.**"

Are you trapped in the dogma of intellectuals, listening to the results of other people who say you must have a master's degree or Ph.D. to become successful in your career or make a 6-figure salary or more?

Like I said earlier, if you have the time, money, opportunity and interest in taking higher education classes, many of which are required courses you know you have absolutely no interest in studying like Steve Jobs, go for it.

But if your time, money and opportunity are limited, and you're like many of us who simply want to follow our heart, intuition, dreams and interests like Steve Jobs, then give that your full attention and focus, even if it makes you look hungry and foolish to others. For many, the way to do that is through following your passion; gaining more experience in your chosen field; concentrating on certifications in specific areas that interest you; and putting those experience and certifications on your resume.

Education's Place among Successful People

As I said, this is not a knock against higher education. Education has its place in society. By all means, pursue higher education if you have the time, money, opportunity and interest. But don't discount the power of pursuing your focused passion and interests through experience and certifications instead of higher college education. Many people have become quite successful in life by pursuing their passion without higher education.

Need more proof? Of course you do. So let's consider a few other people.

Success is Not Defined by Education

Perhaps you're not convinced you can be very successful in your career and make a 6-figure salary or more without higher education. You're not buying the idea that higher education is not needed for success. You feel people like Steve Jobs or Mark Zuckerberg are gifted prodigies who were destined for greatness from birth; an aberration of the normal path to success; and that the rest of us mortals in society must develop our greatness and success in life through higher education.

Then how do you explain these other "mere mortals" who gained great success and wealth in life with only a bachelor's degree?

- Donald Trump (Bachelor's in Economics)
- Barbara Walters (Bachelor's in English)
- Oprah Winfrey (Bachelor's in Speech and Drama)
- Conan O'Brien (Bachelor's in American History and Literature)
- David Letterman (Bachelor's in Broadcasting)
- George Lucas (Bachelors of Fine Arts)
- J.K. Rowling (Bachelor's in French and Classical Studies)
- Jay Leno (Bachelor's in Speech Therapy)
- Jerry Springer (Bachelor's in Political Science)
- Katie Couric (Bachelor's in English)
- Martha Stewart (Bachelor's in History and Architectural History)
- Stephen King (Bachelor's in English)

Successful People without a College Degree

Let's not forget our short list of successful and wealthy people who either **did not attend college** or **dropped out of high school or college** or **have no degree at all**. You could say these people graduated from the school of hard knocks with honors.

- **Amancio Ortega:** A Spanish businessman and founder and chairman of Inditex, a multinational clothing company with multiple stores such as Zara, Massimo Dutti, Bershka, Oysho, Pull and Bear, Stradivarius and Uterque. His 2016 estimated net worth was $73.1 billion making him the 2nd richest person in the world next to Bill Gates whose 2016 net worth was estimated at $82.9 billion. **Ortega dropped out of high school at the age of 14 and has no college education.**

- **Kemmons Wilson:** An American businessman and founder of the Holiday Inn hotel chain. His net worth at the time of his death in 2003 was estimated at $1.5 billion. **He dropped out of high school at the age of 17 and had no college education.**

- **Sean Parker:** An American entrepreneur who was the first president of Facebook and cofounded Napster, Plaxo, Causes, Airtime and Brigade. His 2016 net worth was estimated at $2.4 billion. **He has no college education.**

- **Francois Pinault:** A French businessman who owns Artemis S.A., a holding company for other companies including Gucci, Converse shoes, Puma, Samsonite luggage, Christie's auction house, Chateau Latour which is a ski resort in Vail, Colorado; and is an art collector of one of the largest contemporary art collections in the world. His 2016 net worth was estimated at $14.5 billion. **He dropped out of high school and has no college education.**

- **Haim Saban:** An Israeli and American businessman, media proprietor, investor, musician and TV, record and film producer who founded Saban Entertainment, a children's production and distribution company that produces programs such as Power Rangers. His 2016 net worth was estimated at $2.9 billion. **He has no college education.**

- **Vidal Sassoon:** A British and American businessman, hairstylist who created the Bob cut worn by famous fashion designers and film stars, and founder of Vidal Sassoon hairstyling salons and hair-care products. His net worth at the time of his death in 2012 was estimated at $150 million. **He was a high school dropout and had no college education.**

- **S. Daniel Abraham:** An American businessman and founder of Slim-Fast, a well-known line of diet products. His 2016 net worth was estimated at $2.1 billion. **He has no college education.**

- **Sheldon Adelson:** An American business magnate who is CEO and chairman of the Las Vegas Sands Corporation, and owner of two newspaper companies: Israel Hayom, an Israeli daily newspaper company and Las Vegas Review-Journal. His 2016 estimated net worth was estimated at $31.1 billion. **He dropped out of the City College of New York.**

- **Wally "Famous" Amos:** An American entrepreneur who is the creator of the Famous Amos chocolate chip cookies, and also worked for the prestigious William Morris Agency as a talent agent where he discovered Simon & Garfunkel and worked with Diana Ross, Marvin Gaye and Sam Cooke. His 2016 net worth was estimated at $20 million. **He dropped out of high school at the age of 17 and has no college education.**

- **Ray Bradbury:** An American writer of fantasy, science fiction, horror and mystery fiction who won numerous awards including a 2007 Pulitzer Citation. His net worth at the time of his death in 2012 was $30 million. **He had no college education.**

- **Jim Carrey:** An American actor, comedian, impressionist, screenwriter and producer who starred in roles in films such as *Dumb and Dumber, The Mask Ace Ventura: When Nature Calls, Batman Forever* and *How the Grinch Stole Christmas*. His 2016 net worth was estimated at $150 million. **He dropped out of high school and has no college education.**

- **Alvin Copeland:** An American entrepreneur who founded Popeyes Chicken & Biscuits fast food chain. His net worth in 2004, four years before his death in 2008, was estimated at $319 million.

He dropped out of high school and had no college education.

- **Simon Cowell:** An English entrepreneur, film, record and TV producer and reality TV judge known for his brash but effective talent competition judging in shows such as *American Idol, The X Factor* and *America's Got Talent*. His 2016 net worth was estimated at $550 million. **He dropped out of school at the age of 16 after passing some General Certificate of Education (GCE) Level O courses at Dover College in the UK, a boarding school for boys and girls ages 3-18; and has no college education.** GCE Level O courses are less than GCE Level A courses which are the equivalent to a high school diploma.

- **Tom Cruise:** An American actor and filmmaker starring in roles in films such as Top *Gun, A Few Good Men, Minority Report, Edge of Tomorrow* and *Mission Impossible*. His 2016 net worth was estimated at $480 million. **He has no college education.**

- **Johnny Depp:** An American actor, producer and musician who starred in roles in films such as *Platoon, Edward Scissorhands, Sleepy Hollow, Pirates of the Caribbean* and its sequels and *Alice in Wonderland*. His acting awards include the Golden Globe Award and the Screen Actors Guild Award for Best Actor. His 2016 net worth was estimated at $400 million. **He dropped out of high school at age 15 and has no college education.**

- **Leonardo DiCaprio:** An American actor and film producer starring in roles in films such as *Titanic, The Man in the Iron Mask, Catch Me If You Can, The Aviator, The Great Gatsby* and *The Revenant* which won him the Golden Globe Award for Best Actor. His 2016 net worth was estimated at $217 million. **He** dropped out of high school but later earned his GED diploma, and has no college education.

- **Walt Disney:** An American entrepreneur, animator, voice actor and film producer well-known for his Disney films and Disney theme parks. His net worth at the time of his death in 1966 was $5 billion. **He dropped out of high school at age 16 and had no college education.**

- **Robert Downey Jr.:** An American actor starring in roles in *Chaplin* which won him the BAFTA Award for Best Actor in a Leading Role and multiple Marvel Comics films as Iron Man. His net worth was estimated at $240 million. **He dropped out of high school but later earned his GED while in prison. He has no college education.**

- **David Green:** An American businessman and founder of Hobby Lobby, the arts and crafts chain stores. His 2016 net worth was estimated at $5.8 billion. **He has no college education.**

- **Joyce Hall:** An American businessman and founder of Hallmark Cards. His net worth at the time of his death in 1982 was $1 billion. **He dropped out of grade school and had no college education.**

- **Ernest Hemingway:** An American novelist, short story writer and journalist who won the Nobel Prize in Literature. He wrote the novels *The Sun Also Rises*, *For Whom the Bells Tolls* and *The Old Man and the Sea*. His net worth at the time of his death in 1961 was estimated at $1.4 million. **He had no college education.**

- **Ingvar Kamprad**: A Swedish businessman and founder of IKEA, the popular Swedish retail furniture company. His 2016 net worth was estimated at $3.4 billion. **He has no college education.**

- **Jennifer Lawrence:** An American actress well-known for her starring roles in films such as the *X-Men* and *Hunger Games* franchises; having won an Academy Award for Best Actress, a BAFTA Award for Best Actress in a Supporting Role and three Golden Globe Awards. Her 2016 net worth was estimated at $110 million. **She has no college education.**

- **Stan Lee:** An American comic-book writer, publisher, media producer, TV host, actor and former president and chairman of the popular Marvel Comics that has been converted to the ever-popular *The Avengers*, *X-Men*, *Spider-Man*, *Hulk*, *Fantastic Four*, *Iron Man* and *Thor* films. His 2016 net worth was estimated at $50 million. **He has no college education.**

- **Carl Lindner Jr.:** An American businessman, founder of United Dairy Farmers, former owner of Chiquita Brands and former part owner and CEO of the Cincinnati Reds professional baseball team. His 2006 net worth prior to his death in 2011 was estimated at $2.3 billion. **He dropped out of high school and had no college education.**

- **Katy Perry:** An American singer, songwriter and actress whose album, *Teenage Dream*, earned five Number 1 *Billboard* Hot 100 songs, second only to Michael Jackson's album *Bad*, and has sold over 100 million records globally. Her 2016 net worth was estimated at $125 million. **After she completed her GED requirements at age 15, she left her high school in her freshman year and has no college education.**

- **Kelly Ripa:** An American actress, dancer and TV talk show host popularly known for hosting *Live! With Kelley*. Her 2016 net worth was estimated at $100 million. **She dropped out of Camden County College.**

- **Richard Schulze:** An American businessman and founder and former CEO and Chairman of the Best Buy electronics store chain. His 2016 net worth was estimated at $2.8 billion. **He had no college education but was given honorary doctoral degrees from the University of St. Thomas in Saint Paul, Minnesota and from the University of Minnesota.**

- **Maurice Sendak:** An American author and illustrator of children's books who wrote *Where the Wild Things Are* that sold over 19 million copies worldwide and was made into a movie, *In the Night Kitchen* and *Outside Over There*. His net worth at the time of his death in 2012 was estimated at $20 million. **He had no college education.**

- **Will Smith:** An American actor, producer, rapper and songwriter who starred in *The Fresh Prince of Bel-Air* TV sitcom and starred in roles in films, such as *Bad Boys, Independence Day, Men in Black, Enemy of the State, Wild Wild West, Ali* and the *Pursuit of Happyness*. His 2016 net worth was estimated at $250 million. **He has no college education.**

- **Quentin Tarantino:** An American actor and filmmaker who wrote and directed several films, such as *My Best Friend's Birthday, Reservoir Dogs, Pulp Fiction* and the *Kill Bill* franchise. He won numerous awards including two Academy Awards, two Golden Globe Awards and two BAFTA Awards. His 2016 net worth was estimated at $100 million. **He dropped out of high school and has no college education.**

- **Dave Thomas:** An American businessman and founder and CEO of the Wendy's fast-food restaurant chain. His net worth at the time of his death in 2001 was estimated at $4.2 billion. **He dropped out of high school at the age of 15 and had no**

college education. He later obtained his GED about 46 years after dropping out of high school.

There is too much overwhelming evidence here to say these people are an anomaly of the required path of higher education needed to become successful and wealthy in life. These people are overwhelmingly the norm; not the exception to becoming successful in your career and making 6-figure salaries, millions or even billions of dollars. All of these people did it as a high school or college dropout or as someone without any college education at all.

This list should be good news for those of you without degrees who think you're at a disadvantage going into that job interview room because of the false notion that only a college degree will get the attention of your interviewers.

I'm not saying if you take the long-accepted traditional route of higher education, you can't become successful or wealthy in life. What I am saying is that there are more than one path to a successful career and wealth besides having a master's degree or Ph.D.

Some of you with faith in God would argue that these people made it in life because of God's blessing on their life. Being a man of faith, I agree with you. However, some people prefer to view things from a physical perspective rather than from a spiritual one. Some people need a scientific formula for the overwhelming number of people without high school and college degrees who became successful millionaires and billionaires. To those of you who need an *intellectual* answer, I would say to you that it is because of this passion, drive and determination that Dr. Duckworth calls *grit*.

Passion plus value equals success.

But passion, drive and determination without a goal that eventually becomes something of *value* to others takes you nowhere. All of these people with no high school or college educations became successful and wealthy because of their passion, drive and determination to produce things of value to other people. Albert Einstein said, "*Strive not to be a success, but rather to be of value.*" **Create value to others and you create success**. To many employers, experience and certifications have higher value than college degrees.

Although I purposely chose this lengthy list to prove my point, it is still nonetheless a short list compared to all the people who have accomplished great success and fortune in life without a college education or who dropped out of high school or college. I realize this list of successful people I provided was so long it made your eyes bleed. I get it—this list is long-winded. The amazing thing about this list though is that it is the ***short list*** version. Time would fail us if I tried to tell you about all the people with poor, struggling, difficult upbringings; or who are without college degrees or higher education that became successful, rich and famous. I wanted to share that list with you in order to share what I'm going to tell you next.

SUCCESS DOESN'T PLAY FAVORITES

Success is not prejudice or biased. Success doesn't care if you're well educated or have no education at all. Success won't pass up on you in favor of someone else because of your race, religion, gender or sexual orientation. Success doesn't consider whether you came from the ghetto or a golden palace. Success plays on an even playing field where all players—you and I—have the same opportunity to win.

This should bring great comfort and inspiration to you who feel you are at a disadvantage because of your lack of education or your background. You're not at a disadvantage; you're in that group of millionaires and billionaires who became successful without college degrees or a life handed to them on a silver platter. With so much overwhelming evidence, there's really no excuse for you if you have little or no education to not chase after your dreams like everyone else. Don't let other people talk you out of your dreams. Go after your passion—success will follow.

Arrival at Your Job Interview

When the employer invites you to come in for an in-person interview, they will provide you the address to their worksite where your interview will take place. If the staffing agency is in your local area, the staffing agency recruiter or account manager may be meeting you for the first time at the interview site too; and will introduce you to one of your interviewers who will bring you to the interview room.

One of the things you should do in your pre-interview preparation is make sure you know how to get to the interview location from your home, whether it is by car, train, subway or bus. Once you have the company address, you should take a test drive (or test ride by train or bus if that is your mode of transportation) to the interview site to see how long it will take you to get there; and if there are any roadblocks, construction or other unknowns or possible delays along the way.

Here's where you can make your first of many good impressions by ensuring you arrive several minutes early before your interview time. The key here is you want to give yourself enough time to comfortably make it to your interview on schedule with a few minutes to spare. You should arrive at the company building at least 10–15 minutes early. However, you should not announce your arrival to your interviewers until 5–10 minutes before your interview start time.

I cannot tell you how many times I drove a practice run from my home to the interview site, only to discover obstacles that would have made me late to my interview, such as traffic congestion on a busy street; the road I planned to take ended up in a hotel parking lot (sounds funny now but I would not have been laughing if this happened to me on the day of my interview); the road was blocked or under construction; or the company name had changed on the building of my interview.

Do yourself a favor and discover these surprise obstacles and delays before the day of your interview. It will ensure a stress-free commute to your interview and will start your interview day on the right foot.

Introductions in Your Job Interview

The whole purpose of your job interview is to show your interviewers that you are a much better choice than the other candidates they are interviewing for this job. You do that by showing you are a better **technical fit** and **cultural fit** than the other candidates. One of the best ways to show your technical and cultural fitness for this job is right at the start of your interview in your introduction of yourself to your interviewers.

Our focus in this *Before the Interview* section on introductions will concentrate on what you will prepare to say about yourself to your panel of interviewers after the hiring manager or team lead asks you to "*Tell us a little bit about yourself.*"

Most interviews consist of 3–6 people in the interview room with you. There's usually one person leading the interview, such as the hiring manager or lead person on the team you will be on if you are hired. The remaining interviewers in the room are usually members of the team you will be a part of if you are hired.

Tell us a little bit about yourself.

The person leading the interview will start things off by introducing the other interviewers in the room to you; and oftentimes will break the ice by telling you a little bit about their company. Afterward, the person leading the interview will ask you to tell them a little bit about yourself.

This introduction phase of your interview is much too important for you to talk about yourself off-the-cuff or off the top of your head. You must have a well-prepared introduction plan that you've gone over with a fine-tooth comb to ensure every word you speak carries weight during your introduction.

You want to use your introduction as an opportunity to stand out from the other candidates by incorporating certain things from past jobs (your technical fit) and your personal life (your cultural fit). By using your introduction to show how your past job experiences relate to the job description for this open position, and by sharing a few things about your off-work activities and personal life, you will already be scoring huge bonus points toward successfully completing your interview before answering a single technical question.

How to Prepare Your Introduction for Your Job Interview

You should write out what you are going to say about yourself with an emphasis on your technical and cultural fitness for this job. It's best to do this on a computer so that you can quickly and easily save, update, edit and tailor your introduction for each new job interview.

Once your introduction is well-thought-out and written down, you should begin memorizing and verbally practicing what you are going to say about yourself until you can give your introduction (without reading it) in a relaxed, normal and smooth pace. Later in this *Before the Interview* chapter, we'll cover roll-playing which is a good way to practice being in a job interview giving your introduction to your interviewers.

Technical Fitness and Cultural Fitness in Your Introduction

In the previous section on researching your interviewers, I mentioned that when one of the interviewers asks you to tell them about yourself, this is not a request for you to give them a long-winded account of your work history from beginning to end. Interviewers are looking for something specific when they ask you to tell them about yourself.

What the interviewers are looking for in your introduction are two things:

1. Your **technical fit** in their company.

2. Your **cultural fit** in their company.

The interviewer is asking you to tell them things about your skill sets that can translate to accomplishing the job description of the person they want to hire; and to tell them things about you as a person that would make you a good cultural fit on their team and in their company. Therefore, the way you should tell the interviewers about yourself is through the lens filter of your technical fitness to fulfill the job description and your cultural fitness to fit in with your new team members and the company culture.

Instead of starting out with, "*It all started when I was born in the hills of West Virginia . . .*" or "*My first job was working as a paper boy in the busy metropolis of New York City . . .*"; take what you've learned from your review of the job description and start telling the interviewers specific things you've learned or done in past jobs that relate directly to those items in the job description. This will convince your interviewers that you are a good technical fit for the job without them having to ask you technical questions. Then go on and tell them some personal things about your life—your hobbies, trips, passions or interests. Try to include things you noticed your interviewers are interested in after researching their social media profiles or just share personal things in general to make an emotional or social connection with your interviewers. This will help convince your interviewers that you will be a good cultural fit in their office.

How long should you talk about your technical and cultural fit during your introduction? You should spend about **1–2 minutes** talking about your **technical fit**; and about **15–30 seconds** to talk about your **cultural fitness** during your introduction. This is not a lot of time; so make every word count. You don't want to talk long in your introduction. A long-winded introduction only tells the interviewers that you talk too much; and they will probably pass over you for another candidate they believe won't talk their ear off at work.

How to Include Your Technical Fitness in Your Introduction

When talking about your technical fit, share how things you've done in past jobs relate to the responsibilities in this new job they are interviewing you for. For example, if the job description mentions certain pieces of equipment, tools or processes, share how you worked with those types of equipment, tools or processes in past jobs. If the job description requires knowledge and experience in certain office skills or office software, talk about past job experiences where you used those types of office skills or software. If the job description asks for a person who can operate certain machinery, heavy equipment or vehicles, share how you operated those types of equipment in previous jobs. If the job description states the need for a person who can design, engineer, implement or test certain things, talk about how you performed these duties in former positions. If the job description requires you to provide leadership, training, mentoring of junior personnel or interact with customers, talk about how you handled these types of responsibilities for previous companies.

When you talk about these things you've done in past jobs, make sure you include how what you did had an ***impactful result*** for that workplace or company, just as I explained you should do in your resume. Tell the interviewers how what you did at previous workplaces saved time, energy or money; improved processes, documentation or drawings; met critical deadlines or shortened delivery times; increased productivity or revenue; satisfied customers or stakeholders; supervised, mentored, educated or trained personnel; and troubleshot or repaired critical components that restored or allowed continued service to customers or the company mission.

Don't waste your interviewer's time talking about past job experiences that do not relate to the job description when you're sharing about yourself in your introduction. There is also no need to mention things such as your certifications or degrees because these are plainly shown in your resume. You need to use those precious couple of minutes to address your specific technical and cultural qualities that make you stand out above other job candidates interviewing for the same job as you.

How to Include Your Cultural Fitness in Your Introduction

This is where your research into each interviewer's or the company's social media posts, such as on Facebook or LinkedIn, will be invaluable. When talking about your personal life, try to include things you read about in the interviewer's and company's social network profile. You don't have to mention that you read their posts or saw their pictures engaged in those same interests. Just mention that those are some of your interests if in fact those are your hobbies or interests.

When talking about your cultural fit in their company, share your interests, hobbies, sports, places you like to visit or vacation; books you enjoy reading; music you enjoy listening to; or volunteer work you enjoy doing.

If an interviewer asks you a question, such as *"What are you passionate about?"* or *"How do you spend your free time?"* or *"What do you do for fun?"* they're actually trying to find out if you have anything in common with them—your cultural fit. I've been asked all of these questions in job interviews. So don't be surprised or put off by these types of questions. They just want to know you more as a person instead of as just another job candidate.

So why do interviewers want to hear about your personal life or interests—your cultural fit?

If they hire you, your work area, desks or cubicles are most likely going to be right next to each other at work; and they just want to know if you'll fit in well with them on a daily basis. Use your introduction as an opportunity to mention things that will give your interviewers some assurance they will enjoy working alongside you. So mention things you are interested in that they posted on their social media site, such as a hobby, a book they enjoyed reading, a movie they enjoyed watching, or a place they vacationed or visited. If you couldn't find anything about the interviewers on social media posts or if you were not given the interviewer's names; you should still mention your interests, hobbies, recreation or other off-work activities to the interviewers in your introduction.

You may consider or discount this advice as over the top with too much emphasis on "*who*" you are rather than "*what*" you can do. With all due respect to your career accomplishments, keep in mind that you're probably not the only candidate with that degree, that certification, that knowledge and experience or that skill set. There are several candidates in front of you and behind you in that interview line with similar qualifications and skill sets as you who can do the same things as you in that job. When all candidates look similar in what they can do in the eyes of the interviewers, you can be sure the interviewers are going to lean heavily on each candidate's cultural fit to determine which candidate they would most likely enjoy working with all day long.

So why not take advantage of this social media profile information and make it work to your advantage over your competition? Remember, every word in your introduction counts for or against you in your interview—use that opportunity wisely.

Job Interview Questions and Answers

Interview questions for all jobs fall into one of two areas:

1. Your **technical fitness** for the job.

2. Your **cultural fitness** for the company and your team.

The topics you see in the job description the staffing agency recruiter provides you are the areas where interviewers will be asking you technical questions. The same is true if you get the job description from the job listing on the company's website. How well you answer those technical fit questions will determine if they **hire you for the job**.

The topics you normally don't see in the job description that interviewers oftentimes ask job candidates questions about are areas concerning your cultural fitness. Cultural fit questions cover your soft skills; your ability to communicate and interact with other people; your behavior or response when working in teams or groups; your ability to take criticism, feedback or advice; how you handle difficult bosses, co-workers, customers or other pressures on the job; or how well you can problem-solve issues and provide solutions. How well you answer these cultural fit questions will determine if they **hire you for the team** you'll be on and the company you'll work for.

Notice that **technical fit** questions relate to hiring you for *the job*. **Cultural fit** questions relate to hiring you for *the team*.

Job Interview Questions about Your Technical Fitness

Obviously, the technical fitness questions that interviewers ask candidates will be different for each person's field of work and each type of job in that industry. Therefore, I won't be able to provide the answers to the technical questions that each person reading this book will encounter.

However, I would suggest that after you've gone through an interview; always take the time afterward to write down as many questions you can possibly remember that the interviewers asked you. You'll discover over time, after interviewing with several companies in the same line of work, that many interviewers in different companies ask the same questions. By writing these interview questions down, you'll have the best reference source to go to for technical questions when preparing for your next job interview.

Having been through numerous IT interviews over the years, I've begun to notice the similarities in the questions being asked by different interviewers at different US government agencies and private corporations. I started taking notes on these questions, such as what questions were asked; which questions I knew; and which ones I didn't know. I did this until it got to the point where I had several pages of these notes.

Whenever I had to prepare for an IT job interview, I would always go to these notes first; and afterward I would review books or online material as needed to complete my review based on the job description.

When I identified items on the job description that were new to me, I would study those areas and began anticipating questions that interviewers would ask me; and then I created questions and answers for those subjects too.

As a result of all these notes from interviews and self-study, I have over 400 pages of questions and answers, explanations and network drawings for IT interviews I review to prepare for my job interviews. I've put these IT technical interview questions and answers in my next new book that will be available in summer 2017.

Job Interview Questions about Your Cultural Fitness

A working environment is a team environment, and employers are looking for people who will contribute to the goal of establishing and maintaining a healthy team environment; not hurt, ruin or undermine team cohesiveness and a positive working environment. Employers try to bring in people to their company that will contribute to a healthy working environment by asking cultural fit questions during the job interview process.

Over the years, I've collected a series of cultural fitness questions that interviewers have asked me in many job interviews for both US government and corporate jobs. In this section, I've made these questions and the way you should respond to these questions available to you.

These cultural fit or soft skills questions and answers cover a wide range of questions that interviewers ask to give them a better understanding of how you might behave and interact with different people and situations in the workplace. Questions such as *"Who was your most difficult supervisor and why?"* or *"Explain a workplace experience with a difficult person and how did you deal with them"* are intended to help interviewers uncover your behavioral tendencies in your interpersonal relationships with co-workers under stressful or difficult situations at work. Your answers to these questions help interviewers determine your cultural fit, also referred to as your social qualities, soft skills or emotional quotient (EQ) in the workplace. In chapter 9, I'll explain in greater detail what your emotional quotient is and how it comes into play during your job interview.

Some people refer to these social qualities as *how you are wired*, but that makes it sound as if these qualities are permanently hardwired in you and cannot be changed; when in fact, these are social skills that you can develop and improve.

During your preparation for your next job interview, take the time to go over these cultural fitness questions and prepare well-thought-out answers in advance that show you can handle difficult social situations in the workplace with confidence, maturity and professionalism.

How You Should Respond to the Weakness Question

One cultural fit question that is sometimes asked in job interviews is **"What is your greatest weakness?"** Sometimes this weakness question is asked in different ways, such as *"What area do you need to improve on the most?"* or *"Name one thing about yourself that needs improving."*

This weakness question is a bit tricky to answer because you are trying to put your best foot forward in the job interview. The last thing you want to do is talk about something that places you in a negative light before your interviewers and makes you look worse than your competitors. We all want to show our better selves, not our darkest angels.

So what is a bad response to the weakness question?

The last thing you want to do is ignore preparing for this question; hoping you never encounter it in an interview; only to find yourself fumbling for an answer when you are asked to share your weakness. You should also not try to sidestep this question by telling the interviewers you can't think of any weaknesses or you don't have any weaknesses.

The interviewer is asking this question knowing full well that everyone has weaknesses and each person is aware of most of them. To deny you have weaknesses or to suggest you can't think of any weaknesses makes you appear as if you have something to hide; you didn't prepare well enough for the interview; or you are too proud or conceited to accept or acknowledge the fact that you have weaknesses just like everyone else. Avoiding this question makes you appear as someone who may not accept feedback or constructive criticism well in the workplace.

Any attempt by you to sidestep this question reveals a weakness in you in the eyes of the interviewers—something you were trying to avoid all along. Instead, why not answer this question properly on your terms in a way that makes you look good—something you are trying to do throughout your interview.

Most people who attempt to answer this question about their weaknesses try to put a positive spin on it by using false weaknesses such as, *"I'm too organized"* or *"I'm a perfectionist"* or *"I'm a workaholic"*. This is an old worn-out trick that interviewers see right through as a lame attempt to make yourself look good by squeezing words, such as "organized" or "perfectionist" or "workaholic", into the picture of your weakness. Nice try, but that is a failure in answering the question properly too.

So should you just spill your guts about every nook and cranny of your dark side and worst habits to the shock and horror of everyone in the room? Of course you shouldn't. There's no need to turn your answer into a freak show, horror film or a *Saturday Night Live* skit. You also don't want to mention weaknesses that are necessary or crucial to you functioning properly in this job.

Interviewers who ask this weakness question are gauging your self-awareness; honesty and sincerity about your limitations; and your ability to overcome your weaknesses and limitations through self-improvement.

What you want to provide your interviewers is a carefully crafted answer that reveals one of your weaknesses or flaws that is not a deal-breaker in your interview; can be fixed or developed; and that you are in the process of fixing and developing that area in your life. Don't mention a weakness that you are doing absolutely nothing to fix, develop or improve, such as watching too much sports on TV. (No wait, I think that's a strength, not a weakness.)

A deal-breaker weakness is something about you that would hurt your chances of being hired. Some examples of deal-breakers are stating you don't like working with people; you can't control your temper and tell people off at work; you have a tendency to ridicule people over email; you sleep on the job; you steal supplies from work or people's lunch from the refrigerator (this one should be a crime punishable by law); you're not a morning person and you have a hard time getting up in the morning which makes you late for work at times; you don't like working overtime or unscheduled longer hours; you fart a lot at work (another crime that should be punishable by law); you are a poor speller or reader; you can't handle pressure; you tend to complain a lot at work; or you tend to freeze up and remain quiet in meetings, discussion groups or collaboration sessions.

So how do you respond to the weakness question?

Pick a weakness that is still acceptable and tolerable in the workplace that you are working on to develop and improve. Here are some examples of weaknesses you can use while showing your self-improvement efforts to fix or improve those weaknesses:

- You need more leadership skills but you are reading more about developing leadership qualities or taking leadership classes.

- You lack skill or experience in a particular area but you are studying or practicing that area more.

- You get nervous in interviews but you try to overcome these nerves by preparing and practicing interviews through role-playing and positive visualization techniques as much as possible.

- You've been late to meetings because you lose track of time at work; therefore, you try to always calendar your meetings and set reminders as soon as you're scheduled for one (every interviewer can identify with this weakness).

- You can be too frank or direct at times with your co-workers but you're studying more on proper communications skills, personality types and how to properly influence people.

- Sometimes you'll spend more time than necessary on a project because you can be too critical of your own work, leaving yourself with less time to complete the project before the suspense date; however, you're trying to learn not to waste so much time checking and rechecking things too many times and by studying time management skills.

Cultural Fitness Questions and Answers

Here are some actual questions about cultural fitness or soft skills that job interviewers may ask you. After each question, I provide insight into what the interviewers are looking for when asking each question; and some suggested answers to some of these questions. This way, you can answer each question the way you want to after you understand what the interviewer is looking for when asking the question. Keep in mind that all of these questions interviewers ask are used primarily to help them determine your cultural fit in their company.

- **Question:** Who was your most difficult supervisor and why?
- **Same Question:** Tell me about a time you had to work with a difficult person on your team.
- **Same Question:** Explain a workplace experience with a difficult customer and how did you deal with them.
- **Same Question:** Have you worked with someone you didn't like? If so, how did you handle that situation?

- **Answer:** These questions really aren't about the difficult supervisor, co-worker or customer. The interviewer is not inviting you to start bad mouthing former co-workers; play the blame game; or start throwing people under the bus, backing the bus up, and then running them over again for good measure. Step away from the gas pedal.

  These conflict questions are about **you** and how **you** handle conflict, difficult people or difficult social situations in the workplace.

  With these types of questions, interviewers are checking your interpersonal skills, referred to as soft skills or people skills. The interviewer is trying to gauge your habits, attitudes, tendencies, oral communications, teamwork, problem-solving skills and emotional quotient (EQ) when dealing with difficult people and social situations to determine if you are a good employee and amicable person worth selecting to work for their company.

  It's important that you formulate your answer in a way that shows you can maintain a mature, professional and positive behavior in difficult social situations resulting in ***positive results and outcomes***. If you had some bad bosses or co-workers in past jobs, don't ever call them bad bosses or co-workers. Instead say they were challenging or difficult bosses or co-workers.

  The wrong way to answer this question is responding to conflict *with* conflict. You do not want to appear as the type of person who would escalate the conflict further or someone who turns into a raging Hulk at the slightest provocation.

Instead, you want to show how you can *de-escalate* conflict; how you are willing to communicate professionally during conflict; and how you're able to come to healthy positive resolutions of conflicts. Show the interviewer how you will take the high road in resolving conflicts.

Most people have had or will have some form of conflict at work. If you experienced conflict at a previous job, use one of these past experiences with conflict as an example.

Go over these three areas when talking about that workplace conflict:

1. Pick a specific example of conflict you experienced at a past job. The conflict does not have to involve you directly. It could be two other people in conflict at work.

2. Talk about how **you** responded to the conflict in a professional manner. Share how your words or actions de-escalated the conflict.

3. Then share how your professional response to the conflict helped (not hurt) the situation.

If you haven't experienced conflicts in past workplaces, you can tell the interviewer that you've been fortunate to have had great bosses and co-workers to work with in your past jobs; that you and your co-workers had mutual respect for one another; and that you got along well with everyone in your former jobs.

If you can answer the conflict question in one of these ways, you will pass this question with flying colors.

- **Question:** Who was your best supervisor and why?

- **Answer:** This question really isn't about your best boss, supervisor or manager. It is about *you* and how you interact with people, particularly with workplace management and authority.

  With this question, interviewers are checking your interpersonal skills, primarily your perspective on supervision and authority that will make you a good employee and compatible to work with. It's important that you formulate your answer in a way that shows you can maintain mature, professional and positive behavior interacting with both management personnel and your peers within a workplace setting.

  Use this opportunity to show your interviewers you know how to give compliments and praise to other people in the workplace—bosses or co-workers. Feel free to talk about bosses or co-workers you enjoyed working for or working with; and give specifics about what you liked about the person. Show the interviewer that you are the type of person who speaks well of people and likes to give people pats on the back. Interviewers like this because it shows you can bring a positive attitude and positive vibes to the workplace. People who are upbeat and positive are the type of people employers like to bring into their company culture.

- **Question:** Do you prefer to work independently or on a team?

- **Answer:** There is no right or wrong answer to this question because it is good to be able to work independently and on a team.

  Stating you enjoy working independently shows you are confident in your abilities; however, if you only like working independently, this makes the interviewer think you are not a good team player.

  Stating you enjoy working in a team shows you are a team player; however, if you only like working in a team environment, this makes the interviewer think you are not confident in your own abilities to accomplish tasks on your own.

Therefore, the safe way to answer this question is to tell the recruiter you like both. You enjoy working in a team environment, but you also enjoy work independently when the job requires you to do so. By telling the interviewer you are comfortable working both on a team and independently, you make yourself appear as a person with a broader, more dynamic and complex mix of qualities for the job.

- **Question:** Explain a workplace situation where you had to think outside the box.

- **Answer:** This question really isn't about the inside or outside of the box. It is about *you* and how well you process, manage and solve difficult or complex situations or problems. With this question, interviewers are checking your abilities in problem-solving, acting as a team player, flexibility, adaptability, creativity, innovativeness, initiative and working well under pressure.

    This is another opportunity for you to stand out above other job-seeking candidates because you get to talk about a challenging issue at work that you used your problem-solving skills, creativity, innovativeness or adaptability to solve the problem. It doesn't necessarily have to be an experience where you had to think outside the box; just an experience where you had to *think*. It could be a problem that required careful thought process, insight, investigation, research and application by you to make things work in that previous job. As with your resume, show how what you did provided **good results with a positive impact** to that workplace.

- **Question:** Where do you see yourself in 5 years?
- **Same Question:** What are your long-term career goals?

- **Same Question:** Where do you see yourself in the future?

- **Answer:** This question might come across as odd in an age where many professionals are ready to move on to their next job in 3 to 5 years. The important thing to recognize in this interview question is that interviewers want to know if you are interested in staying long term with their company and workplace.

  It costs the company money to hire you (such as paying a hefty commission to a staffing agency), and it will cost the company money when you leave. Therefore, interviewers want to know if you will give their company some return on their investment after hiring you; or do your career goals indicate that you will potentially leave their company in the near future—1 or 3 years from now.

  Hiring managers also know that candidates that seek long-term relationships with their company are more likely to be more productive workers. Any job-seeking candidates who reveal they plan to move on from their company in a couple of years are oftentimes the first to be eliminated from the selection process.

  Even if you don't plan on being with that company long term, tell your interviewers you hope to be with their company long term or 5 years from now (if the interviewer asks you where you plan to be in 5 years). Remember, there may be 5–15 other applicants waiting in line to interview for the same job as you. When faced with equally qualified job candidates, interviewers are more inclined to select the candidate that will provide the greatest return on their company's investment.

  It's unrealistic in the 21st century to expect any job-hunting candidate to still be with a company beyond 5 years. So you're just answering their unrealistic question and expectation with an equally unrealistic answer. The fact is you, the hiring manager or anyone else doesn't know if you'll be with that company after 1, 2 or 5 years; unless, of course, you know how to work a crystal ball. Who knows, you may like it there and decide to stay beyond 5 years.

So rather than laughing in the face of interviewers for asking this outdated question, simply pat yourself on the back for their interest in wanting you to stay with their company long term. Just play along with their silly reindeer game; take a deep breath of gratitude; and then give the interviewer the assurance they need with a positive answer that indicates you plan to give them a return on their investment. You can share other long-term goals you may have; just make sure they include their company in the long term.

When you do share other goals, make sure all of these goals show how they will make you a better worker for the company. In other words, do not share personal goals that have nothing to do with the job opening or the company. Your goals are in competition with the goals of other candidates seeking that position. Don't waste this opportunity sharing goals that don't make you appear as a better choice than other candidates.

If you have a problem with this approach to this question, just remember this one thing: You could easily be more qualified than the other candidates they will interview; but this company won't hesitate to sweep you under the rug because you suggested you will not commit to the company's ball and chain beyond 1–3 years.

Here are a couple of ways you can answer the goals question:

1. *I hope to gain further experience in this company that will allow me to excel in this position, being one of your top performers and advance in this company.*

2. *My long term goals are to stay with this company, continue growing in knowledge and experience that will benefit me (such as pay increases or other opportunities), this company and this company's customers.*

- **Question:** What are you passionate about?
- **Same Question:** What do you do for fun?
- **Same Question:** How do you spend your free time?

- **Answer:** If you are hired, your work area, desk or cubicle will most likely be right next to the people who are interviewing you for that job. Because of this, the interviewers just want to know if you'll fit in well with them on a daily basis.

  Interviewers also like knowing you are not just another worker who can do the job. They want a well-rounded person with a life outside of work; that you possibly have interests outside the workplace that are similar to the interviewers' lives outside the workplace.

  Here are some suggestions to make a social or emotional connection with your interviewers when answering this question:

  - Share your interests, hobbies, sports, places you like to visit or vacation; books you enjoy reading; music you enjoy listening to; a talent you enjoy developing, such as painting, singing or writing; or volunteer or charitable work you enjoy doing.

  - Try to include things you read about in the interviewer's and company's social network profile. This is where your research into each interviewer's or the company's social media posts, such as on Facebook or LinkedIn, will be invaluable as I previously mentioned.

- **Question:** What is your greatest weakness?
- **Same Question:** What area do you need to improve on the most?
- **Same Question:** Name one thing about yourself that needs improving.
- **Same Question:** What is one thing your previous boss, supervisor or manager would say you need to improve on?

Interview Preparation and Tips

- **Same Question:** Tell me about a time when you failed.

- **Answer:** Interviewers who ask this weakness question are gauging your self-awareness, honesty and sincerity about your limitations; and your ability to overcome your limitations through self-improvement. Since I've gone over this weakness question, we'll move on to the next question.

- **Question:** Why do you want to work here?
- **Same Question:** Why are you here?
- **Same Question:** Why are you interested in this job?
- **Same Question:** Why should we hire you?
- **Same Question:** Why do you think you will be successful at this job?

Answer: Interviewers use this question to not only ask you about your interest in the open position; they are asking you about your interest in their company; and they want to know what you have to offer the company.

Your answer to this question should include three things:

1. What attracted you to this job.

2. Why you chose this company to work for.

3. What you have to offer this company.

Share what attracted you to this job: Use the job description and what information you learned about this job online to explain what attracted you to this job. Share your interest and enthusiasm in the equipment, processes, tasks, people or other aspects about the job description that made you want to work there. Use this opportunity to share how you performed these same aspects of the job description at previous jobs. Interviewers want to know which candidate fits best in this open position; so make sure you take the time to show how your abilities match well with the job description.

Share why you chose this company to work for: The research you performed on the company will provide you several good reasons for why you want to work for the company. This is a good opportunity to show you've done your research into the company; that you like the company culture, mission and industry; and that you're impressed with the company's accomplishments, awards and press releases.

Share what you have to offer this company: Use the job description and what information you learned about the job to explain how your knowledge, experience and skill sets fit in well with this job; how you will be able to contribute to the company to produce positive results and impacts; and how you feel or know you will be successful in this job.

- **Question:** Why did you leave your last job?
- **Same Question:** Why do you want to leave your current job?
- **Same Question:** What were your reasons for leaving your last job?
- **Same Question:** Why didn't you remain at your last position?
- **Same Question:** What was it about your last position that made you decide to move on?

- **Answer:** Interviewers know candidates seeking work are like a box of chocolates: *You never know what you're gonna get.* That's why you can expect them to ask this prying question into your reasons for leaving your current or last job. They want to know if you're as good as Milk Duds or just a dud. Are you as refreshing as sweet, cold lemonade on a hot summer day or are you just another angry, sour lemon bringing your problems to their company. Are they getting another company's finest employee or someone's worst nightmare?

Your goal when answering this question is to ensure the interviewers that you're the real deal when it comes to being a quality employee worth hiring. You want to show the interviewers that you are a stable, reliable and responsible employee.

Regardless if you didn't like your current or previous job, boss, co-workers, customers or salary; don't provide your interviewers negative reasons for leaving your job. If you tell the interviewers you are leaving or left your job because of people or money; your interviewers will automatically assume you won't like their people or salary either. **Translation:** scratch your name off their list of people they would hire. Give them positive reasons for leaving your job. Show your interviewers that you are leaving or left your job for the right reasons—not the wrong reasons. Make your answer more about moving on toward something positive rather than leaving something negative. Remember, interviewers are comparing you with other job-seeking candidates to determine which person they're going to hire. Don't give them a reason to eliminate you from the competition.

You should start your answer off by telling the interviews some positive things you like about your current or last job, and then proceed to tell them positive reasons for why you plan to leave or left that job.

Some examples of positive reasons for leaving a job include looking for a more challenging job; you are looking for a position that will allow you to develop and broaden your skills or provide you more growth potential in your career; you weren't able to utilize all of your talents in your current or previous job, so you felt it was time to move on to opportunities that allow you to contribute more to a company with your skill sets; you've outgrown your current or last position and are looking for new ways to continue growing in your career; although you enjoy your job, you need to find a job closer to your home with a shorter commute time; you were working on a 6-month or 1-year contract, and when the contract ended, you decided to take some time off to hone your skills, work on some other personal projects or hobbies, complete some certifications and take some vacation time off and do some traveling before heading back into the workforce.

By the way, whenever there are large gaps of time in between jobs, you should always try to answer this question by showing you were working on *self-improvement* during your time away from work, such as constantly reading, studying or researching areas of your career field, taking classes, developing your skills through practice, working on certifications, attending workshops, self-employment activities, volunteer work, and so forth.

You should also include the answers from the previous question about "*why you want to work at their company*", such as sharing what attracted you to their company; why you chose their company to work for; and what you have to offer their company. Make the interviewers feel as if their company and this available position is your dream job; a much better position than your previous job.

Questions to Ask the Interviewers and Closure

Once your interview is about to conclude, the hiring manager or another person leading the interview will ask you, "**Do you have any questions for us?**" Don't take this question lightly and pass on the opportunity to ask any questions. Doing so shows your lack of preparation; lack of interest in the company; and will cause you to miss out on another opportunity to shine one last time above other candidates in front of your interviewers.

The entire interview process is about you making yourself stand out above all the other candidates those interviewers will evaluate; and this last part of your interview should be used for that same goal. Use this opportunity to show the interviewers that you are interested enough in their company and this job that you've done your homework—you researched their company and you've prepared your questions.

Prepare 2–3 questions ahead of time that you will ask the interviewers based on your research of the company or areas where you can contribute to their team. Ask smart, thoughtful questions that are focused on how you can contribute to the company, fulfill the job description or enhance their team. Always try to ask the interviewers open-ended questions rather than questions that can be answered with a simple yes or no.

I usually type my questions on my computer; print them out, and take them with me to my job interviews. When interviewers ask me if I have any questions for them, I'll take out this list of questions and start asking my prepared questions.

The following list is suggestions on the types of questions you can ask your interviewers (pick only 2–3 questions to ask):

- *Can you share some of the hot issues, projects or immediate needs you have going on that the candidate you hire would be used in?*

    When the interviewer tells you about projects or needs that you have experience in, continue the conversation by telling them how what you did at past jobs can help them meet those needs.

- *Some teams have established procedures and like things the way they are. Other teams see room for improving their processes. Can you tell me if your team prefers to keep things the way they are or prefers to keep improving their processes?*

    This question is a great one to ask if your resume and skill sets show you have improved processes in past jobs. If the interviewers tell you they like to improve their processes, you can quickly point out how you've done that in past jobs. If they tell you they like to keep things the way they are, you know in advance the modus operandi of their team so that when you are hired, you don't try to change things. In any case, you show the interviewers you are interested in making things better for their team.

- *Based on my resume and my responses in this interview, can my skill sets help with your projects right away?*

As the interviewers try to answer this question, this prompts them to quickly consider how your skill sets can be used to fill the current needs on their team. It also lets the interviewers know you are eager to get started with contributing on their team.

- *For the candidate you select, what are the most important things you want that candidate to accomplish their first 60 days to help your team?*

Again, this lets the interviewers know you are eager to get started with contributing on their team.

- *I've researched your company website and noticed a lot of positive things about your company, such as* [name some positive things you read on their company website]. *What do you like most about your company?*

This not only shows you are interested enough in their company to review their company website and were impressed with what you read; you also complimented them by telling them positive things you read about their company. Now they get to tell you what they like most about their company—this is a win-win question for you and the interviewers.

Just as there are questions you should ask in an interview, there are some questions you should not ask. Asking the wrong questions show you didn't do any research on the company or are more focused on what the job can do for you than what you can do for the job.

When it comes to asking interviewers questions, take some sage advice from President John F. Kennedy's Inaugural Address in Washington D.C. when he took over the helm as our nation's 35th president: *Ask not what your employer can do for you; ask what you can do for your employer.* (Ok, he used the word "country" instead of "employer", but you get the idea.)

Bringing up the wrong topics in the form of these questions I'm going to show you tell interviewers you did not come prepared for the interview or are more interested in yourself than in fulfilling the requirements of the job. Asking poor, shallow or selfish questions will easily turn off the interviewers and lessen your chances of being selected above other candidates.

The following list is questions you should not ask the interviewers:

- Asking a question that is answered by reading the job description. This implies you did not take the time to thoughtfully read the job description. Asking these types of questions make you look like you didn't care enough about the responsibilities of the job to read the description in detail. Get the job description from the staffing agency recruiter before your interview; then review it completely.

- Asking questions related to what the company does that is answered by reading the company's website. This implies you did not care enough about their company to do your homework and research their website.

- Anything related to money. Asking questions about salary or compensation implies you are more interested in the money than in the job.

- Anything related to company benefits, such as health or dental insurance, vacation, training and education, perks and discounts. Asking questions about benefits implies you are more interested in the company benefits than the job.
- Anything related to promotions, transfers to other teams or the possibility of working a second part-time job. These types of questions imply you aren't going to stay with their team for very long. It shows you are not 100 percent focused on this job opportunity.
- Working remotely by telecommuting from home instead of coming in to work. This question implies you don't like working with customers, colleagues or leadership; or lack the available schedule or discipline to work within your scheduled work hours.
- Questions related to drug testing; background or reference checks to get the job; the company's stance on legal use of marijuana; or company policy on Internet use or monitoring of your social network profiles. These types of questions imply there is something wrong in your life that you do not want the company to know about.
- Working hours, working late or on weekends. These types of questions imply your schedule might not fit into the working hours required for this job or you are less inclined to make sacrifices to make it to work for odd hours when the work situation requires your presence. You don't want to come off as a person who is always watching the clock at work, ready at the top or bottom of the hour to leave work for the day. Once you are hired, you will be told your working hours; and may be given the opportunity to flex your hours or work remotely from home on occasion. You may need to know if this job is a swing shift, night shift or on weekends,

but try to get this information from your recruiter before the interview.

- Questions about the previous person who filled this position and why they departed. This question implies you're being nosy. Regardless who previously filled this position and the reasons for their departure; this information is none of your business in the company's eyes.

- Questions about negative things you've read in your research of the company or negative things you may have heard somewhere. These types of questions imply you do not hold the company in high regard. Just as you are trying to put your best foot forward in the interview, so is the employer. Don't bite the hand that feeds you or step on the feet that greet you.

- Questions about who or how many people are on your team to help you accomplish the responsibilities outlined in the job description. This question implies you are not qualified enough to do the job yourself, and shows a lack of confidence in your own abilities.

Closing Statements at the End of Your Job Interview

Once the interviewers have answered your 2–3 questions at the end of your interview, take the initiative to add some closing statements to make one last good impression on the hiring manager and the other interviewers in the room. Don't wait for the interviewers to ask you for closing statements because they won't. Just add them in the conversation immediately after the interviewers have answered your questions at the end of the interview.

There are two things you need to prepare to say in your final closing statements:

1. Thanking the interviewers.

2. Ask for the job.

The first thing you want to close with is thanking the interviewers for taking the time out of their busy schedules to interview you. Let them know you appreciate them giving you the opportunity to be interviewed by them. Gratitude goes a long way when it comes to your cultural fit with the interviewers.

The second thing you want to do in your closing statement is ask for the job. The greatest salesperson in the world will not make a single sale until they ask for the sale. The answer is always no until you ask for the sale. If you don't ask, you can't have. After everything the hiring manager has told you about the company; after all the interview questions they asked you; let the interviewers know you are still interested in the open position and you are still enthusiastic about working with them.

You could combine both the thank you and asking for the job in a couple of closing sentences. You could say something simple such as the following:

I'd like to take this time to say thank you to all of you for taking time out of your busy day to interview me. I'm very interested in this job, and I would enjoy working with all of you on your team.

By simply letting the interviewers know you're interested in the job and would enjoy working with them is telling them you want the job. That's all they need to hear from you to reassure them you still want the job after being grilled by them with so many questions. They can't tell you on the spot that you've got the job because they most likely have to interview other candidates after you.

Don't say, "*I want this job*", because those words make you appear desperate and it sounds like you just want the job and don't care about working with them.

Don't ask, "*When can I start?*", because that makes you come across as arrogant and as if you blindly presume you've already beat out all the competition before all the competition has had a chance to interview.

Role-Playing Job Interviews

Role-playing the interview is an important part to interview preparation. Role-play is especially beneficial if you are new to the job interview process; haven't done an interview in a while; or always seem to be nervous or apprehensive in interviews.

Role-play exercises allow you to act out an imaginary situation that mirrors a real situation to make you feel more natural and comfortable with that situation when it is happening in real life.

Practice Role-Playing with People You Know

By role-playing interviews with someone you know, you give yourself the opportunity to practice your interviewing skills in a friendly, safe, non-threatening, relaxed, controlled environment; gauge and assess how you actually perform in an interview; identify your strengths and weaknesses; receive critiques from trusted family members or friends helping you in the role-play; and make the necessary changes and improvements to your interviewing skills after each role-play. All of these benefits of role-playing can occur before the real interview takes place.

To perform interview role-playing, you take the role of the job candidate and one or several other people will play the role of the interviewers. Use your family members, roommates or friends to help you with this role-playing exercise. You can even use your children or younger siblings and relatives as the interviewers.

As the job-hunting candidate, start with your prepared introduction; then have the person or people playing the role of interviewers ask you questions. Have one of them end the questions and ask you if you have any questions for them. That's when you should ask your prepared questions for the interviewers. Then end the interview by thanking the interviewers for their time and let them know you want the job.

Invest in your children's future—role play.

After you've practiced this several times as the candidate, you can do something really special. If you're role-playing with young family members, such as children or young adults, reverse the roles and let your younger family members be the job candidate. By allowing younger family members experience being interviewed in the candidate role, you will be providing them with one of the most important life skills they will be using throughout their adult life. Why not get them use to the idea of interviewing for a job in a fun, safe family atmosphere. There's an old proverb that says, *"Start children off on the way they should go, and even when they are old they will not turn from it."* Proverbs 22:6 NIV

Have fun with these imaginary interviews and learn to relax, smile and enjoy role-playing the interviewing process. The more you relax and enjoy these role-playing interviews during practice, the more relaxed and comfortable you will be in actual job interviews.

Don't forget that smiling and laughing is allowed in interviews. I've smiled and laughed with interviewers in a lot of actual interviews. Smiling and laughter in an interview is usually a good sign that you and your interviewers are connecting with each other—an important aspect of cultural fitness for a job. Just don't laugh for any reason in your actual interview—that means you're crazy. However, if someone said something funny during the interview, show your lighter side by laughing appropriately if someone cracks a joke in the interview. Laughing shows your interviewers you'll be fun to work with. Don't go overboard with your laugh, such as making snorting sounds or loud vociferous noises when laughing. As with your attire and appearance, keep your laughter in moderation.

In interview role-play, you should select a comfortable place where you can pretend being in the interview room, such as in your dining room, living room, dorm room or any other place where there is at least two chairs and table.

Read through this entire chapter and the following chapter 9 on *During the Interview* before performing role-playing exercises for job interviews.

The following list is some of the things you should include in your interview role-playing:

- Your initial greeting and handshake with the people you first meet at your interview. (This is covered in chapter 9.)

- Your entrance into the interview room and taking your seat. Most interviews are in a small meeting room with a table and chairs. The job candidate usually sits on one end of the table and the interviewers sit side by side on the opposite side of the table. If you don't have a table in the room you are practicing in, that's fine. Just use chairs and sit opposite of each other.

- Your posture and attitude when standing or sitting. (This is covered in chapter 9.)

- Listening to the hiring manager introduce the interviewers and sharing about his or her company. Since this about you and not the interviewers, give the person role-playing as the interviewer a ready-made sheet they can use to introduce their imaginary interviewers and talk about their imaginary company. (This is covered in more detail in chapter 9.)

- Share some things about yourself—your technical fit and cultural fit—when the interviewer asks you to tell them about yourself after their interviewer introductions. **1–2 minutes** talking about your **technical fit** and about **15–30 seconds** to talk about your **cultural fitness**.

- Answering questions from the interviewer/s. Use a checklist of questions the role-playing interviewer can ask you. You can make several lists of questions if you have more than one person playing as the interviewer. If possible, try to list items that are in the job description or general items in your career field that interviewers might ask. (This is covered in more detail in chapter 9.)

- Asking some questions after the interviewer asks you if you have any questions for them at the end of the interviewer.

- Thanking the interviewer/s for their time and let the interviewer/s know you are interested in the job and would enjoy working with them. (This is covered in chapter 9.)

- Repeat this role-play as many times as you can until you feel comfortable and confident with your interview performance.

- Most importantly, have fun doing this. You and your family or friends helping you should enjoy these role-play exercises. The more you enjoy these exercises in practice, the more you'll enjoy these job interviews in real life.

Even the US Military Performs Job Interview Role-Playing for Their Departing Military Members

Each branch of the US military has a transition assistance program (TAP), a program mandated by Congress and implemented by the Department of Defense in partnership with the Labor Department and

Veterans Affairs. TAP training helps military members that are preparing to leave the military to successfully transition back to civilian life and start a new career.

Part of the TAP program are employment workshops provided by the Department of Labor that teaches departing military members valuable lessons on how to be competitive in the job market; covering topics such as employment, training and education opportunities, resume writing, job search strategies, goal setting, interview preparation, negotiating their salary and other job-hunting skills. This training gives our military members the best chance for success in civilian jobs.

When I was in the US Air Force serving my last tour of duty at Ramstein Air Base in Germany, the time had come for me to prepare to retire from the military and return to civilian life. To help prepare me for my transition, I went through the Air Force TAP program.

One of the most beneficial TAP workshops I enjoyed taking part in was the job interview role-playing workshop. This workshop split all of us military participants in groups of two. One person would play the part of the interviewer and the other person was the job-seeking candidate.

After we received lessons from our job counselors on interview best practices, we each took turns interviewing the other person as if we were the employer; and then we would reverse roles and would take a turn at being the job candidate who was being interviewed. Each time we completed our interviews, we and our instructors would provide feedback to each other about our performance as a job candidate.

At first, all of us felt a bit nervous and apprehensive as we went through the role of the job candidate being interviewed. As we repeated this role-playing, we each got more comfortable and confident with talking to our imaginary interviewer; showcasing our skill sets; incorporating our past work history in the conversation; answering interviewer questions; and highlighting how we could be a positive contribution to a company.

Thanks to those job interview role-playing sessions in that TAP workshop, I felt very comfortable and confident in interviews after leaving the military; and I've enjoyed interviewing for jobs ever since.

CHAPTER NINE
It's Game Day—The Job Interview

Be so good they can't ignore you.
Steve Martin

During the Job Interview

Everyone Gets a Little Nervous Before Game Day

It's perfectly normal to feel a little nervous before or during your job interview. Everyone feels a bit nervous before an important event in their life. Lawrence Peter Berra, better known as "Yogi" Berra, a Major League Baseball player, manager and coach for the New York Yankees was an 18-time All-Star and 10-time World Series champion while a player. When it came to being nervous, he said, *"I always got nervous the nights we played in the World Series. First pitch, I was nervous. Then after that, forget it; I'd start playing."*

In this chapter, I'm going to show you how to forget the nerves and start playing and focusing on the game—successfully passing your job interview. I'm going to show you how to beat those nerves into submission so you can feel as confident and comfortable as possible during your job interview.

Sure it takes a little courage to walk in that interview room. But what is courage anyway? It is simply doing things even when you're afraid.

Mark Twain said, *"Courage is not the lack of fear. It is acting in spite of it."*

Major League Baseball player Babe Ruth is famously known for hitting 714 home runs in his career. In 1923, he broke the record for the most home runs in a season and broke the record for the highest batting average. Do you know what other record Babe Ruth broke that year? He struck out more times than any other Major League Baseball player that year. Babe Ruth struck out 1,330 times in his career; a Major League record he held for 30 years; and was known as the king of strikeouts during his career. So what did Babe Ruth have to say about striking out? He said, *"Never let the fear of striking out get in your way."*

Sure, you may strike out a few times during job interviews—so what. Everyone strikes out now and then. Don't let that get in the way of you going at bat again into another job interview and hitting a home run next time.

John Wayne said, *"Courage is being scared to death—and saddling up anyway."*

I'm going to show you how to saddle up, *pilgrim*. We all have to do things that sometimes make us nervous or afraid. The good news is that the more we prepare, practice and do those things; the easier and less fearful those things become.

The Job Interview Process

Not all employers interview their candidates the same way before making a selection on which candidate to hire. One employer may hire a candidate after one in-person interview. Another employer may choose to have two in-person interviews. A third employer may opt to perform phone interviews first as a screening process to decide which candidates they will ask in for an in-person interview. A fourth employer might screen their candidates with written technical questions first, to determine which candidates they will grant a phone or in-person interview.

Most interviews last an average of one hour from the time your scheduled interview starts to the end of your interview when the hiring manager is walking you back to the front entrance of the company building. For starting positions at fast food restaurants or some retail stores, your interview may last only 30 minutes. If your interview goes past one hour, it is usually a good sign that the interviewers are interested in you. A much shorter than normal interview is usually an indication that things are not going so well. When the person leading the interview purposely cuts the interview short, it is because he or she came to the conclusion early in the interview that you are not a good fit for the position.

Any time there is more than one interview in the interview process, it is a good sign each time you are invited back for the next interview. Take a moment to pat yourself on the back for a successful performance each time you are invited back by the employer for the next level of the interview process. It's not a time to worry; it's a time to feel good about how you did in the previous interview.

Your ultimate goal during your job interview is to show and convince all the interviewers in the room, especially the hiring manager, that you are the best fit—*technically* and *culturally*—with their company and team members, many of whom are interviewing you in that room.

By **"technically fit"** I mean you have to answer the interviewer's technical questions well enough to convince them you have the hard skills to do this job well. Your technical fitness determines how well you fit with the responsibilities outlined in the job description.

By **"culturally fit"** I mean your appearance, personality, enthusiasm, interest, sincerity and attitude you display while answering the interviewer's questions has to convince them you can fit in and work well with the members of your new team with your soft skills.

Hard skills define your level of technical ability to perform the job. Soft skills define your level of social skills to fit in and interact with your co-workers, managers and customers.

Measuring your cultural fitness does not mean that the moment you enter the interview room, someone is going to hand you a personality test to complete. What this does mean is that while the interviewers are openly observing your hard skills as they ask you technical questions related to the job description, they are silently observing your soft skills;

your cultural fitness as they watch how you appear in their eyes; and how you respond to their soft skills questions.

This means that your technical fit (hard skills) is observed **objectively and unbiased** by the interviewers—you either know the answers to the technical questions or you don't. The interviewer's personal feelings, emotions and opinions do not come into play in your answers to their technical questions.

Your cultural fitness (soft skills), on the other hand, are observed **subjectively and biased** by the interviewers—their opinion of you is based on their own individual perspective of what makes a person a good fit in their workplace. The interviewer's sense or judgement of your cultural fitness is based on their personal feelings, emotions and opinions.

The good news about the job interview process is that you may not be the best technically fit candidate for the job (other candidates may answer the technical questions better than you), but if you showed a much better cultural fit for the job (you made the interviewers feel they would get along better with you than with the other candidates), interviewers may be more likely to pick you than the other candidates.

The bad news about the job interview process is you may be the best technically fit candidate for the job (you may have answered all the technical questions better than all the other candidates), but because you weren't the most culturally fit person for the job (you made the interviewers feel they would not get along better with you than with the other candidates), the interviewers are more likely to pass on you for another candidate.

Your qualifications and skill sets—your technical fit—are what got you the attention of the ATS system, the recruiter and the hiring manager; and ultimately got you the job interview. But your social skills, your soft skills, your cultural fit is what may be the deciding factor in getting you hired for the job.

The interviewers need to be pleased with what you know about the job, but they also need to like who you are as a person in order to select you for the job above the other candidates. Your task during the interview process is to make them like you both as a professional who can do the job and as a person they would enjoy working with. My job is to help you accomplish both with the information provided in this chapter.

The list below is the key areas you should focus on *during* your job interview:

- Prescreening questions and answers before the job interview

- The phone interview

- Arrival at your job interview

- Introductions in your job interview

- Intelligence quotient (IQ) versus emotional quotient (EQ) for job interviews

- The importance of attitude in your job interview

- Power posture, power thoughts and power words for job interviews

- Other factors that impact your job interview

- Job interview questions and answers

- Questions to ask the interviewers and closure

Prescreening Questions and Answers before the Job Interview

In some rare instances, an employer will screen candidates with technical questions before granting them a phone interview or in-person interview. Employers may use this pre-interview screening process for senior level positions that require a greater depth of knowledge or experience, or they may require candidates at all levels undergo this prescreening process.

Employers use the prescreening process to filter out job-hunting candidates whose resume caught their eye; but the interviewers do not want to waste their time interviewing someone who cannot demonstrate the right level of technical fit they're looking for in candidates. They only want to interview candidates that exhibit a certain level of knowledge and understanding about the different aspects of the job description they want the candidates to possess. Those candidates who answer the prescreening technical questions well are given either a phone interview or in-person interview as the next step, depending on the interviewing process used by the employer.

Employers typically implement this prescreening process in one of two ways:

1. They have the staffing agency recruiter ask you the prescreening questions over the phone.

2. They have the recruiter email you the questions to complete on your own time.

The good thing about prescreening questions—over the phone or email—from the employer is that these questions give you a sense of the type of questions the interviewers plan to ask you in the actual phone interview or in-person interview. If you pass the prescreening questions and the hiring manager wants to interview you; pat yourself on the back because this typically means you have the right technical knowledge to perform well in the actual job interview.

During one job-hunting occasion for a particular IT position I was seeking through a staffing agency, the employer sent me six prescreening questions through my staffing agency recruiter. One question was on Spanning Tree Protocol (STP) and the other five questions were about routing protocols. Most of these questions were accompanied with network drawings having problems I had to decipher and fix before I could properly answer the questions correctly. This is just one example of how prescreening question can be used by employers. Naturally, the employer will tailor these prescreening questions to each person's line of work.

When the Recruiter Asks You the Prescreening Questions

When the recruiter asks you prescreening questions on behalf of the employer, the recruiter may start asking you these questions without warning in your first phone conversation with the recruiter. If this happens to you, the first thing you need to realize is the fact that you are actually being prescreened for an interview with the employer. Therefore, how you respond to the recruiter is crucial at this point.

This unannounced prescreening could easily catch you off guard because you may want to review some subjects before being asked these all-important technical questions.

You can do one of two things in response to these unannounced technical questions from the recruiter:

1. Delay the prescreening for another day.

2. Start answering the prescreening questions on the spot.

Delay the Prescreening for another Day

One option is you can tell the recruiter that you didn't know they were going to ask you some prescreening questions; and you prefer to have a day or two to go over some of your notes before you are prescreened with these questions. Don't be shy about interrupting the recruiter in the middle of them asking you these prescreening questions to tell them you want to postpone any prescreening questions until later.

If you try to answer these questions immediately over the phone and perform poorly, that will end your chances to be interviewed by the employer and you will not hear from that recruiter again—at least not for that job opening.

If you tell the recruiter you want to postpone the questions until you've had a chance to perform a quick review to brush up on some topics, the recruiter will either accept your request and contact you later or try to press you to answer those questions now.

Rarely will the recruiter pass over you and move on to another candidate when you ask to postpone the prescreening questions. Once the recruiter has contacted you, it means the computerized ATS system and the recruiter think your resume is a good fit for the job opening; so the recruiter is not going to walk away from you so easily. That would be like throwing money away, or in recruiter terms, throwing their commission away.

You are only going to have one shot at these prescreening questions. Instead of worrying about what the recruiter might think of you asking them to wait a couple of days for you to answer those prescreening questions, you should be focused more on passing these technical questions that will result in you getting that invitation from the employer for a phone or in-person interview. So if you need to postpone the prescreening questions a couple of days to brush up on some of the items in the job description, tell the recruiter to hold off on the questions a couple of days.

If you haven't even seen the job description from the recruiter yet, ask the recruiter to send you a copy of the job description first before answering the prescreening questions. No doubt, the prescreening questions will cover areas listed in the job description.

Start Answering the Prescreening Questions on the Spot

The second option is you can accept this unexpected challenge on the spot and start answering these prescreening questions off-the-cuff based on your experience, comfort level and confidence in answering these types of technical questions.

I've responded with both of these options at different times in the past when being prescreened over the phone by recruiters who unexpectedly started asking me technical questions. It just depends on how well prepared you are at the time for these prescreening technical questions from recruiters.

When the Recruiter Emails You the Prescreening Questions

In other instances, the staffing agency recruiter or account manager could email you the employer's prescreening questions. When an employer wants to screen candidates this way, the good news is that it is like taking an open book test in school. You can take your time answering these technical questions, reading or researching information found online or in your own books or notes to answer the questions. There's typically no time limit set to complete these questions, but you should complete them as expeditiously as possible.

When you are done answering the technical questions, you will email your answers back to the staffing agent who will forward your answers to the employer for review. If the employer is pleased with your answers and wants to interview you, the recruiter will let you know and ask you when the best day and time is for you to be interviewed by the employer.

Sometimes, it may take over a week before the recruiter provides you feedback from the employer because someone on the interview team who is reviewing your answers may be preoccupied with other work-related priorities or the hiring manager may be on a business or personal trip. If you do not hear back from the recruiter after 1–2 weeks, you should either call or email the recruiter for feedback. Otherwise, accept the recruiter's silence as the recruiter's unprofessional way of letting you know that the employer does not want to interview you.

The Phone Interview

The phone interview we are discussing in this section is not the phone conversations you will have with a staffing agency recruiter or account manager about a job. The phone interview is the job interview you have with the hiring manager and other interviewers over the phone.

After the staffing agency or company HR department forwards your resume over to the hiring manager, it is the hiring manager who makes the final decision if he and his team will interview you by either phone or in-person.

Phone interviews are an elimination process.

The phone interview is oftentimes a vetting and elimination process that interviewers use to determine which job-hunting candidates they want to bring in for an in-person interview.

Make no mistake about it: the phone interview is equally important as an in-person interview because you only get one shot at the phone interview just as with most in-person interviews.

Your ultimate goal in the phone interview is to impress your interviewers enough to make them want to invite you in for an in-person interview. If you do not impress your interviewers over the phone, they will pass over you and that will be the end of any further chances you have of being interviewed in-person with them or being hired for that job.

If you do not pass your phone interview, it will do you no good to try to resubmit your resume to the same employer again through another recruiting agency or through the company's career website. The hiring manager and the rest of the interviewing team have already seen your resume; so they will know it is you again; and they will toss your resume in the trash.

If you pass your phone interview, you will be notified by your staffing agency recruiter or account manager that the hiring manager liked you and wants you to come in for an in-person interview. Passing the phone interview does not necessarily mean you will be hired for the job. It means that you now stand a better chance of being hired because you impressed your interviewers enough during this first elimination round to make them want to interview you in person. You should accept this as a big boost of confidence that the interviewers liked what they heard from you over the phone from both a technical fit and cultural fit standpoint.

Stay on top of your game because you are still competing against other candidates for this job that the employer has already interviewed or plans to interview after you.

Although it is only a phone interview, you should still follow all the applicable guidelines I've pointed out in these *Before the Interview* and *During the Interview* chapters. Don't wait until after a successful phone interview to learn and follow these tips, advice and procedures outlined in these chapters on interview preparation.

How Phone Interviews Benefit the Interviewers

Phone interview conference calls allow the interviewers to either gather together in a company conference room or sit at their separate desks at work while they interview you. A phone interview also allows interviewers in different locations across the country to interview you along with the local interviewers.

If interviewers gather together in a private conference room to interview you over the phone, they will receive your call over the open phone speakers so everyone in the room can hear you speak.

If interviewers are at their individual desks while interviewing you over the phone, each of them typically wear their phone headsets to hear you speak and to ask you questions. This way, everyone in the office does not hear you interviewing for the job.

How Phone Interviews Benefit Job-Hunting Candidates

Phone interviews can also be advantageous to you as the job-hunter as well. A phone interview can be a better option than an in-person interview during times when you are job-hunting while still employed in another job. If you are not working, a phone interview also means you don't have to get dressed up or drive to the interview location.

I've interviewed for jobs while employed by stepping outside of my workplace and going to the privacy of my car to interview for jobs. During a break at work, I've also gotten in my car; drove to a quiet secluded location; and then called in for a phone interview.

When I'm not working, I've interviewed for many jobs via phone at home. I oftentimes preferred the phone interview over the in-person interview because it meant I didn't have to get dressed up and drive to another location for the interview.

A phone interview also provides you the unique advantage of having your computer, resume and notes in front of you while talking to your interviewers over the phone; something I always do when I'm being interviewed over the phone at home.

If you will be interviewed over the phone, pick a location where you can be alone that is quiet and free from distraction. The optimum location for you may be in a room in your home, in your car or some other private area.

How to Call In for a Phone Interview

If the hiring manager wants to interview you by phone, the staffing agency recruiter or account manager will provide you the conference call phone number and a passcode number to call on the day and time of your scheduled interview. The conference call phone recording will tell you when to use the passcode number on your phone.

Just as with arriving early for an in-person interview, you should call the interviewer's number 2–5 minutes before your scheduled interview time. Calling in late for a phone interview is just as bad as arriving late to an in-person interview. It reflects poorly on your ability to plan ahead and perform tasks in a punctual manner.

Once you are on the conference call, the phone system will tell you how many people are currently on the conference call. You should introduce yourself by stating your full name, such as *"Frank McClain is on the line"*, so that if one of the interviewers are already on the line, they'll know you have called in.

If you are the first person on the conference call, wait patiently for someone to arrive. Once you hear someone on the line, again state your full name to let them know you, the job candidate, are on the line for the job interview. One of the interviewers on the conference call will let you know if they are still waiting for other interviewers to call in.

Once all the interviewers have called in to the conference call, the hiring manager or team lead will start things off with introductions just as in an in-person interview; and everything will continue to the end of your interview as it normally would during an in-person interview.

Arrival at Your Job Interview

It's Game Time!

Arrive early to your in-person job interview but not too early; no more than 5–10 minutes early. If you let your interviewers know you've arrived 15 minutes or earlier before your interview start time, they will most likely feel inconvenienced rather than impressed by your "too early" arrival. They're most likely trying to wrap things up with what they're doing at work before your arrival; and now that you've arrived sooner than expected, they'll either feel uncomfortable about making you wait longer or will have to stop what they're doing and come out to greet you.

Either way, it won't start your interview on the right foot like you thought by arriving too early.

It's good to get to the company building 10–15 minutes earlier to make sure you get there in time, but you can wait in your car until 5–10 minutes before your interview start time so that you don't announce your arrival too early to your interviewers. Turn your cell phone off, including the vibrate mode; or better yet, leave your phone in the car prior to entering the employer's building. One of the worst impressions you can make during an interview is having your cell phone go off or the interviewers seeing you look down in a response to the vibration going off. They'll all know what that look means—it means you don't care enough about your job interview to shut off your phone.

Arriving to a Job Interview at a US Government Agency on a Military Installation

Going to a job interview for a US government agency on a military installation presents a few challenges in both getting on the military installation as well as into the government building. Do not fret; there is a process in place to get you on the installation for your interview.

You will not be allowed to enter (walk in or drive in) most US military installations without a military ID card (active or retired military), Common Access Card (CAC) or an escort.

CAC cards are issued to active duty uniformed service personnel, Selected Reserve, DoD civilian employees and eligible contractor personnel. Once you are hired as either a US government civilian employee or contractor, you will be issued a CAC card that is valid for the length of your employment or contract.

Contractor CAC cards are distinguished by a green bar across the front of the card. This CAC card will also provide contractors limited use of other services on the military installation, such as shopping at the military shoppette store (a small convenience store) or filling your car with gas at the gas station.

If you do not have a military ID card or CAC card, someone from the government facility will have to meet you at the front entrance of the military installation to escort you in to your scheduled interview.

Most military installations have a Visitor Center outside one of their gated entrances. The Visitor Center is where you can get a temporary visitor pass to enter the military installation, but you'll need an authorized person with the proper ID credentials to sign you in to get your pass. Therefore, the Visitor Center is where you will most likely meet the person who will escort you to the government agency building where your interview will take place. These Visitor Centers usually have seating areas, restrooms and a drinking fountain while you wait for your escort.

Keep in mind that this whole escort process takes time that might make you late for the start of your interview. Therefore, find out from either the recruiter or from the interviewer (the recruiter will provide you a contact phone number for the interviewer at the government agency) what time should you meet your escort at the Visitor Center.

Introductions in Your Job Interview

When Staffing Agency Recruiters Meet You at Your Job Interview

When you arrive at the employer's building on the day of your interview, you might be greeted by your staffing agency recruiter or account manager if their staffing agency is local to the employer's building. The recruiter or account manager will let you know if they plan to meet you at the interview site. If your staffing agency recruiter or account manager is there to greet you when you arrive, that person normally remains with you until your interviewer comes out to greet you. Sometimes both the staffing agency recruiter and the account manager will be there to meet you; sometimes only one of them will be there; but most times no one from the staffing agency will be at your scheduled interview.

A meeting with staffing agency personnel at your interview is oftentimes the first time you will meet the people who helped you get that job interview at your negotiated salary rate. So use that opportunity to personally thank the staffing agent for their help in getting you that job interview.

When Staffing Agency Recruiters Do Not Meet You at Your Job Interview

If no one from the staffing agency will meet you at your scheduled interview location, the first person you will most likely meet is the person at the reception desk of the employer's building or office. Let the person at the reception desk know you have an appointment with one of the interviewers you were told would meet you.

If the person at the employer's reception desk is the first person you meet, make a good first impression by smiling and being friendly with that person. There's no need to shake the receptionist's hand but always be courteous and friendly with the receptionist. If you treat the receptionist rudely or as if they don't matter, the receptionist can let your interviewers know of your unprofessional behavior which will reflect poorly on you in their evaluation of your cultural fit for their company. Your cultural fitness in a company has to do with how you interact with and treat everyone in the company, including the receptionist.

The same holds true for the person who meets you at the Visitor Center of a military installation to escort you to your interview. This person who escorts you onto the installation is oftentimes a member of the team you will be part of if you are hired.

Your Initial Greeting at Your Job Interview

When greeting staffing agents or your interview party, extend your hand, look them in the eye, smile and give them a firm handshake. Do not give one of those soft, sheepish or wet noodle handshakes. A limp, weak grip in your handshake makes you appear weak, disinterested, insecure or negative. A firm, strong handshake makes you appear strong, confident, assertive, interested and positive.

When greeting your interviewers, smile and give them a pleasant greeting, such as "*Hi, I'm* [state your first name only]. *It's nice to meet you.*"

In your job interview, different types of personnel could be in that room with you, such as a hiring manager, a team lead, and several team members. Typically, all of these individuals are members of the team you will be part of if you are hired.

The Hiring Manager in Your Job Interview

The hiring manager is a manager in the company who requested the position for his or her team be filled. The hiring manager is also the person who makes the final decision on which candidate will be hired for that open job. The title of "hiring manager" is only temporary until the manager hires the candidate for the job. Afterward, the hiring manager uses only their normal manager title. Depending on the size of the company, this manager could manage an entire section of teams; a small portion of teams in a section of the company; or only one team in the section.

The position the hiring manager is requesting to be filled is a position that is under the hiring manager's area of control and leadership. Therefore, although the manager puts in his or her personnel request to the company's HR department, the manager is the one who will take ownership of the recruiting process for this position while the HR department supports and assists the manager along the way. The hiring manager will work with the HR department concerning creating the job description of the available position; conducting the resume reviews and interviews; completing and finalizing the hiring, salary negotiations and job offer process; and establishing the start date of the candidate they select for the job after all the candidate interviews are completed. Since the selected candidate will become a part of the hiring manager's team, this manager has a vested interest in ensuring the right candidate for the job is selected for his or her team members. That means a person who is the best technical and cultural fit for the manager's team.

The hiring manager will most likely become your reporting manager in your section if you are hired for the job. The manager's office could be either in the same office you will be working in or located in another room or building.

The hiring manager could have strong background experience in your line of work; someone that possibly started at the level you're coming in at with this company; and worked through the ranks until they reached the management position they are in now. The hiring manager could also be a person with little to no background experience in your line of work but possesses the necessary managerial skills to be in that position.

It's possible for two managers to be in the interview room with you; a manager for full-time company employees and a manager for contractors. If this is the case in your interview, one of these managers will be your hiring manager depending on whether you are interviewing as a company employee or a contractor.

Such was the case when I was interviewing for a network engineer position for a service provider company. This service provider normally hired job-hunting candidates as contractors first for a 6 month contract. If they liked the contractor's performance after 6 months, they gave the contractor the option to either continue working as a contractor or become a full-time company employee.

If the hiring manager is present in your interview, he or she will introduce you to all the interviewers in the room. The manager will oftentimes share a little bit about their company before asking you to tell them a little bit about yourself. Once all the introductions are out of the way, the manager and the other interviewers will begin asking you technical questions. If the manager does not have a technical background, he or she will pass the interview over to the other interviewers to ask you the technical questions. Regardless if the hiring manager has a technical background or not, you can be sure the manager will be observing you to determine if you are a good cultural fit for his or her team as you are being evaluated for your technical fit.

The Team Lead in Your Job Interview

Each team of workers in US government agencies and corporations usually has a team leader, referred to as the team lead. The team lead is the person who is the technical leader on the team. This person is usually the senior person on the team you will be on if you are hired; is the driving force behind the team; and is responsible to the manager for the rest of the team members, assignments, progress and accomplishments.

The lead person will delegate work assignments from the team manager to you and the rest of the members on your team; however, the team lead is responsible to the manager for the overall success of the team's projects and assignments. Since the team lead is a technical person, the lead will oftentimes work alongside you to complete an assignment, project or goal. If the team lead attends meetings on behalf of the team, the lead will pass on or brief the team on the minutes from the meetings.

As a matter of protocol, when team members have issues to pass on or discuss with leadership, they first go through the team lead; then their team manager; and then to higher leadership.

When it is time assess and evaluate the performance of team members, the manager will seek inputs from the lead person about each team member. The lead may also fill in for the team manager's responsibilities when the manager is out of office.

It's normal to have both the hiring manager and team lead in the room with you during your interview. When the hiring manager cannot make it to your interview, the team lead usually takes over and leads the interview.

When it's Your Turn to Give Your Introduction in Your Job Interview

After the hiring manager, team lead and other interviewers introduce themselves to you, the last introduction during your job interview will be your carefully prepared introduction given to the interviewers. In the *Before the Interview* section, I've gone over how you should prepare and practice for giving this introduction. Now it's time to put all that practice to good use. As Steve Martin said, *"Be so good they can't ignore you."*

In your introduction, remember to talk about things in your past jobs that relate to the job description (your technical fit), and mention a few things in your personal life that the other interviewers can identify with and connect with (your cultural fit).

Remember, your introduction should only be 2–2 ½ minutes long; so relax—you can do this. Nobody knows you better than you, so smile and be confident introducing to these interviewers the person you've known all your life—*you*. Introductions don't get any easier than that. And remember, it's not always the smartest person who gets the job; it's the person who is the best fit, technically and culturally, that usually gets hired.

Intelligence Quotient (IQ) versus Emotional Quotient (EQ) for Job Interviews

For those of you who think the smartest candidates are always going to trump all other candidates in a job interview and be the one who gets hired, think again. Since the 1990s, many scientists, psychologists, researchers and educators have been stating that your emotional intelligence (EI or EQ) and attitude are better predictors of your success in life, including in job interviews, than your IQ.

It's Game Day—The Job Interview

The Importance of Intelligence Quotient (IQ) in Job Interviews

The IQ is, at best, a rough measure of academic intelligence; the ability or capacity of a person to learn, understand and apply information and skills. The first intelligence quotient (IQ) test was invented in 1908 by French psychologist, Alfred Binet, when the French Ministry of Education, who passed a law requiring all French children attend school, needed a way to determine which students were not benefiting from regular classroom education and needed remedial instruction.

Today, there are a variety of IQ tests available; and the test content in each of these tests differs widely from one another. One IQ test may show you only pictures of blocks, circles, triangles and other shapes; another IQ test may ask you questions about words and numbers; and still another IQ test may ask you questions about pictures, words and numbers. Regardless of the test used, the results of each IQ test, called IQ scoring measured in Intelligence Interval and Cognitive Designation is pretty standard across the board regardless of which IQ test you take.

The results of your IQ test are normally compared to other people in your age group to determine your IQ score. You can take one of these IQ tests for free at many Internet websites, such as iqtest.com, free-iqtest.net, seemypersonality.com/IQ-Test, brainmetrix.com/free-iq-test and myiqtested.com.

The average IQ score among Americans is 98, with 99.5% of IQ scores falling between 60 and 140. The following list is the standard IQ scoring ranges and their corresponding cognitive designation; and the IQs of some famous and infamous people who fall within those ranges.

IQ Range to Cognitive Designation

- **1–40 = Mental disability (less than 1% of test takers)**

- **40–54 = Severely challenged (less than 1% of test takers)**

- **55–69 = Mentally challenged (2.3% of test takers)**

- 70–84 = Below average (13.6% of test takers)

- 85–114 = **Average intelligence (68% of test takers):** Andy Warhol (86), Donovan McNabb (88), Henry Lee Lucas (89), OJ Simpson (89), Dan Marino (92), George H.W. Bush (98), Howard Stern (99), Tim Tebow (104), Britney Spears (104), Brett Favre (104), Ronald Reagan (105), Charles Manson (109), Ben Roethlisberger (110), Al Franken, (110), Kobe Bryant (114), Drew Brees (116)

- 115–129 = **Above average; bright (13.6% of test takers):** Peyton Manning (116), David Berkowitz (118), Troy Aikman (118), Lee Harvey Oswald (118), John F. Kennedy (119), Philip Rivers (120), John Elway (120), Gerald Ford (121), Courtney Cox (122), Dwight Eisenhower (122), John Kerry (123), George W. Bush (125), Lyndon B. Johnson (126), Steve Young (126), Tom Brady (126), Abraham Lincoln (128)

- 130–144 = **Moderately gifted (2.3% of test takers):** Aaron Rodgers (130), Harry Truman (132), Jodie Foster (132), Nicole Kidman (132), Al Gore (134), Arnold Schwarzenegger (135), Bill Clinton (137), Rush Limbaugh (137), Geena Davis (140), Hillary Clinton (140), Shakira (140), Madonna (140), Steve Martin (142), Richard Nixon (143), Adolf Hitler (144), Napoleon Bonaparte (145)

- 145–159 = **Highly gifted; Genius (less than 1% of test takers):** Jeffrey Dahmer (145), Hans Christian Andersen (145), Franklin D. Roosevelt (147), Jayne Mansfield (149), Bill O'Reilly (150), Carol Vorderman (154), Sharon Stone (154), Eli Manning (156), Ellen Muth (156), Sigmund Freud (156), Jimmy Carter (156)

- **160–179 = Exceptionally gifted; extraordinary genius (less than 1% of test takers):** Albert Einstein (160), Bill Gates (160), Quentin Tarantino (160), Reggie Jackson (160), Stephen Hawking (160), Dolph Lungren (160), Jill St. John (162), Charles Darwin (165), Johann Sebastian Bach (165), Ludwig Van Beethoven (165), Norman Schwarzkopf (170), Judith Polgar (170), Judy Holliday (172)

- **180 and up = Profoundly gifted; profound intellectual prowess (less than 1% of test takers):** Benjamin Netanyahu (180), John Sununu (180), Charles Dickens (180), Michelangelo (180), Galileo Galilei (185), Bobby Fisher (187), Philip Emeagwali (190), Garry Kasparov (190), Sir Isaac Newton (190), Johann Wolfgang Goethe (210), Leonardo da Vinci (220), Marilyn vos Savant (228)

So what about the importance of IQ in job interviews? To answer that question, I have to talk about the importance of emotional quotient (EQ) in job interviews.

The Importance of Emotional Quotient (EQ) in Job Interviews

When looking at this IQ list, one might be led to believe the person who has the highest IQ is the one who will get the job or is the most successful in life. Unless you are being interviewed by Goggle or some other company that invests twice as much as other companies in recruiting people based primarily on the highest IQ or higher education, many companies would rather consider a person's emotional quotient (EQ) and attitude over IQ and higher degrees in their hiring decisions. Today, many companies are incorporating EQ tests into their interviews and adopting EQ training into their business culture.

Most people are familiar with IQ, but few people are aware of their emotional intelligence (EI) or emotional quotient (EQ). In many cases, employers will hire a candidate whose EQ is higher than their IQ.

Your EQ score rates your ability or capacity to perceive, understand, control, evaluate and express emotions—yours and other people's emotions. How you deal with your emotions determines how well you work with and get along with other people, particularly people in your workplace.

People with high EQ scores are considered confident individuals with good communications and leadership skills that have good control over their emotions. This makes them better suited for group or team environments, such as in the workplace, than people with low EQ scores—characteristics that the IQ scores does not measure or reveal.

Besides controlling their emotions well, people with high EQ scores are highly motivated and productive; face change, variety and challenges head on because they do not fear failure; and show greater endurance and perseverance under long-term struggles and hardship than people with low EQ scores.

If the definition of a high EQ score sounds strangely familiar to the definition of an alpha type person, you would be right because many of the qualities of a person with a high EQ score parallel the qualities of alpha types.

Just as there are IQ tests you can take online, there are many EQ tests and assessments on the Internet you can take for free.

Here are some online EQ tests you can take:

- https://memorado.com/emotional_quotient

- http://www.ihhp.com/free-eq-quiz

- https://www.arealme.com/eq/en

- https://www.mindtools.com/pages/article/ei-quiz.htm

- http://personality-testing.info/tests/EI.php

- http://greatergood.berkeley.edu/ei_quiz

- http://www.iq-test.net/eq-test.html

As I mentioned, many scientists, psychologists, researchers and educators have been stating since the 1990s that your emotional intelligence (EI) or emotional quotient (EQ) is more important than your IQ in determining your overall intelligence and your success in the workplace and in life in general.

Allow me to introduce some of those experts to you.

Travis Bradberry knows all about EQ testing and training. Dr. Bradberry holds a Dual Ph.D. in Clinical and Industrial-Organizational Psychology from the California School of Professional Psychology. He is a world-renowned expert in emotional intelligence, the award-winning coauthor of the 2009 book *Emotional Intelligence 2.0* and cofounder of TalentSmart, the world leader in emotional intelligence tests and training.

TalentSmart provides EQ resources to over 75 percent of Fortune 500 companies; and the talentsmart.com website provides many case studies showing how EQ training and tests have helped many companies.

TalentSmart's own studies of people at all levels of work in different industries of every region of the world reveal that 90 percent of your top performers at work have high EQ scores; and that people with high EQ scores also make an average of $29,000 per year more than people with low EQ scores.

When TalentSmart tested factors that predict a person's greatest chance for success in the workplace, they included emotional intelligence in addition to 33 other necessary workplace skill sets in those tests. The results revealed that of all these skill sets, emotional intelligence provided the strongest predictor of performance success—58 percent—in all types of job markets.

Dr. Bradberry points out that your EQ level is not fixed at birth; it can be developed, reshaped, improved and increased to produce positive impacts in your life. He states that the whole person is made up of IQ, EQ and personality; each independent of each other; and that of the three, only EQ can be developed and altered. Dr. Bradberry argues that you need to increase your EQ level to increases your chances of success in your career as well as all other areas of your life.

Daniel Goleman holds a Ph.D. from Harvard and is the author of the international bestsellers *Emotional Intelligence, Working with Emotional Intelligence, Social Intelligence,* and the acclaimed business bestseller *Primal Leadership.*

In Dr. Goleman's 1996 New York Times #1 Best Seller book *Emotional Intelligence* that sold over 5 million copies worldwide in 40 languages, he suggested your emotional intelligence quotient (EQ) is more important than the traditional intelligence quotient (IQ) in determining your success in life. Dr. Goleman argues that the reason why people with high IQs can fail or flounder in life and people with modest IQs can be successful in life is because the successful person with the modest IQ has a higher emotional intelligence (EQ) than the unsuccessful person with the high IQ but lower EQ.

This argument by Dr. Goleman can also help explain the driving force behind that long list of successful and wealthy people making millions or even billions of dollars; people that are high school or college dropouts or without any college education at all. A **high EQ** that Dr. Goleman points out along with some ***true grit*** that Dr. Duckworth talks about and "The Duke" displayed is a winning combination for great success in life—and in your job interview.

Focusing on developing one's EQ is not just for people seeking to impress hiring managers in job interviewers or current employees seeking to perform better at their jobs. Higher EQ levels also produce better leaders. In his international bestseller, *Primal Leadership: Unleashing The Power of Emotional Intelligence,* Dr. Goleman, along with co-authors Drs. Richard Boyatzis and Annie McKee, performed research on workplaces led by over 3,870 executives. After their research, they discovered that the most effective business leaders are those who understand and harness their emotional intelligence in leading their people.

Like Dr. Bradberry and TalentSmart, Dr. Goleman and his colleagues teach that your emotional intelligence involves malleable traits that can be learned, taught, changed, developed and managed. Rather than focusing on one's IQ in predicting a person's success in life, Goleman suggests people develop their EQ in order to increase their chances for a more successful life.

Clearly, understanding and developing your emotional intelligence will help provide you greater success in your job interviews and career.

If you're convinced in your mind that neither IQ nor EQ levels can be altered to increase your chances of success in job interviews or in life in general, many scientific researchers and educators, such as Carol Dweck, would soundly disagree with you.

Dr. Carol Dweck is a world-renowned research psychologist, a Yale graduate who held professorships at Harvard and Columbia Universities; and is now the Lewis and Virginia Eaton Professor of Psychology at Stanford University. Over the past two decades, she has debunked the idea that intelligence, talents, skills and abilities are fixed, uncontrollable traits from birth that produce success in life. Instead, she advocates the theory that these traits can be developed and changed; and that hard work, learning, training, attitude, persistence and perseverance are what make people successful in life.

In her highly acclaimed book, *Mindset: The New Psychology of Success*, Dr. Dweck explains how people become biased in their thinking or "***mindset***" about their intelligence, skills, talents and abilities. She argues that people can have either a ***fixed mindset*** that believe they can't change their innate intelligence, skills, talents and abilities or they have a ***growth mindset*** that believe they can change and mold their malleable intelligence, skills, talents and abilities through hard work, learning, training and perseverance.

According to Dr. Dweck, having a **fixed mindset** places you at a disadvantage because you believe you can't improve yourself to become more successful in life. Since you think your traits are permanently fixed, that mindset reduces your motivation to try harder to improve and become more successful in life. People with fixed mindsets fear failure because failure to them is a reflection of their perception of a permanent level of intelligence, skills, talents and abilities.

Growth mindset individuals accept failure as part of the learning and growth process to make them better in life. Since these individuals believe failure is part of the process, they continue to persevere and develop themselves to become better in life despite any failures.

Your mindset will also affect your attitude about yourself, your life and your chances of success in a job interview.

Dr. Arthur Poropat of Griffith University's School of Applied Psychology in Australia, a university that is ranked in the top 200 by the QS World University Rankings in 2015, conducted the largest ever study of personality and academic performance based on five fundamental personality traits, also known as the Big Five personality traits or the Five-Factor Model (FFM) of personality—conscientiousness, openness, agreeableness, emotional stability and extraversion.

The results of his research, that included data from tens of thousands of students was published as an article, titled *Other-rated personality and academic performance: Evidence and implications*, in the August 2014 edition of the research journal *Learning and Individual Differences*, Volume 34 that can be viewed on sciencedirect.com.

Dr. Poropat's research concluded that these five factors of personality trump intelligence (IQ) and is more important than intelligence when it comes to success in learning and education. In fact, Dr. Poropat's study showed **conscientiousness** (being thorough, careful, efficient, organized and systematic) and **openness** (being open to experiences) is four times more important than IQ in predicting academic success.

- **Openness** to experience includes active imagination (fantasy); aesthetic sensitivity (toward beauty, appearance, arts and taste); preference for variety and change; intellectual curiosity (the desire to learn, explore, discover and experience new things); and being connected to one's inner feelings (an EQ quality).

- **Agreeableness** (another EQ quality) is being kind, considerate, sympathetic, warm and cooperative.

- **Emotional stability** (another EQ quality) is the ability to remain calm and even keel under pressure or when experiencing stress.

- **Extraversion** is an extrovert who is a highly sociable, talkative, energetic and assertive personality type that tends to be more outgoing and happy than your introvert type.

Dr. Poropat's research study shows that factors other than IQ can produce success not only in school but in the workplace and in life. As with Drs. Travis Bradberry, Daniel Goleman and Carol Dweck and their studies and theories about success, Dr. Poropat also stated that these five personality traits for academic success are malleable traits that can be changed and developed by each individual; and that hard work, effort and perseverance go a long way in predicting a person's success in learning and education.

Even Presidents Go Through the Job Interview Process

These arguments by so many scientists, psychologists, researchers and educators (the experts) explaining why people with high IQs but low EQs can fail or flounder in life, and people with modest IQs but high EQs can be successful in life was born out in our 2016 US presidential election between Hillary Clinton and Donald Trump.

Hillary Clinton went to Yale Law School, an Ivy League school, where she graduated with a Yale Juris Doctor degree. Secretary Clinton has a reported IQ of 140, three points above her husband, Bill Clinton, who has a reported IQ of 137. Together, Hillary and Bill Clinton represented the status quo of the elite, the Clinton political machine, and the political powerhouse in Washington. Everything seemed in Secretary Clinton's favor to win the US presidential election—based on her high IQ and political qualifications that is. As far as money goes, Clinton raised $1.3 billion as of October 19, 2016. Even the exit polls and pundits had Hillary Clinton winning in state after state over Donald Trump.

Donald Trump, on the other hand, graduated with a bachelor's degree in economics from the Wharton School of the University of Pennsylvania—an Ivy League business school. He was a businessman, an outsider to Washington with no political experience and no military background; a first for our nation whose presidents always had either one or both of these qualifications. Many would argue that Donald Trump was the most unqualified person to be our nation's next president. As far as money goes, Trump raised only $795 million as of October 19, 2016.

Despite the odds against Donald Trump, he handedly won the 2016 presidential election over Hillary Clinton. Both candidates went through the fiery trial of their job interview process in front of the American public throughout their campaigns; and yet their hiring manager (over 130 million American voters) selected Donald Trump over Hillary Clinton for the job as our nation's 45th president.

Why? . . . How?

Part of our nation and other nations are scratching their heads in disbelief, shell-shocked by this surprising political upset that many are calling America's "Brexit". The other half of our nation and other nations are celebrating in absolute amazement, joy and happiness. Journalists, pollsters and the rest of the media are spinning out of control at this stunning upset and historic win by Donald Trump. As "The Donald" (excuse me, as "The Mr. President") would say: *"**This is HUGE!**"*

You could say like these "experts" I've quoted that Donald Trump had a higher EQ with perhaps a lower IQ than Hillary Clinton; while Hillary Clinton had a higher IQ with a much lower EQ than Donald Trump. Hillary Clinton had the higher **IQ** and **political experience and**

It's Game Day—The Job Interview

qualifications—the ***technical fit***, but Donald Trump had the ***grit*** and higher ***EQ*** that could connect with the American voters—the ***cultural fit***.

That's why Donald Trump got the job from his new employer—the American people; and started his new job on Friday, January 20, 2017 as our nation's 45th president at his employer's office—the Oval Office—on 1600 Pennsylvania Avenue for a whopping $1. This is not a typo—I said ***one dollar*** because Trump did not want any salary to work for the American people; however, he is required by law to receive payment for his services to the US government.

"***Back the presidential bus up just one minute!***" you exclaim. "*Didn't Hillary Clinton win the popular vote over Donald Trump? How can you say Trump has a higher EQ that could connect with the American voters when Hillary had the higher popular vote?*" you ask.

It's because the **popular vote** in American politics is as misleading as the exit polls, pundits and biased media were about Clinton's "clear victory". True, Hillary is popular among the masses—she has a certain level of EQ (emotional quotient) that connects with American voters. However, her EQ was *not high enough*. In other words, she was "*not popular enough*" to move the voters she needed to come out and vote for her. She was not popular enough to muster the necessary votes to secure the magical 270 (out of a possible 538) **electoral votes** needed to win the presidency. She was not popular enough to convince a few thousand more voters to come out and vote for her in those swing states. Was she popular? Yes. Was she popular enough to win the election? No.

According to the US Elections Project, of the roughly 231,556,622 eligible voters in the 2016 presidential election, roughly over 134,765,650 (58.4%) actually voted. Among those who voted, the New York Times reported on November 21, 2016, the tallied votes that were still coming in showed Clinton's 48% of the popular vote was increasing over Trump's 47% of votes—that's definitely more votes than Trump as far as this "popularity contest" goes.

However, winning the election as the US President is not just about winning more votes; it's about winning more votes in battleground states (swing states that either candidate could win) that provide a larger number of winner-takes-all **electoral votes**. Although the statistics on the **popular vote** do not show it, Trump was *"more popular"* than Clinton in getting enough people to vote for him in those battleground states—the states which gave him the lead in **electoral votes**. Trump didn't use a higher IQ to win those extra votes; he used a higher EQ to win the hearts of those people in those states to get them to come out and vote for him.

When it came down to winning those key battleground states, Trump unexpectedly won those states that all the exit polls, pundits and biased media said Clinton would win. In other words, in those states, Donald Trump was *more popular* than Hillary Clinton—this is what got Trump the **270+ electoral votes** he needed to win the election. Even though Senator Clinton won the **popular vote**, it was Trump who was *more popular* in those swing states that got him the job as President of the United States of America. Was Trump popular? Yes. Was he popular enough to win the election? Yes.

Only a few thousand votes decided who our 45th president would be—**Donald Trump**. For instance, Trump won Wisconsin (a swing state with 10 electoral votes) with just 27,257 more votes than Clinton. Trump won Michigan (16 electoral votes) with only 10,704 more votes than Clinton. One could argue that if Hillary Clinton was popular enough to convince those few thousand more voters in swing states like Wisconsin and Michigan to come out and vote for her, we would have sworn in Hillary Clinton as our 45th president on January 20, 2017.

Translation: *Your vote counts.* Think about that next time you decide *not* to cast your vote, regardless of your political affiliation.

This marks the fourth time in US history that a candidate won the ***popular vote*** but lost the presidency to another candidate who won the ***electoral vote***. Like Hillary Clinton, the three other candidates who

It's Game Day—The Job Interview

won the popular vote but lost the electoral vote were all **Democrats** (Al Gore in 2000; Grover Cleveland in 1888; and Samuel Tilden in 1876). Like Donald Trump, the three other candidates who lost the popular vote but won the electoral vote—and became president—were all **Republicans** (George W. Bush in 2000; Benjamin Harrison in 1888; and Rutherford B. Hayes in 1876).

History does indeed repeat itself.

It's the same way in your job interview—it repeats itself. It probably won't be a higher IQ that's going to get you the votes you need above your job-hunting competition to win that available position. It could come down to who has the higher EQ to win the hearts of those interviewers.

Aesop's fable of the race between *The Tortoise and the Hare* is a parody of Clinton's premature election night *"victory"* celebration party on Election Day, the 8th of November, 2016 at the Jacob K. Javits Convention Center in New York. In attendance were start-studded celebrities, such as Katy Perry, Beyoncé, Jay Z, Jason Derulo, Lady Gaga, Melanie Griffith and Cher. The night was supposed to end with a fireworks display over the Hudson River capping off Secretary Clinton's *"speedy rabbit"* victory over the *"slow but steady tortoise"* Trump as our nation's 45th president. Instead, Clinton and her supporters went home in tears, hanging their heads in painful defeat.

As with my own experience I shared with you in chapter 1 of watching my fellow contractors eating all those delicious meals at the restaurant while I ate vegetables, only to find out I passed my triglycerides medical examinations while they failed their test and had to go home hanging their heads in defeat—the moral of this story once again is: **make sure the race is over before you *party like it's 1999*.**

The Importance of Attitude in Your Job Interview

Attitude is all about how you carry yourself in the job interview. Your attitude, whether it's positive or negative, is affected by your thoughts, beliefs, emotions, feelings and opinions about someone or something.

A person with a positive, optimistic attitude sees themselves, their circumstances and their outlook on life through the lens of confident expectations of good, happiness and success regardless of the situation.

It's important for you to be in the right frame of mind during your job interview. I understand you could think of 50 other places you'd rather be than in a job interview, but during the interview is not the time to let those negative feelings about job interviews undermine the type of attitude you need to display in front of your interviewers.

Don't walk through that doorway into the interview room as if you are the character in the 14th century epic poem *Divine Comedy*, written by Dante Alighieri, who is walking through the vestibule of hell (Dante's Inferno) which bore the inscription over the doorway: *"Abandon all hope, ye who enter here."*

You're not that poor slob in *Divine Comedy* who, in our context about job interviews, allegorically has to make his journey through the chambers of hell filled with interviewers carrying pitch forks; past the purgatory of a barrage of questions; until you finally make your way to the paradise of a new job. You are not Dante in the *Divine Comedy* and your job interview is not a punishment; it is an opportunity for you to move forward to something better in your life.

You want your interviewers to see you as a person who has a positive attitude that they would enjoy working with; someone who is enthusiastic and excited about this job opportunity. Every workplace has its share of whiners, complainers and other types of people with negative, pessimistic attitudes that can pull people down at work. The last person your hiring manager and co-workers want to hire is another person with that type of attitude.

The workplace is going to challenge you with many problems you'll have to solve. Employers want to know if you are the type of person who can face these challenges with a positive attitude that believes he or she can solve problems and produce good results.

So give yourself permission to breathe, relax, smile, and think happy, confident, positive thoughts while you're in that job interview. Learn to loosen up and enjoy the interview experience. Don't be wound so tight that you can't think straight or laugh or respond correctly to humor.

One of my colleagues and I were newly hired network engineers for a major service provider. When he and I had a chance to talk about our interview experience, he told me that after his job interview he immediately went out and bought five new suits for work. Apparently, his interviewers told him tongue-in-cheek that everyone wears suits five days a week at work. They expected him to take that statement lightheartedly, but instead, he took them seriously and spent some hefty cash for five new suits. On his first day of work, when he was the only one wearing a suit and tie while everyone else was in their business casual slacks and jeans; that's when he realized that they were just having fun with him. That's what can happen to you when you are wound too tight during your job interview. So relax; your interviewers are people too. They like to smile and joke with you too during your interview.

As you move from junior to senior positions, your hiring manager and interviewers are going to expect you to display more confidence in yourself. Senior professionals are not only expected to show higher levels of knowledge and experience in a desired role, they are expected to show more leadership qualities which require confidence and a good attitude.

When you walk in that door to the interview room, walk in there with your head held high, your shoulders back and your chest out like you own the place; like you're the most important person in the world. Not with an arrogant air about you, but with a quiet confidence that says, "*I got this.*"

You are not at a disadvantage in the interview; you are on equal footing with your interviewers. After all, **they have just as big a need as you:** they need someone like you to fill a much needed position in their workplace; and you need someone like them to provide you a job.

Think of it like this: your interview with them is going to be either a win-win situation for both of you or lose-lose situation; not a win-lose situation. If they hire you, both of you win by fulfilling your needs: you filled their need for another professional and they fulfilled your need for a job. If they don't hire you, both sides lose in that situation: both you and the company have to continue interviewing; something both sides would rather end by you being the one they hire.

A positive attitude not only helps you have a more successful career; a positive outlook on life is better for your overall health. The well-known Mayo Clinic is one of the world's best hospitals and ranked number 1 on the list of nearly 5,000 "Best Hospitals" on the 2014–2015 U.S. News & World Report. The Mayo Clinic staff posted an article, titled *Positive thinking: Stop negative self-talk to reduce stress*, on their Mayoclinic.org website that suggests an optimistic or pessimistic attitude can affect your health and well-being.

The Mayo Clinic stated that the health benefits of positive thinking include, increased life span; lower rates of depression; lower levels of distress; greater resistance to the common cold; better psychological and physical well-being; reduced risk of death from cardiovascular disease; and better coping skills during hardships and times of stress.

Power Posture, Power Thoughts and Power Words for Job Interviews

Your attitude is also affected by your body posture, your thoughts and your own words while standing or sitting. Having the right posture—standing with your shoulders back and your chest out in a comfortable position or sitting upright or slightly forward in your chair—will not only make you feel more confident in yourself; your interviewers will notice your confidence and enthusiasm based on your posture too. It has long been proven that your posture affects your attitude and confidence just as your thoughts and words do.

How Posture Impacts Your Job Interview

In 2009, **Dr. Richard Petty**, Professor of Psychology at Ohio State University, and two other OSU alumni, Pablo Brinol and Benjamin Wagner, performed a research study of 71 students. In this study, students were asked to either sit upright with their shoulders back and their chest out or slouch in their chairs in front of a computer while they rated themselves as future professionals in a job. The results of the study, titled *Body posture effects on self-evaluation: A self-validation approach* was published in the February 2009 edition of the European Journal of Social Psychology.

This study found that students rated themselves more highly with confident, positive self-attitude for jobs when they sat upright than when they slouched in their chairs. In other words, when the students sat in a position of power—upright—they felt empowered; therefore, they rated themselves highly. When they slouched in their chairs—a position of weakness, they felt less empowered; therefore, they rated themselves low.

In 2012, **Dr. Amy Cuddy**, a social psychologist working as an Associate Professor of Business Administration at Harvard Business School and author of the multi-best seller book, *Presence: Bringing Your Boldest Self to Your Biggest Challenges*, gave a TED talk on TED.com, a nonprofit organization that shares ideas about technology, entertainment and design (TED) worldwide. Dr. Cuddy gave her talk, titled *Your body language shapes who you are*, at TEDGlobal 2012 in Edinburgh, Scotland which has been viewed more than 33 million times on TED.com.

Cuddy shared how her research and experiments along with colleagues Dana Carney and Andy Yap of UC-Berkeley show you can fake confident body postures of dominance and power, something she calls "**power posing**", for as little as two minutes, even when you don't feel confident, to increase testosterone levels in your body; decrease cortisol levels; and increase your desire for risk-taking which causes you to perform better in job interviews.

Dr. Cuddy's research states that power people and leaders—your alpha male types—show significantly higher levels of testosterone and significantly lower levels of cortisol than the less powerful beta male types.

Alpha types are people—male or female—who are more confident, extroverted, dominant, engaging, competitive, calm and non-reactive under pressure, assertive and charismatic than their beta counter-types. They also like standing out and speaking out in a crowd; and are risk takers because of their strong feelings of confidence and optimism, their desire to win in every situation, and their lack of fear in failing.

Beta types—male or female—are more careful and less optimistic about things which make them less confident, vocal, outgoing, confrontational, engaging and assertive than alpha types. They're more passive, timid, shy, quiet, introverted and reserved than their alpha counter-types.

Cortisol is a natural steroid hormone in your body, also referred to as a "stress hormone" that increases your adrenalin to prepare your body for "fight-or-flight" situations. When your cortisol levels increase, your body becomes flooded with glucose; your arteries become narrow and your heart rate increases; making you feel more nervous and excited and less at ease during job interviews.

Dr. Cuddy's research shows that if you posture your body in a way that reflects dominance, power and confidence—the byproduct of alpha types, your brain and mind will also think the same way, triggering your body and emotions to follow suit. This will help give you more confidence and put you at ease and in a stronger frame of mind during job interviews.

What Dr. Cuddy recommends job-hunting candidates do before meeting the interviewers at their job interview is to spend at least two minutes in private, such as in a bathroom, an elevator, a vacant room or at home before they leave, standing in a power position.

A standing power position is any alpha male standing position, such as standing with your shoulders back; your chest out; your head held looking straight ahead; your feet spread apart; and both hands resting confidently at your hips. Hold that position for at least two minutes to give your mind and body time to accept and adjust to that power position.

Dr. Cuddy is basically telling us to do with our bodies (power poses) what motivational speakers have been telling us for decades to do with our mind, thoughts, visualization and imagery techniques (power thoughts), and our words and vocalization (power words) to influence our self-talk in a positive way.

Dr. Cuddy's research on how power postures increase testosterone levels and decrease cortisol levels in your body may also lend a scientific explanation for why power thoughts and words taught by motivational speakers (such as Tony Robbins, Zig Ziglar and Jim Rohn) and by preachers of positive thinking (such as Norman Vincent Peale and Joel Osteen) actually work for so many people.

Whether we choose to listen to Dr. Cuddy or one of your favorite motivational speakers, mentors, life coaches or spiritual leaders; their end goal is the same: to help you become more confident, strong, positive, likeable and optimistic in your life, including in your job interviews.

How Power Thoughts and Power Words Impact Your Job Interview

Dr. Jim Taylor holds a Ph.D. in Psychology from the University of Colorado; is a former Associate Professor in the School of Psychology at Nova University in Ft. Lauderdale; and current adjunct professor at the University of San Francisco and the Wright Institute in Berkeley. He's worked with professional and Olympic athletes in football, baseball, triathlon, golf, cycling, tennis, skiing and other sports. He's been a consultant to the US and Japanese Ski Teams, the US Tennis Association, USA Triathlon; and was invited by Olympic committees of the US, Spain, France and Poland to speak to their athletes and coaches.

In a 2012 *Psychology Today* article, titled *Sport Imagery: Athletes' Most Power Mental Tool*, Dr. Taylor wrote, "*Imagery also isn't just a mental experience that occurs in your head, but rather impacts you in* every way: psychologically, emotionally, physically, technically, and tactically. Think of mental imagery as weight lifting for the mind."

Most of your top athletes and professional sports athletes use imagery techniques, also known as visualization, to rehearse their sport in their mind to maximize their sports performance. For example, football players will use sport imagery to visualize themselves catching the ball and running it in for a touchdown in the Super Bowl; baseball players visualize themselves hitting a homerun in the World Series; basketball players imagine themselves hitting 3-point shots in the NBA Finals; soccer (football) players see themselves kicking the game winning goal during the FIFA World Cup; and Olympians like Michael Phelps see themselves winning another gold medal while beating the living crap out of his South African rival swimmer, Chad Le Clos at the Rio Olympics. (I meant beating him in swimming. Don't send me any angry Phelps memes or *Angry Birds* my way for that remark.) These athletes are taught these imagery techniques to increase their positive self-talk and help them perform at higher levels when they are in competition.

After the Denver Broncos won the 2016 Super Bowl 50 Championship against the Carolina Panthers, Von Miller, the Super Bowl MVP, was surrounded by "Primetime" Deion Sanders and other NFL Network reporters. One of the reporters asked Miller if he ever saw himself where he's at now—at the Super Bowl level as the MVP. Von responded by saying, *"I do a lot of self-visualization and imagery . . . it was easy to say we're going to win the Super Bowl."*

Have you ever noticed how every time when the media asks a professional athlete how they feel about their upcoming championship game, they always respond the same way: *"It's just another game."*? In other words, these athletes are saying this all-important championship game is *no big deal*.

Their response is a visualization technique they've learned in order to make a very big event appear very small in their mind in order to control their emotions; stay focused and mentally tough; reduce their anxiety; and see their own selves as bigger than the championship game. They've trained themselves to make something very big look very small in their mind's eyes. Although they will prepare, train and practice as if it's the biggest event in their life; they train their minds with imagery and positive self-talk to think this game is just like any other regular season game.

You need to do the same thing for your job interviews. You should prepare as if each job interview is the biggest event in your life but you need make this important event appear very small in your mind to control your emotions; reduce your anxiety to help you relax; and make yourself feel bigger and more powerful than this interview.

The reason you become nervous, fearful and anxious about job interviews, speaking in public or other similar life events are because of your *negative* imagery, visualization and self-talk about the situation.

Instead you need to train yourself to think and see yourself in a *positive* light in these situations. Visualize and imagine yourself knocking that job interview out of the park. Imagine yourself being comfortable and confident in your interview. Visualize yourself giving a great introduction and answering your technical questions with great answers in your interview. See yourself feeling and speaking confident in your interview. These visualization and imagery techniques will reinforce your positive self-talk and help give you the confidence and power to perform well in the actual job interview.

Power Postures, Thoughts and Words—Use It or Lose It

With this entire overwhelming evidence showing the advantages and benefits of power postures, power thoughts and power words, why not make use of all of the advice given by these experts?

The best part about these power poses, power thoughts and power words is that they are *free* just like the air you breathe; just take it in. I recommend you try using power thoughts and words from whichever motivational speaker or spiritual leader you choose along with Dr. Cuddy's 2-minute power pose, preferably in front of a full-length mirror if you have one available.

However, I recommend avoiding walking over hot coals prior to a job interview—sorry Tony Robbins; I couldn't resist. You might have heard or read the 2016 news report about Tony Robbins' four-day seminar, called *Unleash the Power Within*, where hot coals were spread outside the Kay Bailey Hutchinson Convention Center in Dallas, Texas where he was speaking. According to reports, more than 30 people were treated for burns and five people were taken to the hospital after the motivational speaker encouraged them to walk on hot coals as a way of conquering their fears; something Robbins regularly encourages his audiences to do at some of his seminars.

Perhaps they should have read the old proverb that asks the question: "*Can one walk on hot coals, and his feet not be seared?*" Proverbs 6:28 NKJV

You don't need to walk on hot coals to conquer your fears right before interviewing for a job, but you might need more than just a single 2-minute confidence boost right before your phone interview or in-person interview. So try these power poses, thoughts and words (including the ones from Tony Robbins if you prefer) several times hours or days before your interview. Give yourself a healthy dose of these confidence boosting techniques before and during your job interviews.

As Dr. Cuddy said at the close of her TED talk, "*Don't fake it 'til you make it. Fake it 'til you become it.*" Keep faking those power postures, power thoughts and power words until they make sense to your mind, emotions and body.

Other Factors That Impact Your Job Interview

How the Chair You're Seated On Impacts Your Job Interview

The chair you're sitting on can also affect your posture in job interviews. I already shared with you Dr. Richard Petty's experiment with students that revealed the way you sit in a chair can affect the way you feel about yourself. If you sit in a position of power—upright—you will feel more empowered and confident. If you slouch in your chair—a position of weakness, you will feel less empowered and confident.

When taking your seat in the interview room, check the height of the chair to ensure it's at a comfortable height that allows you to sit upright. Go ahead and adjust the chair if you need to raise or lower it.

Oftentimes, interviewers will seat you on one of those swivel office chairs that allow you to adjust the height. The height adjuster is a metal lever underneath the right or left side of the seat. The chair lowers with your bodyweight when you pull up on the lever. To raise the seat, reach underneath the chair and pull the lever up with your fingers while rising up with your legs from your seat. The seat of the chair should rise on its own with you.

Some office swivel chairs will lean back when you sit in them. If your chair leans back, try to lock it in the upright position. If there is a lever underneath the chair to adjust the height, there should also be another lever underneath the chair that allows you to lock the chair in an upright position.

How Eye Contact and Head Level Impacts Your Job Interview

Two other areas that impact your job interview are your eye contact and head level.

Always maintain good eye contact when speaking with someone in the interview room. Maintaining eye contact shows you are not only a confident person but also someone interested in what the interviewers have to say. When you don't maintain good eye contact while having a conversation with someone, it makes you appear unsociable, weak and as if you have something to hide.

The type of person you want to project during your interview is a sociable, personable, confident person who is interested in the interviewer's questions and comments, and who is enthusiastic about working on their team. Good eye contact communicates those things to interviewers.

Obviously, your head should move naturally along with your eyes in the direction of the interviewer you are speaking with. Although you want to maintain a power posture when seated, you don't want to become stiff to the point that your eyes move but your head doesn't like a ventriloquist's dummy. Try to relax and allow your body movements to flow naturally with the person you are addressing.

Although your head should be allowed to move freely from side-to-side as you look around the room at your interviewers, your head position should not be looking up toward the ceiling or down toward your hands, your watch, the table or the floor. Looking up makes you look like you're lost in space or at a loss for words. Looking down makes you look weak, a failure or loser, or as if you are lying. Looking down at your watch makes you look disinterested in being in the interview and that you have somewhere else to go. I'm sure the interviewers will oblige you if you give them that impression.

If the interviewer asks you a question you don't know the answer to, don't start looking around the room in desperation, waiting for some epiphany to reveal the answer to you. Just look the interviewer in the eyes and say, *"I don't know the answer to that question."* Your straightforwardness and honesty makes you look much better in the eyes of the interviewer than that "deer in the headlights" look as you ponder the universe for the answer.

Where to Put Your Hands in Your Job Interview

Lastly, your hands and forearms should rest naturally on the desk in front of you. You can use your hands when you talk to emphasize a point, but don't wave your hands around constantly when you talk like a conductor of a symphony or something.

Never put your hands in your pockets while you are standing; don't hide your hands on your lap below the table in front of you; and don't put your hands in your pockets when seated during your interview. Sorry if I sound like your mother taking you to your first day at school when you were 5 years old. And don't forget to flush and wash your hands (just kidding; now I'm acting like your mother when you were 5).

There may be occasions in an interview where it would be acceptable to have your hand resting on your lap. For example, one job opportunity I interviewed for took place in the hiring manager's small office. I sat on a swivel office chair in front of the manager's desk. The front side of the manager's desk was paneled so I could not place my legs under the desk. There were also four other interviewers in the room to my left sitting in chairs against the wall.

In this scenario, I chose to keep my chair stationary up against the manager's desk facing the four interviewers. I placed my right arm and hand on top of the front end of the manager's desk, and my left hand rested comfortably on my left lap. My chair leaned back and it did not have an adjustment lever under the chair; however, I resisted the temptation to sit back in that chair. Instead, I sat upright in my chair the whole time.

I only had to turn my head to the right when talking with the hiring manager, and looked forward when talking with the four other interviewers who asked most of the questions. I was hired for this job interview that paid a six-figure salary that I had negotiated earlier with my staffing agency recruiter.

For another job interview I attended, my interviewers wanted me to meet them at a local restaurant during happy hour. There were four of us that sat on bar stools around a small tall table with just enough room for finger food and beverages which the hiring manager ordered for all of us to enjoy while I was being interviewed by them. Except for the fact that I was wearing a suit and tie while they and everyone else at their tables around us were wearing their normal business casual, this was the ultimate relaxing interview environment.

It was obvious my interviewers wanted to see how I would fare in a relaxed outing with them—my cultural fit. However, this was still an interview, so I maintained good posture sitting upright as best as I could on my bar stool and maintained eye contact when speaking with them. When they asked me a question, I looked them in the eye and did not look down or up when I answered their interview questions. We laughed and joked as well; and overall had an enjoyable time together during the interview as we snacked on finger food and drank beverages. The best part was I got hired for that job too.

When you weigh all the mental (technical fit) and social (cultural fit) factors that go into successfully completing a job interview; the truth is you need IQ, EQ and attitude in your job interview. However, don't assume hiring managers and interviewers are going to weigh IQ above EQ and attitude. You need to show your interviewers you have the ability or capacity to learn, understand and apply information and skills by answering their technical questions satisfactorily—this is part of your IQ which translates to your technical fit. You also need to demonstrate to your interviewers that you have the ability or capacity to work well with other people, particularly people in your workplace and on your team, by your communications skills, personality, mannerisms and behavior—this is your EQ and attitude which translates to your cultural fit.

Job Interview Questions and Answers

The Interviewers that Ask the Questions

After all the introductions are out of the way, the interviewers will begin asking you technical questions. Most job interviews consist of 3–5 people in the interview room with you as they ask you questions. Usually, all the people in the interview room with you will take their turn asking you questions. Typically, the fewer interviewers there are in the room, the more questions each interviewer will ask you. The more interviewers there are the fewer questions each will ask in order to stay within their scheduled interview timeframe. It is also normal for an interviewer who finished asking you questions to ask you a few more questions later on in the interview.

The hiring manager may or may not ask you technical questions depending on the manager's technical knowledge and experience. I've been in an interview with only two people—the hiring manager and the team lead. Both the hiring manager and the lead engineer asked me technical questions in that job interview.

It is also possible that some of the interviewers present in the room won't ask you any questions. That may be the case when the interviewers have different skill sets, experience and qualifications, but they are all on the same team. Take my career field in IT for example. If I am being interviewed for a particular area, such as network engineering, then I may have only the network engineers in the interview room ask me questions. However, if my resume shows I have both network engineering and security engineering experience, then both the network and security engineers may be brought in to interview me in both network and security engineering technologies. I've also been in a rare interview where there were six people in the room but only one person asked me technical questions because that person was the only one who had my type of network experience. The other people in the room had a system administrator experience but were on the same team with the network engineer questioning me.

Although the topics you see in the job description are the areas where the interviewers will focus their questions on; technologies outside the scope of the job description are also open game for questions if those technologies or certifications are listed in your resume.

How to Answer Questions in Your Job Interview

Don't be long-winded when giving your answers to the interviewer's questions. Keep your answers short and concise. Most questions can be answered in 30 seconds or less. With the exception of very few technical questions and your introduction where you would take more time to talk about yourself; if you are going over 30 seconds when answering a question, chances are you are using too many words to answer the question or you are struggling to answer the question.

If you don't know the answer, maintain eye contact with the person asking the question, be direct and tell the person you don't know the answer to that question. If you know part of the answer, go ahead and share what you do know so that the interviewer will at least give you partial credit for knowing portions of the subject. That may be more than what other candidates can answer about that particular question.

Sometimes an interviewer will ask you a question that doesn't make sense to you. It's not that you don't know the answer; you just didn't understand the question. If you don't understand an interviewer's question, let the interviewer know you're not sure what they're asking you. The interviewer asking the question or another interviewer will try to rephrase the question without giving away the answer.

You should demonstrate good communications skills throughout the entire interview process. The way you communicate with each interviewer will give them a sampling of your soft skills, your emotional quotient and your cultural fit with both their team and the company. Your communications skills in the interview reflect how you will communicate with everyone at work once you are hired.

Part of good communications is showing your interviewers you are a good listener. When someone else is talking, don't interrupt them for any reason. Wait until the person is done talking before you inject a comment, answer or question into the conversation. Don't dominate the conversation. Let your interviewers set the pace and focus of the conversation throughout the interview.

Never speak negatively about any past jobs, managers, supervisors, leadership, co-workers or company policies in the interview. Speaking negatively about past workplaces, assignments and people does not reflect negatively on them; it reflects negatively on *you*. It shows you lack the maturity and professionalism to keep those negative comments to yourself.

When asked why you left your last job, don't speak negatively about previous co-workers or managers. Even if those people or companies were the reasons you left those jobs. Try to put a positive spin on why you left those former companies. Show your interviewers that you have the maturity and class to speak well of former employers and colleagues. Talk more in terms of looking for new opportunities, challenges or other ways to increase your knowledge and experience in your field as reasons for deciding to move on from those companies.

These interviewers know that one day you'll leave their company too. If you start griping about former workplaces or colleagues, your interviewers know it will be only a matter of time that you will be griping about them in the future too. No one wants to hire someone like that.

Sometimes interviewers will bait you to see if you'll say negative things about your previous boss, colleagues or employer by asking you soft skill questions, such as *"Tell me about a difficult boss you had in the past and how you dealt with that"* or *"Tell me about a time you had to work with a difficult person on your team."* Don't take the bait and start throwing people under the bus and running over them forwards and backwards as if they were creatures from a zombie apocalypse. That's not what your interviewer wanted to hear from you. Maintain your composure and share how you handled those conflicts in the workplace with confidence, maturity and professionalism.

How to Answer Questions about Salary in Your Job Interview

On rare occasions, one of the interviewers might ask you what is your desired compensation or salary expectation. As I mentioned in *Negotiating Your Salary* in chapter 7, it is taboo for you to bring up your salary or benefits during your interview. Doing so implies you are more interested in the money and benefits than the job; this will most certainly reflect poorly on you in front of your interviewers.

But what do you do when one of the interviewers, such as the hiring manager, brings up the topic of salary?

Do you start negotiating your salary right there on the spot? Do you go over with the interviewers what hourly rate or annual salary you already agreed to with your staffing agency recruiter? The answer to all of these questions is typically **no**. You should not discuss your desired salary or benefits with the interviewers regardless if you previously agreed to a salary with your recruiter. Do not reveal your specific hourly rate or annual salary to the interviewers that you negotiated with a staffing agency recruiter. This rule also applies if you are being interviewed over the phone.

First, let's take the case where you've already agreed to an hourly rate or annual salary with the recruiter.

Once you established your desired compensation with the staffing agency recruiter, the recruiter sent your salary request along with your resume to the employer. The fact that you're sitting in that interview room means the employer—more specifically, the hiring manager and that company's human resources department—has agreed to pay your desired salary. The hiring manager would not have asked to interview you if their company could not afford you.

Interviewers that ask you about your compensation under these conditions are either inexperienced at best or unprofessional at worst. If the hiring manager wants to talk with you about your salary requirements, the manager should do so in private; not with all the other interviewers listening in on that conversation. The interviewer who asks you about your desired salary in front of the other interviewers either doesn't know they're not supposed to ask that question about money in front of everyone or they don't care that you've already arranged your compensation through your recruiter. In either case, you should avoid discussing your desired salary with them.

The only person in the interview room who has the right to ask you about your desired compensation is the hiring manager because he or she is the one who will approve your salary in coordination with the HR department. The hiring manager knows what each person is making for their position on his team you will be joining if you are hired (because he approved their salaries); and some of those team members are in that interview room with you. However, the rest of the interviewers in the room do not have the right to know what your desired compensation is ***before*** or ***after*** you are hired.

If it is someone other than the hiring manager asking you about your salary during your job interview, they are being nosy and out of line. They just want to know if you will be making more or less money than them when you are hired. If the hiring manager or team lead presiding over the interview is professional and on top of things, he or she will intervene and not permit an interviewer to ask you any salary questions.

Those other interviewers in the room should not know what each other's salaries are; nor should they be permitted to know what you will make if you get hired. I've already shared with you the problems that occur when company employees or contractors talk about their salaries amongst themselves: someone is going to come out on the short end of that conversation and realize they are getting paid less for doing the same job as the other person.

The hiring manager should know better not to ask you your desired salary in front of the other interviewers because some of those people sitting across from you in the interview room will become your co-workers if you are hired. Those interviewers are US government or corporate employees or contractors just like you. When you start working with them, they'll already know what you make because you shared your salary information with them in your interview.

Bad things can come out of sharing your salary information with job interviewers because interviewers have egos too. If you quote an hourly rate or annual salary that is more than what these interviewers negotiated for themselves, one or several of them might vote against hiring you because you—a newbie—would be making more money than they who have been working there longer than you. They'll try to get the hiring manager to hire someone who will be making less money than them. This will make it more difficult for the hiring manager to hire you even if he or she thinks you're the best person for the job.

Equally worse is these interviewers might not welcome you with open arms on their team, nor be as helpful as they might have been once you're hired because they know you are making more money than them. Sounds pretty unprofessional and you're right, it is but that's the reality of interviews conducted by company employees and contractors.

Then what should you do when asked about salary in the interview?

You have to be tactful in deflecting the question. By ***deflecting*** I mean you need to simply move or direct the conversation about money from that interview room to your staffing agency. Kindly and respectfully tell the interviewer that you've already agreed to a salary with your staffing agency, so there is no need to go over your salary. This should send a signal to the interviewers that you do not want to discuss salary; and all the interviewers should get the message, back off the salary question and move on to the next topic.

If they don't get the message the first time, you can reword the deflection again by telling them you're satisfied with what your staffing agency or recruiter is offering you for the position; and should they (the hiring manager and HR) offer you the job; you are ready to start working for them.

I've had interviewers ask me about my salary expectations, and I answered them the way I'm suggesting you answer them. It works for me every time.

However, if the interviewer continues to press you for an answer about your desired compensation, you should tell the interviewer that your recruiter would be happy to discuss your salary requirements with them; but you would rather not talk money or benefits in the interview because you're there to talk about the job. The good news is you already know they can afford you—that's the beauty of working through a staffing agency.

Don't be upset when interviewers ask you about your salary. It's a sign the interviewers are interested in hiring you and sometimes they just want to know if they can afford you.

Let's consider another scenario where you didn't get the job interview through a staffing agency.

Suppose you got the interview as a result of submitting your resume on the company's online career website; and during the interview, one of the interviewers pops the question about salary. You can't deflect the question to a staffing agency recruiter because you didn't go through one.

True, but you should still deflect the question for two reasons:

1. You don't want all the interviewers to know your salary.

2. You have greater leverage to negotiate a higher salary after they decide to hire you.

You don't want all the interviewers to know your salary.
First, interviews rarely involve only one interviewer. Jobs where you may experience a one-on-one interview between you and the hiring manager only may occur in businesses such as retail or restaurants. For other types of companies, there may be between 3 to 6 people interviewing you in-person or over the phone for that open position.

With this many people in the interview, there's usually several interviewers in that room who should not be privy to salary information of other workers in their company. The hiring manager or team lead in that interview should understand this just as in the previous situation where you have a recruiter representing you.

By sharing your salary requirements in this situation, you again run the risk of facing the same challenges that come with revealing your salary with your future co-workers.

You have greater leverage to negotiate a higher salary after they decide to hire you.
Secondly, you have greater leverage in negotiating your salary if you wait until after the company has decided to hire you than you would if

you tried to negotiate your salary during your job interview. Once the company's HR department sends you an offer letter, you now have a greater advantage to negotiate a better salary than you did when you were in the interview. Why? Because the offer letter means the hiring manager and the rest of the interview team want you above all the other job-seeking candidates they've interviewed. This gives you some leverage now in your response to the HR department concerning your salary.

If the salary in the offer letter is too low, you can reply with a counter-offer asking for more money. Yes, this is taking a risk. HR can either agree to match your counter-offer or refuse your counter-offer and choose not to hire you. That's the beauty of being a free agent—you control the risk and reward. If your counter-offer is not an outrageous amount above the original offer, the HR department is going to be more willing to pay you the higher amount because you've already gone through the vetting process and have the seal of approval from the hiring manager and the other interviewers that you are the right person for the job.

You are taking a greater risk by asking for that higher salary during the interview process—before their decision to hire you—than you are asking for that higher salary after the decision to hire you. If you try to ask for more money while the hiring manager is still interviewing other candidates for the job, the hiring manager may be more inclined to pick the candidate with a lower salary than you for the job.

The key is to try and deflect and postpone revealing your desired compensation until after the decision to hire you. You do not want to find yourself haggling over your salary with the people who are interviewing you—the people deciding whether or not to hire you. You want to reserve your salary negotiations for the HR department with whom you can be a little more hardheaded without offending your interviewers and negatively impacting their decision to hire you. Once they've decided to hire you, then you can talk money with greater assertiveness and leverage.

So let the employer's HR department make the first move in making you an offer. You might even be pleasantly surprised to find the employer's offer is equal to or higher than the amount you planned to ask for the job.

So how do you deflect their salary question in this situation?

You should use the same strategy as when you are represented by a recruiter: ***deflect*** the question by moving or directing the conversation about money from that interview room to another time and place. In other words, kindly and respectfully tell the interviewers that you would enjoy working with them, but you prefer to not talk about money until they've made a decision to hire you. Again, this should send a signal to the interviewers, especially to the hiring manager, that you do not want to discuss salary, and all the interviewers should get the message and move on to the next topic.

You could also throw in phrases such as, *"I'm willing to stay within the budget projected for this position"* or *"I'll accept any reasonable offer."* This should satisfy their curiosity as to whether or not they could afford you and, hopefully, not press you any further about your salary requirements.

Telling the interviewers that you are willing to stay within budget does not mean you can't negotiate your salary with the HR department after the hiring manager selected you for the job. It just means you are willing to work things out with HR; and if the salary is too low for you, you can either give HR your counter-offer or walk away as a last strategy to get what you want.

If your resources allow you the opportunity to walk away from a low salary offer, let HR know that you mean business about your desired salary and will pass on this job opportunity if you are not paid what you want. HR already knows the hiring manager and his or her team members want you on their team, so they're going to think twice about denying your counter-offer. I've done this several times in the past and it has worked in my favor.

After one job interview, the hiring manager wanted to hire me. I was using a staffing agency recruiter who told me the salary that the employer wanted to pay me. I wanted more, so I gave my counter-offer to the recruiter to pass on to the employer. I specifically told the recruiter to tell the employer that if they did not want to pay me my desired salary, I did not want the job. This was a gutsy move but I was willing to take the risk in order to reap the reward. If the employer decided to pass on me, I had enough resources to continue my job search elsewhere.

I didn't hear from the recruiter for a week and thought the hiring manager decided to pass on my counter-offer. However, at the end of that week, the recruiter contacted me and told me the employer agreed to pay me my desired compensation; and I started working for that employer. The beautiful thing of it was that none of the other colleagues in my office knew how much money I was making for that job because I never talked salary with my interviewers who had now become my colleagues at work.

Lastly on this subject of being asked salary questions, if your personality does not hold up well under the pressure of the hiring manager or another interviewer asking you to talk about salary; and you feel compelled to discuss your salary; then do yourself a favor and start with a salary range instead of a specific salary number. This way you give yourself a better chance of falling within the company's budgeted salary for that position. If you quote a specific salary number that is above what they are offering for the position, you stand the chance of losing out on the job altogether because the hiring manager knows they can't afford what you want or they can hire someone for a lot less.

How to Answer Questions about How Soon Can You Start Working

Oftentimes, at the end of a phone or in-person interview, I'm asked the question: "*How soon can you start*?" Obviously, this is a good sign when you are asked this question because it means your interviewers are interested in hiring you. As tempting as it might be to belch out, *"Right now!"* don't do it. That answer makes you sound desperate; not excited or enthusiastic for the job.

If you are currently employed, tell your interviewers that you need at least two weeks to give your current employer notice of your resignation. This will let your interviewers know you are a person of integrity, respect, responsibility and fairness by doing the right thing in giving your current employer a two-week notice. The hiring manager and interviewers know you will afford them the same courtesy when the time comes for you to leave their company too. This scores huge points in the emotional quotient (EQ) department in the eyes of your interviewers.

If you are currently unemployed, show your interviewers you want the job but also understand there is a process involved by saying, *"I'll need some time to get in-processed and on-boarded with my staffing agency, but as soon as that process is done, I'll be free to start."*

If you need some time to take care of a few personal things before starting work, go ahead and tell your interviewers you can start in a week or two weeks. If you need some extra weeks to move and relocate to your new employer's location, let the hiring manager know of your plans to relocate and the need for extra time for the move.

In one interview, the hiring manager knew I would possibly have to relocate if he hired me because of the distance between my home and the job site. Therefore, he asked me what my plan was concerning my commute to work if I were hired. I told him I planned to move to their location. After the interview, they hired me for the job; at which time I asked for three weeks to move to their location and get settled in which they granted me.

Questions to Ask the Interviewers and Closure

More often than not, the hiring manager or another person leading the interview is going to ask you, **"Do you have any questions for us?"** at the conclusion of your interview. Don't take lightly the interviewer's invitation to you to ask them questions. You would be doing yourself a disservice if you pass on asking them any questions. Doing so shows your lack of preparation; lack of interest in the company; and will cause you to miss out on another opportunity to shine one last time above the other candidates interviewing for this job.

The entire interview process is about you making yourself stand out above all the other job-hunting candidates they plan to interview; and this last part of your interview should be used for that same goal. You should be ready to ask good, engaging *open-ended* questions that will require your interviewers to provide you more than just a yes or no answer.

Hopefully, you did your homework and researched the company; you read through the previous *Before the Interview* section on the do's and don'ts when asking interviewers your questions; and you prepared 2–3 questions ahead of time. You can write or type out these questions and bring them with you to the interview so that you remember to ask them at the end. I usually type these questions on my computer; print it out on one 8 by 11 inch sheet of paper; and then cut the sheet down to size to fit in my small portfolio I normally bring with me to interviews.

Closing Statements at the End of Your Job Interview

After the interviewers have answered your last question, don't wait for them to ask you if you have any closing statements because they might not ask you if you have any last words. Take the initiative to give them your closing statements immediately after they've answered your last question.

In your final closing statements, there are two things you need to do:

1. Thank the interviewers.

2. Ask for the job.

Thank the Interviewers for Inviting You to the Job Interview

First, you should always thank the interviewers for taking time out of their busy schedules to interview you. This lets the interviewers know you get it; you understand that they have work to do but they're in that room with you to make this all about *you*—this is your interview, not theirs.

Ask the Interviewers for the Job

Secondly, ask for the job. The greatest salesperson in the world will not make a single sale until they ask for the sale. The answer is always no until you ask for the sale. If you don't ask, you can't have. After everything the hiring manager has told you about the company; after all the questions you were asked; let the interviewers know you are still interested in the open position and you are still enthusiastic about working with them.

You could say something simple such as, *"I'd like to take this time to say thank you to all of you for taking time out of your busy day to interview me. I'm very interested in this job, and I would enjoy working with all of you on your team."*

Don't say, "***I want this job***", because those words make you appear desperate and it sounds like you just want the job and don't care about working with them.

Don't ask, "***When can I start?***", because that makes you come across as arrogant and as if you blindly presume you've already beat out all the competition before all the competition has had a chance to interview.

Can you take a more aggressive or assertive approach in asking your interviewers for the job?

Certainly, but I recommend doing so only if you sense that the interviewers like you for either your **technical fit** or **cultural fit** or both.

I went through a particularly grueling job interview for a senior network engineer position where I was asked question after question by six interviewers who were also senior network engineers. They asked me a lot of questions that I didn't have the answers to. I was certain I was not the best technically fit engineer for that position but I was still very interested in the job and I wanted to work there.

Although I wasn't the smartest pea in the pod of candidates they would interview for this job, I could sense the interviewers enjoyed talking with me, and I felt I connected with them too. In other words, I knew I nailed it when it came to my emotional quotient (EQ) and cultural fit for the job.

So in my closing statements, I asked for the job more aggressively by putting on a big smile and telling the interviewers that I was very interested in the job and would love to work with each of them. Then I added with a smile, "***So what can I do to convince you guys to hire me?***"

The hiring manager responded, "***Give me a big sack of cash.***" (That tells you how poorly I performed with my technical answers in the interview.)

However, since I showed them my enthusiasm in wanting to work with them; and because we connected in common interests during our discussion that showed my cultural fitness; they hired me for the job that paid a six-figure salary that I previously negotiated with my staffing agency recruiter.

That's the power of asking for the job.

CHAPTER TEN

After the Interview—Now What?

When you reach the end of your rope, tie a knot in it and hang on.
Franklin D. Roosevelt

Congratulations!

You did it! You made it through your interview—Congratulations!

In the closing scene of the 2003 animated movie *Finding Nemo* produced by Pixar, all the fish in the dentist's aquarium finally made their long-awaited escape after many failed attempts to break free from their watery prison in that dentist's office. They successfully turned their fish tank into a place that only Pigpen could love in a Charlie Brown special.

When the dentist placed all of the fish in separate plastic bags to clean the tank, each fish secretly rolled themselves to freedom out the open window like *American Ninja Warrior* contestants or *Spartan Race* competitors. They tumbled across the dangerous obstacles of a busy city street and hurled themselves over the water bank the way Olympic runners would throw themselves across the finishing line into the ocean's winning circle. As they bobbed together on the ocean's welcoming surface within their little plastic bags of freedom rejoicing over their victory; silence settles in among them.

Then one fish asks the all-important question: *"**Now what?**"*

That's sort of the way you feel after you completed your job interview. After jumping through so many hoops and making your way over so many obstacles to get to that all-important interview; you did it and it's over. Now you're finally sitting there in silence, free again to contemplate what just took place. You made it out of the confines of that interview room alive. You breathe a great sigh of relief like someone who was just let out of jail (or *Dante's Inferno*).

Like so many professional sports athletes waiting to find out if they made the team or if they're going to be cut, you're on the bubble waiting for what the future holds for you after completing your job interview.

You feel good about where you are now but you're still in this bubble, like those fish, asking yourself, **"Now what?"**

Here are a few things to consider while you wait out your time after a job interview:

- Sending thank you notes

- Perfecting your craft

- Other job opportunities

- The wait and the response

Sending Thank You Notes

Sending a thank you note to the hiring manager immediately after the interview thanking the manager for giving you the opportunity to interview for the job is still relevant advice today. It shows the hiring manager you do business in a professional and courteous manner. Using the thank you note is also a great opportunity to ask for the job again, as you did toward the end of your interview, by letting the hiring manager know that you are excited about the opportunity to join his or her team.

If you plan to send the hiring manager a thank you note, try to send the note within 24 hours of completing your job interview. With today's technology, your thank you note can easily be sent via email to the hiring manager if you have access to their email address. Snail mail should be avoided due to postal delays that can occur internally and externally to the hiring manager's company.

With advances in technology and services come changes in the way people do business. This is also true with the thank you note after a job interview. When you are working through a staffing agency, chances are you may not have access to the email address or phone number of the hiring manager. Why? Because the middle man—the staffing agency—is there to be a buffer between the employer and you.

Many hiring managers prefer to communicate with candidates through the staffing agency; not directly with candidates. This gives the hiring manager the distance they oftentimes prefer to have between themselves and multiple job-hunting candidates interviewing for the job.

You can attempt to get the hiring manager's email address from your staffing agent, but don't be surprised if you are told the hiring manager prefers not to provide you their email or phone number before or after your interview. Typically, what ends up happening is the staffing agency recruiter or account manager will provide you their own email address and phone number; and you will have to communicate with the hiring manager through the staffing agent.

Understanding how technology and staffing agency services have evolved, I don't bother trying to send thank you notes to hiring managers after the interview if the staffing agent does not provide me the hiring manager's email address. This is an unwritten rule but acceptable practice when you do not have access to the hiring manager's contact information. If I'm provided the hiring manager's email address from the staffing agent, then I'll send the hiring manager a thank you note after the interview.

Perfecting Your Craft

There's no better time to perform a self-evaluation on your interview performance than right after you completed one. Ask yourself what you did well in the interview and what you need work on. Take this time to pat yourself on the back for the things you did well; and don't be so hard on yourself during your self-evaluation for the things you did wrong. You should be your greatest cheerleader whether your team is winning or losing the game.

Here are a few tips for perfecting your interviewing skills for your next job interview:

Tip #1: While the interview questions are still fresh in your mind, try to write down every question that was asked of you whether you knew the answer or not. By writing down these questions, and finding the correct answers to them, you have a better barometer of how well you performed in your technical and cultural fit for the job.

This will also give you valuable interview questions and answers that you can review for future interviews. There's a good chance these same questions may be asked in future job interviews. The one thing that started me on the road to writing this book was my habit of writing down the questions I was asked during job interviews.

Tip #2: Go over in your mind how you presented your introduction to your interviewer panel. Were you cool, calm and collected? Did you remember everything you wanted to say? Did you hit on all the right points that showed you were both a good technical fit as well as a good cultural fit to the company? Make note of the things you could have done better so you can remember to incorporate those corrections in future job interviews.

Tip #3: Evaluate how the effect of using role-playing, power poses, power thoughts and power words helped your confidence in your job interview. Did you remember to smile and maintain eye contact; hold your head up, shoulders back and chest out; and sit upright in a relaxed and comfortable manner? Were there other things you could have done to make yourself feel more comfortable in the interview room? If so, make those adjustments in confidence boosting exercises for future interviews.

Tip #4: How effective was your research on the company or interviewers? Did your research prove useful? Were you able to incorporate that information into the discussion, such as during your introduction? Did you strike a positive chord with any of your interviewers when talking about some of your personal interests, such as your hobbies, sports, volunteer work or other ways you spend your free time?

All of these things added to their perception of your cultural fit in their company. If any interviewers showed interest in your activities outside of work, you might want to consider using those same items in your next interview to establish your cultural fit and rapport with your interviewers.

Other Job Opportunities

Just because you are scheduled for a job interview, that's no reason to discontinue or place on hold your job search activities with other recruiters. I can't tell you how many times I thought the stars had aligned in my favor and I decided to forego pursuing other job opportunities that recruiters were offering me while I waited for the good news from the hiring manager after interviewing for the job. Then I realized those were shooting stars I was looking at because my hopes soon disappeared when I was notified that I was not selected for the job. By the time I tried to re-engage with those other recruiters I had put off, those jobs had already been filled.

Note to self: Stop stargazing after the job interview is over and keep pursuing other job opportunities that are out there. Until you sign your offer letter for the job, nothing is concrete about the outcome of your job interview.

Keep your job search pipeline open for other job opportunities that come your way even if you are scheduled for a job interview. There's nothing illegal or unprofessional about speaking with several recruiters about different job opportunities at the same time. You can be sure both those recruiters and employers are contacting several candidates at the same time, even if they currently have a scheduled interview with you.

If things don't work in your favor after your interview, hopefully you'll have several fallback recruiters you can turn to immediately. The quickest way to get over the post-interview blues is to be communicating with other staffing agency recruiters about other job opportunities.

If you are hired for the job after your interview, you can proudly announce to the other recruiters you were communicating with that you are no longer looking for work.

The Wait and the Response

How long you have to wait after your job interview before you receive a response or feedback depends on the hiring manager or the staffing agency's recruiter or account manager.

If the interviewing panel rated you as a potential fit for their team after your interview, and they still have other candidates to interview, the hiring manager will wait until his interview panel has completed all other interviews before making a decision on which candidate is the best fit for his team. This process could take 1–3 weeks depending on how many candidates are being interviewed and where you are in the interview pecking order.

After all candidates are interviewed, the hiring manager will let your staffing agency recruiter or account manager know if they selected you or not. If you did not use a staffing agency and worked directly with the employer's HR rep, the HR rep will email or call you to inform you of either the good news that you were selected or the bad news that you were passed over by the hiring manager.

What Happens If the Answer is No

If your interview performance convinced the hiring manager and his panel that you are not the best fit for their team, the hiring manager will pass this feedback immediately to the staffing agency recruiter or account manager that set up your interview with the employer. The hiring manager will not wait until all interviews are completed to pass along this bad news to the staffing agency. The manager will let the staffing agency do the dirty work of informing you that you were not selected. If your interview was set up through the employer's HR department instead of through a staffing agency, the HR rep will let you know that you were not selected for this job.

Whether the results about your job interview turn out positive or negative, always show some class and be a professional by thanking the people who made your interview possible—your staffing agents and the hiring manager. If the staffing agent is giving you the news over the phone, thank them there on the spot; otherwise an email to the agent will suffice. As previously mentioned in the section on sending a thank you note, you may not have access to the hiring manager's email address. In this case, you can opt to pass on your appreciation to the hiring manager through the staffing agency if you so desire.

As I mentioned in chapter 6 on *Dealing with Recruiters*, some staffing agencies will not contact you after the hiring manager has informed them that they did not select you for the job.

You have two options when you've waited long enough for feedback about your job interview:

1. The first option is to reach out to your staffing agent for status.

2. The second option is to accept the staffing agent's silence as meaning the hiring manager has not selected you for the job.

The first option is the best option because there could be multiple unplanned reasons that could delay a response back to you. There could be an unexpected number of candidates submitted from various recruiters that the hiring manager wants to interview. The hiring manager or other key members of the interview panel may be out of office for personal or business reasons; so they're waiting for that person to return. One or more pressing company issues or priorities may have placed the job interview process on hold. The company may be undergoing critical changes, such as management, hiring manager or organizational changes, which require the dust to settle on this internal transition before they can refocus on the interview process again.

I've contacted staffing agents for feedback after a week or two of waiting, and oftentimes they've told me the delay was due to the reasons I just mentioned. So be easy on the recruiter. Don't pester the staffing agent or the hiring manager with multiple inquiries each week. Just one inquiry is needed. Maintain a courteous and professional attitude throughout this waiting period.

The second option is to accept the staffing agent's silence as meaning the hiring manager has not selected you for the job. I've used this option when I know I absolutely bombed my job interview. I could not answer the majority of the questions, so I already knew I was not a good technical fit for that job. Under these circumstances, if I chose to contact the staffing agent, it would only be to confirm what the staffing agent and I already knew—I was not selected for the job.

Regardless of the choice you make to learn about your interview results; if it ends up being you were not selected for the job, move on and continue your job search with other staffing agents. Has this happened to me after a job interview? Yes, many times.

How to Handle Rejection after a Job Interview

Rejection is a normal part of the job search process just as in other areas of life. Everyone has to go through it from candidates running for the US presidential office to candidates in search of work in the most menial of jobs. Don't let the rejection from a failed job interview or the silence from Dr. Jekyll and Mr. Hyde recruiters hamstring or derail your momentum, enthusiasm, progress and success in your job search process.

Some people have a hard time with rejection. It makes them feel like a failure. They mistakenly identify an event with who they are as a person. It's not your failures that define you; it's how you respond to failures that matters. Failures refine you; they don't define who you are. You are not a failure just because you didn't get selected after a job interview. You are a successful person who experienced a failure. There's a difference.

Accept failures in life as a good teacher; the way you would accept the scores and remarks your teachers gave you on your paper in school. They are there to help improve your skills in life. Learn from failures the way you would learn from a coach telling you what you're doing wrong so you can improve your skills and performance to do better next time. They are there to make you a success, a winner, a champion in life. Embrace failures the way you did when you first embraced learning to ride a bike or skates or skateboard or snowboard or skis. Falling was all part of the process to rising higher. It is part of the adventure, the risk, the excitement and the fun of learning how to do something well in life. Sure there will be some bumps and bruises along the way when you fall, but when you get back up and move on with your life, you become stronger, better and wiser for having gone through those falls.

Both players and coaches in professional sports know this mentor, teacher and life coach called *failure* all too well. Each year, these professional athletes and coaches fail to win games and are rejected, traded or fired from teams only to find themselves being hired again by another team, performing better and winning games another year. That's what failure produces—**SUCCESS**!

Failure is the secret ingredient to the recipe of success.

During Neo's early developing stages in *The Matrix* film, his trainer Morpheus orders Tank the Operator to load the jump program for Neo. The whole crew of the Nebuchadnezzar hovercraft is watching with anticipation and bated breath to see how Neo will fare during his first-time jump from one rooftop to the next. Most of the crew members are convinced that ***everyone***, including Neo, ***falls the first time***.

As you prepare to jump from one job to the next; remember, everyone falls every now and then. Every great champion has experienced failure and defeat. The key to success is getting back up and trying again.

LeBron James has won three NBA championships; received four NBA MVP Awards, three NBA Finals MVP Awards, two Olympic gold medals; in addition to being selected to 12 NBA All-Star teams, 12 All-NBA teams and six All-Defensive teams. In 2016, LeBron was the key reason the Cleveland Cavaliers won their first NBA Finals championship in franchise history. So what's LeBron's view on failure? He said, *"You have to be able to accept failure to get better . . . You can't be afraid to fail. It's the only way you succeed—you're not gonna succeed all the time, and I know that."*

Theodor Roosevelt, the 26th US President, said, *"Far better is it to dare mighty things, to win glorious triumphs, even though checkered by failure . . . than to rank with those poor spirits who neither enjoy nor suffer much, because they live in a gray twilight that knows not victory nor defeat."*

H. Stanley Judd, author, film producer, communications consultant and president of The Executive Golfer and Golf School Online said, *"Don't waste energy trying to cover up failure. Learn from your failures and go on to the next challenge. It's OK to fail. If you're not failing, you're not growing."*

After the Interview—Now What?

Vince Lombardi, the man the National Football League's Super Bowl trophy is named after, is best known as head coach of the Green Bay Packers during the 1960s where he led his team to three straight and five total NFL championships in seven years including winning the first two Super Bowls following the 1966 and 1967 NFL seasons. Lombardi is considered by many to be one of the best and most successful coaches in NFL history. He said, *"The greatest accomplishment is not in never falling, but in rising again after you fall."*

Abraham Lincoln, the 16th US President, said, *"My great concern is not whether you have failed, but whether you are content with your failure."*

Colin Powell, former US Secretary of State and retired four-star general in the US Army said, *"Success is the result of perfection, hard work, learning from failure, loyalty, and persistence."*

Zig Ziglar, motivational speaker, salesman and author with 10 of his 28 books on the best-seller lists whose books have been translated into more than 38 languages and dialects said, *"Remember that failure is an event, not a person . . . If you learn from defeat, you haven't really lost."*

Michael Jordan led the Chicago Bulls to two separate NBA championship "three-peats" in 1991, 1992, 1993 and again in 1996, 1997, 1998 after coming out of a two-year retirement in 1993 and 1994. He set an NBA record with 72 regular-season wins in the 1995-96 NBA season. Jordan said, *"I've missed more than 9,000 shots in my career. I've lost almost 300 games. Twenty-six times, I've been trusted to take the game winning shot and missed. I've failed over and over and over again in my life. And that is why I succeed . . . I can accept failure, everyone fails at something. But I can't accept not trying."*

Woody Allen is a well-known comic, producer, entertainer, director, Oscar-winner and screen star whose career spans more than 50 years. He won four Academy Awards and has more screenwriting Academy Award nominations than any other writer. Allen said, "*If you're not failing every now and again, it's a sign you're not doing anything very innovative.*"

Denis Waitley is a graduate of the US Naval Academy at Annapolis, motivational speaker and writer. He said, "*Failure should be our teacher, not our undertaker. Failure is delay, not defeat. It is a temporary detour, not a dead end. Failure is something we can avoid only by saying nothing, doing nothing, and being nothing.*"

J. K. Rowling is the British novelist best known for writing the *Harry Potter* fantasy series whose writings became blockbuster films and theme parks. Rowling said, "*It is impossible to live without failing at something, unless you live so cautiously that you might as well not have lived at all, in which case you have failed by default.*"

Benjamin Franklin's face graces our $100 bill. He was a politician, author, printer, postmaster, civic activist, scientist and inventor. Franklin was one of the Founding Fathers of the United States and the first US Ambassador to France. He invented the lightning rod and provided a better understanding of electricity through his famous experiment of flying a kite in lightning. He also invented bifocals and the Franklin stove that was an improvement over fireplaces during his era. Franklin said in response to his many failed experiments, "*I didn't fail the test; I just found 100 ways to do it wrong.*"

Steve Jobs was co-founder and CEO of Apple, CEO of Pixar Animation Studios and NeXT Inc., and on the board of directors of The Walt Disney Company. He was fired from Apple in 1985. Afterward, he founded the company NeXT and helped in the creation of Pixar that produced the first fully computer-animated film, *Toy Story*. Concerning his being fired by Apple, Steve Jobs responded with these words: "*I didn't see it then, but it turned out that getting fired from Apple was the best thing that could have ever happened to me. The heaviness of being successful was replaced by the lightness of being a beginner again, less* sure about everything. It freed me to enter one of the most creative periods of my life."

John Elway is the executive vice president of football operations/General Manager for the Denver Broncos. After losing 43-8 to the Seattle Seahawks in Super Bowl XLVIII (48) in 2014, Mr. Elway said, "We will use this as an experience that we went through, be disappointed that we didn't play better, but the bottom line is this organization and what (team owner) Pat Bowlen wants from this organization—that has not changed and it will not change. The bottom line is we're going to work as hard as we worked this year, if not harder, and continue to do that with the mindset that we want to be world champions and we're going to do everything we can to get there."

Congratulations to the 2016 Denver Broncos Super Bowl 50 champions!

If you failed one of your job interviews; were passed over by the hiring manager for another candidate; consider yourself in good company. People greater than you have fallen a lot farther and harder than you; but they got back up and tried again.

That's what made them great!

That's what made them successful!

That's what made them a champion!

Let your failures teach you; let them refine you; let them improve you; but never let them stop you. Now get back up and try again. There is greatness in you. You are destined for success. **You're a champion!**

Certificate of Achievement

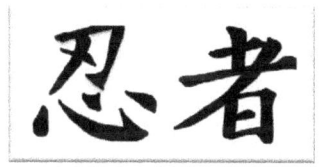

"Ninja"

What would an end to your job-hunting training be without a certificate of achievement? Now that you've read through this book, you have successfully completed your **Job-Hunting Ninja Training Course**. You are now an official job-hunting ninja warrior. Congratulations!

All that is left for you now, *Grasshoppa*, is to go out there and earn your belt. What color is your ninja belt? That depends on how well you apply these ninja principles you've learned to your next job search. You are now a part of the *job-hunting ninja family*. Now go out there and find your dream job, land interviews, negotiate a higher salary and get hired.

Job Hunting Ninja Master

Straight From My Heart

I wrote this book to give you help, wisdom, encouragement, confidence and success in your job search. It is my sincere hope that this book has blessed you, inspired you, strengthened and encouraged you.

I gain no greater satisfaction in life than to pass along to others the things I've learned to help you live a successful, healthy and prosperous life—not just in this life but the next. What do I mean by the *next life*?

The last and most important interview questions: I'm not saying this will happen anytime soon, but if you were to die today, where would you go? If God were to ask you why should He let you into heaven, what would you say?

Here's your answer: The Bible says in Romans 3:23, *"We've all sinned and fallen short of God's glory."* Romans 6:23 says, *"The wages of sin is death and separation from God, but the free gift of God is eternal life and peace from God."* (see also Isaiah 59:2 and Romans 5:1) Romans 10:9 says, *"If you confess with your mouth the Lord Jesus and believe in your heart that God raised Jesus from the dead, you shall be saved."* Romans 10:13 says, *"Whoever calls on the name of the Lord Jesus shall be saved."*

Pray this quick prayer with me: *Heavenly Father, I believe Jesus died on the cross for me and my sins, and rose again from the dead. I give You my life. Lord Jesus, come into my heart and into my life. Amen.*

If you prayed that prayer, you are saved and going to heaven when you die because Jesus paid for all your sins—past, present and future sins. That's your answer to your final and most important interview question of why God should let you into heaven.

Did you like the Job Hunting Ninja Master 2017? Did this book help you? Then please do me this huge favor and write a book review on the Amazon website for this book at http://amzn.to/2rPuojb. This Amazon link will take you to this book's page; then go to the bottom of the page and click the "**Write a customer review**" button. It's that simple. As an indie author seeking customer reviews for my book, I greatly appreciate and value your review—*Thank you*!

Give this book as a gift to a friend or family member as an ebook or paperback.

If this book helped you, inspired you and gave you better insight and understanding of the overall job search process, **tell your connected friends about this book on social media.** It's a great way to let your friends know about a great book that will help both you and them; and your friends will thank you for it. Let me be one of the first to say *THANK YOU* for introducing your friends to a book that will change their careers and their lives for the better.

One Last Thing . . .

Be the first to find out when the next books I'm writing will come out by signing up on my email list at this link: http://bit.ly/2ffZcmx. I will not sell your email to marketers nor contact you for any other reason than to let you know when my next books are out on the market. When you sign up, you'll receive a confirmation email from "**Frank McClain confirmations@madmimi.com**"; so check your spam inbox if you don't see this confirmation email in your Inbox. It's that simple.

Job Hunting Ninja Master

Also By Frank McClain

IT Questions & Answers For IT Job Interviews, Volume 1
IT Questions & Answers For IT Job Interviews, Volume 2
IT Questions & Answers For IT Job Interviews, Volume 3
IT Questions & Answers For IT Job Interviews, Volume 4
IT Questions & Answers For IT Job Interviews, Volume 5
IT Questions & Answers For IT Job Interviews, Volume 6

The 2017 award-winning book ***YOU'RE HIRED!***

About The Author

Frank McClain is a multi-award-winning author who graduated with a BS in Information Systems Management from the University of Maryland. He is a military veteran who served 20 years in the US Air Force both in the US and Europe. He lived and worked in Europe for over 12 years both as a US military member and as a civilian government contractor. He's worked over 15 years as an IT consultant in both US government and corporate jobs in the US and Europe. Frank has extensive experience dealing with the job search process, job recruiters, job interviews and working for many Fortune 500 companies and US government agencies, such as the North American Aerospace Defense Command (NORAD), Missile Defense Agency (MDA) and the Defense Information Systems Agency (DISA). Frank currently resides in Colorado.

www.ingramcontent.com/pod-product-compliance
Lightning Source LLC
Chambersburg PA
CBHW071643090426
42738CB00009B/1414